THE WORLD
OF SWING

VOLUME ONE

THE WORLD OF SWING

162918793

STANLEY DANCE

CHARLES
SCRIBNER'S
SONS,
NEW
YORK

"Back on the Scene," "Coleman Hawkins," "Melody Man at Heart," "Stuff Swings On," "Road Band Perspective" Part II, "Epitaph 1 & 2," "Dud Bascomb," "Barnstorming Days," "Lunceford Ace" and "Woodwind Wizard" are reprinted by permission of *Down Beat Magazine*

"Andy Gibson" edited by Sinclair Trail and the Hon. Gerald Lascelles first appeared in *Just Jazz No. 4* and is reprinted by permission of Souvenir Press Ltd.

"Piano, Organ and Lover Man," "Drummers Odyssey," "The Phone Always Rings" Part I and "Three Score Quiz" are reprinted by special permission of Robert Asen, publisher of *Metronome*.

"Benny Goodman" and "Benny Carter" first appeared in *Jazz*.

Other articles or interviews first appeared in *Saturday Review* and *Jazz Journal*. Copyright © 1971, 1970, 1962 Stanley Dance. Copyright © 1963 Stanley and Helen Dance, Copyright © 1963 Helen Dance.

PICTURE CREDITS

Courtesy: Enzo Archetti, 264; Eddie Barefield, 21 (bottom); Dud Bascomb, 195, 200; Jack Bradley, 5, 158, 333; Doc Cheatham, 312, 313, 323; Columbia Records, 15, 300; Jimmy Crawford, 98, 99; Julian Dash, 217; Frank Driggs, 394; Panama Francis, 378; Andy Gibson, 226; Tiny Grimes, 362, 363; Haywood Henry, 205; Charlie Holmes, 20 (bottom), 255, 258; Claude Hopkins, 37; Pat Jenkins, 86; Jonah Jones, 26, 27, 163, 166, 171 (bottom), 180, 188; Victor Kalin, 137, 309; Bob Kreider, 101, 112; Lawrence Lucie, 146 (bottom), 354; Billy Mackel, 282; Fred Norman, 40, 237; Sy Oliver, 126; Photo Files, 358; Roger Ramirez, 81, 328, 413, 414; Duncan Schiedt, 70 (top); Elmer Snowden, 51, 60; Joe Thomas, 24, 151; Verve Records, 397; Sandy Williams, 65.

Special thanks to Pat Jenkins for Savoy Ballroom flyers used as end-papers. All other photographs from the author's collection.

1 3 5 7 9 11 13 15 17 19 C/H 20 18 16 14 12 10 8 6 4 2

Printed in the United States of America
Library of Congress Catalog Card Number 73–1112
ISBN 0–684–13778–X

In memory of
COLEMAN HAWKINS,
chief among the period's untitled nobility.

CONTENTS

INTRODUCTION   1

SOMETHING TO PAT YOUR FOOT BY (Count Basie and
    Freddie Green)   13

SWINGING: AN INFORMAL SYMPOSIUM (Jonah Jones,
    Sonny White, Jerome Darr, John Brown and Cozy Cole)   17

CLAUDE HOPKINS–Bandleader (piano and arranger)   31

ELMER SNOWDEN–Bandleader (banjo and arranger)   45

SANDY WILLIAMS–Trombone   63

TAFT JORDAN–Trumpet   77

WILLIE SMITH–Alto saxophone   93

ED WILCOX–Piano and arranger   110

JIMMY CRAWFORD–Drums   119

SY OLIVER–Bandleader [trumpet and arranger]   125

BENNY CARTER–Bandleader [alto saxophone,
    trumpet and arranger]   135

COLEMAN HAWKINS–Tenor saxophone   140

ROY ELDRIDGE–Trumpet   148

EDDIE LOCKE–Drums   155

JONAH JONES–Trumpet   161

STUFF SMITH–Violin   176

COZY COLE–Drums   183

DUD BASCOMB–Trumpet   192

HAYWOOD HENRY–Saxophones, clarinet and flute   203

SAMMY LOWE–Trumpet and arranger   212

ANDY GIBSON–Trumpet and arranger   224

FRED NORMAN–Trombone and arranger   232

HOWARD JOHNSON–Alto saxophone   241

CHARLIE HOLMES–Alto saxophone   249

BENNY GOODMAN–Bandleader [clarinet]   260

LIONEL HAMPTON–Bandleader [vibraharp, piano
    and drums]   265

BILLY MACKEL–Guitar   279

BENNY MORTON–Trombone   283

QUENTIN JACKSON–Trombone   293

VIC DICKENSON–Trombone   301

DOC CHEATHAM–Trumpet   307

EDDIE HEYWOOD–Piano   318

ROGER RAMIREZ–Piano and organ   325

NAT PIERCE–Piano and arranger   329

LAWRENCE LUCIE–Guitar   345

AL CASEY–Guitar   356

TINY GRIMES–Guitar   360

MILT HINTON–Bass   366

PANAMA FRANCIS–Drums   375

CHICK WEBB–Bandleader [drums]   384

MILDRED BAILEY–Vocalist   391

BILLIE HOLIDAY–Vocalist   395

SPONTANEOUS OPINIONS   399

BANDS IN HARLEM THEATRES   404

RELEVANT RECORDS   417

INDEX   422

LIST OF ILLUSTRATIONS

Fletcher Henderson and his
  father at home   4

Coleman Hawkins and the
  author at Newport   5

Duke Ellington, Freddie
  Green and Count Basie,
  1961   15

Fletcher Henderson's band
  in its "classic" period   20

Luis Russell's band, 1930   20

Bennie Carter's band at the
  Savoy Ballroom   21

Cab Calloway's band, 1932   21

Buster Bailey, Sidney
  Catlett, Joe Thomas, Israel
  Crosby, Fletcher
  Henderson, Bob Lessey,
  Chu Berry, 1936   24

Jonah Jones and Jerome
  Darr, 1970   26

Stuff Smith's band with Ben
  Webster   27

Sarah Martin and Her Jass
  Fools   37

Claude Hopkins with
  "Ginger Snaps of 1928"   37

Claude Hopkin's band   40

Elmer Snowden, 1965   51

Elmer Snowden's band,
  1933   60

Sandy Williams   65

Savoy Ballroom flyers   70

Cozy Cole, Dick Clarke,
  Taft Jordan, 1936   81

The Savoy Ballroom   86

Taft Jordan, Duke Ellington
  and Ray Nance, 1945   91

Willie Smith   94

Jimmie Lunceford's band in
  Memphis, 1928   98

Jimmie Lunceford's band at
  Lakeside, Ohio, 1929   98

Jimmie Lunceford's glee
  club, 1935   99

Jimmie Lunceford's band,
  1940   99

Joe Thomas, Jimmie
   Lunceford, the author and
   Jimmy Crawford, 1946   101

Ed Wilcox   112

Jimmy Crawford, 1958   121

Sy Oliver, 1973   126

Benny Carter, 1973   137

Fletcher Henderson's reed
   section, 1934   146

Coleman Hawkins's big
   band   146

Fletcher Henderson's brass
   section, with Roy
   Eldridge, 1936   151

Eddie Locke and Coleman
   Hawkins   158

Jonah Jones and Dicky
   Wells in Sunday school
   band   163

Jonah Jones and Tinsley's
   Royal Aces   163

Jonah Jones on the s.s.
   Island Queen   166

Jonah Jones and Clarence
   Olden's band   166

Keg Johnson, Hilton
   Jefferson, Sam Taylor,
   Jonah Jones, 1946   171

Jonah Jones in Baltimore   171

Stuff Smith's "big" band   180

Stuff Smith's septet, 1938   180

Cozy Cole   185

Stuff Smith's sextet, 1937   188

Dud Bascomb   195

Dud Bascomb's band at the
   Savoy Ballroom   200

Marquee of the Savoy
   Ballroom   200

Haywood Henry   205

Erskine Hawkins's band,
   1936   208

Sammy Lowe, 1973   217

Erskine Hawkins, 1973   217

Andy Gibson, 1959   226

Fred Norman, Floyd
   "Stump" Brady, Vic
   Dickenson, 1937   237

Claude Hopkins's band,
   1937   237

Howard Johnson at Jackie
   Robinson's, 1963   244

Luis Russell's reed section,
   with Charlie Holmes   255

John Kirby's band   258

Benny Goodman, Chick
   Webb and Joe Bushkin,
   1937   263

Lionel Hampton   266

Lionel Hampton, Louis
   Armstrong and Lawrence
   Brown   269

Lionel Hampton's band,
   1950   274

Lionel Hampton and some
of his musicians, 1947   274

Billy Mackel   281

Bennie Morton, 1973   286

Fletcher Henderson and
musicians at a fancy dress
party   291

Fletcher Henderson, his
Packard and friends.   291

Quentin Jackson with
combined Basie and
Ellington bands, 1961   300

Vic Dickenson and Charlie
Shavers, 1958   305

Doc Cheatham, 1973   308

Doc Cheatham with Pearl
High School orchestra   312

Doc Cheatham in Chicago,
1926   312

Doc Cheatham in New
Jersey, 1927   313

Doc Cheatham with Juanita
Hall, Buster Bailey,
Coleman Hawkins,
Claude Hopkins, George
Duvivier and Jimmy
Crawford, 1958   313

Eddie Heywood's band,
1944   323

Roger Ramirez   328

Nat Pierce   333

Louis Armstrong's band with
Lawrence Lucie, 1942   354

Al Casey, 1935   357

Tiny Grimes, Slam Stewart
and Art Tatum, 1944   362

Tiny Grimes and His
Rockin' Highlanders   363

Milt Hinton with Danny
Barker and J.C.Heard   370

Panama Francis, 1969   377

Chick Webb and Ella
Fitzgerald   388

Mildred Bailey   393

Billie Holiday   396

Willie Bryant's band, 1936   411

Willie Bryant and the Apollo
Theatre chorus line, 1936   412

Don Redman's band, 1932   421

INTRODUCTION

Histories of the Swing Era have usually been concerned with successful bandleaders and a few outstanding innovators. While their triumphs were usually the result of talent, luck also often played a part, and these musicians did not exist independently of their milieu however much they may have illumined or overshadowed it. They were products of their environment, of the soil and musical climate of their time, and many other musicians contributed valuably to what was, in a sense, the period's spiritual or artistic ferment.

This work is an attempt to examine the Swing Era in depth, to focus on figures in the background as well as the foreground. Here, as in *The World of Duke Ellington,* the musicians speak for themselves, but this time the underlying theme, rather than the personality of a single man, is a particular jazz element—swing.

While no one has succeeded in wholly defining swing, nearly everyone imagines he knows what it is. For most people, it is an exhilarating rhythmic feeling created around a fundamental pulse that suggests—but does not actually realize—a quickening of tempo. Henry Pleasants has likened it to flying. When a band began to swing after the first ensemble chorus, the feeling was much the same as when an airplane—before jets—suddenly took off after roaring along the runway.

Swing is not peculiar to jazz. The Viennese waltz, played by certain musicians under certain circumstances, undeniably swings. Bravely trying to inspire a tired marching column, a military band often swings. So do tziganes when carried away by the emotion inherent in their gypsy music. Black singers and instrumentalists in American churches, however much they may mistrust jazz and blues as Satan's handiwork, swing exceedingly when possessed by the spirit. Surprisingly few rock bands, on the other hand, have managed to swing despite a heavy, emphatic beat.

In essence, swing bears a close relationship to physical movement, especially to dancing. Youngsters dancing to rock bands were often visibly swinging, although the musicians were not. The Second Line, prancing alongside a New Orleans marching band of weary, elderly men, is usually

1

also quite clearly swinging, while the music may very well not be. The musicians in such a case are providing familiar melodic strains above a steady rhythmic foundation on which the dancers improvise. Under the best circumstances, however, there is a mutual exchange of inspiration between musicians and dancers.

Improvisation is regarded as vital in jazz, and it is easy to credit its origin partly to the desire of individual musicians to lift or stimulate dancers. Yet it would be wrong to suppose that swing is dependent on improvisation. An ensemble playing written or oral arrangements, without provision for improvisation, may or may not swing, according to the will and skill of both performers and arrangers. The performers do not necessarily have the technical ability to swing what the arranger writes, while the arranger's intentions or ambitions, alternatively, may virtually inhibit or prohibit swing. The great success of arrangers who were also playing members of the band for which they wrote is explained by their thorough knowledge of the capabilities of their associates. Duke Ellington, Benny Carter, Don Redman, Fletcher Henderson and Claude Hopkins with their own groups; Edgar Sampson with Chick Webb's; Sy Oliver and Ed Wilcox with Jimmie Lunceford's; Mary Lou Williams with Andy Kirk's; Budd Johnson, Cecil Irwin and Jimmy Mundy with Earl Hines's; Eddie Durham, Buck Clayton and Dicky Wells with Count Basie's; Edgar Battle with Willie Bryant's; Sammy Lowe with Erskine Hawkins's; and Fred Norman with Claude Hopkins's—all were writing for musicians whom they knew intimately as players and personalities. The arranger without comparable knowledge was obliged to write primarily for *instruments* rather than for men. The resultant difference might be likened to that between a hand-tailored suit and one factory-produced in a stock size. In fact, the commercial arrangements widely used by bands without either an arranger of their own or the financial resources to hire one were known as "stocks." And even these, often the work of hacks, were swung by bands whose credo was embodied in the title of a famous Duke Ellington composition, *It Don't Mean a Thing If It Ain't Got That Swing.*

That this number was written in 1932, several years ahead of what was to become known as the Swing Era, is significant. Ellington, moreover, has credited the germinal idea to the trumpet player, Bubber Miley, who had left his band three years before. In passing, it should be noted that other anthems of the Swing Era were written by Edgar Sampson as early as 1934, a prolific year in which his *Don't Be That Way, Blue Lou, When Dreams Come True,* and *Stompin' at the Savoy* were all recorded by Chick Webb.

The Savoy Ballroom, where Webb was the uncrowned king, was at Lenox Avenue and 140th Street in Harlem. Its opening on 12 March, 1926, was an event of paramount importance in jazz history. Fletcher Henderson's band was an established attraction at Roseland downtown, but as the leading black band of the day it was brought uptown especially for this occasion. Every band of note, black and white (even Guy Lombardo's) was subsequently to play at The Home of Happy Feet—as the Savoy came to be known—before it closed thirty-two years later. It was there, notably, that Chick Webb, Erskine Hawkins and the Savoy Sultans won their reputations.

The Savoy was renowned not only for its music, and for the "battles" fought out between rival bands, but also for its dancers. Following Charles Lindbergh's transatlantic flight, a new dance was developed and named after him. The Lindy Hop succeeded the immensely popular and exciting Charleston at the Savoy. "In a sense, the Lindy is choreographed swing music," wrote Marshall and Jean Stearns in their invaluable *Jazz Dance* (Macmillan). "Great musicians inspire great dancers—and vice versa—until the combination pyramids into the greatest performances of both. One of the reasons for the early development of big band jazz at the Savoy was the presence of great dancers."

Throughout the country there were, of course, many other ballrooms with inspiring dancers, and in them the shape and character of that purely American institution, the "big band" of brass, reeds and rhythm, were defined. Leaders like Paul Whiteman, with ambitions to concert presentation, fronted bands encumbered with strings and other instrumental impedimenta inimical to swing. Growing out of the years before electrical amplification, the ballroom bands were usually of leaner instrumentation. Fletcher Henderson's combination of three trumpets, trombone, three reeds and four rhythm developed into an accepted norm of four trumpets, three (or four) trombones, five reeds, and four (or three, when guitar was dispensed with) rhythm. This applied to both black and white bands, between which there was a considerable exchange. The uninhibited vitality of the blacks excited the whites, whose technical proficiency, at least, impressed the blacks. Musicians like Frankie Trumbauer, Bix Beiderbecke, Bunny Berigan, Benny Goodman, Jack Teagarden and Tommy Dorsey were admired by black musicians, and were indeed influential in different ways, but it is unarguable that all the most important innovations came from the blacks, among whom Louis Armstrong was the supreme example.

The whole Swing Era was influenced by Armstrong, who gave it its language. His phraseology was used by every kind of instrumentalist, as well as by arrangers for big bands. Perhaps the most striking example of his effect on jazz is provided by the early records of Fletcher Henderson's band. Before Armstrong's arrival, it was a good dance band, but it did not

Fletcher Henderson and his father at home.

Coleman Hawkins and Stanley Dance at the Newport Jazz Festival.

really swing. During Armstrong's stay, his solos dwarfed everything and everybody else, rhythmically and imaginatively. After his departure, the inspiration of his example was reflected in the band's rapid improvement and ascendancy. When Duke Ellington formed a band, it was Henderson's he wanted it to sound like!

Like many of the best early jazz musicians, Armstrong was from New Orleans. The prevalent idiom there has been described as "collective improvisation," yet it was not anarchistic, for each instrument had a well-defined role, and teamwork was essential to its success. The trumpet played the lead, the trombone supported, often indulging in bold glissandi, and the clarinet—the freest of the horns—wove counterpoint around the lead. The rhythm sections were clumsy at first, but there was steady improvement throughout the '20s.

When Armstrong joined King Oliver's band at the Lincoln Gardens in Chicago in 1922, he dutifully and loyally supported the leader in fulfilling the requirements of the New Orleans group idiom, but his virtuosity could not long be contained by it. His power, strong personality and incredible inventiveness, all demanded freedom of expression. This was also true of Sidney Bechet, whose individuality was in so many respects akin to Armstrong's. A marvelous clarinetist, Bechet found in the soprano saxophone an instrument appropriate to his personality, one which enabled him to dominate any ensemble as surely as if he were playing trumpet. He and Armstrong are the prime examples of those musicians who were responsible for an increasing emphasis on the soloist as opposed to the ensemble, an emphasis which grew from the mid-1920s onwards and has persisted in jazz to this day. Even in the hey-day of the big bands, the virtuoso, whether as leader (Armstrong, Hines, Goodman) or as star sideman (Hawkins, Hodges, Berigan), was usually the focal point of attention.

The New Orleans ensemble tradition and instrumentation did not disappear, however. Arrangements, tri-voiced for trumpets, trombones and reeds, often echoed in sections the principles of the New Orleans single horns. This was most obvious in the case of Bob Crosby's band, but Sy Oliver's arrangements for Jimmie Lunceford made effective use of the early New Orleans "two-beat" (two-four) rhythm, while collective improvisation, with the roles re-cast, was embodied very effectively in, for example, his *Baby, Won't You Please Come Home?* Even more important, the rhythmic spirit of the New Orleans musicians persisted in their solos and was highly influential, accounting for increased looseness and swing in the playing of their counterparts in the East. Lessons were imparted more often than not in the course of "cutting contests" and "jam sessions," where the virtuosi of the different bands met in competition. These continued throughout the Swing Era, and their significance in shaping the music was immeasurable.

Harlem in New York and the South Side in Chicago were not the only places where these exchanges of musical "information" occurred. Detroit's Paradise Valley was another. In an article entitled "The Great Black Strip" in *The Detroit Free Press* (7 January, 1973), Toni Jones quoted Jimmy (The Greek) Johnson, who owned a couple of pool halls there, and remembered the period graphically.

"It used to look like a carnival on the weekends," Johnson said. "You could go from club to club and after three in the morning, you'd have the thrill of listening to a jam session.

"Say, for instance, Earl Hines's band was playing somewhere in Flint, Basie's band in Pontiac, and Duke's band would be over here at the Graystone, and maybe Cab's band would be playing somewhere else in the state. They would all stay here (in the Valley) and go to the places by bus and come back here at night.

"When they came back these musicians would get together and stay up and jam all night, playing all of their songs. Sometimes they would jam until 10 or 11 A.M. the next morning."

Besides the big bands, small groups remained vitally active everywhere, and often they could outswing the big bands that overshadowed them in terms of publicity and popularity. The intense violence of Stuff Smith's little band, for example, contrasted with the poise and polish of John Kirby's, yet both swung. So did the happily forthright music of Fats Waller and His Rhythm and the subtle, precise creations of Benny Goodman's Sextet. Small groups assembled especially for recording were responsible for many classic performances of the period, notably in the lengthy series under the leadership of Teddy Wilson (Brunswick) and Lionel Hampton (Victor). In short, there was tremendous energy and invention to be found among the small bands, too.

Swing, as encountered in jazz, was clearly of Afro-American origin. Whether or not New Orleans was the birthplace of jazz is irrelevant here, but that city's musicians certainly seem to have been among the first to sense and stress the importance of swinging. Through the 1930s, this was nurtured in ballrooms, nightclubs and semi-private jam sessions by big bands and small. The trend towards concert halls which developed in the 1940s, led inevitably to less swing, to more ornate "concert" music, and to a reduction in rhythmic clarity. The significance of the pioneering steps in this direction by Paul Whiteman and, to some extent, by Duke Ellington in the 1930s is well known, but what has seldom been acknowledged is the effect of *theatrical* experience on the music.

From the earliest days, jazz musicians were hired either as accompanists or as acts in tent shows, movie houses, vaudeville and burlesque theatres. Zutty Singleton, the greatest of New Orleans drummers, gained invaluable experience in the theatre as a very young man, and Louis Armstrong was a big attraction at the Vendome Theatre in Chicago. Musicians like Claude Hopkins, Elmer Snowden and Eddie Heywood are among those who speak of their comparable experiences here. During the period with which this book is primarily concerned, the big band itself became a major stage attraction in vaudeville theatres and, later, in the larger movie houses. A schedule of appearances by bands in Harlem theatres (Appendix II) shows how important these became in terms of employment opportunities. There were, of course, similar theatres in many other big cities, so that when a band reached a certain level of popularity it could count on spending a considerable part of its working year in theatres.

Clubs like the Cotton Club and Connie's Inn in New York, and the Grand Terrace in Chicago, featured lavish revues that were often superior to those normally presented in the vaudeville theatres (to which they were sometimes transferred en bloc). These in turn demanded a theatrical conception of bands that played both for dancing and the shows. The effect of this can be heard in Duke Ellington's colorful "jungle" music. His experience at the Cotton Club, like Earl Hines's at the Grand Terrace, made a lasting impression upon him. Although these two leaders understood and made good use of theatrical principles in their presentations, the development of the "show" band—a band that was a show in itself—probably reached its zenith with Jimmie Lunceford.

While an increased appreciation of coloristic devices to enhance dramatic and romantic situations resulted in undeniable gains in orchestration, the theatrical context was also inevitably responsible for not a little exhibitionism. Offsetting this was the inspiration derived from accompanying *professional* dancers and enthusiastic chorus lines on stage. Dicky Wells, in *The Night People* (Crescendo) has much to say about the cheerful camaraderie between chorus girls and musicians, whose lifestyles had so much in common.

On balance, it may be said that the theatre enriched jazz even as it encouraged elements inimical to swing. Arrangements became increasingly ambitious and complex, not merely to impress theatre audiences, but also those crowds that forgot about dancing and stood enthralled around the bandstands of the Swing Era. When listeners began to outnumber dancers, the concert hall and seated audiences were the logical next step.

The impact of Count Basie's band, when it came out of Kansas City in 1936, is better comprehended in the light of these developments. Here was a band whose whole intent at that time was to swing. Anything that impeded this was stripped away, and its rhythm section simultaneously furnished an unrivaled incentive and foundation. Its reliance on riffs was not, as has often been claimed, in any way innovative. All the big black bands, as well as the Casa Loma Orchestra, had used them for years, but none with the single-minded, uncompromising zeal of Basie and his men.

Throughout his long career as a leader, Basie consistently stressed in his music what he called a "foot-patting" beat, a factor which unquestionably accounted for his band's enduring popularity. Because of his importance, and that of the many great musicians he employed, the last volume of this work will largely be devoted to his world. The second will deal with Earl Hines and the Chicago scene.

Yet as the present book shows, the story of swing cannot be effectively departmentalized. It may be viewed as a mosaic of men's lives, or a confusing, kaleidoscopic sequence of groups that dissolve and reform in different patterns. Regional divisions—New Orleans, Chicago, Kansas City and New York—are divisions of convenience, mere category labels, temporal as much as geographical, and useful sometimes as a means of quick identification. New York absorbed all the styles, but surprisingly few influential players were born there. Ironically, the musician most responsible for inspiring the so-called "Chicago Style"—Louis Armstrong—was from New Orleans. Count Basie, who led the finest "Kansas City" band, came to it from New Jersey via New York, while his greatest soloist, Lester Young, was born in Mississippi. Duke Ellington and Claude Hopkins were from Washington, D.C.; Coleman Hawkins from St. Joseph, Missouri; Johnny Hodges from Cambridge, Massachusetts; Chick Webb and Elmer Snowden from Baltimore; Earl Hines and Roy Eldridge from Pittsburgh; and many great players came from Texas.

Most of the musicians interviewed are black. This is not solely because of artistic significance, but because white jazz musicians were generally written about more extensively—even disproportionately—in the past. Of course, most writers about jazz have been white, like the author, and they have written mainly for a white public. Important exceptions have been Ralph Ellison, A. B. Spellman and LeRoi Jones, but the last, while adopting a militant, anti-white attitude, nevertheless leaned heavily on the work of earlier white writers in preparing his *Blues People* (Morrow). (The parallels with jazz and blues drawn by Albert Murray in his various books are always enlightening, and they reveal a genuine and deep understanding of the music.)

Environment and upbringing are highly relevant, of course, and it is sometimes said these days that jazz should be written about only by blacks. Were it valid to impose a kind of literary segregation on jazz writers, it might be argued that Shakespeare had no business writing *Othello;* that Carlyle, not being French, should never have written about the French revolution; that it was presumptuous of Washington Irving to write *The Conquest of Granada;* and, from another aspect, that no one born since World War II is qualified to write about what happened before it.

Histories and critiques of art are related, but they should not be confused. If the development of jazz criticism has been farcical at times, its bias can largely be explained by the fact that it has been a matter of whites *interpreting* jazz for whites, just as white musicians had done. The general preference of the white masses for jazz by white musicians was never altogether the result of racial prejudice. Translations, and indeed dilutions, were understandably more to their taste.

In my experience, the chief interest of jazz musicians, black and white alike, is music. Human nature being the same everywhere, there are always some who are equally or even more interested in making money. Talking with musicians either backstage or at home, in buses, cars, planes, trains, ships, record studios, hotel rooms, rehearsal halls or bars, I found that after music their range of interest normally embraced sport, gambling, women and automobiles. Some had less conventional interests. Wild Bill Davis enjoyed flying his own plane. Claude Hopkins was as devoted to carpentry as Milt Hinton to photography. Sandy Williams and Sir Charles Thompson were inveterate golfers, Sy Oliver and Howard Johnson serious chess players. Liquor was the favorite stimulant, pot-smoking being less widespread than in the decades before heroin became a major concern. Liquor, needless to say, destroyed many fine musicians, some of whom drank more heavily when disillusioned by a turn of events that reduced their work opportunities.

Few black musicians of the Swing Era seemed seriously interested in politics, but there was constant awareness of and identification with racial goals. The older musicians did not favor philosophies of hate and division, however, nor believe that those who espoused them would achieve anything of lasting value. They had seen far harder times, and many had bitter memories, but time had made gradualists of them. It had also given them a remarkably sound code of ethics. They would speak frankly and critically about musical ability, but they were consistently opposed to anything appearing in print that might adversely affect the livelihood of others in the profession.

Some of those interviewed here are more articulate than others, and not all the memories are infallible. The vocabularies may occasionally surprise, but they are authentic. Hip slang, surprisingly enough, is not often employed. Wits excepted, most musicians speak English like anybody else. Through their words, photographs, and music (on records), their characters should emerge quite clearly. A certain amount of re-arrangement of taped material is always necessary, otherwise the sequence of events can be too disorderly. The restoration of elisions and the removal of redundancies also serve the reader's interest.

In grouping together the roughly parallel stories of sidemen in such bands as Jimmie Lunceford's and Erskine Hawkins's, there is a risk of boring the casual reader through repetition, yet the confirmations and contradictions they contain should prove of considerable interest to serious students of the period.

Some musicians who ought to have been included here were either inaccessible or had unfortunately died. I particularly regret not having interviewed in time such good friends as Billy Kyle, Buster Bailey and Charlie Shavers, all three prime movers in John Kirby's important little band. (Some interesting data on Bailey's early days were, however, obtained from him for notes to his album, *All About Memphis,* Master Jazz 8125.) Unlike the other stories, those on Chick Webb, Mildred Bailey and Billie Holiday did not derive from taped interviews, but were mainly written by my wife, Helen, who knew these artists well. I have not attempted to update the various pieces, which were gathered together over more than a decade, but reference to the date at the end of each will often explain an unexpected viewpoint. (Perspective is invariably altered by time, and one of the chief purposes here is to present many different perspectives on the scene as a whole.) Editorial cuts made in previously published pieces have in some cases been restored, while occasional deletions of magazine devices may make for smoother development in a book that is not designed to be read at a sitting.

A good deal of supplementary information about some of the musicians mentioned here already exists in book form. The vital importance of Fletcher Henderson and his men is recognized in Walter Allen's definitive *Hendersonia: The Music of Fletcher Henderson and His Musicians* (Jazz Monographs). There is also much illuminating information about Henderson in Dicky Wells's *The Night People* (Crescendo). Where Louis Armstrong is concerned, there is a considerable literature, including *Louis Armstrong* by Hugues Panassié (Scribners), *Satchmo* by Max Jones and John Chilton (Little, Brown), *Louis Armstrong—a Self-Portrait* by Richard Meryman (Eakins), and his own *My Life in New Orleans* (Prentice Hall). Besides *The World of Duke Ellington* (Scribners) by this writer, Ellington's autobiographical *Music Is My Mistress* (Doubleday) was published in 1973.

For a broad picture of the big bands, black and white, swinging or soporific, there is George Simon's best-selling *The Big Bands* (Macmillan). Even broader in scope is Leonard Feather's *Encyclopedia of Jazz* (Horizon). For its pictures especially, *Swing Out* by Gene Fernett (Pendell) deserves attention. Rex Stewart's flavorful vignettes of his contemporaries in *Jazz Masters of the Thirties* (Macmillan) are full of rewarding insights. Nat Hentoff and Nat Shapiro's *Heah Me Talkin' to Ya* (Rinehart), mostly culled from magazines, is an adroitly compiled survey of jazz in the musicians' own words. *The Jazz Makers,* edited by the same pair in 1957, contains twenty-one basic biographies of major figures in jazz history (Rinehart). More analytical is *Early Jazz* by Gunther Schuller (Oxford), which takes the reader to the threshold of the Swing Era. Last but far from least is John Chilton's *Who's Who of Jazz* (Chilton), a comprehensive and indispensable collection of potted biographies of swing musicians.

STANLEY DANCE

Rowayton, Connecticut, 1973.

SOMETHING TO PAT YOUR FOOT BY

Count Basie and Freddie Green probably know more about swing and what it requires than anyone else in the world. Because swinging is as natural as breathing to them, they are not in the habit of putting it into words. In the course of the following short discussion at Philharmonic Hall (between rehearsals for the 1972 Timex All-Star Swing Festival), these two authorities manage to analyze, annotate, and even qualify their experience of swing, revealing its elusive nature in basic, verbal shorthand. Making the accomplishment sound as easy and effortless as the effects he achieves at the piano, Basie describes music that swings as "music you can pat your foot by . . ." This is a typical understatement, but it should be remembered that music which makes a Count Basie or a Freddie Green pat a foot is swing of a very high order.

Dance: Do you have any working definition of what swing is?

Basie: No, I don't. I just think swing is a matter of some good things put together that you can really pat your foot by. I can't define it beyond that.

D. Freddie? Any definition?

G. I think it is the type of rhythm you play that has a lot to do with swing. And it is the rhythm section that determines most whether a band swings.

D. How about tempo?

G. Well, yes. Swing can be thought about tempo-wise. So far as I'm concerned, the best for swinging would be medium tempo. Like Basie says, something you can pat your foot to comfortably, more or less.

D. Swinging has always been your thing, Basie, hasn't it?

B. Yes, I would say so. We've tried to keep it that way.

D. Could we talk of some bands that particularly impressed you as swinging groups?

13

B. Well, I think Jimmie Lunceford had one of the greatest swing bands that ever was. I really do. They'd start to rock, and they'd just rock all night long. For a smaller band, the Savoy Sultans had a great swing thing going. Then, so far as this guy Ellington is concerned, you can never tell what he's going to do. I mean, he'll concert you all, and then he'll swing you all, too. you understand, when he's ready to. He's not limited to anything. Now what era are we speaking of?

D. Any era when the music is swinging, even today.

B. Well, there's Buddy . . . Buddy Rich. He has a lot of swing tunes in the book. And when they turn around and play them, then he has a great swing band.

D. Is that mostly due to Buddy himself?

B. As long as the band is swinging, that's it!

D. Why be analytical, in other words? What about some great individual swingers, as soloists?

G. To me, Lester Young was one of the greatest swingers. I think swing is a thing you reach at a certain period in the music, when the audience says, "Well, they're sure swingin'!" You reach a certain point when everything is going together, and everything is going well, rhythmically, solowise and ensemblewise. Missing out on any one of those may account for the fact that people also sometimes say, "Well, they were all right, but they weren't swinging."

D. Even when a band has been together for some time, it may swing one night and not another.

G. Right.

D. What do you put that down to? Physical condition?

B. You never can tell. Sometimes it's a mood, and sometimes you just don't know what it is. Sometimes it just doesn't get off.

G. Sometimes we get to a point where we're *so* tired, but we get up there and swing like mad. Another time, you can have had an awful lot of rest, and you don't swing at all.

D. You don't have any theories about that?

G. It depends on how *everybody* feels. I can't put my finger on any special thing that determines the possibility or the extent of swing. It just happens. Sometimes it gets off the ground and sometimes it doesn't. The audience has a lot to do with it, too.

D. But the rhythm section is important in triggering . . .

G. The rhythm section is the foundation of it. If the rhythm section isn't swinging, then you can forget about it. If it isn't clicking, moving together . . . Well, I mean, the rest of the band has to rely on it.

D. I remember you spoke that way about Lunceford once before, Basie,

Duke Ellington, Freddie Green and Count Basie.

yet his always seemed to me almost the opposite of your kind of band.

B. It would swing right on . . .

D. I know it would, but yours seemed like a different kind of swing when you came here out of Kansas City. Looser, and closer to Fletcher Henderson's.

B. I don't know. That's how you feel about it. That's your opinion.

D. But wouldn't you say your kind of band was different to Lunceford's?

B. Oh, sure. The style was definitely different.

D. Theirs was closer to Duke's with all that show they put on.

B. But the band could swing.

D. And it had a good drummer, too. What about individuals? Freddie named Lester Young.

B. I won't name any.

D. Because you know too many?

B. Right.

D. But Lester was the one that came into your mind immediately, Freddie?

G. Oh, there were many, you know, but he was my favorite, because of the way he played along with the rhythm section.

D. I always felt that once he got away from you, he could not have been very happy with some of the rhythm sections he had to play with. [No comment. An example of both the correct professional attitude and brotherly love *de facto*.] What is the importance of the guitar in your band? So many seem to have given it up.

B. Given up the guitar?

D. In big bands.

B. To me, it holds things together, but the job is to *find* someone who can hold things together! Guitarists today think they must solo, and they don't see much to just playing along in a section.

D. But there are a few people around who still play rhythm guitar . . . ?

G. So far as big bands are concerned, there aren't very many. Steve Jordan was very good.

D. Who was it you had on some record dates when Freddie was sick?

B. Sam Herman, but he's not a regular.

D. Maybe after the electric guitar came in, everybody wanted to solo on the same footing as the horns.

B. Yeah.

D. What about the relationship of dancers to swinging when you used to play more ballrooms? You mentioned the importance of the audience. Was having dancers in front of you inspiring? Did it lead to your feeling you wanted to swing more?

B. Well, sometimes. I mean, you could have dancers in those days, and you could also have a lot of people in the bandstand audience.

D. At the Savoy or the Ritz in Bridgeport . . .

B. Sure, both of those places had a lot of good dancers—*and* a bandstand audience. There would be a big audience for very slow things, as well as for fast things. And for other, interesting swing things, with a whole lot going on, your big bandstand audience would be standing all around you. Besides, there were all the things the kids used to Lindy Hop to. When they were really good dancers—why, of course, it was inspiring, because you knew then you could play something danceable. And the kids who were doing the Lindy Hop could *really* tell whether you were swinging or not.

D. When the bands began to play concerts instead of dances, with all the people sitting down, didn't that make a difference in the attitude towards the music?

B. Sometimes.

G. In my opinion, if they're dancing it helps, and makes it easier to play. It is a little harder when the people are sitting down.

SWINGING: AN INFORMAL SYMPOSIUM

This discussion with the members of the Jonah Jones Quintet took place at the Rainbow Grill in 1970 during several intermissions. The personnel at that time was: Jonah Jones, trumpet; Sonny White, piano; Jerome Darr, guitar; John Brown, bass; Cozy Cole, drums.

Dance: Jazz musicians were swinging long before the Swing Era, weren't they?

Brown: They used to call the soloists "get-off" men.

Cole: We were listening to records in the '20s, but it wasn't until the '30s that "swing" became a password.

Jones: It was in the '30s that we really got into it, but before that we used to say, "Take a Boston," meaning "get off," or take a "hot" solo, or ad-lib a part.

White: I always thought of a "Boston" as a kind of rhythm.

Darr: Yes, a back-up rhythm, a kind of back beat.

Brown: Well, I always thought of it as a sort of solo.

Jones: We used to say, "That guy took a good Boston. He sure can get off."

Brown: Anyway, the break was the big thing in the early days.

Jones: Yes, when everybody laid out for four bars, except one guy.

Dance: Fletcher Henderson's early records didn't seem to swing, but when Louis Armstrong was in the band, and after he left, they did.

Jones: After Louis, it was what we called a stomp band. Fletcher had the stompingest band in the country, and they called his music stomp music. Before Louis was in it, it hadn't been going long, so I guess it was just getting together.

Brown: When I danced to it in 1924 and 1925, it was the best dance band I ever danced to, and everybody said that about it. They could even play a beautiful waltz.

Jones: But they had those numbers like *Stampede, Jackass Blues, Copenhagen* and *Stockholm Strut,* too.

Brown: And *King Porter Stomp* and *Shanghai Shuffle . . .*

White: Were they playing from arrangements then?

Jones: What I heard on records was arranged. Don Redman was making some stuff, and so was Fletcher Henderson. Coleman Hawkins was making some, too.

Dance: Before we leave the early period: would you say ragtime swung?

Jonah: If you're going back to ragtime, you better speak to Cozy! (Laughter.)

Dance: Because he recorded with Jelly Roll Morton? If you listen to some of the marching bands in New Orleans, those mostly composed of old musicians, you find they have a kind of march rhythm that isn't really swinging, but the people behind and alongside, who're doing a dance step —they're swinging!

Jones: The music inspired them to dance.

Brown: It went back and forth.

Jones: Maybe it wasn't swinging the way we think of swinging today, but it was the best they had, and it moved them.

Cole: Different people kept adding on to it things that were a little different.

Brown: Lloyd and Cecil Scott had a hell of a swing band that used to take charge at the Savoy, although Chick Webb was King up there.

Jones: It was a different kind of swing again, just as there was a difference between the swing of McKinney's Cotton Pickers and Fletcher Henderson's band. Each had a personality of its own.

Dance: Well, when was the importance of swinging first emphasized? Long before the so-called Swing Era, or not?

Cole: Oh, yes, long before. Zack Whyte and Sy Oliver and those guys were on to it.

Jones: There were a lot of bands out there that nobody heard of much that were swinging.

Cole: Bennie Moten . . .

Jones: And the band Pres and them used to belong to—The Kansas City Blue Devils.

Brown: Fate Marable had swinging bands on the riverboats.

Dance: When did the Savoy ballroom open, Jerome?

Darr: I don't know, because the first job I had up there was with Buddy Johnson's band in the late '40s.

Cole: It opened about 1926.

Brown: Chick Webb was strong up there by 1928. I used to dance to his music. John Trueheart was there.

Cole: And wasn't Johnny Hodges with him for a while?

Brown: Yes, he was.

Cole: The ballrooms were all-important then, like the Graystone in Detroit where McKinney's Cotton Pickers were.

Jones: McKinney's were strong in 1927 and 1928, and we used to hear them out west. They didn't come to New York much. It was like Fatha Hines in Chicago. He didn't go to New York much, but he was swinging, too, his own way. We thought of his as a kind of western swing.

Dance: What were the earliest white bands you remember as having some pretensions to swing?

Brown: Mal Hallett's.

Cole: Yes, and didn't Jean Goldkette play opposite Fletcher Henderson at Roseland?

Jones: I believe you're right. But the difference was in the solos. You didn't want to hear anybody else's solos after you'd heard Fletcher's men, like Coleman Hawkins and Buster Bailey. Fastness, getting over your horn, meant something then. Buster was *fast,* and a good musician. Hawk—you know what he was! After Louis Armstrong, Fletcher had Rex Stewart, and he was always a good man. He was fast, exciting, and played third. At that time, trumpet players were hired specially to play the different parts—first, second and third. The first, like Pops Smith, played all the first parts—no

"The Stompingest Band in the Country": Fletcher Henderson's band in the "classic" period. L. to R.: Henderson, Charlie Dixon, Jimmy Harrison, Jerome Pasquall, Benny Morton, Buster Bailey, June Cole, Coleman Hawkins, Kaiser Marshall, Tommy Ladnier, Joe Smith, Russell Smith.

Luis Russell's band, 1930: Greely Walton, Bill Johnson, Charlie Holmes, Albert Nicholas, Russell, Paul Barbarin; Red Allen, Pops Foster, Otis Johnson, J. C. Higginbotham.

An early "Bennie" Carter band at the Savoy ballroom. L. to R.: Theodore McCord, Bobby Sands, Lavert Hutchinson, Carter (with baton), Slim Henderson, Shelton Hemphill, Talcott Reeves (seated), Bill Beason, Wardell "Preacher" Jones, Henry Hicks, Danny Logan. The dedication to Fletcher Henderson reads: "To 'Smack', the finest and most beloved musician of the race. 'Bennie'"

CAB CALLOWAY'S BAND. L. to R.: Lamar Wright, De Priest Wheeler, Ed Swayzee, Harry White, Doc Cheatham, Benny Payne, Calloway, Leroy Maxey, Eddie Barefield, Arville Harris, Maurice White, Al Morgan, Andy Brown, Walter "Foots" Thomas.

solos. The second would be a smooth jazz man, like his brother, Joe Smith. And the third played hot, like Roy Eldridge and Rex Stewart.

Brown: Charlie Johnson used to have a great band, and they would have battles of jazz up at the Rockland Palace with bands like his, Chick Webb's and Luis Russell's.

Cole: Luis had a great band when he had Red Allen, J.C. Higginbotham, Charlie Holmes and, on drums, Paul Barbarin.

Brown: Teddy Hill was in that band.

Dance: This was seven or eight years ahead of the time when Swing mushroomed in the '30s.

Brown: Yes, there were great swing bands in the '20s. Horace Henderson had a school band that used to romp through Ohio.

White: How about the San Domingans?

Brown: I liked that band. They had Claude Green and Howard Johnson. And Steeplehead Brown on trumpet.

Dance: Steeplehead?

Cole: Yes, he had a steeplehead. Jimmy Parker was on drums.

Jones: Luis Russell used to play the hell out of numbers like *Panama!*

Cole: They were playing downstairs at the Capitol. And don't forget that band Claude Hopkins had. That was swinging, and he had a fine drummer in Pete Jacobs. It was a good little riff band, with men like Ovie Alston and Bobby Sands, and we're still talking 'way back, around 1932.

Dance: How about small groups?

Darr: The washboard bands were my beginning. Later, I played in cocktail units, trios, singing and playing behind the bar. I played in most of the uptown places—Covan's, Smalls', Monroe's. Then, later on, I worked with Cootie Williams and Rex Stewart. In the washboard band, I was just jiving. I worked in the tramp bands, too. I started to work the cocktail circuit in the '40s, and that's when I really got to play guitar.

Brown: The Spirits of Rhythm were going in the early '30s.

Jones: Most of the white bands were playing sweet music then. When the swing boom came in, it was good for jazz as a whole.

Brown: The white bands used to play a lot of what they called "symphonic" jazz. They'd take classics and put them in dance tempos.

Cole: When they really started swinging was when Fletcher Henderson and Jimmy Mundy started arranging for Benny Goodman, and Sy Oliver for Tommy Dorsey. And then they began to get colored musicians in the bands, like Teddy Wilson and Charlie Christian.

Dance: But even Fletcher used to play waltzes . . .

Jones: Yes, he had things like *Valse Caprice* in seven sharps, *The Kashmiri Song,* and all that kind of stuff. You had to see around corners to play that *Valse Caprice*. When I played it with Benny Goodman, it was in four sharps!

White: Getting back to what Cozy said about Sy Oliver arranging for Tommy Dorsey. To me, that didn't really swing, or at best it was a syrupy kind of swing. I guess he didn't have the right kind of musicians.

Jones: Sy had a hard time conveying what was wanted to them. They could read, but they didn't feel it.

Brown: To me, when Sy Oliver was with him, Jimmie Lunceford would outswing all of them. I'm not taking anything from Tommy Dorsey, because he had one of the greatest bands in the world, but it wasn't a swing band, not in the way of Fletcher Henderson, or Benny Goodman, or even Paul Tremaine. You remember Paul Tremaine? He was 'way before Benny Goodman.

Jones: He used to play in a Chinese restaurant, and they played things like Archie Bleyer's *I Lost My Gal from Memphis,* but it still wasn't what people like Fletcher Henderson were doing. Fletcher was doing something *else,* and you couldn't do it unless you had men like he had.

Brown: Benny Goodman played arrangements Fletcher had played ten years before.

Jones: But Smack had Coleman Hawkins, Benny Carter and Buster Bailey in his reed section, and what are you going to do about that, especially when it comes to taking solos? They could take care of the section work, too, when they wanted. The band might be raggedy sometimes, but you had to hear it when it got into a battle.

Dance: How would you compare Basie's swing with Lunceford's?

Jones: Well, that's something else. I think of that as western swing— Basie's and Fatha Hines's. In New York, they used to write heavier, more technical arrangements. You know how Benny Carter could write.

Brown: Charlie Dixon, too.

Jones: Yes, those arrangements were hard, and you had to be able to play that stuff to make it swing. The western thing didn't have so many notes, but it would be swinging. Oh, yes!

Cole: They'd get in a groove.

White: If I could compare the Lunceford and Basie bands, I would say Lunceford's was a little more regimented, or perhaps I should say polished.

Jones: It had a different kind of beat. Crawford had his own type of beat.

Cole: Sy always had that two-beat feeling.

Brown: Basie's was a looser type of thing, and Lunceford's swing wasn't as relaxed because the arrangements were more complicated.

Cole: When I was playing at the Primrose Dancehall, my band was called Cozy Cole and His Hot Cinders! Joe Thomas, the tenor player, not

L. to R.: Buster Bailey, Sidney Catlett, Joe Thomas, Israel Crosby, Fletcher Henderson, Bob Lessey, Chu Berry.

the one who played with Lunceford, but the brother of Walter "Foots" Thomas—he gave us that name. I was up there about eight months. Cy St. Clair was in it, Charlie Courcy, Joe Thomas . . .

White: Who was on piano?

Cole: Jack Celestian. He had the band at the Majestic later on. Then Edgar Battle came after me, and I joined Blanche Calloway. The Primrose was a dancing school on 125th and Eighth. The Rose Danceland was at 125th and Seventh. I was the youngest one in the band, and I was afraid to fire anybody. Here I am now, forty-nine (Laughter), so in 1930 I was only ten years old! Walter Thomas used to come there and rehearse all his Cab Calloway arrangements, because his brother was in the band and we didn't charge him anything. That way he would get all the wrong notes out of the arrangements he wrote for Cab. It was good for us, because he would give us arrangements and we ended up with almost the same book as Cab.

Jones: When was it you played with Jelly Roll Morton?

Cole: That was four days before I got the Primrose job, and it was my first time ever in a record studio.

Brown: Did you have to have a permit to work?

Cole: Yes. I had a tutor then, when I went on that gig. I guess it just happened there were no drummers around, but I thought it was the greatest thing in the world for me to record with Jelly.

Jones: It was, it was. Did you have microphones then, or did you have to play into horns?

Cole: In 1930? We had microphones.

White: Was that before James P. Johnson?

Brown: Oh, he went back to World War I.

Jones: How about Bessie Smith? Did you record with her?

Cole: No, but with Jelly Roll, James P., Putney Dandridge . . .

White: Eubie Blake or Luckey Roberts?

Cole: No.

Jones: King Oliver?

Cole: No.

Jones: Now John's father had a band called the Hot Peppers.

Brown: That was about 1917, just before you were born.

Dance: Where was that?

Brown: In Dayton, Ohio. They were playing dance music. Four or five pieces. My father's name was James Brown.

Dance: Off the top of your heads now, whom do you think of as the swingingest of the swingers?

Jones: That's hard, Stanley, because it's a matter of opinion. You can

L. to R.: Sam Price, Bobby Bennett, Jonah Jones, John Jenkins, Stuff Smith, Cozy Cole, Ben Webster.

(Opposite). *Jonah Jones and Jerome Darr, 1970.*

pick out one guy for one thing, and another for another. You take Roy Eldridge and Charlie Shavers: they're both top men, but different types of swingers.

White: Did you know Cuban Bennett, Benny Carter's cousin?

Cole: He was noted for his changes, wasn't he?

Jones: Yes, and they weren't playing them then.

Cole: I'll tell you who I think was a swinging tenor player—Chu Berry.

Jones: In that sense, for a swinging trumpet player—for swing and gut-bucket—I'd have to say "Little Jazz," Roy Eldridge.

Dance: Piano players, Sonny? We know Art Tatum was tremendous, but who to your mind swings the most?

White: Teddy Wilson is my man, in any field, swing, commercial, sentimental, pop. I'm crazy about Oscar Peterson, too, and for outright swinging there's always Earl Hines.

Brown: Three different types.

White: For stride piano there were Fats Waller and Cliff Jackson, God bless 'em.

Dance: Guitar, Jerome?

Darr: If you're still speaking of back in that era, that early, I'd have to say Charlie Christian. In the later period, it would be Wes Montgomery. That's my opinion, but there are a lot of other great guitar players.

Dance: Bass, John?

Brown: Well, Blanton revolutionized the bass.

Jones: He was a swinger, too.

Brown: Junior Raglin was another who could set a band up tempo-wise and everything. Before Blanton, there were a lot of good musicians who hadn't gone into the instrument like he did.

Jones: They played good foundation bass, but they weren't swinging.

White: Back in those days you didn't have bass solos like you do today.

Brown: John Kirby was a good, clean bass player, a little ahead of the rest. Of course, I mustn't forget Milt Hinton. He's been a great man for many years.

Dance: When did Milt first come into prominence?

Jones: Maybe with Joe Bushkin after Cab Calloway's band broke up. Not too many knew about him, although he played great bass. I recommended him to Joe. We had had Charlie Mingus and Joe Shulman. "I'll get you a bass player," I said to Joe. "That boy with Cab?" he asked. "Oh, no!" But finally he agreed to let me bring him in for one night. What had he got to lose? After that one night, Milt never looked back, and it got so Joe wouldn't record without him. I remember saying to him one day, "I thought you were recording." "No," he said, "I cancelled that date out. I couldn't get Milt Hinton."

Dance: Drummers?

Cole: In that period, all of us idolized Chick Webb. Another very good drummer then was George Stafford with Charlie Johnson. There were two with Fletcher Henderson who were also very good—Kaiser Marshall and Walter Johnson. They were the founders. Later there were Sid Catlett and Jo Jones. People like Zutty were great for that Dixieland swing, and in that field I guess Zutty was as big as Chick Webb.

Jones: I thought Kaiser had something none of them had.

Cole: That cymbal?

Jones: Yes, that hand cymbal.

Cole: George Stafford was really the one that brought out the hi-hat cymbal. It used to be on two pieces of board with a strap on them, on the floor. He was the first I ever saw. Then they started bringing it up, so you didn't have to lean over to play it.

White: Freddy Moore used something like that.

Cole: Anyway, swing hasn't gone anywhere yet, because as Duke says, *It Don't Mean a Thing If It Ain't Got That Swing*. A lot of other musics have been publicized more, but swing still means as much as ever when it's heard. Any time they catch a band up there really swinging, people feel the music. That's why Basie has remained so great.

Jones: Duke has survived because of his great arrangements and compositions.

Cole: Basie has survived because he has kept swinging.

White: It's the middle-aged people who seem to want to dance now. On the last set, we played a couple of waltzes and everybody got up. They weren't old people either.

Dance: When bop and progressive jazz became popular for a while, it wasn't being played for dancers.

Cole: You know Ella Fitzgerald can sing all of that stuff, but still and all she's swinging. Back there when she was with Chick Webb, nobody had heard of *Salt Peanuts*. But when *Salt Peanuts* comes in, Ella can get up there and sing it, and still swing.

Brown: People used to stand in front and listen to bop.

Dance: They used to do that to the big bands, too.

White: The people who did that were more musically inclined, but behind them there were always dancers, especially at the Savoy. When I wasn't working, I used to go there myself, and stand in front of the bands, and just listen.

Jones: Then the concert thing came in, and bands like Stan Kenton's went 'way out.

Brown: I don't call it dancing what they're doing to rock now. It's more like gymnastics.

Jones: That's what they used to say when people were doing the Lindy Hop. Older people said that wasn't dancing. People older than that thought the Charleston and even waltzes were crazy.

Dance: It's getting time for the last set. Can we sum up?

Jones: A melody and swing outswing everything, if everybody gets together. It's like what we used to call a "groove," where everybody felt the same thing. Cozy will tell you that. We'd get into that thing and play an hour, and it was no pressure, no strain. It just flowed, and we didn't get tired, because everyone was swinging. That was why little bands always swung better than big ones, because you could never get everybody feeling good in a whole big band of twelve pieces or more. But four or five pieces could swing you into bad health!

Brown: I think Stuff Smith's was the swingingest band I ever heard.

Jones: We used to have people jump up hollering and applauding in the middle of a number.

Cole: I remember when we played a concert in Palomar, Los Angeles. Benny Goodman's band was on the bill, at the time when he had Gene Krupa and that prize brass section of Harry James, Chris Griffin and Ziggy Elman. When they got through playing *Sing, Sing, Sing,* the house just went mad. He could have kept on bowing! When he went off, Stuff had to come on behind with six pieces. We had to set up, put up the drums and everything, and the announcer was telling us to hurry up and get our twenty minutes started and over with. Stuff started playing *Stomping at the Savoy,* and we played *Stomping at the Savoy* for twenty minutes. Do you know, when the papers came out next day they had headlines that said, "There's a New King of Swing—Stuff Smith."

Jones: That happened another time on a broadcast. We played *Stomping at the Savoy* for thirty minutes. But at the Palomar, putting our six pieces on after a house-wrecker like *Sing, Sing, Sing* was something. What we had was a tempo and a groove.

Cole: Clyde Hart was in the band then, and Bobby Bennett.

Jones: They were trying to get us off, but Stuff wouldn't quit. He wouldn't come off. He'd set a pattern, and Cozy was there with his press roll, and the next day Stuff was the New King of Swing in *The Examiner.*

Cole: That goes to show about swing.

CLAUDE HOPKINS

BANDLEADER [PIANO AND ARRANGER]

"My parents were both teachers at Howard University in Washington, D.C., and I began playing piano when I was seven. They wanted me to study medicine, and I had a couple of years of pre-medic, but music seemed to be it, and I got my B.A. in music.

"I was taught by Professor LeRoy Tibbs, a graduate of Oberlin who finished, I think, in Paris. He was a wonderful pianist. Then I had Miss Coleman in harmony and counterpoint when I was sixteen or seventeen. I was really good with classics. In fact, I like classics now. It doesn't have to be jazz. I was always a Chopin lover. When I was in Boston at Mahogh any Hall, I had plenty of time to practice. I was there about three years, and I had a book of Chopin's polonaises and sonatas. I committed the whole book to memory, and I used to play one of his polonaises entirely in its original form, and then switch it around to jazz. That went over very well. I wanted to be a concert pianist back there in Washington, but there wasn't any money in it. Of course, it's different today.

"How did I get into jazz? Well, there were a couple of spots in Washington. One on 7th Street was called Dreamland and a Mr. Moore was the proprietor. There was also a man-about-town named Charlie Johnson, a druggist, who had his fingers into a little bit of this and a little bit of that. He told Mr. Moore he knew a young fellow who played piano, and he asked my mother would she let me work in this place if he looked out for me. She consented, and I went there to work. It was a highspot in Washington. Babe Ruth used to come in all the time, and he'd start out with a fifty-dollar bill in the cut-box. I remember one time he had a double-header, and he didn't leave there till 5:30 in the morning. Stoned! He was something.

"I left and went to work for Louis Thomas. He used to hire Meyer Davis on jobs, and his brother, Andrew Thomas, owned the Howard Theatre. Louis had all the society work around Washington. I went to work at his place, where Duke (Ellington) had worked, too. I went from there to the Poodle Dog, right next to the Griffith Stadium on Georgia Avenue. Around this time, I was visiting a girl called Caroline Thornton, who could *really* play a piano. She worked in the pit at the Howard Theatre, and I used to go and sit in the pit with her and watch her play the acts. She'd say to me, 'You want to take this next act down?' When I'd say no, she'd say, 'Get up there and try it!' So I did, and stumbled through it. And that's how I got my experience, through Caroline Thornton, and also through Marie Lucas, another great pianist, as well as a trombone player and arranger. Her father was a bandleader.

"There were a lot of piano rolls around then by James P. Johnson and Fats Waller, and those two really impressed me the most. I used to go around the bootleggers' homes, where they'd have *all* the rolls. I also learned *Carolina Shout* by playing the roll slow, watching the keys go down, and putting my fingers to them.

"When Luckey Roberts came to the Howard, my mother would take me down. He was more of a showman than James P., and his wife would be singing in the show. They'd throw the spotlight on Luckey in the pit during the band overture, and he'd have two or three choruses, and break it up. He had such *huge* hands, and he could maybe stretch fifteen keys. He was small, but he was a powerful man. He very seldom got angry, but when he did he was dangerous. I saw him turn over a pool table—you know how heavy they are!—in getting to a guy on the other side. Whoo! I remember when he was in an awful automobile accident, and both his hands were crushed. All the knuckles were broken and mashed, but I think it was Barbara Hutton who sent him a bone specialist from the Coast. He was wired up so each hand looked like a banjo for months, but afterwards he could play again.

"He had a big diamond ring, maybe eight carats, and two fellows stuck him up. One had a knife, but he put both of 'em in hospital, just with his fists. He didn't drink or smoke, and he stayed in condition. He was a swimming and boxing instructor at the Y.M.C.A., and I couldn't understand it when he took sick and died. He didn't look any eighty-one.

"Wilbur Sweatman sent for me to join his act, just as he did Duke. I stayed with him a few months. He played three clarinets at once. We had a drummer named Percy Johnson, a great drummer, who later went to Europe with me. But Percy had a kind of sleeping sickness and couldn't stay awake on the stage. So Sweat had him built 'way up, and he had so many drums, cymbals and xylophones that he looked like Manny's Drum Store. One night, during a lull in Sweat's act, Percy fell asleep and came tumbling down. The audience went into hysterics, and there was Sweat chasing him all over the stage with his bass clarinet, trying to get to him.

"After Sweatman, I went to Asbury Park. I had a helluva band, fellows

I'd met in New York: Henry Goodwin (trumpet), Hilton Jefferson and Elmer Williams (saxes), Bernard Addison (guitar), Bass Hill (bass) and Percy Johnson. And we had some comical numbers. Henry Goodwin would put on a frock coat, get a telephone directory on a stand, and start preaching—with his horn.

"Somebody told Caroline Reagan about me. Her husband worked for the embassy in Paris, and she was taking a show to Europe. She had looked at about fifty bands before she came to Asbury Park, but she heard us do this one number and signed me up right then.

"Now I had married when I was nineteen, and I wanted to take my wife with me. Bea Foote, who was a great entertainer, took my wife in the club and worked with her every day, teaching her how to dance, so I could get her in the chorus. She went with me to Europe in 1925. We had eight chorus girls, a dance team, a comedian, Josephine Baker, and what in those days was called a soubrette, Maudie Forrest from Philadelphia. We played the Champs Elysées Theatre in Paris for nine months and the Nelson Theatre in Berlin for thirteen. The show was called *La Revue Nègre*. Joe Hayman, who's a druggist, was on alto sax, Daniel Doy, a great musician, was on trombone. Then there were Henry Goodwin, Bass Hill, Percy Johnson and Sidney Bechet. We got held up several times at the borders because Bechet wasn't with the group. He'd be drunk in Paris or somewhere, and Mrs. Reagan would be going crazy. They held up the train at the Belgian frontier once for five hours.

"There wasn't too much English spoken on the Continent at that time, and I ate ham and eggs for three months in Paris, because that was all I could order. Then I met a Frenchman, with whom I became very good friends, and he started teaching me French. He gave me a cane of solid ivory with a push-button at the top. When you pushed it, a long dagger would come out the bottom. In the handle, there was a vial for whiskey. I'm sorry I lost it, because it would certainly be useful in New York now.

"I used to go to a place called the Flea Pit in Paris. I'd buy drinks, ordering in French, and the bill might come to something like five francs and fifteen centimes. 'Now I'll show you what happens when I order,' my friend said. His bill would be about one franc. Those Frenchmen would really take you. I couldn't get over those cab drivers when I first got there. Some little thing would happen, and they'd get out of the cab, shaking their fists, and you'd think they were going to kill the other guy. I used to take a cab to go to the Champs Elysées Theatre, and it would take thirty-five minutes, until I found out it was only about six blocks away.

"I was about twenty, and wild. Those whorehouses in Paris like to finished me! I used to go every day to the Rue Fontaine, and I bought a whorehouse out one night. It was Madame Blanche's, a fifteen-franc house, and the franc then was twenty to the dollar. I gave her fifteen hundred francs not to let anyone else in. She had about a dozen girls, and there I was, sitting at this great, big gold piano with no clothes on, and naked chicks lying around, all over and under the piano. I even had a tab with Madame Blanche for the guys in the band.

" 'You let them have a girl,' I told her, 'and let me have the bill, and I'll come by at the end of the week and pay you.'

" 'I'll have to give *you* something,' she said.

" 'No, that's all right.'

" 'How about a couple of girls?'

" 'That's fine.'

"If I had stayed in Paris two or three years, they would have had to put me under. We were playing poker in Bricktop's club one night after hours. I had lost about eight thousand francs, and I was playing on my ass. There was an English chick there named Peggy, calling those pots, and she was the meanest. When the game broke up, I owed her about a thousand francs, and I didn't have it. She broke her glass and said, 'I'm going to cut your goddamn head off!' Bricktop gave me five hundred francs, and I told her I'd give her the rest when I got paid. She was known for that habit of breaking her glass, and she was *really* mean. I remember she chased Henry Walker, who was playing trumpet in a dancing school, all up and down Montmartre.

"Besides the theatre, we were doubling for an hour in a nightclub with Gloria Swanson on the bill. But Josephine was really putting her to shame, because she had that beautiful body.

"While we were in Berlin, the guys from the Folies Bergères in Paris came there, for by now Josephine was really upsetting Europe. They spoke to her about joining the Folies, but Mrs. Reagan had a long-term contract with her. Louis Douglas, a comedian who lived in Europe twenty or thirty years, knew all the ropes and got a lawyer. Some said she could break the contract because she was under age, but, as I heard it, the lawyer said the only way it could be broken would be by a serious illness. Whether or not she got sick, Maudie Forrest took her place. The Germans actually liked Maudie better than they did Josephine, who wasn't missed in Berlin too much. Next thing you know though, the papers came out with the news that Josephine had gone to the Folies Bergères. And, of course, she went on from there.

"The Savoy Hotel in Dresden wanted my band. It was owned by a German girl who had married an American named Miller. Josephine had taken Henry Goodwin and Percy Johnson to Paris, so the band was incomplete. I caught a train to Dresden on a Thursday, when I was supposed to open the following Monday. I took Joe Hayman with me, because he could speak good German.

" 'Mr. Miller,' I said, 'I must act in good faith and tell you that I don't really have a band now, but if you will give me a few days I will go to Paris and get some musicians.'

"Although his wife thought he should let me go to Paris, he wouldn't hear of it. 'No,' he insisted, 'he's trying to get out of this.' He was talking in German, and I heard something about the police.

"The telephone was ringing all the time, and he was getting reservations for the opening. The president of the Deutsche Bank and various ambassadors were coming, and he just couldn't see losing all that money. But finally, after giving me a fabulous meal with champagne and everything, he relented and said, 'I'm going to let you go to Paris, but if you're not back by Monday, you'll be picked up and there'll be serious consequences.'

"My wife and I had a suite at the Steinplatz Hotel, and we had with us a dog I had bought, a well-trained dog who knew thirty-five commands.

" 'Look,' I said to her, 'I've got to get out of Germany as fast as I can. I'll take the dog and one of the trunks, and wait for you in Paris.'

"Somewhere in Belgium, the conductors came through the train hollering in Flemish. I got out to find out if I had to change trains. I was standing on the platform, looking around, strange, not knowing which way to turn, my baggage and dog still on the train, when an Englishman came over and offered to help me. When I told him I was going to Paris, he said, 'That train's going to Paris,' and he pointed to the one I had just gotten off, but it was already pulling out! He stayed and helped me get on the next one, but I was worrying, of course, about my dog.

"Evidently a lot of people had made that mistake, because in just one day the dog had gone back to a fence with a pound in Belgium. Luckily, I knew Joe Alex, a fellow from Martinique who used to dance with Josephine in the show. He could speak French, Flemish and German, and he knew just where to go. I paid his fare and everything, and he went to this pound.

" 'No, we haven't a dog of that kind,' they said.

"But he was a helluva fighter, and he cursed them out in French, and raised so much trouble that they finally gave him back my dog. I suppose they would have sold him otherwise. He was a beautiful dog, the pup of a wolf and a Belgian shepherd.

"In Paris, I got an Italian drummer, a German trumpet player, and a French saxophone player. I couldn't talk to any of them except in my broken French to the Frenchman, and he had to tell them what I wanted.

We went to Italy, because I was scared of that Dresden thing. I didn't know whether they would pick me up or not.

"Bechet was working in Paris with Buddy Gilmore, who had four or five spots where he would do a ten-minute drum solo before moving on to the next one. Buddy was supposed to be getting fifteen hundred francs a shot. In fact, he was more popular then than Buddy Rich is today.

"My wife stayed in Paris until I got back, and eventually we came home on the *Mauretania*. My first job here was at the Smile-a-While club in Asbury Park. Then I bought a touring car, and took a band and a girl singer to work for Herman Daniels at the Belmont on North Carolina Avenue in Atlantic City. It was a place for gambling and prostitutes, and he was making money like the Bureau of Printing and Engraving. That was where I had Elmer Snowden on banjo, Artie 'Schiefe' Whetsol (who later went with Duke) on trumpet, Bass Hill, and a drummer.

"Then I went to New York and worked at a dancing school on Eighth Avenue and 57th Street. The band was Charlie Skeete's, and he had a boy named Edwards on trumpet, Pete Jacobs on drums, a bass, and a couple of saxes. I began to write for this group, and it soon became a little different from the average dancing school band, and they suggested I take it over. We played our own arrangements and very few stocks. The *chef* of the pit orchestra (about seventy-five men) at the Champs Elysées had liked me, had had me up in his office at the theatre three or four hours a week, giving me lessons in writing, and showing me a whole lot of things.

"After that, for about a year, I went out on tour with the *Ginger Snaps Revue,* playing the colored T.O.B.A. circuit. We couldn't make any money out of it. Admission was fifteen cents, and you could have a house full of people and not a hundred dollars in the till. It was good experience, but it didn't last. Although we planned on 1928 and 1929 editions of *Ginger Snaps,* we didn't reach them.

"That T.O.B.A. could have been a heck of a thing if they just could have gotten it together. S. H. Dudley, Sr., and a theatre owner from St. Louis, between them had a lot of theatres, in Baltimore, in Pittsburgh, in Indianapolis, in Chicago—at least twenty. They had two in New York, the Lincoln and the Alhambra. But there was a squabble. Negroes didn't trust one another then, and everybody wanted to have an executive position. They couldn't get the thing unified like the Keith circuit, or Pantages, or Balaban and Katz. It was a shame, because it could have kept bands and acts working that weren't working. And it could have been a continuous thing. By the time you'd made the rounds, it would have been time to start out again.

"Next, I played for Joe Ward at the Coconut Grove under the Apollo

Sarah Martin and Her Jass Fools: L. to R.: James McGriff, drums; Artie Whetsol, trumpet; Claude Hopkins, piano; Elmer Snowden, banjo; Shaw, a dancer, posing with soprano saxophone.

Claude Hopkins with "Ginger Snaps of 1928" at the Lincoln Theatre, Kansas City, Mo., 17 Nov., 1927. L. to R.: Bessie Dudley, dancer; unidentified male dancer; girl dancer; Hilton Jefferson; Mabel Hopkins (Claude's wife); Jonas Walker, trombone; Kristina Barnes; Bass Hill, bass; girl dancer; Hopkins; girl dancer; male dancer; girl dancer; Doc Clark, trumpet; girl dancer; Bernard Addison, guitar, girl dancer; Pete Jacobs, drums; girl dancer. In foreground, comedian.

Theatre. The band was so soft, and had such good rhythm, that somebody told Charlie Buchanan about it. He came and heard it, and signed me up for the Savoy ballroom. I was there six or seven months in 1931. Then Lou Brecker heard about the band, and he and Charlie Burgess came up and asked if I would like to go to Roseland. I went in for two weeks, and they had a two-week option. At the end of the first week, Mr. Brecker asked how I would like to stay maybe six months. He signed me for six months, and I stayed from '31 to '34. After a while, Mr. Brecker said, 'Let's form a corporation to protect you.' I was the president, and had about sixty percent of the band. Brecker had a percentage out of the rest, and a newspaper guy had five percent. The basic purpose was protection against lawsuits and to deal with taxes. They handled all the promotion and it worked very well.

"I didn't go out on tour during the first summer, because I was getting such good air time, coast to coast, at Roseland. People didn't get too much entertainment in those days, but the radio audiences were something you don't have today. On matinée days, I'd come on just before Amos 'n' Andy, and people used to run home from work to hear me. Then I would have an 11 o'clock shot from Roseland every night in the week, and that really paid off. I could have made an extra thousand dollars from payola, but I didn't, and that was why those publishers loved me.

"The radio made audiences for you when you went on tour. Wednesday might be the best night in one town, and maybe I'd play there this week. Then two weeks later Earl Hines would come in. That way the people stayed hungry, and were always ready to listen.

"I remember when we played a big theatre in Roanoke, Virginia. The first floor wasn't filled, but the first balcony, the second balcony and the third balcony were jammed. And there were a thousand Negroes out in the street waiting to get in. The manager came to my dressing room.

" 'Well,' he said, 'we're just about ready.'

" 'What are you going to do about all those people waiting to come in?'

" 'Well . . . I mean . . . we . . .'

" 'Your first floor isn't filled. Put 'em down there!'

" 'We can't do that, Claude.'

" 'Why? We're not going to have any trouble. These people are in a joyous mood, and they want to hear the band.'

"He talked to the owner of the theatre, and they agreed to try it, although this was really at the height of segregation. So they moved all the whites over from the centre orchestra seats, and brought all the colored in, and filled up the theatre. At the end, there hadn't been an ill word said, and there wasn't a damn bit of trouble. When they brought the money into my dressing room afterwards, I said, 'Look at the money I've been losing!'

"I always stressed cup mutes and soft rhythm. 'You got to open up at the Savoy,' Buchanan said when I went in there, but I told him that wasn't my cup of tea. And those Lindy Hoppers ate up that soft shuffle! They didn't like the idea of me going to Roseland, but while I was there I got the chance to be in movies like *Dance Team* with Paul Lukas and Irene Dunne, and *Wayward* with Richard Arlen and Nancy Carroll. I made two short subjects with the band alone. Fletcher Henderson had finished at Roseland by this time, and I was the house band on the main bandstand. They'd bring in Glen Gray, Shep Fields and the Dorseys for two weeks at a time on the other stand. I did as many of the arrangements as I could, but I had to get Bill Challis to make some. Fred Norman, who made a career as an arranger, joined me at Roseland on trombone, and he used to do a lot of Bert Williams vocals. I was listening to his *The Preacher and the Bear* on a record recently, and laughing so much people must have thought I was going crazy.

"On our early records, Henry Turner often played tuba, and he was an excellent tuba player, but he also studied string bass with a bassist in the Philharmonic. A tuba is all right on ballads, where you've got whole notes, and it can blend with the trombones. Otherwise, the tuba has got to be light. John Kirby was good at hitting those notes right. Cy St. Clair, too. But that's what a lot of 'em couldn't do. Fill that horn full of air, and you'd be on your next note before the one before it finished sounding.

"After the Roseland engagement, I was at the Cotton Club in '35 and '36, with the same band augmented by Russell Smith. Will Vodery was writing for the shows there then, and Russell was about the only one around who could play the first chair. I guess you could say that by this time my band style was well established. Orlando Roberson was doing those falsetto vocals before Jimmie Lunceford got on it, and Nick Kenny of the Ink Spots got it from Orlando, too. It was strange, I admit, strange as a woman singing bass, but it was very popular. I also had Ovie Alston, who later moved back to Washington. He was a nice little trumpet player, and he had a nice little voice, too. Then, of course, I had Ed Hall, who later became really famous as a clarinet player. Bobby Sands on tenor and Pete Jacobs on drums were also big assets.

"At Roseland, dancing was the thing, but the shows were very important at the Cotton Club. I was with Rockwell O'Keefe at this time, and I understand Rockwell was a personal friend of Bill Duffy, one of the big bosses at the Cotton Club. Duffy also ran the Garden and owned about every fighter that went in there.

"After the Cotton Club, I went into the arranging field for two or three

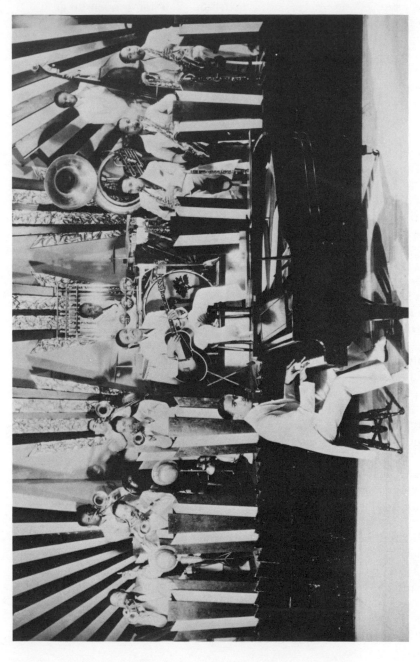

Claude Hopkins's band: L. to R. rear: Fred Norman, Ferdinand Arbello, trombones; Pete Jacobs, drums; Henry Turner, bass. Front: Ovie Alston, Sylvester Lewis, Albert Snaer, trumpets; Joe Jones, guitar; Gene Johnson, Bobby Sands, Eddie Williams, reeds. Hopkins, piano, in foreground.

years. When I went over to C.B.S. the first time, and into the arrangers' room, there were all these old guys—Italians—and they scared me to death. They were writing for the symphony, and they had a score sheet a yard deep for bassoons, oboes, French horns, trombones, violins, violas and everything. They were writing so fast, and all the time they had a conversation going. 'Jeez,' I said to myself, 'I ain't got any business here!'

"I remember doing a couple of numbers for Raymond Scott, but he was worse than Phil Spitalny, and I worked regularly for Spitalny and his all-girl band. He told me, 'I don't want the whole band blowing at any time. It's too big. I want sections working, like eight bars by the reeds with a brass figure, then eight bars by the brass with a reed figure, and maybe the last eight bars—he had fiddles, too—by the ensemble.' So I was a little nervous, but after I got to talking with those Italian guys, they would look on my score sheet and make suggestions, like, 'I'd move him up a third.' They would just be looking at it casually, but I learned from them, picked up a lot of knowledge.

"Spitalny would call me up on a Wednesday. He was at the Park Central and he'd say, 'Claude, come on down. I want you to get this number ready for me to rehearse Monday, because I open at the Palace Friday. And he had twenty-seven pieces! He would sometimes give me numbers that didn't lend themselves to any rhythm, or he would say he wanted the trumpets up hitting an E Flat.

" 'Phil,' I'd say, 'it's too high for those girls. You want this for an opening number? You're doing six shows a day and their lips are not going to stand up to it.'

"Then he'd go into one of his tantrums. 'Goddamn it, that's what I want!' I put up with his eccentricities for a time. You'd make a sketch for him first, before you made the score, and it was really the same as making the score, so you would get paid double. That way, it seemed worthwhile putting up with his hollering and screaming. It made a nervous wreck out of me. I was sitting up all night, smoking two or three packs of cigarettes, trying to get his hurried jobs out, and it began affecting my eyes, so I couldn't take it anymore.

"I formed an entertaining group to play in a lot of Sheraton Hotel cocktail lounges. I had John Brown on bass, Prince Robinson on clarinet, Jimmy McLin on guitar, and a girl named Renee Collins as singer. No drums. I wrote out the parts and it worked very well. We made a couple of records with this group. There was quite a bit of singing, and I even sang myself. That lasted until 1941, when Joe Howard called me.

" 'Hop, can you get a band together in two weeks and open up at the Zanzibar?'

" 'I don't know, Joe. That's awful fast. I've got to build a library and rehearse the show. But I'll try.'

" 'Okay, but don't worry about arrangements. I'll get all the arrangers you need.'

"He did. He got about six, and they were bringing in two arrangements a day. I built up the library to where I had about forty numbers. And I was there till '44.

"I was there on D-Day, when Cab Calloway and I got into a fight. It looked as though the war would soon be over, and he had been celebrating and drinking. I was just getting ready to broadcast, going over a few things behind the curtain with the band, when he came in and started to kid around. 'I'm trying to get the band straight, Cab,' I said. 'I don't interfere with your part of the show.' One word led to another and, to cut a long story short, they arrested him. When the case came up, I was still mad, but all kinds of people put pressure on me to drop it. I remember Bill Robinson and Colonel Julian came up to my house on Cumberland Avenue about it. The newspapers were playing it up for all they were worth. There wasn't any point in Cab having this felony pinned on him, because then he wouldn't have been able to work. And we'd been friends for twenty-five years. So I dropped it. Joe Howard was pleased and gave me a two-week vacation with pay.

"If Earl Hines and I happen to be in the same barbershop, we always act as though we are getting ready to fight, and people get alarmed. But that is just a gag. We've been friends all through the years, and I like Earl. Some people think he is arrogant, but he really isn't.

"When I got back to the Zanzibar, Howard told me Louis Armstrong was coming in next week. 'Hop, he's at the Howard Theatre in Washington,' he said. 'Take these scores down and rehearse the band!' A white fellow named Murray, who had a couple of numbers in the show, went down with me. Louis had a young band that couldn't read. I rehearsed the band Thursday night for about five hours, first the reed section, then the brass, and nothing happened. Murray said, 'Let's go back to New York. This band can't make it.' But Louis and I were friends, and I decided to give it another shot, but still nothing happened. So when we got back, Joe Howard asked, 'Hop, how's the band doing?' And Murray answered him: 'It stinks.'

"The day they were supposed to open, they rehearsed all morning and afternoon. They went past opening time, and Joe Howard decided to do just one show, although they were still rehearsing at midnight. Joe Glaser, Louis' manager was there, and I said to him, 'Joe, I'll conduct the band. At least the tempos will be right.' At that, he turned on me, and began to curse me, because Murray's remark had reached him, and he blamed me for it.

" 'You're a goddamn liar,' I said. 'I didn't tell Joe Howard the band stank. Why would I say that about Louis' band?'

"It was the truth, but I hadn't said it. We both grew angry, and eventually I threw a punch at Joe Glaser. And, you know, he liked that! He was the type of guy who liked you to curse or slap him. He sent for me later, said he wanted to handle me, and he did, for three or four years. I had a small band—five or six pieces—and he was booking me and doing all right. I remember I had John Brown on bass, Toby Brown on clarinet, and Joe Thomas on trumpet. Joe was really blowing then.

"Then I went with Harold Oxley, after he and Jimmie Lunceford split. Oxley was a business man, a helluva guy, and he did an excellent job. But he fell in love with a colored girl, a singer, and divorced his wife, who was the one who had the money. I got a big band together again for him, and he sent me out to the Coast. On the way, we played the University of Texas, the first colored band ever to play there. The band did a great job, and the chairman of the entertainment committee gave the road manager a $400 tip for the band. He also told a colored guy who worked at the university how pleased he had been with our performance, and about giving this tip. The colored guy told me, because I was staying at his house.

"Next morning, when we were getting on the bus to go to El Paso, I said to the road manager, 'Mort, how'd the band do?'

" 'Did great,' he answered.

" 'Any tips?'

" 'Oh, yes. Guy gave me $200.'

"I told the bus driver to stop the first chance he got, because I wanted to make a call. I called Harold Oxley and he said, 'Send that son of a bitch in! You got enough money to put him on a train?' Then he asked me if I thought I could handle the band out to the Coast and back.

" 'Yeah, I think so.'

" 'He had had special tickets printed which couldn't be duplicated, with four or five colors inside when you tore them. This was to prevent promoters from dropping rolls of *their* tickets in on you, because a lot of places I'd go in on a percentage. I knew the business and didn't have too much trouble.

"I was with Oxley several years, until times began to get bad for big bands, and I began to get tired of it. It was hard to get transportation, and when you could get a bus it was eating up everything. You had to guarantee the bus company a thousand miles a week, but if you went into a theatre for a week, or two weeks, the bus would be doing nothing, and you still had to pay for it. Then I bought a bus of my own, and when we were on the way to some town, the motor dropped out on the road! We looked, and there was the motor back there, steaming! We talk and laugh about things like that now, but it was serious business then. I gave up the big band in 1947.

"I took out a show called *The Zanzibar Revue:* six chorus girls, five pieces in the band, with Joe Jordan on trumpet. We played theatres in the South and were booked by Hal Kemp's brother.

"After that, I was in George Wein's Mahoghany Hall in Boston from '52 to '54 with Doc Cheatham, Vic Dickenson, Al Drootin (clarinet), Jimmy Woode and Buzzy Drootin. That was a helluva band. Then I went to the Metropole in New York until '60, when I went to the Nevele Country Club up in the Catskills. I stayed up in the mountains till '66, till I got tired of the woods and began to smell like an ear of corn. You get out of touch, you know, with the run of things in New York.

"I've sure had the full treatment of the business, but I just can't sit down and do nothing. I'll always keep going. I've been through it all, but who needs these musicians nowadays who've *got* to have $450 a week? They lie around New York doing nothing, eating hot dogs and malted milks, and you've got to pay them $450 to work. You're lucky if you get one that isn't a junkie. And when they do work, they mess up so, come in drunk, late, and dressed like nothing.

"In recent years, I've worked a lot with Wild Bill Davison. There isn't a nicer guy anywhere. He talks tough, but underneath he's got a big heart. He cried more than I did when I lost my wife. Of course, I had tears, but I've never been emotional. He isn't as strong as he used to be, but he's got a gift of the gab, and he talks with the customers, and they love it. When someone requests something he doesn't want to play, he says, 'Get your own band!'

"My wife's death last year was a terrific blow, but my son and his wife live with me, and they've been wonderful, and have helped fill the gap. I don't think my wife and I had five arguments in forty years. She would never question me, and I would see she got that money every week. When I was making really big money, she was getting two-thirds of it, and she socked it away. Sometimes, when she was looking through the paper for bargains, I'd suggest she went downtown and shopped.

" 'Oh, no,' she'd say. 'I'm not going to spend like that!'

"I got her a mink coat a few years ago, and she gave me hell for buying it.

" 'That's all money's good for,' I told her, 'to have what you want.' "

(1972)

(Despite the achievements of his lengthy career, Claude Hop-
kins has never had anything like the critical recognition that

is his due. To some extent this was rectified in 1973 by two piano albums, on Chiaroscuro and Sackville respectively, which revealed him to be a talented composer and a refreshing, lyrical soloist with a fine, striding left hand. Too few of his band records have yet been re-issued, but a surprising album on Jazz Archives contains eleven performances recorded in 1932–33 and never previously issued, among them his theme and best-known composition, Anything for You.)

ELMER SNOWDEN

BANDLEADER [BANJO AND GUITAR]

"My father *claimed* he was a drummer in some kind of marching band, but he was jiving. I heard him just once, and he was terrible. 'Look, Dad,' I said, 'forget it!' When I was a kid I played harmonica, or what we called mouth organ then. My mother was always saying, 'I want you to hear my son play his mouth organ!' And I used to play it in church.

"Guitar was my first real instrument. I knew about four chords on it, but I was playing with a fellow named Herbert Faulkner who played mandolin. His father taught me those chords, and then the two of us would get together, and go out on the corners, and sing and play, and take our caps off and pass them around through the crowd. We'd go to barbershops and little bars, too, and the people would say, 'Oh, let the little boys come in.' This was during the first World War, and we were singing the latest stuff like *Put On Your Old Grey Bonnet*—barbershop-type songs. We'd get a little change together that way, but the problem was what to do with it. If we took this money home, we had to explain where we got it. What we did was to roll it up in a paper bag and shove it under the white steps in front of the house, where it would accumulate. I was eight or nine then, and money didn't mean a thing to me. When I got to the point where I worked a steady job, *then* I knew what to do with it. My father was only making eight dollars a week then, and when he found out what I was doing he made a lot of trouble. He took my instrument and broke it up! But my mother said, 'Let the boy play. He's making some money.' And she got me another guitar from the pawnshop for seventy-five cents.

"I was born in Baltimore (in 1900), and that's where I began playing professionally, in a theatre with Eddie Booze, the piano-playing brother of Bea Booze, the blues singer. He got me a job after school playing for the silent pictures in the Carey Street Theatre. As the film changed on the screen, we had to change the mood of our music. I couldn't read, and I didn't start reading until 1917, but I think I was playing better then than I do now, or even at my peak. Why? When I was learning how to read, I started declining, started going back instead of advancing, because I slowed up for the paper. Before I came in contact with the paper, I was nothing but a kid—in short pants—and my mind was real fast at that time.

"They paid me ten dollars a week at the theatre, and I took this money home to my mother. She'd give me two dollars and keep eight. That eight dollars would pay for our food and the rent. See, you could get a loaf for a nickel, and a pound of sugar for three cents. Ours was a two-bedroom house, and the rent was seventy-five cents a week. I had money to buy clothes, and my father stopped working.

" 'If you're making more than I'm making,' he said, 'ain't no sense of me working!'

" 'You've got your nerve,' I told him, 'to quit your job after giving me a beating every time you found me playing!'

"The theatre job lasted a year, or a year-and-a-half, until somebody told Eubie Blake about me. 'Bring him up here,' he said, 'and let me hear him.' He was playing at the Pythian Castle, a fraternity place, where they had a dance floor and a man teaching dancing. It was like a dance school, and Eubie had the band, about five pieces. So he got me to come in on banjo. I still couldn't read, but I had a very quick ear and could play anything. Then I started playing in cabarets as well, and in those days you had to play a lot for singers. You never knew what they were going to sing, and you might not know their songs, but you would just follow the chord construction. 'Just go ahead and sing,' I'd tell 'em. 'We'll pick you up.' And we would, whatever key it was in. Keys didn't make any difference, but that was how I learned to pick up on everything. From that time on, they used to say, 'If you can't play in all the keys, don't play with Snowden, 'cause he plays in all twelve, right around the circle, and in all tempos.' Later, when I got to New York, I learned a lot about the construction of keys from Willie 'The Lion' Smith, just like Duke (Ellington) did.

"In 1919, Eubie Blake's band was taken over by Joe Rochester, an undertaker and a C-Sharp piano player. He played on all the black keys —no white keys. He had one of the best bands at that time, and sometimes we would go to Washington to play. That is when Duke Ellington first heard me, and when I saw him in San Francisco a few years ago he remembered some of the songs we used to play. He was humming them in his dressing room, and he said we ought to record them.

"While I was with Joe Rochester, they sent for me to come down to Atlantic City as a free-lance artist. I was still wearing short pants in the daytime, but at night I wore long pants to work with a group at the New World, at Tennessee and Baltic. They had Ethel Waters, Ethel Williams and another Ethel—there used to be three Ethels—as entertainers. As blues singers they had Mattie Hite, Bessie Smith, and Mary Stafford, the sister of George Stafford the drummer. There was a terrific drummer, a police-man they called Black Diamond, and you never heard a drummer like him! He had a big brass rack, about as wide as a bed, and he kept it shining so it looked like gold. He had everything hanging on it, and when he got through at the end of the band's number the whole place would be in an uproar. Then he'd get up, wipe his head—he was bald—and take his bow. I think the club is still there in the same place with the same name. I was much the youngest guy in the band. There was a clarinet player from Chicago in it, and during the daytime he taught me to read.

"By this time I was playing banjo-mandolin. (I hadn't gotten up to tenor banjo yet.) The neck was like a mandolin's, but the body was a banjo's. That was a C instrument, which you play like a violin or a piano score. The clarinet player was teaching me to read in the bass clef. When the summer ended and we went to Washington, I asked for the cello part, because that was in the bass clef. That would take me into the tenor clef now and then, and soon I got so I could read all the clefs. That made a musician out of me.

"Louis Thomas had been down to Atlantic City and heard me and Black Diamond. He had a kind of booking agency and a nightclub called the Quaker City Jazz Club, and he took us to Washington. Duke Ellington was being booked out of that office then and, although Louis was colored, Meyer Davis worked for him, too. In fact, he had six or seven groups. Our band, Louis Thomas' band, went into the Howard Theatre, playing from a box at the side behind lattice work. We had Doc Perry on piano, Otto Hardwick on sax, Diamond on drums, and I was playing banjo. Oh, we used to perk it up! We had it so they often didn't want to see the show. But then Marie Lucas' band would come out into the pit, and she had sent down to Cuba or wherever it was and got all those musicians like Juan Tizol and Ralph Escudero, and had enlarged her band. They would play the show, and we'd come back and play the intermission and the exit music.

People used to say, 'We don't know who you are back there, but you've got some *damned* good music!' That lasted till 1921, when I stopped playing with the group and married Gertie Wells.

"Gertie was the best piano player in Washington, and she had her own band, but at the time she was having trouble getting musicians. I went back to Baltimore and got four or five guys from the old Eubie Blake band. Then she was tearing up Washington, and nobody could touch her band. I played in it until she got pregnant, and then we had to give it up.

"The fellow who owned the New World also owned the Paradise, the big club in Atlantic City, where Charlie Johnson and the big entertainers worked. His name was Wieloff, or something like that—German or Jewish —and no connection with Ed Smalls who had the Paradise in Harlem. He was booking all the places then, and he sent for me in Washington to open a new place called the Music Box on New York Avenue and the Boardwalk. So I took Artie Whetsol and Otto Hardwick down. When the season was over, we went back to Washington. Claude Hopkins, who had been working the big Belmont, stayed on there. He wanted some musicians and he naturally came to Washington to get them. He asked if I would play with him, and I went down there for quite a while. Claude was a terrific piano player, and he, Cliff Jackson, and a couple of other piano players, used to gang up on Duke, who knew only one or two numbers. Of course, he would play this number he had written, *Poodle Dog Rag,* in half a dozen different keys, and it was supposed to be a different song, but it was the same thing at different tempos. Then Russell Wooding told him he'd hire him for his band if he'd learn to play something besides that rag. *The Siren Song* was popular, and he asked him to learn that. So Duke worked on it all week and went out with the band. He was sitting up there all night waiting to play *The Siren Song,* but they didn't call it till nearly closing time!

"Then I had an eight-piece band working in Murray's Casino, a big dancehall, and at that time Duke was painting the signs for dances. He and another fellow had a studio down in a basement. When another dancehall opened up, the Colonnades, he did the sign-painting for that, too. Besides this and his job as a soda jerk at the Poodle Dog Café, he was always hanging around with us, and asking to sit in. We were sceptical about it and I used to tell him, 'If you'll learn some songs, I'll let you.'

"Clarence Robinson came to play the Gaiety in Washington with a show. Katie Crippen's husband had the band in it, and Fats Waller was the piano player. I hadn't seen any of them before, but one night Clarence came down where we were playing and listened to us. 'This is what I'd like to have,' he said, and asked how I'd like to come to New York. Where they were working was a burlesque house, and I'd heard about burlesque and didn't want that. 'If you come to New York,' he said, 'we'll be on the Keith circuit.' That was supposed to be bigtime, and he made it sound like a lifetime job. So he left me carfare for a full band.

"I had a woman playing piano, but he didn't need her, and my drummer wouldn't go because he also had a job in a bakery shop. In any case, I didn't just walk out, because I had four bands working at that time, and I made up another to play the dances at the Casino when we were gone. I knew Duke and Sonny Greer had been up to New York some time before for about three weeks with Wilbur Sweatman, and that they got themselves stranded. Now Sonny heard about the new job and came over to see me.

" 'You know I've been in New York,' he said, 'and I know about New York. I heard you were approached about a job there and consented to take it.'

"So I understood he was available, and he, Toby Hardwick, Artie Whetsol and myself got into Toby's car, the Dupadilly, and drove to the station. Man, it's a wonder we ever got out of Washington at all! That car used to stall on the rail tracks and all the worst places. We got our tickets, and left it setting right there outside the station. When we got to New York, Toby called his father and told him to go down and get it. Whether he wanted it or not, I don't know, but we never saw it again.

"Fats Waller was supposed to play piano with us, but we were there a week without him or a job. We kept rehearsing, but we didn't even see Clarence Robinson. Finally, Sonny said we should go to his house, which I think was on 130th and Lenox Avenue. 'You know how to get there?' I asked him, because we were living downtown and New York was a big city. We got there and found Clarence in bed.

" 'Well, the reason you're not working is that you don't have a piano player,' Clarence said.

" 'You told us Fats Waller was going to play piano.'

" 'Yes, but Fats is nowhere to be found.'

" 'Well, why didn't you tell us that? We've been here a whole week and haven't touched nothing. We've been setting at our window, looking down, watching other musicians go to work.'

"Next morning, I sent a telegram, and Duke came up at 4 o'clock that afternoon on the Congressional Limited. Sonny met him, and the first thing Sonny wanted to know was whether he had any money on him. But Duke had spent all that his father, Uncle Ed, had given him. I was very close to Uncle Ed, and he had made me promise I would look out for his boy. And Duke is still holding me to that promise!

" 'I'm writing this book,' he told me a year or so ago, 'and I'm going to put in there the promise you made to my father, and about how you stranded me! You don't even come to see how I'm doing now!'

"Then he started asking me about coming back in the band, and this was before I had the heart attack, but I told him he was doing too much traveling, too much flying. He began explaining how easy it was.

" 'Don't talk to me about that,' I said, 'because I remember when *you* wouldn't fly. I remember when you went to Europe on a steamship. The *Bremen,* wasn't it?'

"When he heard about me going over with the Newport Jazz Festival in 1968, he wanted to know how I got there. 'Did they dig a tunnel, or did you go across a bridge? I know you didn't fly, because you told me you would *never* fly!' He was rubbing it in, because he knew it was only by flying that we could have done all those one-nighters in Europe.

"Anyway, after he came to New York the second time in 1923, and we got the band straight, we were off four more weeks. The Washingtonians, which is what we called ourselves, were a good group, and all the other bands used to come and listen to us as we rehearsed. We had only five pieces, but we were all doubling. I was playing C-melody, soprano and baritone saxophones. I had started on sax around 1917, working from the instruction book that came with the instrument, and when I went to Washington in 1919 one of those Cubans in Marie Lucas' band coached me and showed me a lot of stuff on the saxophone. His name was Nulasco, and he was real light. He looked like Juan Tizol, and he was a very good friend of his. He played all the reeds, and thanks to him I got to the point —I'll have to say so myself—where I was very good. I was closer to Toby Hardwick on tone than Rabbit (Johnny Hodges). You could put Toby and me behind a screen, and you wouldn't know which one of us was playing. We had sat side by side in the band, and I had gotten my tone just like his.

"Now we made an audition at a beautiful downstairs club on 48th Street and Broadway called Everglades. We went in, set up, and played. The man was crazy about the group.

" '*This* is what I want,' he said. 'Whoever's the leader, come over here.'

"I started over, but Clarence Robinson shoved me down and went over to talk to him.

" 'Go over and talk to the man for the band,' Sonny Greer said. 'He's asking for the leader, and you're the leader, ain't you?'

"So I went over, and the man said:

" 'Now, wait a minute! Who *is* the leader?'

" 'I am,' I said.

"So we talked, and the money was nice, and he brought up the music,

Elmer Snowden, 1965.

show music, and we played it . . . except for Duke, because he couldn't really read then, but we covered him up. We were getting ready to make a contract when Clarence said, 'You can't do anything without me. I'm in charge of this whole thing. I am the leader.'

"Then the man said, 'When the band played, you didn't get up or do anything. You just sat right there. So what do you do?'

" 'I'm a dancer,' said Clarence.

" 'We've got a floorshow here, and we don't need a dancer.'

" 'Well, if you don't need a dancer, you don't need me, and you don't need my band!'

" 'The hell with all of you!' the man shouted, and he almost threw us out.

"Naturally, we had to get rid of Clarence.

"Bricktop (Ada Smith) used to be a singer in Louis Thomas' club in Washington, and when she heard about us being stranded she was working at Barron's uptown. She spoke to old man Barron about us.

" 'Well, I got a band in here,' he said.

" 'Yeah, but these boys—they're great!'

"The way the thing wound up, we were to work two weeks for nothing while he paid the other band two weeks' salary and let 'em go.

" 'If you don't make forty dollars a week in tips,' Barron told me, 'you let me know and I'll make it up.'

"That was all right with me, because my diamond ring and everything except my underwear was in pawn. When I came out after this talk, the band was standing on the sidewalk, waiting. 'Take it!' they all said when I told them the proposition. And the first night we came out with sixty dollars apiece in tips.

"Sometimes the place would be full of gangsters. When they came in, they would close all the doors. There was one guy who would get fifty-dollars-worth of change—nickels, dimes, quarters, half-dollars and dollars—and sit himself down at a table. Even if it was six o'clock in the morning, he would shout, 'Put on the floorshow!' The girls would come out, and they had four entertainers as well as singing and dancing waiters. When they got through, he'd scoop up all that money and throw it on the floor. Then there was a scramble! Sometimes he would do that about four times, but I'll tell you that he didn't *always* get fifty dollars of change for his paper!

"This was 1923, and I don't think the numbers had reached Harlem then, but there were plenty of other rackets, like gambling and horseracing, besides bootlegging. They used to say they were giving you whiskey straight off the boat—scraped off! They had that Chicken Cock whiskey that was sealed in a can—like a sardine can. You opened it and pulled the whiskey out, the worst stuff you ever tasted in your life. You know it's got to be good because it's in a can! And they would make up the champagne in the kitchen. Ginger ale, some seltzer, and something else they put in. They had a machine to put the cork in so that when it was pulled out— BAM, a lot of noise! They would wrap a towel around the bottle, and it was thirty-two dollars each time.

"From Barron's we went to the Hollywood on 49th and Broadway. Sonny and Duke found Bubber Miley and Charlie Irvis playing at a place down in the basement on 135th Street that they called the Bucket of Blood. I told them to bring them to rehearsal, and I wasn't exactly for their growling stuff, but I could see where it would be an addition to the band. We had been playing like most of the boys downtown before, only doing it with five pieces, and we didn't do any 'jungle style'. When we first recorded for Victor—Elmer Snowden's Novelty Orchestra—Whetsol wasn't doing any of that stuff. He used to use a cup under a hat, and his horn would sound like a saxophone. Toby was playing saxophone on that date, and so was I, and they couldn't understand how we got that sound, because the only saxophone player they knew about was Toby. But our music wasn't the kind of *Negro* music they wanted, so Victor didn't issue it.

"I stayed in the Hollywood about a year. When you went in a place like that, the gangsters took you over and paid you. They paid thirty-five dollars a man, and I was getting forty, but I was only leader in name. One night, I went in there and heard the band talking about me in the girls' dressing room, talking about getting rid of me. Although Toby and I were very close, they were going to put it on him to fire me. The boss had heard about it, too, and he called me in the furnace room.

" 'We hired *you*,' he said, 'Why don't you get another band?'

" 'I don't know no musicians in New York,' I answered, 'but I know some in Washington.'

" 'How much would it cost to bring them up here?'

"At that time the fare was about four dollars, so he gave me the money. But Sonny had been sitting on the steps behind the furnace where it was warm, and he heard all this, so he goes and tells the group.

" 'Wait a minute! We're planning to get rid of Poppa, and Frank just told him to go to Washington and get another band!'

"Oh, it was a mess, but I got out, and went to Washington, and brought a band back. Right then the place burned up for the first time. Whetsol left and went back to school, and Freddy Guy took my place. Duke didn't really want the job as leader, because all he wanted to do was write songs and get them published, but I think the bosses were afraid he was going to take the band into a hotel.

"There was a singer called Broadway Jones who was working at the

Bamville Club on 129th and Lenox. He had the band there, and some of his musicians told him about me, so he had me come and sit in one night. His banjo player, Henri Saparo, was a barber. He couldn't read and he wasn't a soloist. He was the guy Duke later got Harry Carney from. I borrowed his banjo and they put the music up. Okay, I cut the mustard just like that! Then they put up a number I'd never seen, and it had a banjo solo in the middle. The pianist had been playing it, because Saparo couldn't. This time the pianist laid out and they listened to me.

    " 'Is that on the paper?' they asked.

    " 'Sure it's on the paper,' the piano player said.

    " 'Well, that's the first time we've heard it,' they all said.

    "So right away they all wanted to hire me, and after a time, when Broadway Jones left to go with a big show downtown, they made me leader in his place. In that band were Horace Holmes and Gene Aiken (Gus Aiken's brother) on trumpets. Gene usually played trombone, but I had Jake Frazier on that instrument. Bob Ysaguirre, I remember, was on tuba. Alex Jackson, who's a preacher now in Oakland, and Ernie Bullock were on saxes. The pianist, a beautiful concert pianist, later went to Europe and sent for me, but the woman I was with didn't want to go. Everybody was coming up to listen to this band, because I had some symphonic arrangements. We were all doubling on instruments, and we used bassoon and English horn. When you walked downstairs into the room the band sounded like a big pipe organ.

    "At one time, I had Jimmie Lunceford playing piano in this band, but he switched to saxophone when Count Basie came in. It was one of Basie's first jobs in New York, and he could not read too well, so then I got Claude Hopkins for a while.

    "The same man who owned the Bamville also owned the Nest at 133rd and Seventh. It was a small place, longer maybe, but nowhere near as wide as the Bamville, which had a dance floor and floorshow. We played both places, and one morning, about 6:30, I was at the Nest. Most of the musicians had gone home, and I was packing up my instrument and talking to the boss. The guy upstairs pressed a button that meant some cash customers were coming down. When the door opened, in came Duke, the whole band, and the three bosses from the Kentucky Club, the new name for the Hollywood. They patted me on the shoulder and had me sit down. I could smell a rat.

    " 'Bring us some champagne,' they said, 'because Elmer likes champagne!'

    "Now I never drank no champagne in my life, but they filled up the glasses.

" 'I'll tell you one thing,' I said, 'you fellows came down too late. The band has left.'

" 'Who wants a band? We've got our own. Don't you see the band here?'

"They had all the Washingtonians except Freddy Guy, and now they got to talking and reminiscing about the things we used to do, and how the band used to sound.

" 'Elmer, it doesn't sound like that no more since you left.'

" 'Oh, that's too bad,' I said.

" 'But starting tomorrow night,' one of the bosses said, 'it's going to be right back where it was, ain't it, old pal?'

" 'What do you mean?'

" ''Cause you're going to be right back on the bandstand.'

" 'Hold it!' I said. 'I've got the band here. What *do* you mean?'

" 'You're going to come back with the group. We're telling you now.'

"They went to the boss and said, 'See that Elmer gets you a band, a nice band, for your place, 'cause he's gonna be back down at the Kentucky Club tomorrow night.'

"Evidently the boss had been used to things like this happening to him before, because after they had gone he said, 'Okay, you go ahead with 'em.'

" 'You firing me?' I asked.

" 'No, no, I'm looking out for your health. You're young. You want to stay alive, don't you?'

" 'Yes, but I'm perfectly satisfied, and I've got a good band here.'

" 'Baby,' he said, 'you go ahead and put somebody else in here.'

"So I got Bernard Addison and put him in charge of the band, and went down to the Kentucky Club for six or eight months until they burned the place down again. We were still just the Washingtonians. Duke didn't want to use his name, and when he first went in the Cotton Club it just said *The Cotton Club Band*. He didn't want to be a bandleader then, but his wife, Edna, she kept pushing him.

"All the white musicians downtown used to come to the Kentucky Club. Colored musicians couldn't even get near because it was so expensive, and, besides, they'd be working at the same time. Paul Whiteman used to send his spies out, and Henri Busse was the main one. He sat in beside Bubber Miley, and he was trying to steal his stuff, but Bubber was too fast with that plunger. He never let nobody know what was inside that! He and Charlie Irvis had a whole lot of different mutes. Sometimes Charlie used half a yo-yo! After Busse had been to hear us a couple of times, Whiteman came himself.

"One night, the boss called me over in a corner and said, 'When you get through tonight, Elmer, take your instruments home.'

" 'Wait a minute, Frank! They tell me that's what you said once before. You're not going to set the place on fire again, are you?'

"He didn't say yes or no, but just looked at me and said, 'Uh-huh.'

" 'You *must* be kidding!'

"But I took him at his word, put my saxophones, guitar and banjo in a cab, and went home with them. He didn't tell the other guys. Sonny's drums were burned up. Bubber had hung his horn in the furnace room, and all it got was tarnished. Later on, I remember, Duke was sitting back and laughing.

" 'It's their piano. I didn't buy it. Ha-ha-ha!'

"I went back to the Bamville and organized an eight-piece band there with Rex Stewart on cornet, TeRoy Williams on trombone, Prince Robinson and Joe Garland on reeds, Freddy Johnson on piano, Bob Ysaguirre on bass and Walter Johnson on drums. I played banjo. Even while I was at the Kentucky Club, I had five bands of my own working. Cliff Jackson, the piano player, was in one called Elmer Snowden's Westerners. So was Tricky Sam Nanton. The new band almost caused a riot in New York. We were well rehearsed and we had as many as three arrangements on the same number in some cases. Everybody came to hear us. There was a battle going on then between Coleman Hawkins and Prince Robinson, because people used to tell Hawk that Prince was greater than he was, and that sort of thing.

"We were playing a breakfast dance at the Bamville one morning. The band was swinging and everybody's fingers were popping when, all of a sudden, over at the entrance, here come Fletcher Henderson, Coleman Hawkins and Louis Armstrong. The three of them got a table right in front of the band.

"Rex was only a kid, about seventeen then. He had never met Louis Armstrong, but he idolized him and had heard all his records. He was sitting right behind me, and now he suddenly got sick.

" 'Pop,' he said to me, 'I got terrible pains in my stomach.'

" 'That's bullshit,' I told him.

" 'I can't go on. I can't make it.'

" 'Sit down and play your horn,' I said to him, and hit him hard on the shins. He looked like he was going to cry, but I wouldn't let him get up. Every time he tried, I'd hit him on the shins again. So he got mad, and started blowing.

"Louis came over afterwards and said, 'Hot damn, I ain't never heard nothing like that before in my life! Where did you get this kid from? And who is he?'

"He took Rex in the men's room, and gave him some of his special lip salve, and they got to talking, and became good friends. A couple of nights later, when we were over at the Nest, there was a telephone call for Rex. It was Louis, and he wanted him to take his place with Fletcher Henderson. Rex didn't want to go.

" 'If you don't take the job, I'm going to fire you anyway,' I told him, because I wanted to see him get somewhere, and Fletcher Henderson had the biggest name at that time.*

"The Washingtonians hadn't really liked Freddy Guy's playing when he first went with them, and during 1927 he was rehearsing with a Broadway show called *Rang-Tang* that Flournoy Miller and Aubrey Lyles were producing. They had forty-two banjo players in it, the whole chorus line, and their nails were done in fluorescent paint, so in one scene, when the stage was dark, all you could see were the nails fingering the instruments. They heard about me from somebody and called me to a rehearsal, and as soon as I made that audition Freddy Guy went back with Duke. It was about the time they went in the Cotton Club.

"I had what I thought was a good banjo, but Arnold Rothstein, who was at the rehearsal, didn't like it. He had money in all the big shows at that time, and he told me to go out and get a banjo with a lot of flash to it. So I went to a store and found one that cost $790 with the case. All the plate-work was gold, there was pearl on the back, and it had a lot of stones —like diamonds and rubies—so that when the lights hit it the whole theatre lit up.

" 'That's what we want,' Rothstein said. 'I told you to get a good one.' He paid for it, and I did a good job, and stayed with that show about two and a half years. At first, I played on the stage and in the pit, but the union objected to that on the grounds that I was doing two men's work. So they had me do the feature from the pit. I'd stand up and put my foot on a chair, and then they'd put a baby blue spot on me, and a spot on the people on the stage, and we would co-ordinate between the two.

"After that show closed, they opened up with another called *Keep Shufflin'*, and Miller and Lyles had me doing much the same thing. Fats Waller was on one piano and James P. Johnson on another, and they set

---

*In a letter to Snowden written on 24 December, 1965, Stewart looked back appreciatively: "I'll never get over being sorry that we did not record your band when we had Prince Robinson and Jimmie Harrison in there playing things like *Bass Ale Blues, Spanish Shawl,* etc. Well, Pop, I guess I've bent your eyes enough. But I want you to know that you are responsible for whatever I may do in this chicken-shit business and I am eternally indebted to you for giving me my start. Love, Rex."

me in the middle between the two of them. I was with that show about eight months. Then in 1930 came another *Blackbirds,* and Miller and Lyles were in that, too. Miller liked my work and insisted on having me wherever he was. The big number turned out to be *Memories of You,* which Minto Cato sang. Ethel Waters hit the ceiling, because she was singing *You're Lucky to Me,* and they had all expected that to be the hit. This was the show Ethel brought little Sammy Davis, Jr., out on stage in her arms.

"The people who have written stories about me didn't know about this period. They've said I went into 'obscurity,' or 'passed out of the picture,' but I was doing Broadway shows. Claude Hopkins and I were in one called *Make Me Know It,* an all-white show except for us. Claude had the band, but the show only ran about two weeks, and we never got paid.

"I went back to bandleading at the Hot Feet Club in the Village. It was run strictly by gangsters. Fats Waller was on piano, Chick Webb was on drums, and the saxes were Toby Hardwick, Garvin Bushell and Al Sears. I was playing banjo and saxophones, but we used no trumpet, trombone or bass. We went on the air every night from 1–1:30, and everybody swore we were a big band. Toby was an A-1 musician and he used to take the stock arrangements and transpose the violin part for fourth saxophone. The other three saxes would be playing the regular sax parts. When they started putting out four saxophone parts in stocks, then we had four saxes and Toby would be playing from the violin part and the melody, so we had five-part harmony. We'd come on so heavy you'd forget there was no brass there. Sometimes Toby and I would be playing two baritones, and sometimes he'd play the bass sax. Our sign-off was *Looking for Another Sweetie,* and we had the four waiters and the four entertainers singing it in harmony. A little short guy, Chris Smith, wrote it. He was a piano player, but later on somebody else got hold of it, changed the words, and it became *Confessin'.*

"From the Hot Feet I went to Smalls' Paradise in Harlem. To tell the truth, I had been doubling there in 1930, even while I was with *Blackbirds.* When I got off the stage around eleven, I'd jump in a cab and join the band on the stand, and be there till six in the morning. Many days, when they had the breakfast dances, I'd come out there around ten-thirty or even twelve o'clock. We worked seven days a week, and the stuff we were drinking is not like you get now. They'd make it and serve it to you in fifteen minutes. Did you want it hot or cold? Or red or white? If you wanted white whiskey, you got corn. If you wanted red whiskey, which was supposed to be rye, bourbon or whatever, they'd put a few drops of iodine in and shake it up. I could name a lot of musicians that went blind, went topsy-turvy and every other thing over that stuff.

"I took most of the men from the Hot Feet to Smalls' to play the Sunday matinées. We weren't working there nights, but Ed Smalls liked what he heard there Sundays. People were coming from downtown, because word about the band got around, and the place would be crowded. After Chick Webb left me, I got a fellow named Walter Conyers on drums. He made some records, and he's still around. Later, I got Sidney Catlett. I had Gene Aiken on trumpet, but then I changed and had his brother, whose real name was Gus, but they all called him 'Rice.' Or 'Geechee.' All of 'em from North or South Carolina were called 'Geechee.' I had Rice on trumpet until I got Roy Eldridge. Norman Lester was the pianist when we first went in. I think he had diabetes or something, but while the show was on the floor—bright lights shining, girls kicking up their heels, and the band blasting!—he'd be sitting bent over as though asleep.

" 'That guy is drunk,' Ed Smalls said.

" 'No, he's not.'

" 'Don't tell me that! Get rid of him.'

"So then I got Don Kirkpatrick, and now the band began to shape up. I had hired Dicky Wells from Cecil Scott, and Dicky knew Roy Eldridge from Pittsburgh or somewhere. I was looking for somebody to play hot stuff, because, although Gus Aiken was a good first man, I already had Red Holland, who was a *beautiful* first man. Dicky knew about this situation and told me about a kid he knew, Roy Eldridge. After I heard him, I hired him, and when Louis Armstrong came in, Louis' eyes got big. 'Where'd you find him?' he wanted to know.

"John Hammond used to say that band up at Smalls' Paradise was the greatest band he ever heard in his life, and that it was the cause of him quitting Yale. Duke Ellington used to come down there and just shake his head. We had a weird sign-off that Garvin Bushell wrote. We used flute, clarinet and bassoon on it. Roy was playing muted trumpet, and I was using a tipple. It was something from India, and Duke always wanted to know what it was. The first time he heard it, he was on the floor dancing, and his mouth came open. It was only about six bars, but it tore him up. He couldn't figure how we got that sound. Bushell used to arrange a lot of heavy, symphonic stuff, too.

"Although he was only eighteen, John Hammond used to come down every night. He brought the head man at Columbia to listen to us, and he thought the band was just terrific. Arrangements were all made to record us, and then Petrillo pulled a band strike. This was in 1931, and after that we didn't get to record, although we made a movie short called *Stash Your Baggage* with the Paradise review.

"We were at Smalls' from 1930 until about the middle of 1933, when

Elmer Snowden's Band, in 1933 movie short. Snowden, banjo; Toby Hardwick, Al Sears, Wayman Carver, saxophones; Leonard Davies, Red Holland, Roy Eldridge, trumpets; Dicky Wells, trombone; Richard Fullbright, bass; Sidney Catlett, drums.

I practically gave up playing and started teaching. There were very few good jobs for bands, and there was a deal where musicians got $22.50 a week and all the tips were turned over to the clubowners. I had an eight-piece group at the Congress Casino, a club on 133rd Street and Seventh, up over the Rhythm Club. The union had started putting on some colored agents—*black* agents they'd call 'em now—and these guys were trying to make a name for themselves. One of them came in one night and said I was working under scale, although he didn't know what scale was when I asked him! When they had me before the board, I asked again what scale was, and they said they would let me know later. When they finally let me know, it was the same as what I had been paying, but they cancelled me out anyway. So from 1935 to 1939, I worked with Luckey Roberts, doing society work for the Hitchcocks. We'd go to Aiken, South Carolina, until September, and then go to all the millionaire places, following the horsey set. Nobody knew what I was doing, but I was making good money and I just stayed quiet. When I made some Bluebird records in 1934 with Cliff Jackson, they came out as by the Sepia Serenaders, and other records I did earlier came out with names like the Three Hot Eskimos, the Kansas City Five, the Three Monkey Chasers, the Choo Choo Chasers, and the Rocky Mountain Trio. We made a lot, too, with Monette Moore and Rosa Henderson.

"I suppose I might have made money in the Swing Era with a big band, but when I went back to New York in 1942 to work at the Samoa Club on 52nd Street, the union put pickets outside. Fortunately, I was very thick with John Hammond, and he took up my case and they found out they had been wrong. When they discovered I had a man like him behind me, they gave me back my card paid up for a year, and took their pickets away from the club door. That was supposed to soothe me down, but I was raving.

" 'What about all the time they've stopped me working,' I wanted to know, 'and all the money I've lost?'

"In more recent years, I worked with my own quartet in and around Philadelphia and New York, and taught. I went to California to live in 1963, taught at Berkeley, played with Turk Murphy, and led my own group. The album I made for Riverside in 1960 with Cliff Jackson had brought me a lot of attention here and abroad. In 1968, I toured Europe for the first time, with George Wein.

"We opened in London and there were seven guitar players. I don't think George had ever heard me in person or any of my recordings. John Hammond got me on the trip. It was arranged that each of us should play with just bass and drums, because nobody seemed to want to play with

Thelonious Monk. When we got to the theatre, George said, 'You open up.' He shoved me out on stage, but he had Baney Kessel waiting in the wings with his instrument in case the old man faltered. I started playing, and started rocking the joint. I think George was afraid I was going to mess up, because he went through to the bar to get a drink. When he came back, he asked who was on.

" 'Elmer Snowden.'

" 'He's *still* on?'

"I had that audience in the palm of my hand. When I took my bow, they didn't want me to leave the stage. 'Go back and take another bow,' George said, 'and this time bow to the people in the back.' I looked back then, and there seemed to be as many people behind as in front. Right there, George Wein told me he wanted to book me for the Newport Festival. The newspapers didn't give much credit to the guitar players, but they said the drummers hadn't given them the cooperation they needed. A boy from Brazil, Baden Powell, joined us in Berlin, and he was nervous and wanted to know what it had been like in London. But he was all right. He played by himself and got an ovation.

"Which do I prefer, guitar or banjo? At a certain time, banjo, because I get more recognition on it. Nowadays, it's more unusual, although the way I play it doesn't have the razzmatazz people expect, and it doesn't cut through with that sharp edge. Ralph Gleason, the critic, said he didn't understand how I got that tone from the instrument, because it sounded to him more like an unamplified guitar. Patrick Scott in Toronto and Whitney Balliett in New York said much the same thing. A lot of people around the country have bought banjos, and then taken them back because they couldn't get that tone. I get letters about it, too, but I don't explain. I think I should keep that part of my musical identify to myself."

(1972)

(Elmer Snowden died 15 May, 1973. The secret of his unique sound on banjo, which he did not wish revealed while he was still professionally active, was his use of Gibson heavy duty guitar strings.)

SANDY WILLIAMS

TROMBONE

"I dream about that damned horn right now," Sandy Williams said. "There's never a day passes I don't fool with my mouthpiece, and I get the horn out and play for a couple of hours now and then. It would take me some time to get my embouchure together, but if I did I think I would play ten times better, because my mind is clear. I know what I want to do, and I wouldn't reach for a note I couldn't make. I'd know my limits. Right now, when I'm lying in my bed, I can hear myself playing this tune or that tune. It's in my mind and I go to sleep with it in my mind.

"Once in a while I play some records I'm on. I hear how this should have been in tune, or that passage so much cleaner. I guess I must think I'm still young. I still figure I'm going to be able to play. I'll never give up.

"Trummy Young did a whole lot to help me. He tried his best. (He's a fine cat, and he made a hell of a contribution when he was with Louis Armstrong!) But unless I can get my teeth smoothed down exactly as I want them, I'm not going to bother.

"It's three years since I accepted a gig. The regular job gives me two days off a week, and every day I have free I play golf. When I work a night shift, I may take my horn and mute down in the basement. I know the state of the business and I wouldn't try to make a living in music. I know there's not too much happening, and I'd never *ask* for a job."

The release of three Chick Webb albums within a year drew attention to Williams' importance in the little drummer's band. By all odds its most consistently rewarding soloist, he was also one of the best trombonists of the Swing Era. His taste, tone and execution were excellent. It is hard to find anything overly dramatic, emphatic or sentimental in his solos. Even the humor is under control, as was that of his great model, Jimmy Harrison. Like his friends of the Fletcher Henderson band, Bobby Stark and Coleman Hawkins, he epitomizes the "hot" musician of the period. Intensely independent spirits, they were bold, disinterested in personal publicity, hardy in adversity, scornful of the exaggerated, the affected and the corny, and not a little proud. They retained their self-respect as men in conditions

63

which make those experienced by today's jazz musicians seem positively enlightened.

Sandy Williams was born in Somerville, South Carolina, where his father was a minister. There were eleven children (six boys and five girls), and the family moved to Washington, D.C., while he was still very young. There both his parents died, six months apart, during the 'flu epidemic of 1918. As the oldest of four young boys, he was sent to an orphanage, St. Joseph's Industrial School, in Delaware.

"Like most schools," Williams said, "they had a band, and I asked the teacher if I could join. He put me on E-flat bass first, which I didn't like —*boomp-boomp,* you know! I begged him to let me have a trombone, but he wouldn't do it.

"Everybody had to work there and I'd been assigned to the baker shop. I had to get up at 3 in the morning, and we'd make enough bread for the day. We'd be through about 11, when I'd go over to the gymnasium and sneak into the band room, and get one of the trombones and practice. I wanted that long horn! In all the parades, the trombones were in front, leading the way. I kept fooling with it until the teacher, George Polk, finally let me have one. He'd been a bandmaster in World War I and he could play every instrument in the band, although his main instrument was the euphonium. He played it beautifully, and I used to try to get the same sound on the trombone.

"I was in that school two years, and as the oldest of the four brothers I was fighting all the time. If someone bothered those kids, I had to fight. They had a system of demerits, which meant that if you got more than a certain number you had to spend Sunday in the guardhouse. I never forget that I once spent thirteen Sundays straight in there. In the summertime, when it was too hot, they had another punishment. There was a long walkway from the No. 9 Dormitory to the dining hall, and along it were the stumps of trees. You'd have to stand on these stumps with your arms stretched out sideways for periods of a half-hour before you could take 'em down. It would get so it would feel as though you had two tons on each hand, and that would go on all day Sunday. Somebody was watching you all the time, too. It was kind of rough, and after two years of it I ran away and went back to Washington, where my sister and an older brother looked after me.

"I got myself a little dishwashing job, because that way I was certain of something to eat, and I got a room at the YMCA for two dollars and fifty cents a week. Then I tried to go to school. The restaurant where I worked was only two blocks away, so I'd work in the morning before school, come back at lunchtime to rest and eat, go back, and then wash dishes until

Sandy Williams

about 9. After that, I'd go home and do my homework. All the time I was figuring on how I could get myself a trombone. Although I couldn't play too well when I left the orphanage, they'd taught me to read.

"I used to get those Western magazines, and in the back of one of them I saw an advertisement where I could have a brand new trombone for twenty dollars—two dollars down and two dollars a month. Right now I owe them twelve dollars for that first horn!"

Williams took lessons from the music teacher at Armstrong High School in Washington, Professor James Miller, who charged him seventy-five cents a time. Miller's sons were first-class musicians, Bill and Felix playing saxophone, and a third, known as "Devil," drums. Williams got to know them, and occasionally they would give him a gig, which, he remembered, might pay as much as a dollar-and-a-half a night, a sum very useful to him in those days.

"I kept studying," he resumed, "and they wanted to put me out of the Y because when I came home at night I was going to blow that horn anyhow. I didn't have enough money to buy a mute, but I'd take a hat and put over the top.

"On Sundays, I'd do a little parade work with Professor Miller's band, or any kind of work that came my way. The sons' band played jazz and they had quite a repertoire. It wasn't just barrelhouse. They used to have stocks sent them from different publishers in New York, and you had to be able to read music to play with them. I worked with two or three other little bands before I was really making a living from music, and I ended up in the pit band of the Lincoln Theater, a movie house. It was a regular theater band—four fiddles, two trumpets, trombone—about fourteen pieces. The music score would come right down with the picture, and the night before a change of program we would have a run-over, and you had to be able to see those notes. Nothing would ever come in an easy key. The easiest key we would ever get, I'd say, was two sharps, the key of D. It was then I appreciated the foundation I got in the school.

"I kept that job for quite a while, and I was making a whole lot of money, about thirty dollars a week, but I wanted to get into some gutbucket. I was about seventeen when I joined the Miller Brothers band at the Howard Theater, where they had all the shows from New York every week. I was already catching up with the boys, and that was where I wanted to be. In the three years I was there, I saw every band that came down from New York. Some of them wanted me to go back with them, but I wouldn't go. I remember Charlie Johnson's band, but Fletcher Henderson didn't play the Howard, although he would play dances around. I used to go out of my way to hear that band. If I heard he was playing in Baltimore, I'd be in Baltimore that night, one way or another, in order to hear Jimmy Harrison. I had all his records, and I thought the sun rose and set on him. I loved his playing. I'd also heard Wilbur De Paris when he came through with different bands, and I thought highly of his playing, too, which I do today. Another trombonist you may have heard of was TeRoy Williams. Then there was a guy called Johnny Forrester. I think he spent a lot of time in Europe. He was a nice-looking fellow with a streak of grey in his hair. He came through one time and he played so much trombone! The guy who owned the theater didn't want to get rid of me, but he liked Johnny and had him stay with us about two weeks. It wasn't that he was so much of a jazzman, but that he was a very good trombonist who knew the horn backwards. It has always seemed like a dream to me, because I've never heard of him since.*

"Another who could play beautiful horn was Daniel Doy, a boy who died early. 'Way back in those days, he had one of those Tommy Dorsey tones. He had been in Paris with Claude Hopkins and Josephine Baker. He was a good pianist, too, and he was playing piano with the Miller Brothers when my horn fell to pieces. Because he had a bad chest, he had to stop playing trombone. He made a pretty good living playing piano, and I kept the horn.

"While I was at the Howard, I used to double around the corner in a nightclub called The Oriental Gardens, a hole-in-the-wall. You didn't get much of a salary in those days, and you played mostly for tips. Claude Hopkins came in one night and made me an offer to go to the Belmont Café in Atlantic City for the summer of 1927. I went, in his seven-piece band. Everything we played, we played very soft. It was a terrific band. Hilton Jefferson was on alto, Elmer Williams on tenor, Bernard Addison on banjo, Bob Brown on drums, and Doc Clark, from Philadelphia, on trumpet. Doc was no tear-off man, but he played a good lead.

"The job didn't last too long, so we went to Asbury Park and played at a joint called Smile-a-While Inn. It was during Prohibition and the club was selling whiskey. When the place was raided, they locked everybody up. They kept us in jail all night, let us out next day, and we went right back to work. When they took us to jail a second time, in Freehold, New Jersey, everybody took a bottle out of the bar. They had all the chorus girls downstairs and the band upstairs. We raised so much hell, I think they were glad to see the back of us."

Horace Henderson had heard of Williams and sent for him to join his

---

*Brian Rust's *Jazz Records: 1897–1931* lists him and Arthur Briggs as members of Pollard's Six, a group which recorded in Paris during 1923.

second band (not the one he brought out of Wilberforce University). Among its twelve members were Jack Butler (trumpet), Bob Carroll (tenor) and Manzie Johnson (drums). From this band, in 1932, the trombonist went to Fletcher Henderson's for a period of two years.

"It was the height of my ambition to get into that band," Williams continued, "where I was beside Higgy (J.C. Higginbotham) and with guys like Rex Stewart, Bobby Stark and Coleman Hawkins. All this time, Jimmy Harrison had remained my idol, because even back in those days he was playing like guys are trying to play today. He always played as though he were trying to tell you something. I got to know him very well. In fact, he died right around the corner from me, just a block away. I used to visit him in hospital, and saw him a couple of days before he died. Everything was fun with him, and I think I copied that from him, too. Just live and be happy! I even tried to sing like him. When I was with Rex Stewart in Europe, we did *Somebody Loves Me* with Jimmy's ending:

> Somebody loves me.
> I wonder who.
> Yes, I wonder who,
> Oh, my, my, my. . . ."

The job with Henderson came to an untimely end in 1934 as a result of an incident on July 4th.

"Bobby Stark and I got a big roll of firecrackers like they use in Chinatown," Williams recalled. "We were at the Hollywood Gardens in Pelham, and we let 'em go in the dressing room, which was right under the dance floor. It sounded as though the joint was blowing up. I think I got two weeks' notice. Bobby and I were known as Bar and Grill in those days, Mr. Bar and Mr. Grill. We hung out together, and I don't care whether it was the middle of the desert, we'd find a bar and get a drink. We were playing the State Theater in Chicago once, 'way down in the Loop, during Prohibition, and we didn't know where to get any whiskey there. So during intermission we took a cab to the South Side to get a bottle. We got all the way back to the theater and Bobby dropped it right outside the stage door. Such cussing I never heard in all my life! That made the day a lot harder."

Following a well-established pattern of traffic and exchanges between the two bands, Williams went from Fletcher Henderson to Chick Webb.

"Chick sent for me when Higgy was leaving," he remembered, "and I think Big Green was still there then. I'd been with Edgar Sampson in Fletcher's band and we were very close. When I joined it, Chick's was already the house band at the Savoy. That was our home base except when they sent us on those long tours of one-nighters. I used to hate that. It was practically all we used to do with Fletcher. And I never liked traveling, as much of it as I had to do. I'd get very homesick. I was married in 1925, and no matter where I was, if I had two days off, I'd make it my business to get home somehow.

"Chick's band was known in New York, but it wasn't known nationally like Fletcher's or Duke's. His big ambition was to have a band good enough to cut Fletcher Henderson's. He always wanted to have a hit with a good band record, but when he got Ella (Fitzgerald) the picture changed. From *A-Tisket, A-Tasket* on, the band automatically became secondary. Taft Jordan was a terrific showman and had really been the star of the band before Ella. At the time when Louis Armstrong was in Europe, he had been doing all Louis' hit numbers and winning quite a bit of fame.

"I never had much to do with Louis Armstrong, but I liked him and he seemed to like me. Years and years ago, I went down to hear him at the Paramount. 'You like my style, don't you?' he said. 'I sure do,' I said. 'Don't try to play a million notes in a bar,' he said. 'Put two or three notes from here'—and he put his hand on his heart—'and place 'em right.'

"What does it mean," Williams asked with a shrug, "if you can get over your trombone so fast it sounds like a clarinet? Some of them today ought to be playing valve trombone, not slide trombone. As a rule, I don't talk about other trombone players, and I do admire the way J. J. Johnson can get over the horn, but I heard him one morning when he was a guest on Arthur Godfrey's show. Lou McGarity was there, and after they had played something together, Godfrey had J.J. play a straight melody. My God, he sounded like a dying cat in a thunderstorm! It was horrible. And it's the trouble today. They play a whole lot of notes that don't mean a damn thing.

"I've always been taught to paint a picture, to tell a story. Now I saw a guy on TV last week painting a picture by dipping fishing lines in paint and dragging them over paper. That was supposed to be a picture? Art?"

Williams overcame his indignation, chuckled, and returned to his consideration of the Chick Webb band:

"Though Elmer Williams wasn't too much of a get-off man, he'd sweet you to death with that beautiful tone when he took solos. Most of the instrumental arrangements were written to feature him, Taft Jordan, Bobby Stark, Edgar Sampson or myself.

"A lot of the arrangements had to be chopped up to fit three-minute records. Some of those we played would last ten or fifteen minutes. I remember one Christmas at the Apollo Theater, we were playing a special midnight benefit for the *Amsterdam News* fund for needy people, and it

Savoy Ballroom flyers.

was being broadcast over WNTA. That night, I counted the choruses I played on *King Porter Stomp*—twenty-three.

"Bobby Stark and I could play as many choruses as we felt like on that, so long as each chorus was a little more exciting. That was *our* tune, and sometimes it used to be a matter of seeing which of us could play the most choruses. But don't let down! As long as you could keep it going, Chick would let you go, but he had a special little beat to tell you when to stop. He was a lot of fun.

"Just once towards the end he was a little pitiful. 'When I was young and playing for peanuts,' he told me, 'I could eat anything you guys eat, but now I have all this money and can only eat certain things. I can't even take a little nip when I want to.'

"The battles at the Savoy were a big thing. He knew the crowd up there and everybody liked him, but we used to go into training like a prize-fighter. We'd have special rehearsals. The brass used to be downstairs, the saxophones upstairs, and the rhythm would get together somewhere else. We had the reputation of running any band out that came to the Savoy. But just forget about Duke! The night he came, the place was packed and jammed, so you couldn't move. We opened, and just about broke up the house. After all, it was our crowd up there. Then Duke started, and he'd go from one tune right into another. The whole room was just swinging right along with him. I looked over and saw Chick sneaking around the other side into the office.

" 'I can't take it,' he said. 'This is the first time we've ever really been washed out.'

" 'You're right tonight, Boss Man,' I said. 'They're laying it on us.'

"They outswung us, they out-everythinged us.

"The only band other than Duke's that really gave us a headache was the Casa Loma band. I hate to say it, but they outplayed us. We used to have an arrangement on *Chinatown* that featured Taft Jordan, and he'd end up on high C, or something like that. The Casa Loma came in when we finished, playing the same tune, but their trumpet man started where we left off, and went on up. And then they started swinging. That was a big let-down that night. But Basie and Lunceford couldn't do it. That was because the crowd was with us. Maybe if they'd caught us in some other dancehall it would have been different.

"In my estimation, Chick was the top drummer. I guess Gene Krupa was the closest he had to competition in his last years. And, incidentally, Benny Goodman gave us a rough night at the Savoy when he came up there with Krupa, Harry James, Teddy Wilson and Lionel Hampton. Krupa and Buddy Rich used to hang around Chick in those days. Of course, Sidney Catlett was a hell of a drummer, too. But Chick didn't take no from anybody. He thought he was the best and he'd tell you he was the best, right quick. He couldn't read a note, but he was a topnotcher.

"Everything was funny to Chick. He would laugh at anything. He made me hot as hell one time when we were in Texas. There you just ride, ride and ride. We had one of those big Greyhound buses, and we stopped for about seventy-five gallons of gas and seven or eight quarts of oil. The bus had one of those big water coolers that held about twenty gallons, and everybody in the band was supposed to take his turn to fill it up with ice before we left town. That particular day, somebody had forgotten, and it was hot, hot. We all bought sandwiches and soda, but when you're thirsty after drinking you want water. Now there was a little, old, funny-looking woman had charge of this gas station.

" 'Madam,' I said to her, 'would you mind giving me a glass of water, please?'

" 'We don't give your kind no water down here,' she said. 'There's the river over there. Go help yourself.'

"Chick laughed like hell. That was funny to him. 'Ha, ha, ha,' he went, and then the guys started laughing, too. It burnt me up.

" 'I'm going to quit the first big town we come to,' I told Chick. 'I'm going back home.'

"I don't remember coming to a big town, but I was evil that day. Look at the money we'd spent there! With the valets, road manager, bus driver, and all of us, there were about twenty guys altogether, and everybody bought two or three sandwiches.

"I haven't been that way in a long time, and I'm not going either. I couldn't take that stuff nowadays. But to Chick it was funny. I guess he thought I should have had more sense than to ask.

"When Chick died, I had been with him over eight years. I stayed on another eight months, but I lost interest in everything. Something was really missing. I guess I was often a headache to Chick, because he would give me hell sometimes, but I think he liked me. At one time, there had been a lot of guys in and out of that band. When things were getting rough, they'd quit. Once, when there was a question about money, Chick named those who had stuck with him when times were tough. They included Taft, Bobby and myself, and the one who was closest of all to him, almost like a father—John Trueheart. I've seen the time when we sat beside the highway and split a loaf of bread and a can of beans together."

In 1943, Williams was with Duke Ellington for ten weeks while Lawrence Brown was on vacation.

"I loved it," he recalled, "but during that time the bottle was really beginning to get to me. A drink will pick you up, but it gets to the point

where you say you can't get on the bandstand unless you've got a bottle
—in case you get tired. The road had a lot to do with it, because doing
those one-nighters you were tired all the time, and back in those days the
hotel accommodation wasn't like it is now. You took a room wherever you
could, even if it was in a barn. Some places, the hotels were so lousy I'd
sleep in the bus. Traveling by bus, sleeping in it, just getting a sandwich
here and a sandwich there, you were naturally tired all the time. Then
you'd say, 'To hell with it! I'm going to get a drink.'

   "When we worked at the Savoy, it was different, but I'd have my own
hour for getting home. Sometimes we used to rehearse after we got
through, and Sunday was a breakneck day—from 3 in the afternoon till 3
next morning. The rest of the week, we'd start at 9 and play till 3, or some
nights 4. There were always two bands—a top band and another that was
mediocre. Usually, we'd play a half-hour on and a half-hour off. I think
when the Savoy Sultans were first there we'd play forty minutes and they'd
play twenty, but eventually they got a big following themselves. Sometimes
we'd go on the road for two or three months, and then they'd naturally
take over.

   "Most of the tours were in the South. Business was good there, and
that's why the office sent us there. We might hit Chicago on a theatre date,
but in the hot summer we always seemed to be in Texas. That was how
Moe Gale booked us. For a Christmas present, he'd give us a piece of
luggage, a nice suitcase maybe, or an alarm clock. Oh, brother!

   "Some parts of Texas were as bad as Mississippi. Going through states
like Mississippi and Alabama, you wouldn't have any trouble in the big
cities, but the highways were bad in those days. You might have to make
a detour, get stuck in muddy roads, or make a stop at one of those dinky
gas stations. With Fletcher, we mostly traveled in cars, but with Chick it
was in a bus, very seldom in trains. I preferred cars, and I used to ride with
Russell Smith, Old Pop, all the time. I rode with Coleman Hawkins later
when he had his big band, and that caused some trouble, too, because all
the rest of the guys had to leave on the bus. They hated that. He drove
fast, always left much later, and arrived after the band had started. 'Here
come the two bosses,' the guys would say. They called me Strawboss, but
I just rode with Hawk because we were close.

   "I remember coming with him and Walter Johnson from Philly once,
and he had just got a new Imperial. He decided to open it up on a long
stretch, and he had it up to 103 miles an hour. That was the first time I
ever did over a hundred an hour, but Hawk was a good driver. 'Hell, I
don't want to kill myself,' he'd tell you right quick. 'What are you worried
about?'

   "I remember once we were playing Tennessee—another nasty state—

when some guy came up on the floor and said something ugly to me or Higgy. We took our mouthpieces out to use in our hands as a weight, and we were really going to start something that night. After that, Fletcher put his trombones behind his trumpets. Somewhere else—Bradford, Pennsylvania—we had to have a police escort out of town. The bully of the town wanted to start something. Fletcher asked for an escort and got it. Two motorcycle cops took us about twenty miles out of town. You'd run into all that kind of mess.

"In those days, everybody would have his own gun, because when you're traveling on the road like that you would go through a lot of states where you could buy a gun as easy as a pack of cigarettes—no license at all. On the highways, where there were dairy farms, they used to have big cans of milk out waiting to be collected by a truck. When Bobby Stark had been drinking, and if he saw them standing there, he'd get out his pistol and—bam! He used to like to see the milk spout out.

"We'd play some white dances in the South, and some Negro. Some had a rope stretched across the floor, so the whites danced on one side and the Negroes on the other. In others, the whites would be dancing and the Negroes would be sitting upstairs listening, and they all paid the same price. That used to burn me up and make me evil. And that was another excuse to take a drink."

Among Chicago engagements Williams remembered were those at the Grand Terrace when he was a member of first Fletcher Henderson's band and then Cootie Williams'.

"We had to play four shows a night there," he said, "and I'd been on to Cootie for a raise. When it didn't come, I got mad, because I couldn't send enough money home. I went to the hotel that night and let my bags and golf clubs out the window at the back. I just had enough money to take the bus home, and when I got to New York I had one nickel in my pocket—subway fare uptown.

"I started playing golf in 1930, and I used to take my clubs on the road with me when I was with Fletcher and Chick. In 1941, when I was with Fletcher again, I used to play with Freddy Mitchell, the tenor player. When we hit one town in Louisiana—and that's a bad state—we had our clubs on the bus. It was early in the morning and the nightclub sat up on top of a hill with a big, beautiful golf course all around it. Freddy and I looked at each other.

" 'I'm going to ask,' I said.

" 'We'd like to play a round if you don't mind,' I said to the boss of the place. 'We've got our clubs with us.'

" 'Where in the hell did you ever learn to play golf?' he asked.

" 'I'm from the South,' Freddy said. 'I used to caddy, but since I've been in New York I've learned to play.'

" 'All right, but I'm going to give each one of you a caddy, and they're going to keep score. So you better shoot a good score. Go out and play.'

"We shot a good game that day. Those caddies just wouldn't lie, and they took the scorecards right to the boss.

" 'You guys shoot that score?'

" 'Your boy here was keeping the score.'

" 'Okay,' he said. 'Open up the bar.' And he set up a round of drinks for everybody in the band."

The two years Williams was with Henderson in the early '40s were not a notably happy period. Besides Mitchell, Peanuts Holland, George Dorsey, Benny Morton and Walter Johnson were in the band.

"We had a chance to go back to Roseland," Williams resumed. "The manager came to Pittsburgh and begged Fletcher to come back. That's when Peanuts and I stole an obbligato and wrote the tune *Let's Go Home*. I named it because I was hot with Fletcher. He wanted to stay on the road and go to Chicago, but I wanted to go back to New York. I lost some of my respect for him then. It was an opportunity he passed up. He wasn't too happy home, and when he was on the road he could play around.

"Another tune I named was *Fish Market,* when I was in the big band Roy Eldridge had, and we were up in Boston several weeks. I remember we had four trombones on that date—Vic Dickenson, George Stevenson, Wilbur De Paris, and myself. *Fish Market* was a blues, the kind of thing you can play for a month, so long as you don't play the same thing over and over. It was a very good band Roy had, and we did a lot of dances, theater dates and records, but it didn't last too long."

Most of the reference books also credit Williams with working for Lucky Millinder, but it was a brief engagement, honorably terminated on an artistic difference.

"We played a week at the Apollo and a week in Baltimore," the trombonist said. "On one tune, I had a break to make, and I always used to say to myself that I didn't make the same break twice. I'd always change it, but Lucky didn't like that.

" 'I never play the same thing twice,' I told him.

" 'In my band you will,' he said.

" 'That's it! Give me my ticket.'

"He did, too, and paid me for the whole week."

Williams was an important contributor to one of the greatest record sessions ever made under Sidney Bechet's name, that on Victor from which *Shake It and Break It, Old Man Blues, Wild Man Blues,* and

Nobody Knows the Way I Feel This Morning resulted. He later played a summer engagement with the New Orleans veteran "in the mountains" during World War II, and got to know him well.

"I used to get a kick out of Bechet," he said with a reminiscent chuckle, "but he was a moody guy. He'd be happy and jolly one minute, and the next he'd be off by himself, walking through the woods. He'd tell you he was thinking. Other times, he'd go out on the lake in a boat by himself. I used to go in a boat myself, with a jug of wine and a camera. One day I was standing up to take some pictures when the boat turned over with me. Henry Goodwin, the trumpet player, had his camera and took a picture of me climbing out of the water, still with my pipe in my mouth —but no jug. I was mad.

"That reminds me of when I was in Atlantic City with Fletcher Henderson. Edgar Sampson, Russell Procope and I used to go down to the boat wharf. We'd throw a jug of gin in the water and dive for it, and whoever got it kept it. One day, I was full of my juice and got a long way further out than I realized. I got tired, put my feet down, and found there was no bottom. That's a hell of a feeling!"

Ultimately, liquor struck Sandy Williams down. When he picked himself up again, problems with his embouchure prevented a full return to his musical career.

"I never did much writing," he continued, "but I used to play things to Harry White (the arranger and trombonist) and have him copy them down. He used to come by when he knew my wife was out and take a bath. Sometimes he'd have a suit someone had given him, and I'd take his old stuff and throw it down the incinerator. I used to try to get him to eat, but I never could pass him by without giving him enough to get a drink, because I know what that is. I know you're doing wrong in a way, but I've been through that, and it's murder. Bob Carroll was a hell of a musician, with a beautiful tone and good ideas, but he ended up like those guys on the Bowery, lying in hallways and everything.

"I used to go down there just to try to make myself disgusted by seeing those guys. I'd go down with three or four dollars in my pocket, but I'd end up buying them a drink and drinking with them. I was lucky, because I always had a home to go to. I can thank my wife for that, and that's why I'm about the only guy left of the bunch I used to drink with. She'd always leave me something to eat on the stove when she was going out to work. Sometimes I'd pretend I'd eaten it and throw it down the incinerator. Or if I could make a sandwich out of it, I might take it around to a bar where I could trade it for a big slug. One time, I went over two weeks without a mouthful of food. I just couldn't eat it."

Asked to sum up his career, Williams was quick to answer.

"I guess my biggest kicks were with Fletcher. And with Chick, naturally, because I was home there. I could play the whole night without opening my book. I got a kick out of being in Europe, too. If I'm ever lucky enough to win a sweepstake, I'm going to take my wife on the same trip. It's beautiful over there, and now I quit drinking I know I'd appreciate it even more."

(1968)

TAFT JORDAN

TRUMPET

"I was born in Florence, South Carolina, in 1915. No one else in the family was musical, but after we moved to Norfolk, Virginia, I was living next door to a fellow who played trumpet. (Later on, he became my brother-in-law —we married two sisters.) I asked my mother if she would get me a trumpet, and she said she would 'see.' I knew I could blow it, because a friend of mine, who was in the Boy Scouts, had a bugle he would let me blow. One Saturday, Mom asked me to get dressed, because she wanted to take me downtown. We went down and walked in the music store, where she asked the salesman to show me a trumpet. He showed me a Gretsch American, and that was my first horn. I guess it was a beginner's trumpet, and I think I have only seen that kind once since, but Mom bought it.

"Now there was a friend of the family, a Mr. Spooner, who lived two or three miles away in Norfolk. He played baritone horn, which I knew fingered like trumpet, so I walked over to his place. He wrote out some scales for me, and wrote the fingering down, and I started playing that over and over again. At St. Joseph's, the Catholic high school I went to when I was thirteen, there was a music teacher named Dr. Bailey, and I asked him if he would give me lessons. 'On what?' he asked. 'The trumpet,' I said.

He told me it would be twenty-five cents a lesson, which was a lot of money in those days. Mom said we would have to see what Dad had to say about it. He was the breadwinner, a longshoreman. Norfolk is one of the largest naval bases in the world, and it is where the sailors and marines get their leave of absence.

"Dad decided I could have a lesson a week, and I evidently progressed so rapidly that after three or four months Dr. Bailey told me I could come over and try out with the school band. This was the first time I'd ever seen two notes on one stem! Every time I think about it now, I have to laugh. I was playing fourth or fifth trumpet, and I was trying to play *all* the notes! Consequently, when the tune was over, I was still playing! The guys turned around and laughed at me, and I felt bad. So I waited around until the band left and asked Dr. Bailey, 'How do you play these two notes with the rest of the guys?'

" 'You don't,' he said. 'You only play either the top or the bottom note.'

"I asked if I could take the piece of music home, so the next day I was prepared. I made quite a few mistakes, but at least I finished with 'em! I kept on trying, and after three or four months I could play fair trumpet, with ease, no sweat. One day, when the guy who played solo on baritone horn had left and gone to college, Dr. Bailey asked if I would like to try his instrument. It had a double bell and there were five valves. The fifth was to change the pitch one tone. When you pressed the fourth valve, the sound came out of the big trombone bell. Anyway, I played the baritone, and I didn't play trumpet in the band any more. It was nice for me to be playing two instruments. I played the baritone at school, in marches and parades, and at home I played trumpet again.

"There was a band around Norfolk led by Ben Jones, a saxophone player, and during my second year at high school his second trumpet left him. He had heard about me, and sent for me. So I went around, but I'd never played dance music. That was another thing, too! The first time I'd seen stock arrangements with two sets of five lines and four spaces. The one on top was the first trumpet, the one on the bottom the second, and every time you got to the end you had to skip two lines. I'd never seen that before, and I didn't do too hot the first night. Ben Jones wanted to get rid of me, but the first trumpet player said, 'Give the kid a chance!' I wouldn't ask anybody, and I figured it out for myself, because I knew the music had to be right—because everyone else was right. I'd get there early, take the music out and study, and all of a sudden it dawned on me what I was supposed to be playing. I did better and better, until Ben Jones was happy with me. In fact, when the other trumpet player asked for his job back, Jones told him, 'No, we've got a kid now, and he's doing all right.'

Besides the two trumpets, the band had a trombone, three saxes and four rhythm. Joe Garland and Prince Robinson were in it before me, and when I met them later, and told them I used to work with Ben Jones, they both said, 'What, you, too!' I played with him until I finished high school.

By this time, I was doing all Louis Armstrong's things, although Ben Jones never knew it. When I heard *Fireworks* I thought, 'Is it possible anyone can play a trumpet like that?' Later on, I heard his recording of *When You're Smiling,* and every trumpet player around Norfolk tried to play that, but they'd begin petering out when they got around the last eight bars. The best of them even put out a rumor that Pops (Armstrong) was playing a special kind of trumpet, that it was the instrument and not the man.

When Louis' band first came to Norfolk, they came in late, and my father and I were standing on the corner when the bus went by.

" 'Dad, that's the world's greatest trumpet player gone by there in the bus.'

" 'Yeah.'

" 'That's the world's greatest trumpet player . . .' I began again.

" 'Yeah,' was all he said.

" 'Can I go to the dance, Dad?'

" 'If it's okay with your mother, it's all right with me.'

"I ran home and Mom said, 'If it's okay with your father, it's okay with me.'

"I had never asked my father for more than a nickel or a dime, but when I got back and told him what Mom said, he asked what it cost to get in. I was reluctant to tell him.

" 'Well, how much does it cost?' he demanded.

" 'Fifty cents,' I whispered.

" 'What!'

" 'That's the world's greatest trumpet player, Dad.'

"He gave me the money and I ran all the way to the dance. I guess I was about fourteen, and I was afraid I wouldn't be able to get in before they started to turn people away, but I got my ticket and kept easing by people on the steps until I was in the place. It was a long hall, about sixty yards long, and I could hear the orchestra tuning up. People were packed and jammed all around, but I kept easing through 'em, and when Pops hit the first tune I was standing right up there next to the bandstand. And he played and played. And people kept asking for *When You're Smiling.* That was the big thing then. All the trumpet players around town were there, and I knew 'em all, but they didn't know me because I was still in the school band. They were all standing around with their horns, watching the way he fingered his. They thought it was probably not the same one he played *When You're Smiling* on, but they kept asking him to play that song.

" 'Okay,' he said. 'I'll play it for you later.'

"Well, right after intermission they went into *When You're Smiling,* and the house was in an uproar. And just as suddenly it quieted down, because everybody wanted to hear this. After Louis got through singing it, the saxes came in for eight bars, and then he played, and they screamed again—and came right back down. Then he really got into playing *When You're Smiling!* He had a great big Turkish towel around his neck, and perspiration was coming out like rain water. When he got to the last eight bars, he was getting stronger and stronger. Then he hit that top note and completed the tune.

"The trumpet players were all looking up at him, and one of them asked him, 'May I see your horn?'

" 'Yeah,' Pops said, and handed it to him.

" 'Mind if I blow it?'

" 'Right,' Pops said. 'Got your mouthpiece?'

"So the guy put his mouthpiece in and sounded C on Pops's horn and C on his own. He ran the scale on his, and he ran the scale on Pops's. It was all the same. It was no trick horn. It was just the man, the difference of the man.

"Nobody bothers with *When You're Smiling* now. All these high-note specialists, all these strong-lipped fellows—they jump over that. (They went for *Shine* later because he was faster on it.) The feel Pops had on that tune, the way he delivered it . . . Even the fellows who played much higher than Pops ever recorded—and I've heard him play extremely high in practice—none of them bothered with *When You're Smiling* at that tempo. I've heard guys play it fast, but they're cheating. Pops *sang* it, you know, on trumpet.

"I played *When You're Smiling* only twice. Once was in a theatre called the New Jewel, on Norris Street in Philly, between 18th and 19th. (When my mother and father separated, Mom and I went to live with her parents in Philly.) On Sunday nights, they used to have a midnight show, and the fellows in the neighborhood would go over and play during intermission. The next time I played it was with Chick Webb down at the old NBC studios. I never cheated on it, but it got harder, and I said to myself, 'That's the last time I'll attempt it.' There was a physical thing involved. Pops was so powerful, and a little guy like me . . . I could do his other stuff, but when it came to something like that, it was too tough.

"There were exceptions, but most trumpet players were trying to imitate him then. No matter how individualistic a trumpet player might try to be,

L. to R.: Cozy Cole, Dick Clarke, Taft Jordan. 1936.

there'd have to be some Louis in him somewhere if he played jazz. Another thing people have probably forgotten is that in the late '20s, when I started listening to him, he used to incorporate a lot of quotations from operas and other unexpected places. It was a fun thing for trumpet players. How the hell does he figure to put that there, in that spot? No one else had done this sort of thing until he started it. I used to remember all the quotes he had in different tunes. He had *Rhapsody in Blue* in *Ain't Misbehavin'*, something else in *Tiger Rag,* and so on.

"I went around with five or six bands in Philly. There was Ted Tinsley and His Jungle Band, a ten-piece orchestra that played nothing but Ellington. I had never been an Ellington man, and I didn't know half the things they were playing. I just sat there waiting for them to pull the music out, but there wasn't any—it was all off the records, by ear. Then I joined Jimmy Gorham, a trombone player, who had twelve pieces. Later, I was with Doc Hyder. I lived in Northfield, and I don't know how he heard about me. Lincoln Mills, the first trumpet player, and Hyder's drummer came to get me. It was in the daytime, in the summer, and I had gone to the New Jewel to see the movie. Some of my gang told them where I was, and they asked an usher to get me.

"Doc Hyder's was the biggest band around Philly, so I came out right away, and the usher pointed out where they were sitting in a car. I was about eighteen then, and wearing a sweater.

"You want to see me?'

"No, we're looking for Taft Jordan.' They thought I'd be bigger, and older.

" 'That's me.'

" 'You a trumpet player?'

" 'Yes.'

"So then they introduced themselves. I didn't know anyone in Hyder's band and had never seen it, but I knew they played the big clubs and the bigger dances, while we just played club and social dances. They asked me if I could make the rehearsal next day, and I said I'd be there.

"Herman Autrey was the second trumpet and Bernard Archer was the trombone player. Ellis Reynolds, who wrote *I'm Confessin'*, was the pianist. They started rehearsing and nobody called me until Doc Hyder asked, 'What happened to the fellow who was supposed to come and play third trumpet?'

" 'He's standing right there,' Mills said, pointing at me.

" 'That kid!' Doc said. 'Well, get your horn out and pull up a chair.'

We were rehearsing in his home, and I was waiting for the book when he told Herman to let me play second. It was nothing at all, because I'd been playing six years by then, and playing first in the other orchestras. I played everything they had there, then went back and sat in the third chair, and I made up the third part as we went along. I did that for four or five months, from the second part, because chords weren't as complicated at that time as they are now, and you could anticipate what the next would be. They progressed very evenly, but now you never know what's going to be added. The brass section sounded fuller because of the notes I was adding.

"Hyder himself played saxophone, and he was working out at a place called the Pierre Roof Garden, at 63rd and Market. He told me I'd have to have a tuxedo, and you never saw such a tuxedo as I got from some secondhand place! It had a white vest and one of those stiff shirts. The pants were too short for me, and when I pulled them down as far as I could, the shirt would blouse over. The sleeves were too short, too. If it had been winter, I could have hidden it all under an overcoat, but it was full summertime.

"Hyder heard I did a little bit of singing and trumpet playing like Armstrong. I knew all his songs and I think the singing must have started with Jimmy Gorham, because prior to that I'd been with Billy Watson's society orchestra, and they wouldn't have gone for that at those social clubs. And, of course, it would be out with the Jungle Band. But for me, it was a lot of fun, and it proved popular.

"When that job closed, we came over to New York to rehearse a show at a place called the Brown Studio between 121st and 122nd on Lenox Avenue. It was only my second time in New York. The first time had been when I was asked to record with a washboard band. I came over, recorded downtown, got in the car, and went right back to Philly. That's all I saw of New York, and that was my first recording date.

"Now, in Philly, I used to get home every night and listen to all the bands from New York and Chicago on the radio. Ellington, Don Redman, Earl Hines, Cab Calloway, Luis Russell, Isham Jones . . . Mom would be upstairs sleeping, and I'd lie on the floor with the radio on real quiet. I knew all their theme songs, and I knew what time the different bands came on. I knew where all the places were when I got to New York, because they used to announce what street they were on. So after we got through rehearsing, I took my horn and walked right straight up Lenox Avenue, from 121st to 139th, where I knew the Saratoga Club had to be. After I found it, I saw a big sign for the Savoy in the next block. Then I went on up the street and looked at the Cotton Club. All the time I was looking to see some of the musicians. Although I had never met them, I knew them all, because I used to see all the bands when they played at the Pearl

Theatre in Philly. I'd go and watch them come out backstage, but not talk to 'em, because those were the *greats*.

"After I'd looked at the Cotton Club, I wondered what was up the street a little further. Then I heard this playing upstairs. It was the Radium Club, a community-type thing that was never popular. A fellow named Leon Englund had the band and I asked if I could sit in. 'You got a union card?' he wanted to know. When I said I had, he told me to go ahead. They were playing things like *Honeysuckle Rose* and *I Got Rhythm,* everything by head, no music. I think Cliff Jackson was on piano. When someone called for *I Can't Give You Anything But Love,* I asked if I could sing it. They had a megaphone—no mike. When I got through singing, I played the solo Pops had played, and got a nice ovation. They asked if I knew more things like that, so we went into *Chinatown.* I played all night and had a ball, and they wanted me to stop by tomorrow.

"The next night, when I went there, Rex Stewart and Red Allen came in to see who this new trumpet player in town was. That didn't frighten me, because I was there for only a few days and then going back to Philly. But then Chick Webb came by between sets at the Savoy and asked Leon if I could do some of the Louis Armstrong stuff. So I did *I'm Confessin'* and *Chinatown,* and Chick asked if I would like to join his band. I told him I'd have to give two weeks' notice.

"The last night I was with Doc Hyder, at the Howard Theatre in Washington, I was doing some thinking. How am I gonna get to New York, and where am I going to stay when I get there? It was lucky our bus driver was going back to New York, so I got a free ride. He dropped me off and I made it uptown. I was walking along Seventh Avenue, and again I knew where everything was. I checked into a hotel on the next block to the Lafayette Theatre, between 132nd and 133rd, and found out when Chick Webb began playing at the Savoy.

"When I got to the Savoy with my horn, the doorman said, 'Hey, kid, where d'ya think you're going?' I told him I was supposed to join Chick Webb, but he said he hadn't heard anything about it, and he told me to stand outside and wait. Instead, I bought a ticket and went on upstairs and stood in front of the bandstand. On a Sunday, the first band played from 4:00 to 5:00 there. Then the house band played from 5:00 to 5:30, and they did half-hour sets until the first band got an hour off for dinner. Chick's band always played the *last* hour and the other band the first.

"So I was standing in front of the bandstand, and I smiled at Chick and he smiled at me, but he had forgotten who I was. When he came off, I said, 'Hiya, Mr. Webb!' He said, 'Hiya, kid,' and walked on by. 'I guess he's busy,' I said to myself. Then I stood in front of Teddy Hill's band and listened.

"When Chick came back, I asked him, 'Mr. Webb, don't you remember me?'

" 'No.'

" 'You told me to come back to New York. You wanted me to play trumpet.'

" 'Oh, you the trumpet player?'

" 'Yeah,' I said, and I was getting scared now.

" 'Okay. You got your horn with you?'

" 'Yeah, right here.'

" 'Well, be ready to play in the next set.'

"He told the second trumpet, a fellow by the name of Scotty, to let me sit down and play second chair. This was 1934 and Mario Bauza was playing first and Reunald Jones third. So I pulled out the music, and I read everything they put up there. When they called for *Darktown Strutters Ball,* I looked to see where my signs and things were, and saw C's and D's up there on the last page. I said to myself, 'If I'm playing C's and D's, that guy's going to be playing F's and G's, but I never heard anybody play that high when Chick came to Philly. When I get to this last chorus, I've got to be real strong!' I'm paid to play, and when we came to it I was ready. I was nice and strong.

" 'Who was playing an E back there in the last chorus?' Chick asked Mario when we were through.

" 'The kid.'

"I was under the impression Mario had the top part, and I was trying to get up so that it wouldn't sound as though I wasn't there. But I was playing the lead and didn't know it until we were through. That's the way Charlie Dixon used to write! In the next set, Chick asked me to do some of the newer stuff, and they liked me pretty well. I started to work for him that night, and I stuck with the band till he died.

"I got along with Chick beautifully. I only had one run-in with him, and that was nothing serious. He was very well liked by all musicians, and he thought there were no musicians greater than those in his band, and he stood up for them. Edgar Sampson was one, and Edgar wrote great hits for him like *Stomping at the Savoy, Don't Be That Way, Blue Lou, When Dreams Come True,* and the band's theme, *Let's Get Together.* Edgar was retiring, easy-going, and I understand some other bands he wrote for didn't like his voicing, but he should never have gotten out of the field. Some people have a tendency to concentrate on the sound of a reed section or a brass section, but you have to listen to the overall thing when it's all consolidated.

"We didn't have outstanding saxophone players, but we had a good tight section with Edgar, Pete Clarke, Wayman Carver and Elmer Williams.

SAVOY NEWS

VOL. 1 No. 2   PUBLISHED BY SAVOY BALLROOM AT LENOX AVENUE & 140th-141st ST.

THE BEAUTIFUL SAVOY, THE MOST TALKED-ABOUT DANCING ROOM IN AMERICA

A GENERAL VIEW OF THE SAVOY SHOWING THE SPACIOUS LOUNGING ROOM AND BOXES
THE BANDSTANDS CAN BE SEEN AT THE RIGHT

A NEWLY-LAID FLOOR
INVITING YOU TO DANCE

A CORNER OF THE SAVOY
SHOWING ONE OF THE FAMOUS MURALS

And that Elmer—ooh, he had the sound! Then Chauncey Haughton came in. On trombone, we had Sandy Williams, and no one *sounded* like him. And no one sounded like Bobby Stark when he came back on trumpet. His wasn't an Armstrong thing. That solo he used to play on *Squeeze Me* was just Bobby Stark and nobody else.

"When I had the run-in with Chick in 1936, I went with Willie Bryant for a few weeks. We were playing at some club that closed at 4:00, and the Savoy closed at 2:00 every night but Saturday, when it also ran until 4:00. When I went in the house one morning, Chick was there, talking to my wife, telling her how he trusted me, and how he wanted me back. I wanted to go back, too, because I enjoyed the music in that band.

"Chick never got a chance to record most of the stuff he won the battles of music with. Just like the Casa Loma Orchestra. Ooh, that was a terrible band to battle! The only things we recorded that we used to battle with were *Clap Hands, Here Comes Charlie* and *Harlem Congo*. The general public remembers Sampson and Al Feldman, but Charlie Dixon's were the tough arrangements, and we never got to record most of them. When Ella Fitzgerald came in, we had to go with the tide, and she really put the band over.

"I remember the first day she sang with us. I was doing a tune called *Judy*. Bardu Ali brought Ella backstage at the Harlem Opera House for Chick to listen to, and he called up Moe Gale, who handled the band. Moe came and looked at her.

" 'Ah, no, Chick,' he said. 'No, no.'

" 'Listen to the voice,' Chick said. 'Don't look at her.'

"When he listened, Moe Gale said, 'Unh . . .'

" 'Okay, I'll hire her,' Chick said.

"So they had her go on the next show and asked her what she wanted to sing. Her choice was *Judy!* She tore the house up. What was I going to do now? Well, one thing, it took a lot of work off me, because I had been featuring a lot, playing all the high notes and most all of the solos.

"In the early days, I used to ask Chick if I could play some leads, too. 'Now, kid, you've got plenty of time,' he'd say. That was a case of opening your big mouth, because I wanted to play lead as well as solo. He didn't let me until 1938, on a day when he called an impromptu rehearsal and Mario had bought a ticket for the Yankees ballgame. We kept waiting for Mario, and Chick was outside, not even on the bandstand, when Al Feldman said, 'Let Taft try it.' When Chick came running back and wanting to know who was playing lead trumpet, Feldman told him it was me. So then Chick wanted to start the arrangement from the top again. That was my undoing! Every arrangement that came in, he would give me a little more lead to play, and after a while I was playing *all* the lead, all of the high notes, and most of the solos. It didn't bother me when we were playing dances, but it got to me one night in Canada. We were broadcasting, and we had the world's fastest announcer. Before you had even closed your music up, he had announced the next tune, was walking away from the mike, and we were stomping off. We played about fourteen tunes in half an hour. When we got through, I said, 'Chick, you've got to do something about this. I can't make it.' At a dance you have time to put your music back and get a little breather, but this was too much—fourteen tunes, bam, bam, bam . . . 'I understand,' Chick said. 'I understand.'

"After Chick died, I had charge of the band for a while, but I was young. A bit later there was a lot of resentment. When Ted McRae had charge of the band, he gave me my notice, but Eddie Barefield hired me back when he took the band over. We were drawing okay, but not as when Chick was alive, and there was a trend towards smaller groups then, like that led by Louis Jordan, the same Louis, oddly enough, who used to play and sing a ballad with us.

"What was wrong in that era wasn't jealousy. The higher-ups didn't want too many attractions within the orchestra, which I think was foolish, because the more attractions the more drawing power you have. And they didn't want to pay anybody any money. I think we were making seventy-five dollars a week, while guys in other big orchestras, that were not drawing as much as we were, were making twenty-five to thirty-five a week more.

"Chick's drumming had been very important to the band. He had a way of playing the bass drum I've only known two other guys to play anything like. They were Louis Bellson, for one, and Walter Johnson who used to be with Fletcher Henderson. Those are the only two guys I worked with, besides Chick, who really played the bass drum, and that was the secret of the big beat, and that's where you got all your fullness. The fullness doesn't come from the other instruments. The style today makes me reluctant to play on jazz sessions, because invariably I'll be put with some drummer who'll be trying to play what he thinks I'm gonna play, instead of just sitting back there, and driving, and letting you do *your* thing. Yet he'll have plenty of time to do *his* thing. I became so disgusted, but in another field I found I could throw things out of my mind and not even think of them any more. I just forgot about jazz. I did *Hello, Dolly!* for seven years. When a fellow called me to a jazz session over at the Strawhat Club, I said I hadn't played any jazz for so long. He told me not to worry, but just to do my thing. I went down, and I got a fine write-up in the N.Y. *Times.* They didn't fight me there. Jo Jones worked with me beautifully— he and Beau McCain on tenor.

"When bop came in, it didn't sound like anything to me at first. After a while it began making more sense, but not from *all* those who played it. When a bunch of musicians get together, and they all try to play the same way, I start wondering where the personality is. Where is the individualism? It seems as though it has been lost, because everyone has been trying to see how fast he can play. And then they call it soul, and all that stuff! My idea of soul would be misinterpreted in reference to jazz. Now they play very free, but with*out* soul. Everything is dead, and there's no life in the sound today. I don't play that way. I've got to be myself.

"After Chick Webb, I had a group of my own uptown at a place called Murrain's on 132nd and Seventh Avenue. Bob Carroll was on tenor, Tommy Fulford on piano, Dick Vance on trumpet, Pete Clarke on alto, and a bass player and a drummer whose names I can't remember. We were seven pieces, and after about a year-and-a-half we went up to the Savoy. It was a good little group. We played shows beautifully—no sweat!—and we also played nice dance music. I liked that combination: two trumpets, two saxes, three rhythm. You can get a lot of color with those four horns —from brilliant to pretty to low. I had an idea for voicing those four instruments that I used when I wrote my theme song. It was melodic and haunting, and whenever we played it everybody would crowd around in front. I never gave it a name and never had a chance to record it. I wouldn't want to do it with more than the seven pieces, because the way I voiced it seemed so foolish, but it came off. If I had been playing with a fifteen-piece orchestra, I would have thought about it another way, because I would have heard more instruments, but with just four horns it was real nice and tight.

"Bob Carroll was a guy everybody told me not to hire, because he wouldn't make time, but all the while he was with me he was not late one day. They said he had been a big boozer, but he didn't act up with me. I think the reason was that he heard a conversation I had with the manager of the place one day. He wanted us to play a tea dance on Sunday, but wouldn't pay what I asked for the *band.* 'But we'll give *you* some money,' he said, meaning me personally. I turned him down, and a day or so later Bob said, 'Man, you know, you're okay. I heard Frank when he was talking to you.' Well, whenever I formed a group, I just wanted every man to know what he had to do and be able to do it. As simple as that. I can't stand prima donnas and all that stuff.

After the job at the Savoy ended, I actually talked about giving up music. I was so disgusted. I thought I should have been into something, but nothing ever seemed to jell. Some months went by while I was trying to find out what I could get into, and then one day I went home and found a note that read: 'The Man wants to see you. The Man . . . Duke Ellington.

Be down at the Hurricane tonight.' I hadn't touched my horn for about three weeks and wasn't about to go down there. So I forgot about it, and went on a binge instead. But a few days later, I got another note. So I took my horn out and blew all day till my lips swelled up. Then I put some ice on 'em until they were back almost to normal, and went down there.

"They had extra uniforms and I found one that almost fit me. Jonesy (the band valet) showed me how to get down to the bandstand, and I sat down there at the time I was told to be there. The guys started straggling in. I knew all of them, too, and they probably knew me by name. Wallace Jones told me which chair to take, and Harry Carney came in, called the tune, and we started down. I played when I had to play. After a while, Tizol turned around and said, 'What've you been doing? Listening to Ellington records?' Which was a nice compliment. When we got through, I had to face The Man. He wanted to know how much I wanted to work with him, and I asked him how much he was paying me. I forget what he told me, but I upped it about fifteen dollars, and after we had argued a little I joined the band.

"I was with him four years, and I enjoyed it. I never shall forget one Sunday afternoon in the Civic Opera House in Chicago. He had called a rehearsal and he brought in a thing called *Jam-a-Ditty* that featured Lawrence Brown, Jimmy Hamilton and myself. 'Oh, we're going to do this tonight,' he said, while we were wondering how the hell it was going to sound. Then, just before the concert he told us, 'Fellows, you're going out front to play that tonight!'

" 'What you mean, go out front? We just got the thing today. We don't know it.'

" 'Take the music out front and put it on the floor.'

" 'Put it on the floor? In the Civic Opera House?'

" 'Yeah.'

"So we did that, and stood up there and played it. I wouldn't be able to do it now, because I can't see that well with glasses. But he got away with it, made the audience be a part of it, like it was a big rehearsal.

"When I left Duke, I was so tired I slept almost a whole year. I had had too much road. For a long time I actually slept two or three times a day, and not cat naps, but for two or three hours. I hadn't realized how tired I was while I was out there.

"After that, I played in Lucille Dixon's band at the Savannah Club down in the Village. Then I was in Don Redman's band with Pearl Bailey and Louis Bellson. Don was a sweetheart, and always the same every time you saw him. There was no put-on about him. A very sincere guy.

"In 1958, I went to Europe in Benny Goodman's band. It was all right,

R.: Taft Jordan, Duke Ellington, Ray Nance, 1945.

too, although Benny wouldn't let the band *go*. One night, his sacroiliac condition was acting up very bad and he had to leave the bandstand. When Jimmy Rushing came on, the band started to let it go, to sound like a big band should, and not like four or five pieces. Benny couldn't stand that, and he soon came back from the dressing room.

"I had plenty of work for years around New York. Sometimes I'd record six or seven times in a week, but about four times on an average. Then I had my gigs, and I could never turn down a gig. When that scene fell off, the shows proved a wonderful thing. Sure, you get tired of a show in a long run, but not *that* tired, because it is more security than working in a big band. You also get what are known in the brass world as 'show chops'. You play the same thing over and over again, and your chops seems to know what's gonna happen. In fact, your chops can get into a rut unless you're fortunate enough to be in three fields at one time as I was— recordings, playing dance music, plus the show. Then it's no sweat. After *Hello, Dolly!* I was in *Follies,* and we'd be off six or seven minutes before 10:00, and most of the gigs start at 11:00. The subway in New York will put you any place in the city within an hour.

"I think I've become a man of melodies. I like to play them with my own variations, and I don't sound like anyone else. Tonight I'll maybe play them one way; tomorrow night another; and the next night another . . . the way I feel. But it will be myself, and no one else.

"Of course, I've still got all my Louis Armstrong records from 'way back —*Skip the Gutter, That's My Home,* and that beautiful song, *Someday.* I wore out a record of *Someday* after he died. Would you believe that my German shepherd knows when Louis Armstrong is playing? He may be lying by the window in the bedroom, or in the bathroom, but he'll get up and come in the living room, and lie right down in front of the stereo, and stretch out on his side. He only does that when I play Louis Armstrong."

(1972)

WILLIE SMITH

ALTO SAXOPHONE

"It was the most precise saxophone section I ever heard, and I've worked in an awful lot of good ones. As a rule, there was absolutely no error at all. If a guy made the slightest mistake, he felt very badly."

Willie Smith was reminiscing about his years as a member of Jimmie Lunceford's orchestra, when he led the reeds. In New York at Basin Street East with Charlie Barnet, he was again at the head of an excellent section, but characteristically he took no personal credit for its sound, preferring to dilate on the advantages of the lengthy rehearsals Barnet had made possible. The night before, however, Paul Gonsalves had paid a visit to the club after a record date, and he was in no doubt where much of the credit lay.

"And did you hear the way the saxes played Ben Webster's chorus on *Cottontail?*" he asked, an expression of astonished delight on his face.

In the years before Charlie Parker, Smith was the third member of an alto saxophone triumvirate, the other two being Johnny Hodges and Benny Carter. After World War II and forays as a star of *Jazz at the Philharmonic,* he lived in Los Angeles, where he was much in demand for recording when not working with Harry James. Although he was featured in the latter's band, the jazz audience of the '50s and '60s was decreasingly aware of him as a jazz soloist, and his fame as a lead saxophonist suffered, *outside* the profession, as a consequence of the long eclipse of the big bands.

Yet anyone who heard him at Basin Street East could recognize that Willie Smith remained one of the great masters of his instrument, and probably the greatest leader of a saxophone section that the business has known.

He was born in Charleston, South Carolina. His grandfather on his mother's side was Scottish, whence came his unusual second name, McLeish. His parents were religious people, and they made him work as soon as he was old enough.

"I had two newspaper routes," he recalled. "I used to get up every

Willie Smith

morning at 4 o'clock, though it was dark, go out and carry my papers, come back, eat breakfast, go off to school, come back, get some exercise, and then back to the books. Later, I got a job hammering down boards with my father, who was a contractor. I liked reading, and I used to read like mad, so that they had to take books away from me. But the books must have helped me, because I skipped a couple of grades and went to college when I was fourteen."

Smith's mother played piano, his father sang in the church choir, and his sister—now a teacher—was an accomplished pianist. While quite young, he decided he would like to play clarinet, and his father bought him one.

"I was very diligent in my practicing," he said, "and when I was fourteen I could play the instrument very well, if I do say so myself. I had an old German teacher, a very fine clarinetist, and he didn't have any trouble with me about practicing. My first real job was with a coloratura soprano. That is, my sister played piano and I played the obbligato.

"That was how I started out, but I couldn't play any jazz at all. If it was something written down—okay, I could eat that up, but I couldn't take a chorus on *anything*. I started playing in a little symphony band at college, but as I grew up I got to feel I'd like to blow some jazz. Then one night they talked me into going on a little job and I borrowed a saxophone.

" 'Take the next chorus,' the leader said, after we'd played a while.

" 'What do you mean?' I said. 'What do I play?'

"I didn't know how to get off, how to improvise. I went through the scene, goofed up everything good, and struggled along. But I soon found a chord would fit here, and a few notes not written on the page would fit there. It's always bound to be a long tedious process until you automatically see not just a note but the chord that goes along with it.

"Swinging is something else. You can either swing or you can't. There are some musicians who can't, but can make you think they can. When you listen to them a little more carefully, you find out."

The saxophone, he discovered, was much easier to play than the clarinet.

"The clarinet is ten times as hard," he insisted, "because as you change each octave the fingering is different, whereas it remains practically the same on saxophone. I was playing Albert then, but there are several notes you can make in a simpler way with the Boehm system. Or, to put it another way, Boehm gives you a choice of making notes several ways, whereas on Albert you have only one. If you're facile enough, the Albert can be played very well, and some of the great old symphony guys preferred it. Then they used to say—and this is hard to pin down—that the

Albert had a little bit broader or heavier tone. I play both systems now, but I still play Albert much better and feel more at home on it. All I've done lately is to play a few parts in the kind of big band I work with in California. I don't really feel I play it well enough to solo, because clarinet is an instrument you have to play all the time to keep up on. They had a lot of clarinet parts in the Lunceford band, so I kept up and even took a couple of solos, including a chorus on *What's Your Story, Morning Glory?"*

(His clarinet is also heard on Lunceford's *I'll Take the South, On the Beach at Bali Bali, Put on Your Old Grey Bonnet, Rose Room, Black and Tan Fantasy, Rain, Hittin' the Bottle, Organ Grinder's Swing* and *Raggin' the Scale*.)

The fact that the clarinet is hard to play may account for its present relative unpopularity, but Smith also referred to the dislike for it harbored by certain arrangers:

"Take Billy May, who I work with all the time—he doesn't like clarinets at all. Why? I haven't any idea. He likes the full sound of saxophones and brass at all times. He likes fiddles and cellos, too, but he doesn't like clarinets. I must have played on hundreds of arrangements by Billy, but he's never written a clarinet part.

"It's different with Duke Ellington. I know I had quite a few clarinet parts in that band! Johnny Hodges never would play them, although at one time he played soprano. That's an instrument I never played. It's hard to find one that's in tune, though they're all made in the same mold. The tiniest fraction of a millimeter difference and they blow different. It's true of all saxophones, but particularly of sopranos. They say the curved one is more often in tune, but any soprano player who finds a good one, with the intonation fairly good in each register—well, you can't get that away from him for love nor money."

Jimmie Lunceford was a senior at Fisk University in Nashville when Smith, a freshman, first met him. After graduating, Lunceford accepted a post as a music teacher and athletic instructor at Manassa High School in Memphis. Out of the school band, he formed a jazz group, which soon began to show a great deal of promise. When Smith had finished his four years at Fisk, majoring in chemistry, he went to Memphis to help Lunceford with the band.

"My parents were very straitlaced people and they were completely disgusted," he said. "To be a saxophone player was about as low as you could get at that time. They didn't allow card-playing in the house, and even after college I didn't have nerve enough to light a cigarette there. I finally got long pants the last year I was in school, and then I naturally got interested in women. The first time I ever had a drink was when I joined a fraternity, and then somebody got me drunk.''

Lunceford had taught most of the men in the band, drummer Jimmy Crawford and bassist Moses Allen being among his high-school students. The saxophones became Smith's responsibility, and pianist Ed Wilcox also came in to help when he graduated from Fisk. These two also wrote most of the arrangements, and the band soon improved to such an extent that the fourteen musicians decided to "make the big plunge."

A Memphis doctor, Dr. Crow, owned a dancehall at Lakeside, Ohio, and he gave Lunceford the job there for the summers of 1928 and 1929. Playing every day, the band continued to progress steadily.

"We decided to forget about Memphis and go from there to Cleveland," Smith resumed. "We didn't have any money or any job, but we were all full of 'the exuberance of youth.' We experienced a series of bad promotions. Although Lunceford was a good businessman, guys took advantage of us because we didn't know any better. They'd get us to try out, tell us we sounded pretty good, that something was sure to come of it, and in the meantime they'd be getting paid without letting us know.

"It got so bad after two or three months that we came as close to starving as anyone ever did. There were seven guys in each hotel room, and we always owed rent. Whenever anyone got a job, they shared out the money. Maybe I'd come back with five bucks, and I'd give everyone thirty cents, or however it would divide. Our regular meal was a glass of milk and a piece of raisin cake, which is why I don't like raisin cake right to this day. We had only two overcoats between the fourteen of us, so sometimes we had to wait for guys to come back to get the milk and cake. And Cleveland was terrible that winter—blizzards and everything. Sometimes we had only a handful of peanuts from a machine for breakfast and dinner. But we were a bunch of friends and we didn't care. It was just a lark. 'How're you getting along?' the folks back home would want to know. 'Fine,' we'd write right back.''

Eventually, Lunceford and his men left Cleveland and went to Buffalo, where they fared better. Despite their plight during the winter, they had practiced and rehearsed all the time. Now they made an impression, and added tenor saxophonist Joe Thomas to their company.

"Stuff Smith was playing at a famous cabaret called Ann Montgomery's," Willie Smith remembered. "It's still there, I believe. That was the day of chorus girls and the whole bit. She had a chorus line and entertainment, and there were about half a dozen nightclubs within two blocks, for Buffalo was a real jumping town at that time.''

The next significant engagement was at Lake Caroga, a resort near

Jimmie Lunceford's band in 1928 at the Chisca Hotel, Memphis. L. to R.: T. J. Johnson, trombone; Henry Clay, trumpet; Mose Allen, bass; Charles Douglas, trumpet; Jimmy Crawford, drums; Alfred Kahn, banjo; Bobbie Brown, piano; Lunceford; Williams, alto saxophone; George Clark, tenor saxophone; Chris Johnson, baritone saxophone.

Jimmie Lunceford's band at Lakeside, Ohio, 1929. Standing L. to R. Henry Wells, trombone; George Clark, tenor saxophone; Alfred Kahn, banjo and guitar; Jimmy Crawford, drums; Mose Allen, bass; Ed Wilcox, piano; Henry Clay, trumpet; Charlie Douglas, trumpet. Seated L. to R.: Christopher Johnson, alto saxophone; Lunceford; Willie Smith, reeds.

Jimmie Lunceford and His Glee Club: (1935) L. to R.: Jock Carruthers, Ed Wilcox, Ed Tompkins, Sy Oliver, Al Norris, Tommy Stevenson, Jimmie Lunceford, Russell Bowles, Willie Smith, Joe Thomas, Henry Wells, Jimmie Crawford, Mose Allen.

Jimmie Lunceford Orchestra, 1940: L. to R.: Jimmie Crawford, Jock Carruthers, Willie Smith, Trummie Young, Elmer Crumbley, Joe Thomas, Dan Grissom, Russell Bowles, Lunceford, Ted Buckner, Dutch Williams, Mose Allen, Eddie Wilcox, Eddie Tompkins, Gerald Wilson, Al Norris, Paul Webster.

Gloversville in upstate New York. All that summer they continued to rehearse and rehearse, until finally they received an offer to go to New York. This was the opportunity for which they had worked, struggled and suffered so long.

"We opened at the Lafayette Theater," Smith said, "and the band was *terrible*. The guys got stage fright and were scared to death. They messed up for the chorus girls—played the wrong tempos and even quit playing before they were through. They also goofed up the singers' music. We felt so bad, we all sat on the stand in complete darkness after they brought the movie screen down. We sat through the whole intermission because we didn't dare go off. The big and very good chorus there was known as the Number One Chorus, and what those girls were saying as they were going out was unprintable. They detailed what kind of little so-and-sos we were, and how we ought to be sent back where they found us. The whole works! Jimmie had goofed the show up, too, because he had been excited—the first time on a stage like that, in New York, the greatest place in the world. But it wasn't just his fault. The whole band was scared, because before that we had only played dances.

"This was when Jimmy Crawford got his first experience and lesson as a 'show' drummer. He got his baptism the hard way, a way he could never forget. Right now, he's considered the best in the business, and he has played big Broadway shows for years."

Somehow or other the band climbed out of the depths of its despair, got over its stage fright, and went on to play other theaters. With its glee club, vocal trio and varied book, it was such an entertaining proposition that when it went into the Cotton Club the entire second show was devoted to it. Sy Oliver, who had been playing with Zack Whyte's Beau Brummels ("the hot band around Cincinnati"), had come in as a trumpet player and arranger, and was by this time responsible, with Wilcox, for most of the arrangements.

"I didn't do many after he arrived," Smith explained. "I used to like to write, but it took me so long, and I was much more interested in playing. Arranging is tedious work, but the more interested in it you are, and the more experienced, the less tedious it becomes. That's like anything else. You make mistakes and you remember not to make them again. Sy wrote a lot of wonderful arrangements for the band, and really became a great man at it, which he still is today. We always liked Wilcox, too, because he had the ability to write very good saxophone choruses.

"We made so many hit records, the record company would get mad, because there was a hit on both sides. We became one of the biggest theatre attractions and we used to make a circuit of theatres in New York,

L. to R.: Joe Thomas, Jimmie Lunceford, Stanley Dance, Jimmy Crawford, 1946.

Baltimore, Washington and Philadelphia. The same girls who had cursed us out the first time used to cry when we left, and ask us to write them. They even made up special routines to our records, so when we went into their theatre they'd ask, 'Can we do our routine to your *For Dancers Only?',* or to some other number they liked. 'Okay,' we'd say, very big, 'if you want to.' And it worked so well, the chorus used to take encores. They'd break up the show, just like the band did, and you didn't see that happen often.

"Our appearance meant a lot, too. We had the most expensive clothes in the world. If we did seven shows, we wore seven different uniforms. That included shirts, socks, shoes and ties, all made specially for us. We were getting good money then, and the clothes had to be sent ahead in wardrobe trunks."

Everything the band did was done with such precision that the musicians were often described by friendly rivals as "the trained seals." Smith explained how this precision was achieved:

"For example, we used to go to rehearsal and rehearse *bows.* We didn't take our horns. We had four different bows—a regular bow, a serpentine bow, and so on—and they'd call out a number for which one they wanted you to do. When we did a gleeclub number, we had a diagram showing how to get out of your seat and down to your spot on the stage without bumping into or crossing in front of anyone. It had to be accomplished in so many seconds, and it was.

"The saxophone section used to rehearse all by itself, and we'd play some real difficult music. 'Later, for you,' we'd tell the brass. We might rehearse just three numbers all day. Start in the morning, go out for lunch, and then rehearse all the rest of the afternoon. There was no compulsion about it. We just wanted to have the best saxophone section in the world, and we did have. We worked on it, so it sounded like one guy playing five saxophones. Everything had to be marked, breath had to be taken at the same place, and all the crescendos were rehearsed over and over. So far as worry was concerned, the notes were the smallest part of it.

"The brass rehearsed in the same way. We'd join up and put it all together the next day. I may be prejudiced in favor of the reed men, but I don't think the brass quite reached our level, although they included some outstanding musicians and great showmen. Tommy Stevenson was about the first to start making all those screeches and high B-flats. There were the two Websters, Paul and Freddie. Freddie was a beautiful player. Then there were Sy Oliver and Gerald Wilson. Eddie Tompkins was one of the best first trumpet players I ever heard. At that time, if you took a first trumpet part away from a first trumpet player, he was insulted and

likely to fight you. Nowadays, they say, 'Well, you play this, while I get
my chops straight, and the other guy can play that.' Eddie Tompkins played
the first parts all night long. Snooky Young is an outstanding first today, and
also one of the best I ever heard."

Harry Carney and other Ellington musicians have credited the Lunceford
orchestra with giving them more competition than any other, but the result
of the two bands' meeting on one celebrated occasion has long been a
matter of debate.

"We only played one real battle of music with them," Smith said, "and
in my opinion we won it. Another time, though, I *know* we had the edge
and made Duke's guys mad. It was a big dance at Cornell University,
where they had three bandstands. We had the biggest, the one in the
middle. On the other two were Duke Ellington and Guy Lombardo. We
were very hot then and had a lot of bookings, and we could only give them
an hour of our valuable time this particular night. So we came in there very
sharp, in our best uniforms, played just the hour, and then stepped out
again, very big time."

The band had begun as a co-operative and its spirit as a group effort
continued for years. When Lunceford decided to build a casino at Larch-
mont, the musicians' regular salaries were discontinued and they worked
for just room rent and board. Although the roof was not finished, they
opened at the casino as scheduled.

"We had to," Smith said, "because we couldn't disappoint our legions
of fans. And it rained! There were inches of water on the floor, but all the
people were there. They stayed and danced in the water. We got wet, too,
but we didn't care."

Tommy Dorsey, one of the band's greatest admirers, went out to Larch-
mont one night. Afterwards, he gave Smith a lift back to New York.

"I want to talk to you a minute," he said when they stopped outside
where Smith was living. He pulled out a checkbook and signed his name
on a check.

"You see this line up here, *Pay to the Order of?*"

"Yeah," Smith said.

"Put whatever you want on that line and it's yours."

The saxophonist had to tell him that he couldn't leave Lunceford, although all he was getting was room and board. "I felt it would be a terrible
breach on my part," he recalled. "That was the spirit we all had. Nobody
would quit regardless of what happened."

Later, the musicians began to be dissatisfied when they felt Lunceford
was not treating them fairly in view of their past sacrifices.

"We knew he was making a lot of money," Smith said, "because he was buying airplanes, wrecking them, and buying new ones. The places we played were still packed, but it got so that we never knew what money they made. Before that, we used to know. So when Tommy Dorsey offered him a big salary, Sy Oliver quit. He couldn't be blamed, in view of what was happening. I always understood, too, that he got just five dollars for making the arrangement of *My Blue Heaven,* which was a big hit, and he did the copying himself. Work like that may have made his reputation, but he deserved twenty times that much money, because the band was on pretty big time by then (1935)."

Eventually, in 1942, Smith himself left, to join Charlie Spivak. After Trummy Young and Jimmy Crawford left, the band rapidly deteriorated. "Not that Lunceford didn't get good musicians," Smith reflected, "but the spirit wasn't there. That do-or-die-for-good-old-Boopadoola was gone! I went to hear the band a couple of times and it was like day and night."

Spivak played at the Pennsylvania Hotel and Smith was with him for about a year. Although it was a more commercial band, Spivak had a lot of swing arrangements by Jimmy Mundy and Sonny Burke. Dave Tough was on drums, and Nelson Riddle played fourth trombone and wrote the "sweet stuff." Spivak left jazz to others, but Smith admired his sound on ballads.

From there, the same year, he went to the Navy and Great Lakes, a training center where a hundred thousand men were stationed.

"Our job," Smith explained, "was to train bands to go other places. We'd look over the recruits, find likely prospects, put them together, teach them a few marches and pop tunes, and send them off to Guadalcanal or some place. Music was a big deal up there. They had a huge symphony and there were four separate bands in the barracks I was in. We had everything to work with, including arrangers—Gerald Wilson was ours—and our own repair shop for instruments. You could get any size group you wanted. All you had to do was call Administration and say, 'I want twenty fiddles and thirty singers. Send 'em right over.' Herman McCoy, who worked with Duke Ellington on his first sacred concert, was in charge of the choral groups.

"We had continuous leave, because we belonged to what they called Ship's Company, which gave us privileges the rest of the guys didn't have. Chicago was only forty miles away and we went there nearly every night. We musicians were really very fortunate, but at least we provided handsome entertainment for the massive concentration of people they had there."

When he came out of the Navy, Smith hadn't a job. He decided to call Harry James and see if he needed a saxophonist. As he picked up the 'phone, a voice said, "Hello!" It was his old friend, Juan Tizol, calling from New Jersey to ask him to join the band. As a result of this remarkable coincidence, Smith's long association with James began at Frank Dailey's Meadowbrook forthwith. It was broken only by engagements with *Jazz at the Philharmonic* and Duke Ellington.

"Duke and Tizol are lifelong friends," Smith said. "They're almost like brothers. Tizol and I are, too. Anyway, Duke asked Tizol if he, Louis Bellson and I would like to go with him for a year. We had no contract. The four of us just shook hands, but then we had to go tell Harry.

"He wasn't working very steady then, sometimes taking off a couple of months at a time, but we needed to keep blowing to meet expenses. When we went to see him, nobody wanted to speak up first, but somebody very haltingly explained how sorry we were, that we needed to make some money and had this chance to go with Duke for a year.

"Louis had the hardest time saying anything. He's one of the nicest men I ever met in my life. He never changes, morning, noon or night. He, Billy Strayhorn and I used to room together. We'd get a suite, and while Billy and I were drinking up all the whiskey, Louis would be eating apples and having more fun than we were. He had good taste and always wore good clothes. If you said to him, 'Gee, I like that sports shirt you're wearing,' he'd go out of his way to say how much he hated it, and how sorry he was he bought it, so that he could give it to you. He'd insist that you take it. And that's the kind of man he is."

With its new members, the Ellington band went east and played Birdland, where it created a sensation that is still vividly remembered by many, including Count Basie.

"For some reason or other, the band decided to wake up and really play," Smith explained. "Great as they are, it's very seldom you can get all those guys to want to play together at one time. Some spark got into them and for six months the band was unbelievable. It had so much fire and determination—every set, no lulls, no letdowns. People used to get up in the middle of a number at Birdland and start yelling. They couldn't contain themselves and wait until the end of the number to applaud. *Diminuendo and Crescendo* was one of the numbers on which this used to happen. I couldn't believe what I was hearing either, and I was sitting in the band playing a part.

"After about six months, they went back to their old habits, and I went with them. It seemed as though I would always be at the bar with Paul Gonsalves during intermissions, and sometimes we would be just about to wend our way back to the bandstand when we'd hear Duke play his little band call. 'Hey, it's almost time for us to go back,' Paul would say. 'Let's get us another double!' Then Cat Anderson would sometimes lean over and tap me on the shoulder when someone got up to take a three-or four-chorus solo. 'Let's go back and have a drink,' he'd say. 'No, we can't do that,' I'd answer, from force of habit and training. 'Don't worry, we'll be back in time,' he'd say. So I got like the rest of them, and when I felt like it I'd go out in the wings and have another drink.

"This sort of thing used to make Tizol so mad, because he is the most punctilious man in the world. He gets everywhere a half-hour early, rarin' to go. So when I got into these bad habits, he was really disgusted. It was one of those things. But I had a lot of fun playing with Duke—great music and everything. And he was always real nice. He told me once that he made up his mind a long time ago that he wasn't going to let those guys worry him to death."

Smith left in 1952 at a time when the Ellington band was spending nearly all its time on the road. He joined an old friend, Billy May, who was living in California and had had a number of hit records. May took a band out on a cross-country tour, but he didn't like the experience. When he got back, according to Smith, he said, "To hell with it!" and broke up the band.

A tour with *Jazz at the Philharmonic* followed. "Fun" is a word Smith often used in reference to musical experiences, and to him that was what the Granz tours were.

"I enjoyed them," he said, grinning, and falling into the laconic humor familiar from his vocals on records. "No music to read. Easy. Go out on the town every night. Big deal."

He had been a star of the first enormously popular J.A.T.P. album with Howard McGhee, Illinois Jacquet, Charlie Ventura and Gene Krupa. Subsequently, he found himself playing alongside such musicians as Coleman Hawkins, Lester Young and Charlie Parker. Mention of their names provoked a series of reflections on the art of the saxophone.

"When I first heard Charlie Parker," he said, "I thought the style was very unusual, and it was a little while before I could understand it. He and Dizzy Gillespie evolved a much more intricate method of expressing this music, and it required a lot of study and a lot of practice, which they must have done. So far as modern music is concerned, they were a couple of this century's geniuses.

"My favorite players when I was coming up were Johnny Hodges and Benny Carter, and I used to steal their stuff off the records. In their way, they were just as much masters as Charlie Parker was. What he played required a vast knowledge of chords and also a great technique, but the style has been prostituted to quite an extent by guys attempting to play it who didn't really know what they were doing.

"I've heard Ornette Coleman and I have to be honest and admit that I don't understand *him*. He seems to be interested in making a lot of strange sounds, but Charlie Parker wasn't. Everything Charlie played can be analyzed, and it is what was supposed to be there.

"The way I see it, if you're going to run a race, you've got to accept certain conditions: to run a certain distance on a certain track at a certain time. You can run any *way* you want, but you have to observe those conditions. The way it was with Parker and all the others was that you said, 'Here's the track, here are these chords! All you guys who are going to play will have the same chords. Let's see what you can do with them!'

"This has nothing to do with the guys who just make strange sounds. My honest opinion is that most of what is going on is a promotion. I don't believe it when they claim the touch of genius. I could take my horn, go out there, look straight up in the air, act real strange, blow anything I wanted, and say I'm getting a message. Who's supposed to believe that? And I've got to know what a man is trying to play. Is he trying to play *Body and Soul* or *I Think I'll Go Back to the Mountains Tonight?*"

Smith also likened much of the new music to abstract painting, and its fans to those who pretended to see images on a canvas that were not really there. He spoke of Leonardo da Vinci and Van Gogh.

"They didn't just walk out there and say, 'I'm going to paint me a picture.' There was technique involved, and they spent a lot of their lives acquiring it. A lot of the new guys can't really play their horns. It would be impossible to use them in a section. If you asked them to play the melody—nice, pleasant-sounding—they'd be completely lost. No tone. No technique. Ask them to just play the melody as Johnny Hodges would. Just play the tune—don't run the changes. They couldn't do it. And it even took Johnny a long time to learn to play melody like that. Tommy Dorsey the same way. He wasn't what you'd call a jazzman, but every trombone player in the world was trying to get a bit of that sound. If you could play melody half as well as he could, you didn't have to worry about jazz.

"Tone takes a whole lot of time and practice. What the modern guys mostly play doesn't require a good tone, because everything goes by so fast. Everything is eighth notes, or sixteenth notes, or thirty-seconds, and tone goes inversely to the number of notes you play. When you forget about tone, you are losing something valuable, because the first thing you're supposed to learn is to get a good sound. When you've got that, you go after something else. And when you put a whole lot of notes before sound, you're getting into a mathematical area. You can tell whether a guy has any sound when he has to play a few whole notes. If he hasn't, he may try to hide it by never playing any, and just keep running all the time."

On the other hand, Smith regarded Lester Young's sound and what he played as an unusual combination, one that nobody else could have put together so well as he did.

"Coleman Hawkins' tone was big, heavy and strong, the kind that should be," Smith said. "It was full of force and power, and he was fortunate in having the technique and imagination to go along with it. Although Lester's tone was small, it fitted what he played perfectly. From Coleman, you always expected a big, pretty note every now and then, and then he would go into the runs. Lester never did that, or very seldom. Up until his time, all the big guys had beautiful tones—Coleman Hawkins, Benny Carter, and Johnny Hodges. So in a way Lester paved the way for bop, although Charlie Parker had his own thing."

When Harry James began going to Las Vegas, it opened up a whole new field for his band, which soon found itself working almost half the year on a little circuit of Las Vegas, Reno and Lake Tahoe. This suited the musicians, including Smith, very well. The short trips in between were nothing like the long stretches of one-nighters everyone dreaded.

"There were times with Lunceford," Smith recalled, "when we'd go on the road for 364 days and play in New York one night—at the Renaissance. That night, you'd have to be somebody special to get in, and there would be a whole lot of famous musicians sitting along at the back of the stage listening to us. When we were young, the traveling was a lot of fun and nobody cared. After a time, the novelty wore off, and you knew which hotel and which restaurant to go to, even the names of the streets, in every town you visited.

"I think drinking enters into it partly from boredom and lack of sleep. Up to a certain point, too, it speeds you up a bit, so far as your feelings are concerned. You feel more like playing. Then you find you need more and more whiskey to reach the same level. Over a certain point, it destroys your coordination, your thinking, and everything else. You finally end up a drunkard. I think it was some freakish thing about my physical system, but I never had a headache, and Lord knows I should have had some big ones. It would probably have been better if I had, because drinking is an insidious process that finally traps you.

"Without the whiskey, I was a nervous wreck. It took about a fifth to get me to normal. It was just like dope. The nerves start to scream, and you've got to cool 'em off, so what do you do? You take a double shot and another double shot until they stop shaking. Then you need more and more to stop them from shaking, until the day comes when they don't stop. I got to the point, too, where food was distasteful and I ate maybe just a hamburger every other day.

"Eventually, I got so sick I had to quit drinking and go into hospital. I'd never had anything wrong with my stomach, but I found I had an ulcer, malnutrition, anemia, an enlarged liver, and a few other assorted ailments. I was in bed quite a while, because I was so weak I couldn't stand up. I'd just been starving myself to death. It was as simple as that. Now I was right off whiskey and they gave me some tranquilizers two or three times a day. I lay there trying to make it back, to get me an appetite. I finally did, too. The doctor couldn't understand it. He said he never knew anyone stay alive who drank that much and ate so little."

Back on the scene and on the wagon, Smith found plenty of band work and recording in Los Angeles, where he preferred to live. "There's not so much hurry and bustle, and the climate is a lot better, but coming to New York now is fun. Maybe it will snow tonight?" He recalled recent record dates with Nancy Wilson, Brook Benton, Matt Munro, Frankie Randall, and one with John Gary on which he played bass clarinet. He had recorded an album for his friend, Harry Lim, with musicians like Tommy Gumina, Johnny Guarneri, Irving Ashby, Bill Perkins and Jimmy Rowles.

Asked about favorite records on which he played, he answered: "I usually forget 'em as soon as I make 'em, but I liked the record I made with Harry James of *Man with a Horn*. That's a nice tune. Then there was *It's Been a Long, Long Time. I'm Confessin'* was just a head. There were a *lot* of Lunceford records I liked, and *How High the Moon* with *Jazz at the Philharmonic . . .*"

It was time to go down through the hotel into Basin Street East. Soon the Barnet band began to blow—an excellent ensemble with manifest *esprit de corps.* Smith led the saxes with enthusiasm and energy, hunching and twisting his shoulders to indicate shading and accents, the section's phrases issuing with an accuracy that bespoke two years of togetherness rather than two weeks. Halfway through the set, Barnet called a waiter.

"Sidney, you know what we want?"

"Yes, sir."

When Sidney returned, he carried a large tray on which were eighteen drinks, one for each member of the band. Smith, in the middle of his section, gravely handed them up one by one. Then, as Nat Pierce played *Cocktails for Two* at the piano, the band toasted the customers and Smith grimaced over his ginger ale.

There weren't many people in the room, because it was a few days before Christmas. When he came off at intermission, he said, "You know what they always used to say in show business? Watch out for Christmas Week, Holy Week and St. Paul! I never played in St. Paul, but they said it was like Holy Week every week there.''

(1966)

Willie Smith died 7 March, 1967.

ED WILCOX

PIANO AND ARRANGER

It is many years since Jimmie Lunceford died, but the memory of the man and the band he led remains strong in the minds of those who knew them. Lunceford devices, moreover, still echo in many forms of contemporary popular music.

Probably the most significant event in the entire 1969 Newport Jazz Festival occurred when Lunceford's tenor star, Joe Thomas, returned to play with Count Basie's band. More than an exercise in nostalgia, as was much of the music heard that night, their performance of *For Dancers Only* became a demonstration of the artistic durability of great jazz arrangements in the hands of skilled and sympathetic musicians. Certainly, Thomas and Basie were there as guarantors in the all-important matter of tempo, but many also remarked how appropriately Al Aarons and Harold Jones—both relatively young—played in the context of Sy Oliver's marvelous arrangement.

Oliver was, of course, a member of the vital triumvirate behind Lunceford. Willie Smith, the alto saxophonist, was another. The third and least publicized was Ed Wilcox, pianist and arranger, who contributed over a longer period of time than anyone else in the band.

He was born in Method, near Raleigh, North Carolina, in 1909, the youngest of three girls and five boys. He took piano lessons in order to please his oldest sister, who helped with the children. He played in a local dance band during his last year at high school, and on graduating his father tried to persuade him to abandon music and take over management of the family farm. When he enrolled at Fisk University, Nashville, in 1925, his sister urged him to take music and his mother, medicine. He took both before making a decision.

A bad cotton crop ultimately made it difficult for his father to help with his expenses, so he decided to forego the longer medical course. He graduated in 1927 with a degree in music.

Meanwhile, he had met Lunceford, who was a senior at Fisk, and Willie Smith, who was in his second year. Lunceford had a campus band that played in the Nashville area, and Wilcox joined as pianist. In his first summer, they played an engagement at Belmar, New Jersey; the following year, they were at Asbury Park.

"I never heard any of the great names among pianists around Raleigh," Wilcox said. "I heard records, but nothing really impressed me so much until I heard an excellent pianist called Charlie Lewis in Nashville. I think he's in Paris now, and they call him 'Dizzy.' He was a classmate of Jimmie's, a music student, and when I heard him play I realized for the first time how much you could do with the instrument. You see, when you hear something on record, it's not so impressive as when you *see* somebody do it. I saw this guy, his fingers flying like lightning, and making anything he wanted to make. 'This is what I've got to learn to do,' I said to myself. Then I really began to enjoy hearing men like Fats Waller. I listened to Earl Hines, James P. Johnson, Willie The Lion—all of them.

"After my father died, I decided I'd better study something about music, besides playing the piano. We had orchestration, harmony and counterpoint at Fisk, but when I came out of school I had only orchestrated things like *America*. Willie Smith had had a little of it, in high school or some place, enough to know chords, but I took the course. Little of it meant anything where dance bands were concerned. It was leveled at the symphony, and the difference is like day and night. So when I got out with our band, and we heard all the others with special stuff, I decided I'd better learn how to write fast. I knew all the chords, but I didn't know the instruments so well, nor the particular styles that went with them. Technically and theoretically, what I wrote might be correct, but I didn't know whether it would be the sound I meant.

"When the guys started playing, I would say, 'What is that note? Show it to me on the staff.' Then I associated the position on the staff with the sound I heard. For a long time, it was a matter of trial and error. If I didn't like what I'd written, I'd have the guy play something I liked, and then decide where it should be on the paper. I only had to see it once. From then on, I'd got it. And after you've done that a long time, you cannot write bad. To show how important that was, many years later when I went to

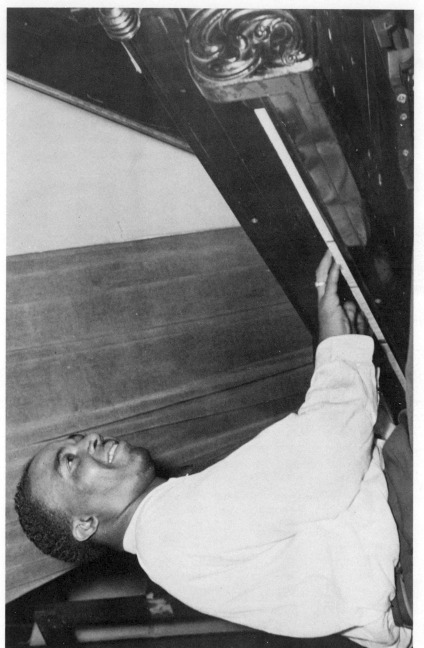

Juilliard to take an advanced course, I found the kids there were getting the same things I already had. I *know* what it's going to sound like now before it comes off. But at that time, I had to wait to hear it. Sometimes it would be better than I expected, sometimes worse."

When Lunceford graduated from Fisk, he took a job as a teacher at a school in Memphis, where first Willie Smith and then Ed Wilcox joined him to help in the development of an eleven-piece band. It was while playing a summer engagement at Lakeside, Ohio, in 1929, that the band's progress resulted in the decision to go professional full time.

"The guys who wrote the arrangements were more responsible for the character of the band's music than Jimmie," Wilcox continued, "but he was responsible for seeing that it was played the way they wanted it played. In the beginning, we were all young and stimulated by new ideas, and he left the writing up to us, but he demanded our best effort. We were all just out of school, and used to discipline, and Jimmie was several years older than most of us.

"He was serious-minded, good at discipline and organization, and he meant everything to be done right when you were working. When you were out playing baseball, or talking about airplanes, he was a lot of fun, but when you got on the stand, he was very serious.

"The relationship between Jimmie, Willie Smith and myself was close. There was never a boss relationship, but we were intelligent enough to respect him as a musician. He played guitar, banjo, clarinet, flute, trombone, and the whole saxophone family. He was also an excellent basketball player, an excellent football player, and an excellent track man. Whatever he decided to do, he concentrated on. He didn't like anything done sloppily, and that carried into the music."

The "Lunceford style," Wilcox insisted, definitely started before Sy Oliver joined the band. Records, particularly the 1933 Columbia performances of *While Love Lasts* and *Flaming Reeds*—both recently issued for the first time, and both arranged by Wilcox—bear him out.

"It started between Willie Smith and myself," Wilcox explained. "We didn't really hear bands that gave us ideas. It was what we wanted to do. The melodic quality I had came from studying classical piano. That was how I wanted it to sound. If you have a good classical teacher, melodic structure is implanted in you so strongly that even when you find yourself wanting to do something else you don't lose it. Willie was influential in the way the reed section phrased from the beginning, because he was so positive in what he wanted to do, and so dominating in tone and quality. And he had good ideas. A lot of people have good ideas, but they're not positive enough in the presentation of them. Willie was always more concerned with being able to play the horn well, and arranging was a lot of work.

"*Runnin' Wild* was arranged by him, and we had it in the book a long time before we recorded it. He wrote the whole arrangement with the pickup inside, instead of outside. He couldn't figure it. He didn't get the down beat at the right place. We played it all right, but it just felt wrong all the way. That disgusted him so much, he decided to quit arranging. It was a pity he didn't keep on, because what he did was good, although unorthodox."

The young musicians spent their first professional winter the hard way, nearly starving, in Cleveland. It was there that Wilcox's ambition was spurred in a strange way.

"McKinney's Cotton Pickers were having themselves a big Thanksgiving dinner there," he recalled, "and there were a lot of girls around. We were all hungry and poor, and we saw these famous guys like Don Redman, and we wanted to talk to them. But we were nobodies, and younger, too, and they didn't have anything to say to us. I wanted to have just a word with Don, just to be able to say I'd talked to him.

" 'Oh, kid, I ain't got time to talk,' he said to me, just like a lot of people would when they were busy and didn't want to talk music at a time like that.

"Instead of discouraging me, I told the rest of the guys, 'I'm going to make that man respect me one of these days. I'm going to learn how to write something, and I'm going to be in competition with him.' They looked at me and said, 'Oh, you're crazy!' But it happened.

"When Sugar Ray Robinson started to make his musical debut about twenty-five years later, they got Don Redman, Jimmy Mundy, Fred Norman and myself to write arrangements. 'Here's my chance,' I said. 'I'm going to do my music so well—and no tricks with the band—that it will make the singer sound good.' I did about twelve arrangements and they were the only ones used. I especially remember *It's Nice to Go Traveling*. Now Sugar Ray was not a real singer, and that a singer has got to be if he's going to top a band behind him when a lot of crazy stuff is going on, but I had had a lot of experience writing for singers by then. When Don Redman came up and said, 'That's very, very good,' I thanked him, but I didn't remind him of our encounter years before. I thought about it, but then I decided it would be too small. So that was one of the things that was influential with me, that created determination."

After Cleveland, the band went to Buffalo, where it became necessary to acquire financial backing. Lunceford's age and extra experience made him the man to do it, and when he was successful the original three-way partnership with Smith and Wilcox was virtually dissolved. More than money was acquired in Buffalo, however.

"Jonah Jones was with us a short time, and Joe Thomas joined the band there," Wilcox continued. "Joe had a lot of personality, and a lot of tricks on the horn. He had a way of slopping over notes, too, instead of making all the notes in a run. Willie Smith wouldn't settle for that kind of stuff. He would turn his back on you, refuse to listen if you played that way. 'Play all the notes in the run, man,' Willie would say. 'Don't play like that.' Joe was a good tenor player when we first got him, but sitting beside a man like that he naturally got better, for Willie was a perfectionist. He believed in doing everything right. And that made three of us, because Lunceford and I were the same way.

"I was instrumental in Sy Oliver coming into the band. Jimmie didn't particularly like his personality until he got to know him. 'You've got to recognize that he has a lot of talent,' I told him. 'He's a great arranger and he can play enough trumpet to be in the section, too. He's a stylist, and we need somebody else to help us out on arranging.'

"After Sy was in, I gradually got entrusted with the ballads and vocal arrangements, because he couldn't do those so well as he could the jump and jazz. Sy used to do the old things like *St. Louis Blues,* but one day I said to him, 'Why don't you do some of this pop stuff. You'd learn something. It's got different kinds of changes in it.' So he tried his hand on *Woodenhead Puddinhead Jones,* but when he'd finished he'd got the chords wrong. 'Use the changes the man gave you,' I told him. So he took it back and made another arrangement that turned out better, but was still not right. He wound up making three arrangements, and fussing with me each time. He'd get mad, but as a result he started writing pop things, and learned a lot he didn't know. Many things were contrived in that way. We weren't exactly in competition with one another, but each of us wanted his thing to be as good as possible. That applied right through the band. It was what you call *esprit de corps.*

"Eddie Durham came in the band because he was a good trombone player, and at that time (1935) it was much harder to find good trombone players. Besides, he could write music and double on guitar. He was among the first to use the electric guitar. We collaborated on the arrangements of Duke Ellington's *Bird of Paradise* and *Rhapsody Junior* because there were a lot of things in there for the piano player. We had to get together, because he didn't know whether I could play it, and I didn't know how he wanted me to play!

"A lot of the band's ideas came from the arrangers—presentation and everything. We knew we had to have something different if we were going to make it. The band didn't have many *great* soloists. We had enough to cover, but we had to have something nobody else was doing. The glee club did numbers like *It's the Talk of the Town* and *Don't Blame Me*. All the guys would be singing except the rhythm section. We turned it loose when we didn't need it any longer, and when everybody else started copying it. We were the only Negro band doing it originally. In fact, the only other band with a glee club that we knew of was Fred Waring's."

Another musician for whom Wilcox evinced the highest regard, and one about whom so little has been written, was Eddie Tompkins.

"Eddie," the pianist said, "was not only a great first trumpet player, but a great all-round trumpet man, and the best we ever had. The split lip he suffered from may have kept him from making the F's and G's, but he could make everything else. He could play any part. I remember one in *Rhythm Is Our Business* that Steve (Tommy Stevenson) used to play. When Steve got sick, everybody was wondering who was going to play it, and Lunceford himself was getting worried. 'Don't worry about it,' Eddie said. 'I'll play it.' He got up and played it better than Steve—didn't miss, split a note, or anything. He could do everything. When the band was rehearsing the acts for a show, and didn't know where to come in, he'd get up and do the steps, and tell the band, 'That's where you hit!' He never got the credit he deserved, but that happens in life."

Paul Webster, who eventually took over the high-note chair after a period with Bennie Moten, was no accidental or casual choice.

"We knew of him because he had been at school with me at Fisk," Wilcox explained. "Earl Carruthers, the baritone saxophonist, was another classmate of mine. And Henry Wells, the singer and trombonist, and Mrs. Lunceford, had gone to Fisk, too."

The spirit that made the band such a success for a decade was a subject that Wilcox touched on repeatedly in different ways, in anecdote after anecdote.

"When we started out, we were a bunch of ambitious youngsters," he said. "Money wasn't important. It was being able to play good. When anybody made a mistake, hit a bad note, the guys would all stomp their feet out of time. It didn't matter what we were doing—recording, broadcasting, or anything. The trumpet guys used to take a mute and hit it on their derbies. It got so bad, Lunceford eventually had to stop it. But it used to make you try hard to avoid being stomped on! If you had something you couldn't play, they'd let you go at a rehearsal, but when it came the time, they'd stomp on you. So what you had to do was to take your part home and work on it. That kind of spirit you can't buy.

"I remember the arrangement Sy made on *The Shoemaker's Holiday*. It wasn't hard, but somebody who writes for piano and doesn't play piano can write the most awkward stuff in the world, because it doesn't fit the instrument. It doesn't lay right for the fingers. 'I've played sonatas by Chopin that weren't this hard,' I said. I took it home and worked on it. It was all a matter of the fingering and the key. Sy didn't write it that way deliberately. Things like that just happen. It was the kind of number we played as dinner music, and we had a library that would fit no matter where we played. *The Shoemaker's Holiday* was a little, light, airy piece, and Jimmie never called it unless he knew I had a good piano. So I didn't play it often, but on the occasion I'm thinking of, when they thought I was going to stumble, I ate it up alive.

"I remember once when we were playing our concert arrangement of *Sonata Pathetique* in the Oriental Theater, Chicago. I didn't know our light man, Dutch Williams, was going to give the cue when I came in so that a pinpoint light hit me. It was like an electric ray. It shocked me so bad, I don't think I played five notes out of that first run. I felt so ashamed, but the band was tied up in knots. I had a brandy between shows and was ready the next time. It taught me a lesson, that you always had to be prepared.

"I mention this because when you see a guy doing something fairly easy, you don't know what price he has paid to learn how to do it easy. That's why, when people sometimes ask me how I do something, I tell them, 'It takes a long time.' "

When the band first went to New York, it was faced with a union problem.

"Because the union wouldn't let us in," Wilcox remembered, "we started doing gigs all around, and from that our years of tough itineraries really began. The band got so hot that Harold Oxley, the manager, had no difficulty booking us. The real reason we did all those one-nighters was that the location jobs didn't pay the same money. It suited Jimmie to do one-nighters, because he could make twice as much money that way."

The attitude towards money had, in Wilcox' opinion, much to do with the band's decline and fall.

"It was Jimmie's fault that the band began to break up," he said. "When you're young, you can go a long way on ambition, but when you get older you want some of the things older people have, and Jimmie didn't want to give enough money. Those that did stay, after several had quit, he treated better, but it was late then. I know that when Willie Smith left, he cried. He didn't want to leave, but the money was wrong. Jimmie was used to treating us like little boys who left Memphis with him, but we had become grown men and we needed more. He wanted to keep us on the same scale financially, and it ruined the whole thing.

"Something else that hurt us badly was that leaders of most other bands gave their men a vacation with pay. We'd have a vacation sometimes, but it would be like a lay-off, with no money. I blamed Jimmie rather than Oxley, because we told him what the trouble was."

When Lunceford died, Wilcox set about re-organizing the band.

"I planned to revamp the whole thing with a bunch of young and energetic musicians, not ones filled with lethargy," he said. "I wanted a little more inspiration, and although I didn't plan to do it at one time, I was going to cut down from eighteen pieces to twelve."

Although he found a sponsor, and although the band had been doing good business right up to Lunceford's death, too many problems doomed the project after a short spell in which he and Joe Thomas were the band's nominal leaders.

"I couldn't make the same money, even if I had had the same men and the same music," Wilcox explained, "because everybody knew Jimmie was dead, anyway. And 1947 was a rough time for big bands."

After he let the band go, he worked as arranger for the Derby record company, for which he wrote the all-important chart on Sunny Gale's hit *Wheel of Fortune.* Having paid off the debts incurred with the band by arranging, he decided he ought to be able to work as a pianist, too.

"So I sharpened up at a little club in the Village called the Riviera, and stayed there about ten years. Then I had a trio in the Garden Café for two-and-a-half years. On the side, I wrote orchestrations and did vocal coaching, as I still do. I was at Banjo Inn eighteen months, and now I'm at the Pink Poodle. I've been playing in a Dixieland group Sundays at the Club Eleven in Brooklyn, where we've had guys like Roy Eldridge, Ray Nance and Big Chief Moore."

A student was waiting for a vocal lesson. Wilcox got up from his desk to say goodbye, a frank, firm, articulate man with an air of disciplined self-reliance that characterizes so many Lunceford alumni. The arranger of *Sophisticated Lady, Rhythm Is Our Business, Sleepy Time Gal,* and *I'm Walking through Heaven with You,* and so many other significant numbers in the band's book, he obviously knew full well what he had personally contributed to the Lunceford story. Somehow, his final words on Eddie Tompkins came to mind: "He never got the credit he deserved, but that happens in life."

(1968)

Ed Wilcox died 29 September, 1968.

JIMMY CRAWFORD

DRUMS

"The drummer situation is unbelievable. There are not many big-band drummers around. The young guys don't know how to assert authority. They have no experience whatsoever except in small groups. So I use Jimmy Crawford a lot. He can give me spirit, time, enthusiasm, sympathy with the musical situation, a professional attitude and—very important —musical discipline.

"The thing we did with Dinah Washington (Swingin' Miss D) was one of the best albums we ever made, and Crawford played drums on it. Guys like him and Milt Hinton are irreplaceable. There is nobody anywhere in the world like them."

QUINCY JONES

"When I was a kid in Memphis, Tennessee," Jimmy Crawford recalled, "my aunt used to carry me to the old Palace Theatre. It would be around 1924, I guess, and there I saw Ma Rainey, Bessie Smith, Ida Cox, Baby Cox, and Butterbeans and Susie. That was the time of the TOBA circuit and there was an orchestra in the pit led by Charlie Williams. Booker Washington was the drummer and he was sensational. He just thrilled the whole audience. When the overture hit, this man would do things—throwing sticks twirling in the air, shooting pistols, blowing horns, and everything. He was a nice-looking fellow with a beautiful smile, and, when you saw him on the street in a derby, he was quite a dude. He was so good he went to New Orleans later on. All the good musicians used to leave Memphis then for New Orleans or Chicago. I understand he got tuberculosis down there and passed.

"My interest in drumming began right there, in the theatre.

"Then Jimmie Lunceford came on the scene. He had attended Fisk University and gone north after he graduated to see what he could do with the bands of that time; but he couldn't quite make it, although he was a great instrumentalist. So he came back to Memphis and accepted a job at Manassa High School as music teacher and athletic instructor. He formed the school band and out of it we finally got a little dance group.

"I was always interested in drums, of course, but I was just too poor to own a drum outfit, and whoever was well enough off to afford a set of drums played in the band. I borrowed one of the school horns, a peck horn, just to be in the band. When eventually the drummer left, the school acquired drums, and I sat back behind them. I thought I had a natural gift, but I was just keeping time, and I kept going without any instruction. Drummers were really timekeepers in those days. They weren't solo men like they are today.

"We used to play gigs around town and we became very popular, although we were really only a lot of amateurs. Moses Allen, who played bass with Lunceford so long, was in the band, and we had a girl pianist named Bobbie Brown who was a real professional and much better than the rest of us. John Williams, who married Mary Lou, was from Memphis, and they came through with a package show from Pittsburgh. They quit the show and ran a little band that gave us plenty of competition. As compared with Bobbie, Mary was boss.

"Our first professional job was in the summer of 1928, in a hotel in Lakeside, Ohio. We were eleven pieces* and we went back to school after the engagement. Willie Smith and Eddie Wilcox graduated from Fisk the following year and joined us for fourteen weeks at the same summer resort. So did Henry Wells, the trombone player. After that, we agreed to keep going north, to get out of the South, and to try to make it somewhere else. We had heard so much about the northern bands that we wanted to listen and learn. Of course, when I first heard Alphonso Trent in Memphis, I thought his band the greatest thing I ever heard in my life, and it was pretty close to what we were to hear up north, because he had musicians like Stuff Smith, Snub Mosley and Jeter Pilars, and other good men, although a lot of them fell by the wayside.

"In the fall of 1929, we had a job to go to in Cleveland, Ohio, but the depression had started and there was a waiters' and musicians' strike on, so we were stranded, broke, hungry, and everything else. I spent my last dollar there to hear Fletcher Henderson. I'd heard so much about that band, and Coleman Hawkins. We lived on peanuts and water. If anyone made a gig, the money was shared.

"We laid around there three or four months until we got a gig in Cincin-

---

*Lunceford, leader and reeds; Henry Clay, Charlie "Bruno" Douglass, trumpets; H.B. Hall, trombone; Chris Johnson, (?) Williams, altos; George Clarke, tenor; Bobbie Brown, piano; Alfred Cahns, banjo; Moses Allen, tuba; Jimmy Crawford, drums.

Jimmy Crawford

nati, where we ran into the Zack Whyte and Speed Webb bands. Webb had one of the swingingest bands in the world, with musicians like Roy and Joe Eldridge, Vic Dickenson, Eli Robinson, Teddy Wilson and his brother Gus, who was a good arranger. We were coming up then, but our band didn't compare to those, for though they were young the musicians in them were real pros. But Cincinnati was a hellhole for all bands. Even Fletcher's band used to get stranded there at that time, about 1930.

"Later, we worked in Buffalo, where we picked up Jonah Jones and Joe Thomas. They were playing at the Vendome Hotel in a little combo led by a drummer named Jackson. Everyone knows about Jonah, but what Joe became with Lunceford may be forgotten. He was a ball of fire when he was playing. He played more soul, more funk in two beats than most guys do in a chorus.

"I think it was in Columbus, Ohio, that Sy Oliver left Zack Whyte and joined us. He had been arranging for Zack in a way that was to help make Lunceford famous. Sy did such a lot for our band. He really organized it, told us about two beats, and many other things. I always wanted to play in four, but Sy said, 'No, put it in two, and keep it right there!' That was the beginning of a lot of that two-beat rhythm.

"Willie Smith used to write arrangements, but he stopped after Sy had been with us a while. Lunceford wrote some, too, and Wilcox stayed with it, but I guess when Willie saw another fellow come along with talent and ambition he felt he didn't want to run too much competition within the band. Willie was another very valuable man, and he probably thought it was enough that he took solos, led the saxes, and sang.

"We came to New York in 1933, played the Lafayette Theatre, and hit it off very good. Besides Sy and Eddie Tompkins in the trumpet section, we had Tommy Stevenson on trumpet to play the high notes, and he'd really peck 'em—peck 'em up and down. We did so well they booked us into the Cotton Club, which was uptown then. When you went in there, you were supposed to have it made. Only three bands played there in those days—Ellington's, Cab's and the Blue Rhythm Band. We stayed there six or eight months, broadcasting every night, working for Irving Mills.

"After that, we kept on for fourteen years, until I'd had enough of traveling. We were the biggest one-nighter band in the world, year in and year out, from Maine to Florida, from New York to California, over and over again, all the time, until I was sick of it. I wasn't getting anywhere, living from hand to mouth, and I could see the handwriting on the wall. Sy had already left. I put my notice in and only went back for ten days to help Joe Marshall work in.

"I really learned all I knew within that band. I wasn't tired of working with it, but tired of traveling. I laid around New York until, like they say, my 'capital was exhausted,' and then I worked in the shipyards for a month or so. It was 1943, wartime. I went to 52nd Street one night to hear the boys. Specs Powell was leaving Ben Webster at The Three Deuces to go to CBS, where he's been ever since—a good drummer, fast as lightning. So I sat in there with Ben, opposite Art Tatum, Tiny Grimes and Slam Stewart, the most wonderful trio you could ever hear in your life. Ben's combo included Billy Taylor (piano), Teddy Walters (guitar) and Charlie Drayton (bass), and I was offered the gig.

"I went back the next night thinking I could cover the scene, but I got butterflies in the stomach after the first set. After playing with Lunceford for fourteen years, with all that power and volume, to make a transition into this little, smooth group was a great thing. Shelly Manne used to come and sit in, and I'd listen and watch him, and he'd take me in back and show me a lot. 'Just take the brushes and relax,' he'd say. I kept going, but after the first week I told Ben:

" 'I got to quit.'

" 'No, please don't,' he was nice enough to say. 'Just stick around and everything will jell eventually.'

" 'I'll come back tomorrow night,' I'd say, 'but I'll have to quit. I just can't fit in this.'

"A week or so later, something did jell. I was relaxing, fitting in. Making that transition was my greatest achievement. Nowadays, you have to be a flexible drummer. That's something about guys like Osie Johnson—they're so flexible. There are others, though, who I feel play for musicians or other drummers rather than the group or artist they're working with. If their name is on the record especially, they don't want to play dead straight time. They're thinking, 'I've got to show 'em a few tricks.' But I don't think they're right, especially when the spotlight is on a singer. I remember what Pearl Bailey used to say:

" 'I thought you were here to accompany me, not to destroy me.'

"Well, eventually I was asked to carry my own little group into The Three Deuces, and that made me very happy, but just as I was getting organized the Army stretched out its long arm and said, 'Come hither.' I was lucky enough to be stationed at Camp Kilmer, which is only about thirty miles from New York. They had a great orchestra out there and they sent for Sy Oliver and Buck Clayton. When I came out of the service in 1945, I ran into Mary Lou Williams one day and she was instrumental in getting me a job with Ed Hall at Café Society. I worked there, uptown and downtown, for about three years, until the recording scene was really under way.

"Billy Kyle had been in the Army, too, and he got a job as rehearsal pianist for a Broadway revue called *Alive and Kicking*. They asked him about a suitable drummer, because there were a lot of jazz-like numbers, and solo spots for drums in different times, three-four, six-eight, and so on. Billy recommended me, and although it only lasted six weeks, I must have impressed someone, somewhere, somehow, because they called me for another show, *Pal Joey*. From that time on I've been mostly in Broadway musicals like *Delilah, Mr. Wonderful, Jamaica* and *Gypsy*. Recommendations for those shows often come from the stars themselves.

"When you're in the pit, you watch the stick. You can't watch the star and the stick at the same time. To me, it's always pretty perturbing when a star says, 'Watch me—don't pay any attention to him.' After all, there are thirty other guys in the pit with you.

"It was different when we played vaudeville houses with Lunceford. He would bring his stick down for the opening beat, but from then on the drummer had to control the tempo, make the transitions, watch the music, the feet of the dancers, the gestures of the singers, and everything. They had their music and set routines, but if I didn't look at the dancers' feet as well as at the music, I couldn't make those transitions right.

"Dancers influenced the music a whole lot in those days. Sometimes we'd have jam sessions with just tap dancers, buck dancers and drums. Big Sid Catlett was one of the greatest show drummers who ever lived. He could accompany, add on, improvise, so well. And believe me, those rhythm dancers really used to inspire you. In ballrooms, where there's dancing like I was raised on, when everybody is giving to the beat, and just moving, and the house is bouncing—that inspires you to play. It's different when you go to those places where it's 'cool' and the people just sit listening. I don't care too much for the 'cool,' harsh pulsation. I don't like music where it's simply a matter of 'Listen to my changes, man!', and there's no emotion or swing. I think Louis Armstrong has done more to promote good feeling among earthy people than anyone. He can't speak all those foreign languages, but he lets a certain feeling speak for him. You can play too many notes, but if you make it simple, make it an ass-shaker, then the music speaks to people."

For many years, Jimmy Crawford played Broadway shows without ever missing a performance and without ever having been late, despite the fact that he may have had colds and, as he wryly admitted, an occasional hangover. For this, he gave credit to the discipline of the Lunceford band, and he recalled the amazed reaction of one famous newcomer to it: "How can you guys always be on time? It's bad for your personal prestige."

Crawford did not feel that way. One of the warmest, friendliest and most modest musicians in the profession, his conscientious attitude towards his commitments was exemplary. His unselfish consideration of others was extremely uplifting, particularly on record sessions, for which he was always very much in demand. He recorded with Count Basie, Quincy Jones, Jackie Gleason, Frank Sinatra, Sarah Vaughan, Ella Fitzgerald, Rosemary Clooney, Perry Como and many other stars, as well as on hundreds of jazz sessions by studio groups. Even were he not one of the greatest and most dependable of drummers, his cheerful personality would often make all the difference between the success or failure of a date. His solos were relatively few, not because he lacked any. ability in that direction, but because of his conception of the drummer's role. He practiced xylophone two-and-a-half hours a day, not to improvise, but just, he said, "to feel more adequate in the pit."

In the words he uses admiringly of so many other musicians, Jimmy Crawford is "a real professional." One of his old associates put it another way: "You don't feel nervous with Craw sitting back there."

(1961)

SY OLIVER

BANDLEADER [TRUMPET AND ARRANGER]

When Sy Oliver left Jimmie Lunceford's band in 1939, he was the most acclaimed arranger in jazz, but by that time he thought he had had enough of music. He had been with Lunceford six years, with Zack Whyte and Alphonso Trent before that, and he knew he could afford to realize a lifetime ambition. He had always wanted to go to college.

As it happened, Bobby Burns, Tommy Dorsey's road manager, was present the night he put in his notice, and Dorsey had been trying for a long time to get Oliver to write arrangements for him. Burns promptly called his boss.

"Try to get him to come over to the hotel," Dorsey said.

"There's no point, Bobby," Oliver told Burns. "I'm not interested in being a musician. I want to go to college."

Sy Oliver

"Ride in with me anyway," Burns replied, "and say hello to the Old Man."

Oliver acquiesced and went up to the bandleader's room. Dorsey was in the middle of shaving.

"Whatever Lunceford paid you last year for playing and arranging," he said immediately, "I'll pay you $5000 a year more."

"Sold," said Oliver.

In the three decades that followed, his services were consistently in demand. He wrote arrangements for Dorsey, for the band he led while in the Army, for a big band of his own, and subsequently for all kinds of singers in every kind of context. Greatly gifted, richly experienced, and everywhere respected in the profession, he went to Paris in December, 1967, at the request of Bruno Coquatrix, the songwriter whom he describes as "the Irving Berlin of France."

"He had a lot of big hits going all the way back to the '40s," Oliver said, "and he wanted to update and record them. After we had done that, in three albums, he asked me to stay and write for the orchestra at the Olympia Theater in Paris. The orchestra there is a gas, one of the best I've ever worked with. Basically, it's the regular size—four trumpets, four trombones, five reeds and four rhythm—but it's augmented depending on the acts, and in those European music halls they play *everything*, from opera to circus music, rock 'n' roll, the whole bit. So they'd have strings and extra percussion, depending on the kind of show. There was an American producer, George Reich, who used to do the shows at the Copa and the Latin Quarter. There was an American chorus, too, girls and boys, white and colored."

Oliver became musical director of the theater. Each show contained two "ballets" about ten minutes long. He wrote original music for these, and he also wrote for the acts that came in without music.

"I got to speak workable French," he continued, "but there was never any problem. The language of music was the same. Most of the musicians spoke some English, and between their smattering of English and my smattering of French, we got along all right. For a while, I conducted, too, but I had to stop because there was just too much work. The time we were on the stage, and the time required immediately before and after, killed the day. The programs changed about every three weeks, so what with rehearsals and everything my writing time was too restricted. What I continued to do, however, with every new show, was to conduct the ballets until the French conductor got with it. Lester Wilson, a terrific dancer who used to work with Sammy Davis, did some of the choreography. You get the routines at the last minute in shows of that kind, and then you have to work two or three days without sleep. Lester would come in and say,

'Sy, the number's to go like this: *Ta-da-cha-cha-da, ta-doo, bop-bop, ta-doo, bop-bop!*' And I had to write music to that! I soon decided the only way I could do it was to tape him whenever he came to the office. It was very interesting, and I put some tapes together where he sings the routine and the music for it follows."

Oliver had a comfortable apartment not far from the Étoile, and he was very happy there—so long as his family was with him. His wife speaks French well, and his younger son, who wants to be a writer, had the valuable experience of going to school in Paris. Afterwards, a period ensued when shows done earlier in the year were being repeated at the Olympia.

"There was no necessity for me to stay, and I prefer New York," Oliver said. "I've paid my dues, and I've got a nice home there. For me, it's the only place to live. I came back intending to go into the usual commercial work, but after being away more than a year I suddenly realized I wasn't involved in anything. I'd go home, read, watch television, play chess. My life seemed to have come to a dead end. I wasn't even interested in music. There was no problem picking up the threads again, but when I picked them up they just weren't interesting. It was a surprise to realize that I was bored. So I decided to go to school. I enrolled in three classes at the New School down in the Village—psychology, philosophy, and one of the humanities courses, *Planning New Life Styles.*"

Even when Oliver first went to New York with Jimmie Lunceford, it was not with the intention of staying with the band, but of going to college, taking a course in the liberal arts, and eventually studying law. However, because he was still young, and because the band became an overnight success, it seemed logical to stay in music.

"But I always had an interest in the law, and wanted to be an attorney," he explained. "The fact that Lunceford and a lot of his guys had been to Fisk had nothing to do with it. The college thing was bred in my bones, and I get it from my father. The only salvation for a Negro in America when I was born, in 1910, was education. People don't always realize it, but there are several strata in Negro society. The educated Negro is at one pole, the uneducated at another—a different life, a different world. My father had a stroke when I was a sophomore in high school. Had he lived, I would never have been in the music business. He was a professional singer, and he taught all the string and brass instruments. I was the oldest of six kids and I began to play trumpet professionally to earn money to stay in high school.

"I had grown up in a musical atmosphere, and my parents started me on piano when I was quite young, before I went to school, but I didn't like it, didn't like to practice, and they didn't insist. My father taught practically every kid in southeastern Ohio but me! I can't remember when I couldn't read music. It seems as though I'd been able to read it all my life. After they settled in Zanesville, a city of about 30,000, my parents had become very active in the church. My father was choir director, and my mother was church organist, and I was well aware that music didn't just come on a printed sheet, because I used to see my father writing it all the time. He had a very famous choir, made up of youngsters and called the Junior Choir, and he travelled all over the Mid-West with it.

"Al Sears (the saxophone player) and I were buddies, and he was playing in the local orchestra. They used to rehearse at night, but I had to be home by dark. They needed a trumpet player, and my only interest in learning trumpet was so that I could join Cliff Barnett's band and stay out at night.

"When I told my dad that I wanted to play trumpet, he was delighted, and he got me an instrument right away. He showed me how to run the scale, and I learned to play the thing very quickly. I guess I have some innate talent. In a matter of months, I was ready to play with the band, so I went to him and said, 'Dad, I have a job.'

"Meanwhile, college had always been uppermost in my mind. It was understood that I would work and save money for it, and when my dad got sick I had almost $4000 in the bank. I was thirteen years old and I had grown men cutting grass for me in what I called Oliver's Horticultural Society. I'd get around, get the jobs, supply the tools, and take fifty percent of the take.

"Although my father was very conservative in some ways, he was 'way ahead in his appreciation of the value of education. When I told him about the job, that I wanted to play in Cliff Barnett's orchestra, he said very firmly, 'No, you're not.' In those days, a musician who played in a dance band was regarded as the equivalent of a pimp or a bootlegger. So that was the end of it, until unfortunately a year later he had the stroke. Then I started playing with Barnett to earn money. The other five children were all younger than I, and none of them went into music."

Oliver worked with Barnett for three years until he finished high school. At seventeen, he joined Zack Whyte's Cincinnati-based band, which was the most popular and successful in the area. As a member of it, he went to New York and toured extensively.

"Here's how I can explain the musicians in Zack Whyte's band," he said. "Those ignorant guys had never heard anyone speak English. They used to follow me around at parties and write down things I said. I didn't use slang of the kind in which they usually communicated, so they started calling me 'Professor,' but that didn't work, because a seventeen-year-old kid with glasses looked too young to be a professor, especially when he'd just got through blacking your eye. So the drummer, who was the so-called wit in the band, started calling me 'Psychology,' for no reason except that it was a big word, which they abbreviated to 'Sy.'

"I started writing just to avoid arguments. Smoke Richardson was musical director, and we used to make head arrangements, but they'd give out the harmony all ass-backwards, and it was hard to remember. It was so much simpler to run the voices along consecutively. And I had ideas about introductions and things, but I was only seventeen years old. 'Oh, shut up, kid!' they'd say, those musicians who were so much older than I, and I'd literally get into fights with them.

"When I was eighteen, I also used to box in Cincinnati to earn money. Look at those knuckles! I'd come off the road with Zack Whyte's band and go down to the place where they had fights, and get on the preliminary bills. I'd get in the ring for four or five rounds with one of those old cats that hang around the fight scene, and he'd say, 'Now take it easy, kid, and I'll carry you!' They're in there trying to make a buck, too, and the first couple of times I believed them. So we'd spar around, and all of a sudden, POW! I soon got hip to that though.

"Andy Gibson was several years younger than me, a baby when I left home, and I was only an influence in the sense that we were both from the same town, Zanesville. But my mother took him under her wing as he grew up. She was a very fine pianist."

After three years with Whyte, Oliver went to Columbus, where he taught and made arrangements for collegiate bands at Ohio State. He also led a small group in a nightclub there until he joined the famous Alphonso Trent band.

"I went with Trent to write them a new book," he explained, "because they lost their music when they were burned out of a club in Cleveland where they were working. Stuff Smith had been fronting the band, and I took his place. It was a great band, the smoothest Negro band I ever heard back in those days. They were class—a bunch of good-looking guys who used to dress beautifully—and they played well. I didn't record with them, but it's conceivable they recorded some of my arrangements later. Snub Mosley was one of the guiding lights. They were traveling all the time, and I was only with them a few months in 1930 or 1931. I went back to Columbus, and it was there I joined Lunceford."

Oliver was again hired primarily for his ability as an arranger, and there is no reasonable doubt that his contributions were vital to Lunceford's success. He has modestly referred to himself as the "band's Boswell," but after due respect has been paid the arrangements of Ed Wilcox, Willie Smith, Ed Durham and Billy Moore, it is obvious that no one brought the essential Lunceford style—particularly its rhythmic values—so sharply into focus.

"Lunceford's guys were like a lot of other musicians in some respects," Oliver said. "They liked to play for other musicians, and any time you said 'solo' they were gone. Willie Smith often wouldn't play melody where I wanted it in an arrangement. He was ambitious, and he just wanted to play. One of the problems we had when the records became popular was that the guys wouldn't learn to play the same solo. We'd get in a dancehall where everybody knew all the solos on the records, and when they started playing something different, the people would be disappointed. 'Learn to play the solo like it is on the record,' I'd say.

"I was constantly fighting those cats, too, and Lunceford spent all his time trying to keep the peace. 'Sy,' he'd say, 'you've got to give these fellows a chance. They'll get the idea eventually. Let it sink in. If they all thought like you, they wouldn't need you. They'd all be Sy Olivers.'"

Despite these problems, Oliver found it much more difficult to write for Tommy Dorsey's band than for Lunceford's.

"Things just grew and happened naturally in Lunceford's," he remembered. "I had to write *down* for Dorsey's guys, because this was before the days when you couldn't tell the difference between a Negro and a white musician. There was a polarization in performance then—their approach to music and swing was completely different. But even so, it wasn't just white musicians, because I don't think there ever was another band that phrased like Lunceford's did. It was a way uniquely theirs. That was how I thought and wrote, and that was how they thought and played. We evolved together and the music was all of a piece. My original feeling for two-beat rhythm was a natural feeling, just as some people are right-handed and some left-handed. That's my stick."

Partly as a result of the courses at the New School after his return from Paris in 1969, Oliver found it necessary to assess potential and determine which direction he should take. He recognized that he had years of experience in every facet of popular music, natural ability as a leader, and a good understanding of elementary psychology.

"I know how to get people to do what I want without hitting them over the head," he said. "I've learned a lot about living since the time I was constantly active in the record field, and I wouldn't run a record date the way I used to. I know I have a lot of goodwill going for me. Down through the years, I've written for people like Frank Sinatra, Louis Armstrong and Sammy Davis, but I've never asked them for anything, never asked them to get me this or that, nor to do my tunes. And although I've never really been a performer, my name is well known in certain areas. Above all, I realize that people of our generation have no place to hear the kind of music they were raised on. There's nobody presenting it any place. Neither Ellington nor Basie present what I'm talking about."

Oliver accordingly decided that the time was ripe to put a band together again, and early in April, 1969, he opened at the Downbeat on Lexington Avenue, New York, with a nine-piece group. The response was immediately enthusiastic. Old favorites from the Lunceford and Dorsey books were recognized and welcomed back affectionately, while Oliver's continuing flair as an arranger was demonstrated in many new compositions and arrangements.

"Our music is rhythmic," he emphasized, "but it appeals to people who are not musicians. We have the vocal trio, for one thing. I could reach Lawrence Welk's audience if I had the opportunity, just as Lunceford's band could have done. In the way he combined things, Lunceford had something no other Negro band ever had. It was an interesting band for musicians, and an interesting band for non-musicians. That's why he had such a following. The band was musically exciting, and it was still exciting if you knew absolutely nothing about music. That's what we're after now —presenting a general spectrum!"

The size of the band was determined by economic considerations, Oliver being thoroughly aware of the condition of the band business.

"One of the reasons there's no band business as we knew it," he explained, "is that it simply isn't feasible economically. There just isn't that much money around, or the number of places to support it. A band of this size can play anywhere a sixteen- or eighteen-piece orchestra can play. We don't need that much volume because there are no ballrooms, but even if there were they would present no problem. With amplification as it is today, guitar bands play Madison Square Garden.

"I'm not presuming to reproduce the big-band sound in its entirety, because we don't have that much instrumentation, but we're going to get as much out of the framework as is humanly possible. There'll be abundant color, and it won't be boring. Where I have the two saxophones playing lead and the two trombones playing with them, it sounds just like a full saxophone section."

Except for the time he was in the Army during World War II, Oliver had not played trumpet since he left Lunceford. Although he always deprecated his ability as a player, he was, in fact, a stylist whose use of the plunger mute was distinctly and pleasingly individual. His return to a playing role was certainly an additional, gratifying aspect of the appearance at the Downbeat.

"As a trumpet player, I've never considered myself a soloist like Roy Eldridge and those guys," he said, "but being an arranger I have one thing going for me—I can frame myself. You know, if you put a zircon in the proper setting it will look like a diamond! Moreover, the plunger does result in an interesting sound, and there are only a few guys like Cootie Williams who use it now. But playing the trumpet again was part of my therapy, you might say, and economics had some bearing on it, too. I'm getting my chops back. The whole time I was writing the band's book, I'd practice holding tones for ten minutes every hour on the hour."

Oliver proved personable and exceptionally articulate as a leader. He was also the band's chief vocalist, not only on the numbers which he originally sang, but also on those which had featured Trummy Young, Willie Smith and Joe Thomas. The band backed him with skill and zeal, and its personnel was indicative of his experience in recognizing talent. Money Johnson (trumpet), Britt Woodman (trombone), Candy Ross (trombone), George Dorsey (saxophones), Cliff Smalls (piano) and Leonard Gaskin (bass) were veterans with years of experience in big bands and the recording field, while Bobby Jones (saxophones) and Bobby Pike (drums) were obviously musicians of whom much more would be heard in future. With those of the leader and Ross, Buddy Smith's was the third voice in the vocal trio.

"Buddy Smith is from Washington," Oliver explained. "He has worked with me before, and he sang with the Billy Williams group. He's an electronic engineer and an a. and r. man. He mixes records all day. He can do anything. He has been a road manager. This time last year he was the manager of the big restaurant by the boating lake in Central Park. He loves music, and he picks up the parts in the vocal trio quicker than Candy Ross, the trombone player, although he isn't a musician and can't read. He has been invaluable to me.

"I think I can do as good a job in front of a band as anybody in the business. I really do. I know how to work an audience. For instance, I tell them that *Five Four Blues* presents some problems. I ask them to try to count the first two bars, and then I kick it off—'One, two, three, four, five!' —and they're trying to snap their fingers to it. It's a gag, but they love it.

"I always try to impress on the fellows that every second we're on the stand somebody, somewhere has his eyes focused on *you.* You can't pick your nose or scratch your balls. Another thing I've stressed to them is: when people applaud, acknowledge it. Musicians don't realize the difference things like that make."

The group's flexibility was quickly apparent in a program that included not only well-remembered hits like *For Dancers Only, Four or Five Times, 'Tain't What You Do, By the River Sainte Marie, Margie,* and *On the*

Sunny Side of the Street, but also Oliver's arrangements of such numbers as *How High the Moon, Undecided, Zonky, My Baby, Easy Walker, Lover, Come Back to Me, Rumble* and *If You Believe in Me.* The spectrum was broad indeed, and the fact that new music was handed out on the stand every night was a measure of the leader's confidence in his men.

"By the end of this engagement," Oliver said confidently, "I'll have around eighty numbers in the book. After the first week, the band was at a stage I thought it would take at least two weeks to reach. We're presenting good entertainment, but I'm not looking for critical acclaim, and I'm not trying to convert anyone. The analysts can analyze to their hearts' content, and I couldn't care less. We as a people have a great addiction to labelling. There's hard rock, semi-hard rock, New Orleans jazz, Chicago jazz, Kansas City jazz—that's a crock of shit, man! All I'm doing is presenting what I like, and if you like it, come on in and enjoy it!"

(1970)

In an interview with Bill Coss in Metronome *(November, 1960), Sy Oliver was amusingly frank about his relationship with Jimmie Lunceford:*

"Oddly enough, I resented him all the time I was associated with him. I loved Jimmie and hated him, too. I never understood that. I think he's the only guy I ever knew—I think the phrase is intellectual modesty—something about that guy I couldn't help looking up to. I think I resented it. Because this guy was the world's greatest square. But he just had something, the minute he walked on the scene. He was a great man. Actually, he made that organization what it was without contributing a darn thing musically; he was the leader. *The whole thing was focused around him, though not in a musical sense."*

Lunceford was equally frank when Oliver, complaining about not getting his support, asked why he had been hired:

"Well, you know I always investigate everyone carefully before I have them join the band, and you're the only man I ever investigated that no one had a good word to say for. If you can alienate the world, you must have something."

BENNY CARTER

BANDLEADER [ALTO SAXOPHONE, TRUMPET AND ARRANGER]

At the time when bandleaders were being allotted noble titles, Benny Carter received one. Characteristically, he didn't use it long, but the earliest version of his famous composition, *Blues in My Heart,* came out on record as being by "King Carter and His Orchestra," and this was a title a great many musicians felt he deserved.

"His bands used to sound so good because of the book," Dicky Wells has said.* "All he would ask you to do was play the notes—nothing extra. If you accidentally played a wrong note, he'd stop the band and ask you what note you played. 'The one on the paper,' you'd answer. 'You'd better look again,' he'd say.

"He was very well liked because he knew how to rub his men down, get what he wanted out of them, and leave them smiling. It was very rare for anyone to be late, because the guys liked playing his music so much. The band always came first with him, and if ever there was any trouble where we were playing, the proprietor had to speak to him about it, *not* to the guys in the band."

Bassist Hayes Alvis is another musician who recalls his days in Benny Carter's orchestra with pride and pleasure:

"Working with Benny was the happiest period in my life," he told Johnny Simmen (*Jazz Journal,* May, 1966). "Benny is just about the greatest musician and the nicest fellow there is. We didn't make much money, but when one has the privilege to play in Benny Carter's band one does not think of such things. If you are able to hold a chair with Benny, you are made. Every bandleader will hire you after you made the grade with Benny Carter. Having worked under Benny's baton is a real recommendation in the entire music world."

The fact that Carter no longer leads a band regularly in public is certainly a loss to jazz, but he has mixed feelings about a return to his early role.

* *The Night People* (Crescendo, Boston)

"Sometimes I think it would be nice to have a big band again," he said. "If someone offered me an engagement for two or three weeks . . . but then, again, I might get frightened to death at the prospect of going into the preparation. That's the thing: what you've got to do to get ready!"

The rapidity with which he attained an ascendancy in the profession has never been adequately explained, but the route was partially delineated in the discussion that followed.

"So far as I can remember," he said, "my first real step in music was when I bought a trumpet and took it home on a weekend. I'd been paying for it for weeks—thirty-three weeks, a dollar a week—and I picked it up on a Saturday. Over the weekend, I found I couldn't play it. I thought I was going to be an instant Bubber Miley. He lived just around the corner and I admired him very much. On the Monday, I took the trumpet back and traded it for a saxophone, because I had been told—erroneously, of course—that a saxophone was easier to learn. Nothing is easy to learn. There was a wonderful man in the neighborhood called Harold Proctor, who offered me some lessons. I was fourteen. He gave me three or four lessons, and then I went to a couple of teachers. I can't say I was really self-taught, because I studied saxophone with Eugene Mikell and with the late Arthur Reeves, who was a very fine teacher. It was in and out. I'd study for a while and then go off and come back.

"When I went to Wilberforce, Horace Henderson was leading the band, and I joined it. It was a ten-piece group: three saxophones, two trumpets, trombone, piano, bass, guitar and drums. When it went out on its annual summer tour, I went along. How old was I? I was very young! The greater number of the fellows in the band had graduated, but those of us who hadn't decided to forget the university, just to keep the band together.

"Bubber Miley was an early inspiration to me, but Cuban Bennett was the greatest. It's just a pity he never recorded. One reason why I never talked about him was that he was my cousin, but he was absolutely unbelievable. You would not believe that anyone played that way in the '20s, yet it's hard to talk about him if you've nothing to substantiate it with. He just never got the opportunity to record. After all, how many people did get the opportunity in the '20s? Unless they were with Fletcher Henderson or someone like that? And he was so advanced. They're doing today what he was doing then. This is not exaggerating. Roy Eldridge can tell you about him, because he was from Pittsburgh, around where Roy was. He was the reason why I always wanted to play trumpet, and after my first experience of changing from trumpet to saxophone, I went back to trumpet in later years because of Cuban Bennett. He was about two years older than I was, and I'd never before heard anyone do what he did.

Benny Carter.

He didn't play like Bubber. He had a big, beautiful tone, no gimmicks, and he was just very, very musical. Whatever gift I had, I got from him. I was certainly inspired by him. When I blew trumpet, I always wanted to feel that it related to what he did. At least, I'd be flattered to feel that it did."

Dicky Wells is one of those, like Roy Eldridge, who remember Bennett vividly.

"He played changes like I've never heard," he said. "And he would play four or five entirely different choruses, and try to end on a high note. If he couldn't make it, he would play four or five more choruses until he finally got it. Then he would cream."

Eldridge was more terse. "Cuban Bennett was a bitch," he said. "And really ahead of his time."

Despite his aspirations and success on trumpet, Carter really made his name first as an alto saxophonist.

"My original inspiration on the saxophone," he continued, "was Frank Trumbauer. I don't think I ever had his facility. He was a great technician on the instrument, but he wasn't an exhibitionist. He played beautiful solos, but very seldom would you hear him make a fast run. When he did, you knew he had that instrument under control, the mastery of it beneath his fingers and thumbs. Do you remember a thing he did called *Trumbology?* That told you what he could do with the instrument, but when he played a solo he just played something simple and beautiful. That's the kind of thing I like to hear. He never tried to display his technique, but he had it.

"Who were my arranging influences? That's a very good question. I guess there the real, basic influences were people like Archie Bleyer, Jimmy Dale and Jack Mason—the people who did the stock arrangements. I would also add the name of Bill Challis, and one arrangement in particular that he did for the Goldkette orchestra on *Blue Room.* It was kind of revolutionary for its day. Even before then I was attempting to arrange. I started off by writing saxophone choruses, along the chord structures I knew the rhythm section would be playing. From there on, I would take each part from an orchestration, put them on the floor and study them, part by part. And I started arranging like that. It was many years before I learned to make a score. I used to do each part for the orchestra. That was the hard way. So this was the meagre beginning, as I've heard somebody say!

"I liked the way both Horace Henderson and Smack wrote, and one of the first to impress me in the field of jazz arranging was Don Redman. I still remember his *I'm Coming, Virginia* and *Whiteman Stomp.* Joining the Fletcher Henderson orchestra naturally made a great impression on me, too. My goodness, that was the band everybody was hoping to play with! It was the acid test. If you could make it with Fletcher, you could make it with anybody. It was the hardest music and the best music around."

But Carter resisted the idea that he himself brought something new to the Henderson band, and also that his technique was markedly advanced. "After all," he insisted, "Hawk moved around a lot on that tenor, and so did Buster Bailey on clarinet."

When he was asked what he did about keeping up on the horn today, he replied:

"Almost nothing. When I get something to do, I grab it and rehearse for a couple of days. When I had my own band, I'd pick up the different instruments and play them, because nobody could tell me not to play this or not to do that! It was my band! Earlier, of course, clarinet was a natural double. As regards the trumpet, I always found that playing one horn sort of stimulated the lip for the other as well. It didn't keep the embouchure, but it certainly helped. I never had any serious trouble when I played them both. Every now and then I blow some trumpet, but to really do something on it I guess I'd have to practice for three or four hours every day for a couple of weeks. Soprano is not hard to play—it's just another saxophone —but it is hard to play in tune. That's what Johnny Hodges always knew, but he played it very well. I heard an album of Lucky Thompson playing Jerome Kern about a couple of months ago. I thought he was fantastic. He played great on that—great tenor, great soprano, both. I was so impressed with it, because I hadn't heard him play for a long time. I heard it just once over an FM station in California, and ever since I've been saying I must get it.

"When I went to Europe the first time," he said, "it was to join Willie Lewis in Paris. I was there nine months, and then I went to England to work for the B.B.C., thanks to Leonard Feather. I didn't know him personally at that time, but I knew him through his writing and he knew me through my music. Altogether, I think I was there about twenty-two months. I enjoyed England very much, and still do. I had to get out of the country every now and then to renew my visa. I always had a limited work permit and I wasn't allowed to play at any time, with one exception when we did a big concert at The Hippodrome.

"The job with Henry Hall at the B.B.C. meant, so far as I can remember, that I did about six arrangements a week. It was a full orchestra with a string section. The programs were more varied then, because they were played live on radio. It was almost like writing for the Hit Parade, which I did after coming back here. All the bands were playing the pop tunes of the day. I could still do it—an arrangement a day, and two if it were just a matter of vocal backgrounds. It wasn't a question often then of composing a tune, but of doing a treatment of a song."

"I originally got into the movie field when I went out to Los Angeles with the orchestra to work on a film, *Stormy Weather*. All the time I was doing that, we were playing there, and there was a club, the Swing Club, that we came back to every year—in '43, '44, '45, and '46. Then I started doing studio work, and by the time I gave up the band I'd decided that that was going to be it, and I'd bought a home. There's a lot of scope in TV and pictures, and a lot of recording is done out there, too."

Nobody writes for saxophones with such skill and flair as Benny Carter. This was axiomatic even before the famous Paris recording of *Crazy Rhythm* and *Honeysuckle Rose*. It was especially evident when he himself led the section, and it is as true now as it was three decades ago. ("Then and now, he's timeless," Oliver Nelson maintains.) His arrangements and playing are equally imbued with suppleness, mobility, lyricism and unsugared richness. In short, his music "sings" and moves with a graceful distinction—and certainly it swings. In the years before Charlie Parker, he and Johnny Hodges reigned supreme as soloists in a kind of dualism, each with a specific, complementary sphere of influence. Today, his style reflects his awareness of the last quarter-century's innovations, and his taste and selectivity in incorporating what is appropriate to his own musical personality.

(1966)

COLEMAN HAWKINS

TENOR SAXOPHONE

"It's surprising that a musician with his knowledge and experience should take time out to listen to younger musicians, but then his thinking isn't limited by the past. And he doesn't just listen to saxophones. He listens to all instruments. He always retains his personal flavor, but you find young musicians on his dates, and he's just as comfortable with them as with the older guys.''

Lockjaw Davis was talking about Coleman Hawkins, a senior he holds in high regard. His recognition of the great tenor star's perennial freshness was echoed by Johnny Hodges.

"The older he gets, the better he gets," Hodges said. "If ever you think he's through, you find he's just gone right on ahead again. He's a bitch!''

Paul Gonsalves, himself one of the most formidable technicians of the tenor saxophone, has never hesitated to express his admiration.

"Coleman Hawkins is more than a stylist," Gonsalves claimed. "He is a great stylist, of course, but he is also a very, very good musician. He plays jazz and he also plays the instrument the way it should be played. I'm sure he could take a place among symphony musicians and command their respect. You might say that the secret of his success has been that he had a natural gift, and that he took trouble to develop it, just like Duke. You can't rely on natural talent alone in today's competitive music world. There certainly aren't many guys around with talent like Hawk's, and there are even fewer with what I'd call the humility to recognize any need for developing that talent."

The subject of those perceptive comments was indeed a jazz phenomenon. In terms of durable artistic accomplishment and growth, the only parallel to his career is provided by Duke Ellington. He was challenged by different stylists several times, as Paul Gonsalves implied, but his supremacy was soon reasserted. Basic to this, and to his ability to go on adding creatively, was his sound.

Discussing "the wide range of tonal approaches" to the instrument in *The Book of Jazz,* Leonard Feather referred to the "manly sonorities of a Coleman Hawkins." There have been many approaches, but for the majority of musicians and listeners the Hawkins tone has consistently represented the ultimate. The tones of some others have been appealing, permissible deviations, though they have often suggested loyalties split between alto and tenor. Others again have sought to match the Hawkins tone, but they have never quite attained its full, rounded power and authority.

Despite his own strong convictions about tone, Hawkins' appreciation of another musician's ideas was unaffected by a differing tonal approach.

"I like most music unless it's wrong," he said. "I liked Lester Young the first time I heard him, and I always got along very well with him. We were on a lot of tours together, and I spent a lot of time with him, talking and drinking, in hotel rooms and places like that. People forgot that Chu Berry's sound wasn't like mine either.

"As for mine, sometimes when people think I'm blowing harder or softer, I'm really blowing with just the same power, but the difference is due to the reed. I like my reed to speak. It's supposed to sound just like a voice. On records, the engineering can do things, too—make the sound harder or sharper. I dropped the buzz a long time ago and just play with a clear tone now."

His attitude towards contemporary activities was unambiguous.

"I've got all that current scene," he said. "If I play with you, I've got you. Coltrane, Lockjaw, Charlie Rouse, Paul Gonsalves, Johnny Griffin— I hear what they're doing and I've played with all of them. And, good gracious, I nearly forgot Sonny Rollins! He's a favorite of mine."

He kidded the members of the quintet he and Roy Eldridge led jointly: "Last night you had Coltrane. Tonight you're going to get plenty of Ornette!"

On his nocturnal rounds and in record studios he heard plenty of jazz, but at home the records he played were almost entirely classical.

"I love all the operas. I like Stravinsky when I'm listening to Stravinsky, Bach when I'm listening to Bach, and Beethoven when I'm listening to Beethoven. I have no prejudices. I think Tchaikovsky was a great composer, but I guess his music became too popular to be chic.

"You see this sheet music here—*Deux Arabesques* by Debussy. I must have bought it ten times, but I always seem to lose it. I play it on piano and on my horn.

"I'd been telling Roy for a year that I'd write out the melody of *I Mean You* for him, the number I did with Fats Navarro. Well, today I decided to do it, and I went out and bought some music paper and a couple of pencils, and there was this piece lying in the store right under my nose."

Almost every night, between sets, the length of Hawkins' musical career became the subject of discussion or argument. The talk might at first sound unkind, even malicious, but with familiarity the outlines of a kind of game emerged, the object being to prove Coleman Hawkins older than he really was. The players did not expect to win. Their pleasure rather lay in seeing how he would extricate himself from the traps they set, or how their arguments would be refuted. Two notably talented players were Sonny Stitt and Roy Eldridge. The latter, in fact, through long association, had come to regard himself as Hawkins' straight man.

"Yeah?" someone would say. "Then how about the time when you were working with Mamie Smith?"

"That was somebody else using my name," Hawkins replied with crushing finality.

"I can remember you, a grown man, playing with Fletcher Henderson when I was still a child," said a Swing-Era veteran.

Reminiscences flooded in. Hawkins himself talked with more animation, to give the impression that his guard was down. Then:

"I don't think," he said, suddenly and airily, "that I ever was a child!"

When the Eldridge-Hawkins quintet was once playing the Heublein Lounge in Hartford, an eight-year-old girl insisted on getting the autograph of Coleman Hawkins, and his only.

"How is it, Roy," he asked afterwards, "that all your fans are *old* people? They come in here with canes and crutches. They must be anywhere from fifty-eight to a hundred-and-eight. But my fans are all young, from eight to fifty-eight years old!"

"That little girl thought you were Santa Claus," said drummer Eddie Locke.

"Is that so? Well, who's got more fans than Santa Claus?"

An often-cited example of Hawk's mischievous and sometimes macabre sense of humor goes back to the early *Jazz at the Philharmonic* tours. Several musicians in the package were unaccustomed to flying and fearful of it. On this occasion, the plane took off uneventfully. No sooner were safety belts unloosed, however, than Hawkins was on his feet, slowly pacing the aisle, his head behind an opened tabloid, the big black headlines of which proclaimed the number of dead in a catastrophic air crash.

Unsentimental about the past, he preferred to talk about today—and tomorrow. For instance, of Jimmie Harrison, one of the great pace-setters on trombone, with whom he had a close friendship, he would simply say:

"Yes, Jimmie and I were real tight. He could play. He had a good beat, and he could swing."

As Dicky Wells remembered it, Hawkins' relationship with Harrison was something like that he later had with Eldridge. "One time," Wells said, "Hawk told Jimmie:

" 'I won't be here tomorrow at the matinee. I'm sick of this stuff, coming down here and blowing—for what?'

" 'You're not coming?' Jimmie asked.

" 'No,' said Hawk.

"So next day Jimmie went down about ten minutes before the matinee ended, with some kind of story all ready to tell Smack (Fletcher Henderson). As he went in, he heard a tenor that sounded real good, and sure enough Hawk had been there all the time. So when he spoke to Hawk, Hawk said:

" 'Don't pay me no mind, man. I was only fooling.' "*

The Night People by Dicky Wells, (Crescendo, Boston, 1971.)

One story Hawk tells against himself concerns Miles Davis. He had been kidding Miles about leaving the stand when he finished his solo, about not acknowledging applause, and so on.

"I played with you on 52nd Street, didn't I?" Davis asked.

"Yes."

"What kind of example were you? Sometimes you didn't show up at all."

In comparison with those days, Hawkins became very punctilious in the matter of time-keeping.

"That isn't the only way I've changed. I don't eat like I used to." (The slimmer outline offered visible proof.)

"I used to order a great big T-bone steak. When the waiter brought it, I'd order another, and I was always good for three of them, but now one little medium-sized steak is enough."

Cars used to be a sure-fire topic for conversation. He had driven a Rolls, regarded it as good value and a good investment, and seriously considered buying one. But although renowned as a fast driver from Fletcher Henderson days on, he laid that aside, too.

"You know that last car I bought. I've had it two years and there's not much more than a thousand miles on the clock. It just sits in the garage.

"Why?" He snorted bitterly. "That radar! I was driving back from Jamestown after a gig, alone. They must have pulled about twenty cars.

"Jamestown? That would be about four hundred miles. I'd never feel sleepy if I was driving fast, not even when I'd been drinking. If I had a big meal—now that *would* make me sleepy. And so would that driving along at those slow speeds. Sixty miles an hour on those fine thruways is just a shame!"

One change in recent years that Hawkins felt had not been beneficial to the business, or to musicians, was the policy of short engagements favored by many club-owners.

"They have a different group in their place every week, or every two weeks. You don't get to know the people and they don't get to know you. They don't get into the *habit* of coming to hear you. They may like what you're doing, but when they come back they find a totally different group and music. You take when Red Allen was at the Metropole all those years. People liked him and knew he was there and kept on coming back. Same thing with Wilbur De Paris at Ryan's. Engagements used to be much longer, and then you had a chance to build up a following. The combo would be identified with the place and the place with the combo."

Hawkins and Eldridge returned to the Metropole after too long an interval. One night, as Hawkins was swinging his way through *Stuffy,* a customer from Texas yelled up at Eldridge:

"How about some Dixie? *South Rampart. . . ?*"

To placate him, Eldridge called *Tin Roof Blues* next.

"Coleman doesn't like that kind of request," he said later, "but when we play those numbers we play them our way."

Their "way" was, of course, highly rewarding. They did not coast and they did not compromise. Their vitality, their invention and their sound were all equally impressive. The rhythm section of Tommy Flanagan, Major Holley and Eddie Locke gave them good support. Hawkins appreciated Flanagan very much.

"He plays piano. He plays it like the great instrument it is, not like some kind of drum."

Thinking about Flanagan's playing led to further reflection:

"Yes, I think a solo should tell a story, but to most people that's as much a matter of shape as of what the story is about. Romanticism, and sorrow, and greed—they can all be put into music. I can definitely recognize greed. I know when a man is playing for money. And, good gracious, there's plenty of that going on right now!

"Tempo is important, too, of course. Tempo should go according to the piece. Certain pieces are written so that the right tempo—fast, medium, slow—is really quite clear. If you play a slow ballad fast, you lose everything. There's plenty of that going on, too!"

"Some of my biggest moments," Hawkins said, "have been in jam sessions, but I don't want to talk about them. There were always other people involved! A big kick of another kind was when I opened at The Palladium with Jack Hylton. It was my first experience of an audience in Europe. And it was a huge stage. Just to walk out there was something! And then I was very well received."

Paul Gonsalves had a theory about Hawkins' success in Europe during the '30s: "It wasn't only due to the fact that he was a good musician. It was his manner, his dignity, the way he carried himself, and the way he dressed. I think it was the same with Benny Carter."

Hawkins saw great changes in Europe after the war, not all of them for the better. New attitudes reflected world movements and the presence of U.S. armed forces. "London and Paris were great cosmopolitan cities when I first went there. If you were good or if you were bad, you were treated accordingly, and that was that. But since those days New York has become a very cosmopolitan city, too.

"When I came back here the first time, I was disappointed with what had happened in the music. Charlie Parker and Dizzy were getting started, but they needed help. What they were doing was 'far out' to a lot of people, but it was just music to me. Joe Guy was playing their way when he started with me in 1939.

Fletcher Henderson's reed section, 1934. L. to R.: Hilton Jefferson, Russell Procope, Buster Bailey, Coleman Hawkins.

Coleman Hawkins and his big band at the Apollo Theatre, Lawrence Lucie on guitar.

"Another kick was when I opened with my own big band at the Golden Gate in 1940. They wouldn't let us off the stand. I enjoyed that period very much, and being leader didn't worry me. The band was very good—too good in some ways. We had fine arrangements, by Andy Gibson, Buster Tolliver and Buster Harding. And every now and then I wrote one.

"I always used to write when I felt like it. I remember writing an arrangement of *Singin' in the Rain* for Fletcher Henderson when that song was popular. I don't think Smack was recording then, because we never made a record of it. I also wrote a theme for him. We didn't give it a name, but it was written for the saxes and rhythm including tuba.

"Since my own band broke up, I haven't worked regularly with a big band, and I like blowing with a big band just as much as with a small combo. I don't know how it is, but I never have played with Duke's band. I'd like to. I hope I can record with him some day.*

"A date I did last November was one I'll remember. Benny Carter came into New York to do some work with Basie before going on to Europe again, and we recorded together for Impulse with the same instrumentation we used on a session in Paris in 1937, the one where we made *Crazy Rhythm* and *Honeysuckle Rose*. We made those titles again, but this time we had Phil Woods and Charlie Rouse. They can play, those two—and read! For rhythm, we had Dick Katz, John Collins, Jimmy Garrison and Jo Jones."

"Nobody likes hometown," Hawkins said, and sometimes he did not seem to be adequately appreciated in his own country. He was, after all, one of the five greatest musicians jazz has produced, and a true aristocrat in his profession. In club after club he stood, detached, serene, distinguished, listening maybe to Eldridge solo with a semi-benign smile, a figure of pronounced intelligence and sophistication. Then he would begin to blow. Sometimes the audience listened appreciatively and sometimes it didn't. Sometimes it continued its unknowing babble and ignored the quality of the music flowing all around. A poor audience deserved a poor performance, but it didn't get it. Eyes closed, Hawkins was immediately in flight. His muse claimed him body and soul.

(1961)

Coleman Hawkins died 19 May, 1969.

---

*This came about shortly afterwards, in 1962.

ROY ELDRIDGE

TRUMPET

Roy Eldridge's story needs a book to itself, and it is one he has often spoken of writing. Here he refers to a few episodes in his long and eventful career. Born in Pittsburgh in 1911, he is often cited with Louis Armstrong and Dizzy Gillespie as one of the three major innovators on jazz trumpet, and it is well known that he was one of Gillespie's early inspirations. Attempts to classify the trumpet hierarchy under these names should, however, be avoided. As with most such musical categorization, the subjects will prove all too elusive. King Oliver, Joe Smith, Bubber Miley, Bix Beiderbecke, Rex Stewart, Henry Allen and Frank Newton, for example, were all trumpet players of decided individuality.

"My mother played piano, but no one encouraged me to be a musician. I didn't want to be one, but I was playing drums when I was six! Then my brother, Joe, had the idea for me to switch from drums to trumpet. He told me I was never going to be too big, so lugging those drums around—and they had big sets of drums then—didn't make sense. He had my folks get me a trumpet for Christmas. A barber named P. M. Williams taught me. He used to play in parades and things, and he was something else, too. You could hear him ten blocks down the street.

"I never bothered then about reading music, because whatever he played, I could play. Just like that. I could play classical music or anything else if I heard it. Sure, not reading was bad, but I started to catch up in 1928, when I went to Detroit with Horace Henderson. I broke it up there, and I thought I was really something, but my brother would say, 'Put your notice in. You don't know nothing about any music!' He knew I was jiving. He tried to get me a couple of jobs with good bands around there, and I couldn't play the music at auditions. So he started schooling me then—how to read, the chords, and all of that. Then I got with some cats that ended up being called McKinney's Chocolate Dandies. It was a little seven- or eight-piece band, and they could swing. They played a lot of good heads, but they couldn't read too good either. So that was right up my alley while Joe was getting me going with the music. Jean Goldkette had the official band that was McKinney's Cotton Pickers, but this little band got so popular around there that they gave us that name.

"After that I went with Zack Whyte for two weeks in Cincinnati. Then in 1929 I went with Speed Webb for a while. Teddy Wilson and his brother, Gus, were in that band, and Teddy wrote an arrangement with a modulation for me to play, and it came out sounding just like Louis Armstrong. Would you believe that, before I ever heard Louis? Gus Wilson arranged for that band, too. So did Eli Robinson. In fact, everybody arranged but me.

"I didn't stay with anybody too long in those days. It wasn't that they were hard to get along with or anything like that, but nobody was paying any money. If you saw me crying or acting like I was drunk, you look next morning and I'd be gone. If I was not getting any money, I'd tear out in a minute then.

"In the beginning, I didn't hear Louis Armstrong, but I heard guys like Rex Stewart and Bobby Stark. I liked Rex because he was very fiery. I heard Red Nichols and liked what he played, not because it was clean, but because it was different. It's always a matter of what you're exposed to when you're young. Really, I liked saxophones better than I did trumpet. That's how I got my first job with the carnival band in 1927, playing Coleman Hawkins's chorus on *Stampede*. They had never heard a trumpet play like that, and that's one of the reasons why I never could growl or use a plunger good.

"First time I ever heard trumpet played like that was in St. Louis, where I got stranded. I got a job in the Grand Central Hotel, and every Sunday those guys would come down there—Dewey Jackson, Baby James, five or six of them—and they all knew Louis Armstrong's things like *Cornet Shop Suey* and *Big Butter and Eggs Man,* too. I thought that was 'southern' trumpet playing, but they used to wipe me out every Sunday. One cat in particular, real big, taller than Louis—I never did know his name, but he could play! Sleepy Tomlin, Ed Swayzee, both good trumpet players—they used to be in the crowd that would come.

"Another reason why I was familiar with Red Nichols, I remember, was when I went out on the road with a little band called Roy Elliott and His Panama Band from New York City. I was fifteen and had never been to New York, but the show people changed my name and gave the band that title. I would never have thought of it. We used to play some of the arrangements Red Nichols and His Five Pennies played on the records, so that kinda got me in his bag. Another feature I used to do was *East St. Louis Toodle-oo.* I had a tin can painted gold for a mute, and I used to do the Camel Walk while I was playing. The Lon Chaney Walk they called it, and I'd get 'way down.

"I'll tell you who really used to wipe me out when I was playing in an after-hours spot in Detroit—Joe Smith. I used to *hate* him when he came in there, because otherwise I had the joint locked up. He'd come in there and play so pretty. They talk a lot about Bix, but this cat was too much. Just listen to what he plays in the middle of Fletcher Henderson's *Stampede*.

"I never actually heard Bubber Miley. We used to call him and Tricky Sam the 'Jungle Men.' But at that time I didn't really like Duke's band. I liked Fletcher Henderson's, because they played more different kinds of music, things I could really get with.

"I heard Louis Armstrong for the first time at the Lafayette Theatre in 1931, and it made a big impression on me. That was when I really learned to appreciate him. I had changed my embouchure back in '28 or '29, and I played fast all the time. In fact, I couldn't play anything else, because I had no feeling for it. I was like the younger cats today. If they play *Stardust,* they have to play it triple time. It goes with wanting to be speedy. Really, it takes more energy and more thinking to play slow than it does to play fast, because you can do a lot of jiving when you're playing fast. You've got to put more in it when it's slow. Well, the change is like you're growing up. I can tell the difference in myself when I listen to tapes of things I did 'way back. Not that there was anything specially wrong with 'em, but there was a completely different approach between then and now."

After going to New York in 1930 and playing with Cecil Scott, Elmer Snowden, Charlie Johnson and Teddy Hill, Eldridge returned to Pittsburgh in 1933 and helped his brother, who played alto saxophone, get a band together.

"It was called the Eldridge Brothers' Rhythm Team, and we had four saxophones, five trumpets and three trombones. Outside of my brother, the only guy in it I can now remember was Kenny Clarke on drums. The band lasted about six months. We played in contests against all the local bands, and we won them all hands down. But after winning the contests, attitudes of the guys started changing, and my brother and I said, 'Well, we better let these cats go!'

"We went to work with the Original Cotton Pickers as they were then called, because McKinney had gone. It was still a good band, with people like Prince Robinson and Dave Wilborn in it. We stayed with them a while, and then I went back to New York and rejoined Teddy Hill at the Savoy in 1935. I had my first little band in New York that same year at the Famous Door. From there I went with Fletcher Henderson until I opened at the Three Deuces in Chicago on 5 September, 1936. That was the best little band I ever had. There was a good feeling, and those guys would *think* so good. Some groups, you have to actually draw 'em blueprints for them

L. to R.: Dick Vance, Joe Thomas, Roy Eldridge, trumpets; Ed Cuffee, Ferdinand Arbello, trombones.

to do anything. My brother, Scoops Carry and Dave Young, they were *down,* you know. I was pretty good at making up melodies in those days, and we'd get some chords and soon have a piece that fitted when we were tied up for a program. We were on the air seven nights a week, and we never had any problems.

"I had another very good band in 1939, when I had ten pieces at the Arcadia Ballroom in New York. Don Redman did some of the arrangements, and *The King of Bongo Bong* was his number. My brother, Clyde Hart, Prince Robinson, Eli Robinson, Franz Jackson, Ted Sturgis, Bob Williams and Panama Francis were all in that band, and Laurel Watson was singing."

In the '40s, Eldridge was with Gene Krupa, and often played drums while that leader was conducting. During this period he became a national figure as a result of record hits like *Rockin' Chair* and the celebrated duet with Anita O'Day on *Let Me Off Uptown.* He joined Artie Shaw in 1944 for about a year, and then got together a big band of his own.

"I don't know why. It was a headache. I had a lot of cats who could play good, but they couldn't hold their whiskey. Yes, that band was good in 1946, when I had Lockjaw Davis and Porter Kilbert in it. Buster Harding was arranging, and we had a publishing company then. I had arrangements by Eddie Lowth, too. He was a white guy, and a good arranger. And Elton Hill was doing some. I was featured, but I never made it a one-man thing like Pops (Armstrong) did. Business began to go down the drain for big bands that year. I noticed lots of dates getting canceled, and I saw the handwriting on the wall. We did one-nighters, played the Apollo, the El Grotto in the Pershing Hotel in Chicago . . . The last gig with that band was at the Spotlight in New York.

"After that, after all the money I lost, you couldn't *give* me a big band! I didn't have anyone backing me. I did it all myself. The guys all got uniforms, and I paid for them. I had to pay for four trumpets, a set of drums, cymbals, and all the music. I saw myself as taking care of some lowly musicians nobody else ever looked after. I just blew all my bread, man, and I ain't had nothing since! But at least I didn't owe anybody, because I paid as I went along. A lot of guys who got big bands ended up owing a lot of bread to somebody who backed them. I really don't see how they can make it today. There was a time you could get a hotel room for five or six dollars, but you can't get a room in the YMCA for that now. And food was so much cheaper.

"My brother died in 1950. He got sick before I went back to Pittsburgh, and died while I was working there. I never did know the real cause. There was no autopsy, but he had got real overweight, drinking wine and stuff. It could have been his heart. The night he died, my father made me go to work anyway. 'Nothing you can do,' he said. 'Might as well go.' And I'd go to play something, and I'd remember the things he had taught me, like running the changes, and all that. You don't think about it till the cat's gone, and then every time you play something you hear him. Sure was a drag, man.

"That was one reason I went to Europe, and stayed in Europe. When I came back I got a quintet, and sometimes Coleman (Hawkins) and I would be booked together. Now it seems like we played together all our lives! They did us an injustice though, because we'd only get the same money I'd get with my own group. There should have been more, but they'd never let us break through.

"Another reason I stayed in Paris was a concert I did with a lot of guys at Carnegie Hall, when I felt I was out of step. Then Norman Granz brought a record of it over, and I found I wasn't out of step. You see, I was torn between whether I should do that sort of thing or go for myself. Rhythm sections . . . I didn't know what they were doing, but it sure was mean. I never actually put anything down. I give it every chance in the world, to see what's happening, to see if I can get any feeling out of it. I used to go and dig different groups, and I couldn't see how they could come back in together when there was a break. To me, they were always messed up. It got to be so I really needed a pencil and some score pads to figure out what was going on. It stopped being fun any more. I don't think with jazz you should have to figure out what's going on. You should be able to *feel* it, pat your feet, and enjoy it.

"Coleman and I had some drummers you wouldn't believe! We picked one up in Philadelphia. I guess we were juiced and the band was swinging. We took this cat up to Boston, and I was the first to notice what was wrong. Coleman and I both blew heavy, and you needed some weight behind us, but he wouldn't say anything, you know.

" 'I don't think this cat is playing any bass drum,' I said.

" 'No, he just hits it every once in a while,' Coleman said after we'd played another tune. So I went over to the drummer and said:

" 'Hey, baby, when you get to play with some old-time cats, they like to hear that bass drum so they can get some *time*. There ain't but five of us, and that'll make the band sound heavier, too.'

" 'Man, cats don't do that now!'

" 'Don't tell me what cats don't do! You ain't playing with some cats that don't do that. That's what we *want!*'

"So we played some more tunes, and he sat and played, but he couldn't actually do it.

" 'What happened?' I asked.

" 'Well, I hurt my foot in the war.' That was his cop-out.

"I played drums a couple of times while I was with Count Basie in 1966, when Sonny Payne was late. Basie kept me up there, but, goddam, I could hardly play my trumpet when I got through with that. I don't play drums any more, and I'll tell you what stopped me.

"There's a clarinet player on Long Island named Herb Myers, who used to be a policeman. Naturally, he liked Benny Goodman, and I did a lot of club dates with him. He got a date playing for the policemen, with an organ player, a singer and me. Gene Krupa had given me a drum set one Christmas, and after Herb got through playing forty minutes with the tom-toms going, I'd play a thirty-minute drum solo! I knew all Gene's solos, and everything went along nice. We played about two hours overtime, and when we got through, I had forgotten how to tear those damn' drums down. I'd been juicing and was pretty well out of it by then, but when I used to play drums as a kid, they didn't have stands like they have now. When I played with Gene Krupa, Gene had always set them up. So they were like a crossword puzzle to me. Man, I messed around there and couldn't get those drums broken down for nothin'!

" 'Come on, Roy,' the man said, 'we've got to close.'

"Eventually, he got a couple of waiters, picked up the drums just like they were, and put 'em in my station wagon. When I got up, and was sober, and remembered how to break 'em down, I put 'em up, and they ain't been out since. And, oh, I was sore! My arms and legs ached from playing those long solos. That was six or seven years ago.

"You get a lot of rough nights in this business. Sometime in the '50s, Coleman Hawkins and I played till four o'clock in the morning in St. Louis. We got in our cars then—he had a Cadillac and I had a Lincoln—and drove to Buffalo, through ice and snow, one behind the other, often at a hundred miles an hour and over. That's one way to get killed, especially if you've been juicing. I drove all through Cleveland, didn't run into anything, stopped at all the lights, they said, and everything. I don't know how that happened, because I didn't remember a damn place in the city. When I came to myself and looked down, I saw I needed some gas.

" 'How far are we from Cleveland?' I asked at the gas station.

" 'Man, you just come through Cleveland!'

"We played Buffalo that night, got something to eat when we were through, and then tore out for Boston. I've got a picture of us on the stand there, and if we don't look like two sick cats . . . ! Well, our resistance was low after that, and I broke out with the 'flu first. Coleman got it right behind me.''

Their remarkable friendship and musical partnership had a melancholy coda in 1969, when Coleman Hawkins died. To many, this marked the end of an era, but after a brief, depressed interval, Eldridge made a splendid recovery. He returned to 52nd Street, the scene of earlier triumphs, and played nightly at Ryan's with much of his old enthusiasm. At the 1973 Newport Jazz Festival, he made two extremely successful appearances, his performance of *Stardust* in Carnegie Hall being one of that festival's unquestionable artistic peaks.

(1973)

EDDIE LOCKE

DRUMS

Eddie Locke, the youngest musician interviewed in this book, was born in Detroit, Michigan, in 1930. He was educated at Miller High School and Wayne University, and while in high school he met Oliver Jackson, with whom he began a long friendship. They formed an act called *Bop and Lock,* and played theatres in and around Detroit, singing, dancing and drumming. Cozy Cole saw and encouraged them, and in 1954 they appeared in the show at the Apollo Theatre in New York on a bill which included Arnett Cobb's group. After working around New York for some time, they split up and found work individually as drummers in different groups at the Metropole.

Locke was too young to have experienced the best days of the Swing Era, but he was unusual in his ability to comprehend and adjust to the requirements of two of its greatest figures, Roy Eldridge and Coleman Hawkins. His close association with them, and his affection and admiration for them, together enable him to shed valuable light on their beliefs and way of life.

"The first time I worked with Roy Eldridge was at a club in Brooklyn with Harold Singer on tenor, Al Williams on piano and, I think, Gene Ramey on bass. He had heard me playing at the Metropole in the afternoons with Tony Parenti and Dick Wellstood. J.C.Heard had been playing drums with Roy and Hawk (Coleman Hawkins) there, and when J.C. went to Europe for a month they got another drummer who was just terrible and couldn't make it with them. So Roy called me, but I couldn't do the afternoons *and* evenings, too. That was when I introduced Oliver Jackson to them, and got him the gig. Then Sol Yaged, the clarinet player, heard Oliver there, and hired him for his rhythm section, and when Roy was going out with a quartet, I went with him.

"Roy knows a lot about drumming, and he wants that *time*. Time is his thing. He taught me a whole lot about drumming, and helped me build that solo I do on *Caravan*. Cozy Cole was first, though, because I had met him in Detroit when he was still with Louis Armstrong and Earl Hines. But the main influence on me was Jo Jones, and I'd go on record dates in New York where he was playing, help carry his drums, and so on. My own first record date was with Roy for Norman Granz, when we made the quartet album called *Swingin' on the Town* with Ronnie Ball on piano and Benny Moten on bass.

"Soon after I started playing with Roy—just a quartet—we were up in Toronto, and something happened that had never happened to me before. I was doing my solo on *Caravan,* and when we got to the bridge, where we swing, Roy played so much he scared me to death, and I forgot what I was doing. I'm used to it now, but I hadn't any experience then of anyone playing with that kind of power. It practically lifted me off my drum seat.

"I've played some funny jobs with him since then. One I never forget was for four days at an air base near Limestone, Maine. I don't know how we got booked up there. We were playing in the non-commissioned officers' club, and the people there knew absolutely nothing about jazz. They'd sit and look at us, wondering what the hell we were doing there, but we made the gig, played calypsos, cha-cha-chas and everything. What upset Roy was that we were confined to a very small area, and we couldn't go out. They had dogs, and all kinds of security stuff. Roy is very sensitive, and he wanted to get out of there *so* bad!

"The first time I ever played with Coleman Hawkins was on Fire Island. I'd played with Roy by then, but I'd never worked with Bean (Hawkins), and I didn't really know him. From that time on, I played with him nearly all the time. That was some night! Besides him and Roy, there were Dicky Wells, Ray Bryant and a bass player out of Jersey. We had driven out from Manhattan in a couple of cars, and we were taken to the island in motorboats. There was no air-conditioning in the place and it was terribly hot. Bean and Roy each had a half-gallon of gin, and during the course of the night they drank it all. I remember Bean wiping himself with a towel between sets, and then wringing the sweat out of it, as though he had come in wet from swimming or something. But the heat and the gin didn't seem to affect their playing, and it was one of those nights when the music was really exciting.

"You had to be a fairly strong drummer for Coleman, because he played so heavy. And when you got him and Roy together . . . ! In 1958, when we got the gig at the Metropole, Bean said, 'I'll get the piano player,' and he got Tommy Flanagan. Roy said, 'I'll get the drummer,' and he got me. We had four or five basses at different times. I kept working with them when we went over to places like the Coronet in Brooklyn and the Heublein House in Hartford. The trouble when he and Roy were working together was that the price was too high for a lot of clubs. They played great together, but when they played separately it was like playing in two entirely different quartets. Their approach to music was quite different. That first night at the Metropole, Bean listened to me backing Roy and seemed to like it, because he smiled and asked, 'Are you playing like that for me, too?'

"You remember when we made the record at the Village Gate with Johnny Hodges in 1962? On one number, when Johnny finished his chorus, he stepped back and looked at Bean for him to go up to the mike and blow. But Bean, he just stood there with his hands on his hips, and said, 'Ain't no sense in no tenor following no tenor!' Only someone who appreciated the sound Johnny had would dig the wit in that. He didn't follow him either, but let the piano take a chorus. All the time Johnny was playing, Bean must have been thinking about that, because he came up with it right away. Later, when we were packing up our instruments, he said, 'You know, I really learned something about Johnny Hodges tonight. He's got a lot of jive on that horn.' That was one of his favorite words, 'jive.' He had so much humor, but it didn't come out unless you were around him a lot.

"John Coltrane used to come and listen to him wherever he went, and one night Coltrane came in the Metropole with Eric Dolphy. Bean stopped to talk to Coltrane when he came off that long bandstand. They were talking about music when Eric interrupted him. 'I don't have to worry about *you,*' Coleman said, 'because I can out-melody you!' It was true, of course, because Bean was *the* Melody Man.

"Later on, we were working at the Village Vanguard, and Coltrane and Pharoah Sanders were also there. Usually, Coleman would just sit through

Eddie Locke and Coleman Hawkins.

other people's sets, but this time he couldn't. It was really funny for him to make the effort to go up all those stairs to get outside. 'I can't stand that any longer,' he said. But he never closed his mind to anything, and that was the only time I remember something like that happening.

"He wouldn't talk to interviewers. We went to the Latin Casino in Philadelphia where a boy who wrote for the newspaper came in.

" 'I want to interview you,' he said.

" 'You a writer?' Bean asked.

" 'Yes,' said this young, brash kid.

" 'What you want to know? Where I was born, and all that? You can get it all from any record album. But if you're a writer, you come downstairs and *listen* when I play the next set. Then you go and write your article.'

"Bean had lost his license so many times that I ended up as his driver as well as his drummer. He sold his car, and then one day he came out from his place and couldn't get a cab for a long time. When he finally got one, he told the guy to drive him right to the showroom, where he bought his last car, the Imperial. Because he had no license, I was the only person to drive it. The furthest it ever went was one weekend in the summer, when we had a job at Canaan, near Pittsfield, Mass. He had that car two years, but I don't suppose it had a thousand miles on the clock!

"The first time he called me up about it was funny. 'Come over,' he said. 'Let's go downtown in my car. It's just sitting there.' So I got dressed, and when we went out to the car we couldn't discover how to get the emergency brake off. We were out in the lot about an hour. We had the hood up, pressed every button inside, had the lights come on and the windshield wipers work—everything. It was brand new, and nobody had driven it since the man from the showroom delivered it and put it back of his place. I'd never driven a Chrysler before, but finally Bean said, 'Well, Eddie, let's try to move it.' As soon as I put it in gear, it went *ssssh,* and the emergency brake came off! 'Why didn't you read the manual?' I asked him. For a time, we took it out quite often, but later it just sat there again.

"Classical music was his big love, and he would often talk to me about it. Now, you know, he would never take his horn out to practice, no matter how long he was off. One day, he was talking about Rubinstein.

" 'If I could get you a gig to record with Rubinstein, just you and him . . .' I began.

" 'Eddie, if you did that,' he said, 'I would practice.'

"He loved pretty music, and I never forget one day when he came to my place on West End Avenue to dinner. My wife is a good cook, and so am I. And so was he. We used to talk a lot about what we would cook, just as he did with Roy. Those two would talk about food and cooking by the hour. Anyway, he was sitting there eating, and I had put on a record of *Encores,* short pieces by Rubinstein. It shook me up when I saw tears streaming out of his eyes.

" 'Honey,' he said to my wife, 'don't pay me any mind, but that music is *so* pretty!'

"I think I was as close to him as anyone towards the end, even closer than some who had known him much longer. I was lucky to spend so much time with him, and I got to know the musicians he liked and disliked very well—at least, during the time I was around him. Tommy Flanagan was his favorite among piano players. Bean was a competitive man himself, and I remember a night when he had four top-flight piano players up in his apartment. Then Tommy came in and played, and after that nobody played any more.

" 'You cats,' Coleman said, 'you make all those runs and think you're so fast, but Tommy plays all those notes you leave out—the choice notes!'

"You remember that introduction Tommy played on *Love Song from 'Apache',* a tune Coleman liked as soon as he saw the music in the studio? That session was one of the great ones, I think. (*Today and Now,* Impulse AS-34.)

"Roy Eldridge, of course, was another musician he really did like. 'You've got to go a long way,' he told me, 'to find a trumpet player with chops who can swing like that.' He didn't talk about tenor players very much, but I never forget his amused expression when a guy came in one night and said, 'Hawk, I heard that record you made with Sonny Rollins. Don't ever do it again!' Although there were times when he would say there was nothing for him to listen to, he was always interested in what the younger cats were doing.

"When he talked about Fletcher Henderson, he often told me how hard he tried to get him to keep Cootie Williams. He reckoned that was the worst thing Fletcher ever did, when he let Cootie go to Duke. He liked that big-bodied sound Cootie had. When he told you he didn't like Russell Smith's lead, he meant it, because he was serious about music, and when he did pass an opinion he wasn't bullshitting.

"He told me that originally, when he was still playing piano and cello, he went around and listened to *all* the saxophone players. He said there were many good pianists then, but none of the saxophonists were playing anything. 'If I played saxophone,' he said to himself, 'I could easily be the best.' So he played it, and he was."

(1973)

JONAH JONES

TRUMPET

"My father played a little piano by ear, but the main reason I got into music had to do with a kid band coming down the street in a parade when I was about eleven. This was in Louisville, Kentucky, and the band was the Booker T. Washington Community Centre Band, the one Dicky Wells was in. It was about forty or fifty pieces, and the trombones were always out in front of the band.

"I went running back to my mother and grandmother crying, 'I want a trombone! I want a trombone!'

" 'What's wrong with him?' my grandmother said. 'He must be crazy. He wants a trombone, and we can't buy bread!'

"Things were rough then, because of the depression. They thought I would get over it, but I kept crying about a trombone for days. So they called a fellow whose name was Hense Grundy, a good trombone player, and asked him how much a trombone and lessons would cost. He told them they'd be expensive, but that the band I'd seen in the parade would give me a trombone and teach me free. The requirements were that I had to go to band rehearsal every day after school, and stay in Sunday School all day Sunday.

"My mother took me over there, and Mrs. Bessie L. Allen, who ran the whole Sunday School, asked, 'What kind of horn you want, Sonny?'

" 'Trombone, ma'am,' I said. 'I want a trombone.'

" 'Okay, let's see if you can reach the seventh position,' she said when she gave me the trombone. I tried and tried, but I couldn't quite make it, because the seventh position is at the bottom of the horn, and my arms were too short. So then she gave me an alto horn. I had sense enough to know it wasn't what I wanted, because in a big band the alto horn just carries a thing like *um-tah, um-tah, um-tah-tah-tah*. But I would have settled for anything to get in that band, and I stayed on alto horn for two years. Then, when I was thirteen, I switched to trumpet, and I've been on that ever since. By that time, I'd been listening to records by Fletcher Henderson and Louis Armstrong, and I didn't hear any alto horn on them!

I wanted to play something with some melody in it.

"I got my nickname from the conductor of that band, Lockwood Lewis. He was excitable and stammered all the time. We were rehearsing *Our Director March,* and when you came to the trio on it, everybody got down nice and soft. I didn't know my sharps and flats then, and I was making E natural when it was supposed to be E flat. He heard this wrong note and stopped us. 'Let's take it down again,' he said. We did it again, and he began to holler and get more excited. He caught me the third time and threw his baton at me. He called all the kids by their last names, and now he began, 'J-j-j-j-Jones, don't you see . . . ?' All the kids laughed, and from then on I was 'Jonah', for life, although my real name is Robert Elliott Jones.

"Another teacher, a great trumpet player from Louisville, was 'Kid' Mitch, George Mitchell. He'd come home from Chicago and help teach the kids in the band. I go out to say hello to him sometimes when we play Chicago. He's way up there and doesn't play any more. Bob Shoffner always comes by to see us, too.

"I think the instruction we had was good. We played music like the *Poet and Peasant Overture,* hymns like *Onward, Christian Soldiers,* and heavy marches—all of John Philip Sousa's. Since it was a Sunday School, they didn't allow you to play any jazz there, because they figured jazz was dirty.

"Bessie Allen was a wonderful woman. She'd get money from lawyers and department stores around the town after telling them about the work she was doing for the kids in the West End. With their contributions, she bought instruments, hired a beginner's teacher and a conductor for the big band. She turned out a lot of good musicians like Dicky Wells, Bill Beason, Bob Carroll, Les Carr (a good clarinet player), Hal McFerran, and several other guys who later played with Cecil Scott. When girls came in the band, Helen Humes played trumpet and sang, and then got on piano. I met my wife in that band, when she was fourteen or fifteen, and playing trumpet and clarinet. Her brother, Russell Bowles, was in it, too, and he later played with Jimmie Lunceford. A great trumpet player who came out of there, who played at Smalls's with Charlie Johnson or someone like that, was Matthew 'Red' Holland. He was also in Horace Henderson's band, and when he left I replaced him. That would be around 1927, when I was eighteen.

"I had played around Louisville with the local bands before that, while still playing in the Sunday School band. The jazz things we were playing were numbers like *Blue Skies* and *Sweet Georgia Brown.* I didn't know about Dixieland then, about *That's a-Plenty* and *Tin Roof Blues,* although I bet older guys like Hense Grundy did.

Sunday School Band: Dicky Wells is the foremost trombonist. Jonah Jones is on his left, with peck horn.

Tinsley's Royal Aces, Jonah Jones's first band in Louisville after the Sunday school band. Jones is at the extreme left. Mack Walker is on bass, Bob Carroll on tenor saxophone.

"Wallace Bryant out of Paducah came to Louisville, and he was looking for a trumpet player and a clarinet player for the band on a riverboat called the *Island Queen*. Somebody told him about me. The job paid forty dollars a week, with room and board on the boat, and that was not bad in those days. I didn't want to leave town by myself, but I told him I'd go if he'd take my buddy, William Grainger, who also played trumpet. He already had one trumpet, and really wanted a clarinet, but he ended up by taking us both.

"This *Island Queen* used to run in summer from Cincinnati to a park called Coney Island, about twelve miles away. Then in September it would go down the Ohio River, taking out moonlight excursions. We got on the Mississippi at Memphis, and went on down till we hit New Orleans. We stayed around there about a month, and ran into all the other boats, from St. Louis, the Streckfus boats . . . and they all had bands on them. After the boats got back from excursions around one o'clock, we'd go out and jam all night. I guess the guys I played with down there were names, but I didn't know about them at that time.

"Our band had three trumpets, trombone, three saxes and four rhythm. Charlie Stamps, who used to be with the Missourians, was playing banjo. It was all an interesting experience for me. Round about November, the band came back up the river, and when the weather got cold we went to Paducah, trying to keep the band intact, but there wasn't much work, so Grainger and I went on back to Louisville.

"In March, 1928, I joined Horace Henderson, who was working out of Cleveland. A lot of guys out of our kid band were with him, Russell Bowles and Red Holland among them. Roy Eldridge and Bernice Morton were playing trumpet, and he had a very good guitar player, Luke Stewart, who was with Stuff Smith later.

"Louisville was really quite a breeding ground for musicians. There were several good banjo and guitar players—single-string, you know. Luke Stewart's brother George was great. Then there was Carroll Smith, who played with Clifford Hayes. My brother, James W. Jones, was eight years younger than me, and he played good trumpet, but he was one of those guys you couldn't hold down. He wanted to play music, but he didn't want to take orders, and he had to have his own way about everything. He just didn't want anybody to boss him around, but everybody said what a fine trumpet player he was. He's still down there, but I don't think he ever plays any more.

"Buck Washington, of Buck and Bubbles, the piano player, was from Louisville, and I think he recorded with Clifford Hayes sometimes. So did Dan Briscoe, another piano player out of Louisville. His brother was Sylvester Briscoe, who played trombone in the Jenkins Orphanage Band. Elmer Whitlock, the trumpet player who was with Louis Armstrong in 1933, was in that band, too. They had a nice band, but we always called them the 'bad' boys, because it was a sort of detention home.

"Bandleaders got in the way of picking up musicians in Louisville, and when Horace Henderson came there Red Holland left him. Then all the other Louisville boys in the band said, 'Send for Jonah!' So Horace sent for me.

"We played a lot of Fletcher Henderson's arrangements, because Horace was always getting Fletcher's stuff. I played first, Bernice second, and Roy took all the jazz stuff. Oh, Roy was blowing! He always did blow! Ever since I heard of him, he was blowing. Of course, he was playing a lot of Louis Armstrong's stuff then. He could play *Beau Koo Jack* note for note. He was serious, about seventeen years old, a fantastic trumpet player, one of the naturals. I don't think he could read too good then, but he could play so well that he could put his own third part to the stuff.

"In Columbus, Ohio, we picked up Joe Thomas, who later played tenor with Jimmie Lunceford. He was a waiter in a hotel, and he played alto sax then on weekend gigs. When Bernice Morton left, I sent for my buddy, Grainger. And we added another trombone player, a great guy named Archie Hall. After about nine months we got stranded in Buffalo—getting stranded was nothing in those days!—and Grainger and I went back to Cleveland, stayed with my wife's auntie a few weeks, and then went home to Louisville. That was in October, 1929, when Grainger said, 'I've had it. This is enough for me.' But by now I'd made up my mind I wanted to play in those big bands I'd been listening to on records and the radio.

"Horace Henderson came over to Louisville again from Kentucky in January. 'Hey, Fathead,' he said, and that was the nickname he'd given me. 'I need a trumpet and a trombone.' He was fronting the Hardy Brothers band in the pit at the Walker Theatre in Indianapolis. I figured I couldn't get hurt too bad, since it was only a hundred-and-ten miles away. I had another friend out of the kid band, Milton Robinson, who later played trombone for Andy Kirk and Benny Carter. So we went and worked in that pit band a couple of months, and then went on tour playing all the colored theatres in cities like Cincinnati, Cleveland and Detroit. By now I'd learned a bit, and I'd make it my business to meet the bandleaders in the different towns. After working around Richmond, Indiana, which was the Hardy Brothers' hometown, work started to slack off, so I called Wesley Helvey in Cincinnati.

" 'Sure, come on,' he said, 'we'd like to have you.'

"Two-thirds of that band was from Louisville—Milt Robinson on trom-

Jonah Jones (at far left) on the S.S. Island Queen. His friend Wm. Grainger is the third trumpet from left. Wallace Bryant is the trombonist, Charlie Stamps the banjoist, and "Popcorn" the drummer.

Clarence Olden's band: Jonah Jones at far left; Olden, third trumpet from left; Milt Robinson, trombone; Pete Suggs, drums; Chick Carter, conductor.

bone, both altos, the piano player and the drummer. Alec Baker, the tenor player, was from Cincinnati. I was playing first *and* the jazz, because I had learned a lot from Roy. We played through Ohio and Pennsylvania, until I got a call in August from Luke Stewart, the guitar player. He had a quartet in the Vendome Hotel in Buffalo and wanted to add a horn. He said it would be a steady job, so I quit Helvey.

"Luke had Pops Diemer on bass, Wallace Jackson on drums, and Benny Thompson, who played great piano and is still around Buffalo. The job paid only thirty-five to forty dollars a week, but every night we'd split up fifty dollars in tips, and that was good money for that time. Of course, we threw it away as fast as we got it, because we knew we'd get more the next night.

"Then Jimmie Lunceford came to town, and I liked his band and I liked his guys. They lived in the Vendome Hotel, so I got to meet 'em. They needed a trumpet when Paul Webster quit. This was before Tommy Stevenson, and when I joined they had Eddie Tompkins and a fellow named McRae on trumpet, and only one trombone, Henry Wells. They put my brother-in-law, Russell Bowles, on while I was there. When Eddie and I left, they got Tommy Stevenson and a very good trumpet from St. Louis named Sleepy Tomlin. Before they got Joe Thomas on tenor, they had George Clark and a good, fast player from around Buffalo, Clarence Ford. They got Earl Carruthers while I was in the band, too.

"We had a chance to come down to New York and try out for a job, but we missed it because a girl called Cora La Redd had a band they liked better. When we went back to Buffalo, I quit, because we were doing only a couple of nights a week and money was slow.

"That's when I joined Stuff Smith. He had six pieces in a club called Little Harlem. After about a year, he decided to put on more pieces and have a big band. We got some of the best guys in Buffalo and went on down and played the Lafayette Theatre in New York, and the Lincoln Theatre in Philadelphia. We were stranded there, and started going back to Buffalo one by one. This is now 1934, and luckily Lil Armstrong came to town and took over practically the same band Stuff had had. Teddy McRae, the tenor player, had joined us in New York, and we also had George Clark, who had been with Lunceford. Teddy Wilson's brother, Gus, a great arranger and trombone player, was in the band, but Stuff was the main feature.

"Lil started featuring me as King Louis the Second, because at that time I was playing things Louis Armstrong had done on records note for note, like *I'm a Ding Dong Daddy* and *Confessin'*. We had a lot of fun and played good places like the Graystone in Detroit, where I got talking with McKinney of McKinney's Cotton Pickers. When work began to fall off in the early part of '35, four of us quit and went with them. It wasn't the band it used to be, and I stayed only about six weeks before going back to Buffalo. By this time, Stuff Smith had got another little group that was working at a place called the Silver Grill, and he asked me to come on out with him. Ben Bernie came through there when Dick Stabile was playing with him, and Dick came by the club and said, 'How'd you guys like to have a job at the Onyx Club in New York?' We said we would, not thinking it would happen, but a guy came up from New York to listen to us.

"Riley and Farley had had a hit with *The Music Goes 'Round and Around* while in the Onyx, and they were getting ready to go to California. When we went down to New York and got the job, we soon had a hit called *I'se a-Muggin'*. We did a lot of novelty stuff there along with the playing, although we hadn't done so much before. We got such a good response with one novelty number that we made up another. We'd make 'em up on the bandstand, and clown around. All of us had different, funny hats.

"With Stuff, if a number got to going good, in what we called a groove, you could set back and never want to stop playing. Stuff might play twenty-five choruses, and then I'd play twenty-five, and all the time Cozy would be getting stronger and stronger. I told you how we once played *Stomping at the Savoy* for a whole half-hour on the radio—WOR, I think —and we went on playing it for another half-hour when we went off the air! It was nothing for us to play one number for forty-five minutes or an hour. They would accept it at that time.

"We stayed in the Onyx sixteen months, mostly with just the two horns and four rhythm. Mack Walker, who came out of the Louisville band, played bass fiddle. He used to play bass horn in Louisville and with Cecil Scott, and he could play that thing like a trumpet. He could play the cadenza Louis played on *West End Blues* on the bass horn. Bobby Bennett was the guitar player. On piano, we had Raymond Smith from Buffalo, then Jimmy Sherman who was with the Charioteers, and then Clyde Hart. After Johnny Washington left, we got Cozy Cole on drums.

"Cozy was recording with Billie Holiday at that time, and he helped me get a lot of things. That guy could *swing*. Oh, God, he would swing everybody every way! I never forget the first date he took me on at at 1776 Broadway. Bernie Hanighen was the a. and r. man, and John Hammond had a lot to do with it. Because I was working every night, I hadn't yet had much of a chance to get to know the guys around New York, and here I was working with Billie Holiday, Johnny Hodges, Harry Carney, Teddy Wilson, Lawrence Lucie, John Kirby and Cozy. I was a little bit nervous playing in that company! I wasn't known much in New York then, only down on 52nd Street, but after this I started to record with a lot of different guys.

"I remember a date in 1937 when I did *Slappin' the Bass* with Adrian Rollini. I was on another session with Billie Holiday and Benny Goodman. Then I made a lot of sides with Georgia White and Peetie Wheatstraw, the Devil's Son-in-Law. We'd go in the studio and stay all day, just Big Sid Catlett on drums, Lil Armstrong on piano, the singer and myself. We made some stuff under Lil's name for Decca, too, and *Sixth Street* was one of the best things I ever did in those days.

"When Tommy Dorsey was going to play a battle of music with Chick Webb at the Savoy, he got me to go in there with him. He had to do something, because Chick was just waiting for *everybody!* But I didn't help none. Chick blew everybody right out, me along with them. Chick asked me to join his band after that, but I was happy with Stuff and I only did that with Tommy as an extra. Tommy wanted me to join him, too, and he kept after me, but we never got together on the price.

" 'We have to talk price,' I'd say.

" 'Don't worry about that!'

" 'Yeah, but I *am* worrying about it!'

"Then he'd tell me how, in addition to the salary, I was going to lead a small band out of the big band, and record with it, and make extra money. He was so sure I was going to join him, he even had Sy Oliver write parts with my name on them.

" 'Give me an idea,' I'd say. 'Send me a letter with a price, so I'll know if I'll be doing better than I'm doing now.'

"Stuff's group was still hot, and he was paying me $125, which wasn't bad then. Finally, when we were at the Famous Door in Hollywood, Tommy sent me an airline ticket to join him in Indianapolis in two days. When I sent it back, he called and asked why, and I told him because he hadn't told me the price. So then he sent me a letter that I've always kept. I didn't bother to answer it, because I found I was doing better with Stuff.

"Tommy was always very nice to me though. After I played the job with him at the Savoy, I never asked him for any money, figuring he'd pay me when he got around to it. One night, when we were passing through Cleveland, I went backstage where he was playing to say hello. He called me up to his room, and we sat around and had some drinks.

" 'Where are you going now?' he asked when I got ready to leave.

" 'My wife and I are just going out to dinner.'

" 'You and your wife have dinner on me tonight,' he said, and laid fifty dollars on me.

"I guess he had the same idea in mind when he got Charlie Shavers. I don't think I would have held up as well as Charlie did. But then again, I'm the kind of guy who can play more when the conditions are such that I have to.

"Anyway, I was still with Stuff, and we were very close. I liked his way of playing so much, and never got tired of listening to him. He always looked after me, although he did so many crazy things. He was a nice guy, and he had a heart, and he would give you the shirt off his back. He'd run into somebody on the street and spend his money on him. He was a whiskey drinker—didn't like anything else—and eventually he got cirrhosis. You had to drink to play with him.

"Sometimes Cozy and I would come on the job and say, 'Let's take it easy tonight. Let's don't get drunk.' But we'd drink every night, a fifth apiece, and all people would give us in that Onyx Club. One of those nights when we decided not to get high, Stuff looked around during the first set and said, 'Eh, things don't *sound* right tonight! Let's play so-and-so.' We went to another number, and he said, 'I don't know—there's something wrong with you tonight. We ain't swinging!' Finally, he asked, 'Jonah, you high?'

" 'No, I decided to take it easy tonight.'

" 'Cozy, you high?'

" 'No, the whole group decided to take it easy and stay sober one night.'

" 'Oh, no! Everybody that's not high on the next set gets a ten-dollar fine. We can't play sober. We got to be high!'

"So that gave us an excuse to start again. Of course, we were young then, but when you get older liquor works the other way, and you can't play nothing when you're drinking. I've seen so many doing that and thinking they were playing. I'm glad I got off. The doctor took me off around 1940 when I had a little flutter in my heart. He said I didn't have a bad heart, but it was just tired. 'If you stop drinking, you'll live to be a hundred,' he said. Now I just drink a little beer, and a little Harvey's Bristol Cream, but no whiskey.

"In order to stop, I had to quit Stuff's band. He had begun to say to me, 'You're not the same any more.' The group broke up anyway, because he was messing up so much with the money, not paying commissions, taking all of it to buy an automobile, and things like that. The guys got together, and for a time the agents sent the checks to me, but Stuff didn't like that!

"I went with Benny Carter next, for a short time, off and on, when he had a record date or a one-nighter. Benny had some good bands, but he never had any luck with them. The greatest thing we did together was when he did all the arrangements for the Capitol album I made with Glen Gray. I never forget that record he made on trumpet of *I Surrender, Dear* either. Every time I see him, I say, 'Leave the trumpet alone! There's enough trumpet players out here now!' He could pick up that trumpet and play more than anybody. I heard his cousin Cuban Bennett when I was

(Above). *Record date: Keg Johnson, Hilton Jefferson, Sam Taylor, Jonah Jones.*

(Right). *Jonah Jones and young autograph hunter outside the Royal Theatre, Baltimore.*

young, and they say he was running the chords like they do now, but I
didn't have enough knowledge to appreciate what he was doing.

"Russell Smith, the reed section and I went from Benny's band to
Fletcher Henderson in December, 1940, when Fletcher got a job in Roseland. Then on February 21st, 1941, I joined Cab Calloway—and stayed
with him until 1952. Cozy Cole had left Stuff and gone to Cab in 1938.
We were very close friends, Cozy and I, and we always kept in touch. He
had told me that Cab liked me, and eventually they sent me a ticket to join
the band in Pittsburgh. The bread was pretty good, and Lammar Wright
and Dizzy Gillespie were in the trumpet section with me. I enjoyed that
band, because it was like security. Every week they were looking for you
to pay you; you didn't have to look for them. I'd had the other kind of
experience, had a lot of fun, but now I'd got four kids who had to go to
school. Not everybody was featured as in Duke's band, but Cab had Buster
Harding write a number specially for me called *Jonah Joins the Cab*.

"I did what I was supposed to do in the eleven years I was with him.
When you went in that band, he'd say, 'We'll get along all right, but I want
you to make time, play my music like it is, and have on your uniform.' He
bought the uniforms, and he expected you to wear brown socks, not black.
When he'd brought that stick down, he'd look down the stage to see who
had the wrong socks. He was a good businessman, you know, and if you
came in high, he'd as soon give you your two-weeks' money and train fare
home. Oh, he took care of business!

"Every man traveled by Pullman, and we had our own baggage car.
When you joined, you'd go and get a trunk, which Cab paid for, and you
paid it off weekly. All the trunks went into the baggage car, and when you
wanted to change clothes, you just went in there. Everybody had his own
berth number—mine was Lower 5. When we were playing one-nighters,
the train would drop us off at a town, and we'd get up, wash up, put on
our uniforms, go play the gig, come on back to the Pullman, and go to
sleep. By next day, the engine would have been in, pulled us out, and
dropped us off at another town.

"It was a great band, too, with people like Keg Johnson, Quentin Jackson, Tyree Glenn, Chu Berry, Illinois Jacquet, Ike Quebec, Sam Taylor and
Hilton Jefferson in it. After Dizzy left, we got Shad Collins, a great trumpet
player, and Russell 'Pops' Smith. Pops played first and was a wonderful
leader for the trumpet section. He had had so much experience with
Fletcher Henderson. In the rhythm section, besides Milt Hinton on bass,
we had first Cozy, then J. C. Heard, and then Panama Francis on drums.

"When things began to go slow, Cab cut down to seven pieces. We tried
that for about a year, and then cut down to four—just one horn (me), Dave
Riviera on piano, Milt Hinton and Panama Francis. We knew how to back

Cab on things like *Minnie the Moocher,* which was what the public wanted to hear from him, and we played like an act at the Roxy Theatre. But in 1951, he decided to have a big band again, and we went down to play a festival in Montevideo, Uruguay. When we came back, our last job was in Birdland, in 1952, and after that we broke up.

"Joe Bushkin and I were friends from 'way back, when he was playing at the Hickory House on 52nd Street with Joe Marsala, and he persuaded me to go into the Embers with him. Charlie Mingus was on bass, Jo Jones on drums. When Mingus quit, I talked Joe into hiring Milt Hinton. He brought Milt in for just one night, because he didn't know him then, but after that he wouldn't even make a record date unless Milt was on it. Nobody but Joe would take a trumpet in the Embers with them, and before me he had Buck Clayton, but I think Buck was out of town this time. I wasn't really a muted trumpet player, but I found out what to do with a mute there. I was strong, and had played a lot of firsts in all the bands. In fact, Cab would rather have me play first than anybody, because I could punch it strong.

"Then Earl Hines started an all-star group. He got me, Benny Green on trombone, Art Blakey on drums, Tommy Potter on bass, Harold Clark on tenor, six of us, and Etta Jones was singing. When Clark quit, he got Aaron Sachs, and when Blakey quit, he got Osie Johnson. We played around, and went into Snooky's in New York.

"Meanwhile, I always kept in touch with Cab, and he'd been playing Sportin' Life in *Porgy and Bess* in London. He asked me if I'd be interested in playing in the pit band at the Ziegfeld Theatre. The conductor was trying to get some soul brothers in there, and they ended up with four out of forty musicians—Buster Bailey on clarinet, Al Brown on viola, Winston Cullamore on violin, and me.

"They had a guy named Howard Roberts who used to play a trumpet solo on stage, thirty-two bars or something like that. He played good, too. When his vacation came up, I'd been in the show four or five months, and they were all up in the air looking for someone to take this guy's part. Cab recommended me, but I played hard to get, and said, 'Get Bill Dillard. He can do it.' Finally they came up with what I thought was fair money, and I went in the wings that night without rehearsal. Cab put his arm around my shoulder and said, 'Now go out there and start blowin'!' They didn't know I was a jazz man, and they were real surprised! They thought I was a legit man, because I had had some training and my reading was good. As a matter of fact, I'd studied with William Vacchiano, the first trumpet in the New York Philharmonic, and a good teacher is like a good doctor —cure your ills and tell you what you need.

"After about a year in that show, I was tired of it. You know it note for note after three or four months, but you've still got to take the book out every night. There were tricks to learn, of course. When you first go in, you must hit your A. After about a half-hour, you've got to find you another A, because the strings have gone up from the heat of the bodies in the place. At intermission, they throw open the doors and everybody goes out, and when you come back you've got to tune up all over again. It was important to find out things like that, and *Porgy and Bess* was the toughest score on Broadway.

"That was '53. In '54, I played around New York for Lester Lanin with Stuff Smith, Urbie Green and Big Chief Moore. Then Charles Delaunay invited me to France with a three-month guarantee, and I played in Paris and Belgium, and made some records. That was where I met André Persiany, the piano player, who later worked with me over here. When I came back in '55, things were so rough. Big bands were in trouble, and if anybody was doing anything it was the 'progressive jazz' people. 'Oh, what the heck!' I said to myself. 'I'll get a day job and just do weekend gigs.'

"Then I was walking around downtown when I ran into Sam Berk, who used to book Cab and Duke and all of 'em. He told me to forget about big bands, and he'd see what he could do for me. He got me to go into the Embers on George Shearing's night off. I told the drummer to stay on brushes. I knew I had to use a mute, and I mixed a lot of show tunes with jazz numbers. Ralph Watkins, who ran the place, liked what I did and asked if I'd like to go in for a week. I took John Brown, the same bass player I have now; Hal Austin on drums; and George Rhodes, who is now conductor for Sammy Davis, on piano. Later, I had Lanny Scott and then Teddy Brannon on piano, and George Foster on drums. And I got Buster Harding to arrange for me.

"We made an album for Victor, Dixieland on one side and show tunes on the other. Then Dave Cavanaugh kept calling me, and we went over to Capitol, where we got a better sound. First pop out of the box was a hit album that sold 'way over a million. *On the Street Where You Live* was the single that did it, and we made that in the last twenty minutes of the session at Dave's suggestion. 'Make up a little introduction, and put a shuffle beat behind it,' he said. *Rose Room* was on the other side of the single, and was supposed to be the hit, but the disc jockeys turned it over and played *On the Street*. Then, when we did the next album, Dave suggested a tune I'd never heard, *Baubles, Bangles and Beads*. We got a head introduction on it, played one chorus straight and one swinging, and it sold even bigger than *On the Street Where You Live*. So you never know!

"There was a melody, and it was swinging, and there was a lot of experience in the phrasing. Guys were writing me for the arrangements, and I soon had a lot of imitators. Some were saying, as they always do if anyone makes a couple of bucks, that I had gone commercial, but we'd come right up through rock 'n' roll, right up through 'progressive' and everything, at a time when I'd been talking about taking a day job! These things happen. Sure, there's an element of luck. There's *got* to be.

"I played the Embers from 1955 to 1964, and had a contract for twenty weeks a year. When I first went in there, I had one mute. That started to get monotonous, so I looked around for others. I got the buzz mute and the bucket. The bucket's closest to playing open. Then I got a plunger, and with it I used the old brass mute that used to come with the Conn trumpet. That's the only one you're going to get that sound with. You can't get it with the mutes they make today. They don't put the good brass in the horns like they used to, either. Those old horns would last a lifetime. I also got a Harmon mute, the kind Harry Edison uses a lot with the stem out. But I haven't used a derby since I've had the small band. You don't need to 'fan it' no more! Since Cozy Cole joined me in 1969, I've played open more, because I can't make *him* use brushes all the time. So when he uses sticks, I play open, which I'd rather do anyway, because it helps me keep my lip.

"That Embers engagement and the Capitol albums opened a lot of doors for me. I remember when Benny Goodman asked me over to his house for a jam session in honor of the King of Thailand. 'Hey, King, this is Jonah Jones!' he said when he introduced me. I enjoyed making two television shows with Fred Astaire. We played at President Johnson's inauguration, and went to Monaco at the invitation of Prince Rainier. We've played in Bangkok and Honolulu, and we went to Australia in a package with Dizzy Gillespie and Sarah Vaughan. What I've learned about this business is that the better you are equipped to do different things, the more you are on your way."

(1970)

STUFF SMITH

VIOLIN

"Louis Armstrong was my inspiration," Stuff Smith said. "I was supposed to be practising classics, but I'd get my little victrola and go into the woodshed and listen to Louis. And practice Louis!"

Born in Portsmouth, Ohio, Smith was the son of a barber-musician and a schoolteacher. His father, who could play all the string and reed instruments, made his son his first violin and taught him to play. By the age of seven, he was dutifully in his father's band, but a couple of years later he heard Armstrong and began his attempt to capture the trumpet player's style on violin.

"Joe Venuti and Eddie Lang came through our town," he recalled, "and I snuck in with my dad, into a saloon, and heard Joe. 'That's the way I'm going to play, Dad,' I said, but he had other ideas for me. 'No, no,' he said. And as it turned out, it was just Louis who influenced me. I got some Venuti records, and they were pretty, but they didn't push me enough."

When he was fifteen, Smith left Johnson C. Smith University in Charlotte, North Carolina, where he had won a musical scholarship, and joined the Aunt Jemima Revue band for a couple of years. It was during this period that Hezekiah Leroy Gordon Smith was nicknamed "Stuff," because of his habit of thus addressing those whose name he could not remember.

Next, he joined Alphonso Trent, who led an extremely successful band in Dallas. "I conducted it and was a sort of comic," Stuff said, chuckling. "This was when you might say I developed my act." Trent played piano and the brains of the band were James Jeter, the alto saxophonist, and Edwin "King" Swayzee, the trumpet player who was later with Cab Calloway. "Swayzee taught me a lot about music and how to read a manuscript," Smith added.

The band, an extremely versatile one, played the Adolphus Hotel in Dallas for a year and a half. While Smith was a member, it included such musicians as Irving "Mouse" Randolph, George Hudson, Chester Clark and Peanuts Holland on trumpet; Snub Mosley on trombone; Hayes and Chester Pillars on saxes; and A.G. Godley, "a great showman and a fine drummer."

176

When he was eighteen, Smith could no longer resist the urge to go to New York, and he and Swayzee joined Jelly Roll Morton, who was playing in a dancehall.

"Louis Metcalf and Foots Thomas were in that band," he remembered. "Jelly Roll just had men who could play choruses. He wouldn't have the whole band on each chorus, but as soon as one man finished a chorus, we'd go right into another number. They'd clean the floor off in between, and then it would be five cents more for another dance. They had about a hundred hostesses.

"When we got through, Jelly Roll would go on up to the Rhythm Club, and he and Chick Webb would get into arguments about who had the best band. Jelly Roll carried more money than Chick and had more diamonds. He even had a diamond in his tooth.

" 'Oh, you little shortstuff,' he'd say, 'you can't play nothin'! Your band —it stinks! If you want to hear something, you come up to the Rose Danceland and hear Jelly Roll's band. And see who it is on that big picture outside. That's me!'

"That was before Chick got Ella Fitzgerald, of course, but he always had a fine band. I remember he had Jimmie Harrison, Ward Pinkett and, I think, Prince Robinson. I believe Rex Stewart was in it, too. And Edgar Sampson, a great musician, who also played violin.

"After we had had our fifth of Gordon's Dry Gin, we would go to bed. One morning, I went to bed and set the whole place on fire. We were living above an undertaking parlor. When I woke up, a fireman was squirting water in my face! We burnt the whole apartment up, and everything went except the violin, the trumpet and the saxophone. We grabbed them first —Swayzee, Foots Thomas and me—but it left us without any clothes, so we had to go to the pawnshop to get something to put on."

Because Jelly Roll Morton's band played so loud that his violin could not be heard, Smith left and rejoined Alphonso Trent in Little Rock, Arkansas.

"I always had a problem before I had an amplifier," Smith continued. "I used to cut off my bridges to make the violin louder, and I would get the band to play soft so I could be heard. The Trent band used to play waltzes real sweet. A.G. Godley and I tried to make an electric amplifier, but, when we got through, the guts of the amplifier were as big as a room. We had everything in it and it would pick up what I was playing, but only a tiny sound would come out.

"At first, I used to use a violin with a horn. It came out from underneath the bridge, and it was just like the horn on an old-time victrola—about eight inches in diameter and maybe fourteen long. There was a little disc under the bridge which took the sound and passed it through the horn. It wasn't too effective, but it was louder than the regular violin. The Selmer people put it out, and it was quite common in those days, although it looked very funny. Mine got burned up in the Three Deuces, Chicago."

The fame of the Trent band was widespread. Dallas and Cincinnati were its bases, and it traveled extensively. Smith continued to reminisce:

"We traveled in cars mostly in those days—about four cars, for suitcases, instruments and us. We had our troubles with bad roads, breakdowns and accommodation, and we couldn't always sleep where we wanted, especially in the South, but we usually managed to get around those things.

"What made Trent so big was the comedy, and the fact that all of us could sing. We had a vocal trio—I was in it—and we used to sing those unison parts, and that's where I think Sy Oliver actually got some of his stuff for Lunceford and Dorsey. Sy came in when I left, and stayed about a year. He left a whole bunch of arrangements. They also had a lot by Smack and Horace Henderson, as well as others by guys in the band. When we played in Memphis, Lunceford used to come and stand right under the band, and that was when his band was still in college. Mary Lou and Johnny Williams would stand right there, too, when they were in Memphis. It was a terrific band and McKinney's Cotton Pickers was the only one that ever blew us down. That happened in Port Arthur, Canada, right out from London, Ontario. They came there and I never heard such a band in my life! Don Redman was in charge and they had everything right.

"We weren't afraid of Fletcher Henderson or the Casa Loma, because we had run across them and could battle them. Wherever we played, we packed the halls. Besides the originals and the comedy, we could play sweeter than any colored band you ever heard in your life. The Paul Whiteman of the South is what Trent was called.

"We started to come to New York, but Trent was afraid. He had had a lot of success and was a wealthy man, though his band was paid better than the New York bands. He was afraid to come east because of Duke Ellington. But the band wasn't. We wanted to come. And he wouldn't have lost his men, because we were all paid the same and were more like brothers.

"The fact that we didn't record much held us back, but I do remember making a record for Gennett in Richmond, Virginia, of *Gilded Kisses* and *Louder and Funnier*. We had a nice long run at the Palais Royal in Buffalo, New York, right on Main Street. I married a girl in Buffalo and eventually left Trent in Syracuse when my son was born. 'I gotta be beside him, so I'm going home now,' I said."

Smith stayed in Buffalo for several years, working mostly with small groups. At one time he led a sixteen-piece band which played successfully against that of Jimmie Lunceford, whose musicians he sometimes employed when Lunceford was not working. He was in a comfortable position and he remembered Buffalo as a great place for jam sessions. Among the fine musicians he met there was Jonah Jones, who was to find fame with him in New York. "Jonah's a sweetheart," he said, "and in all my years with him I never had an argument."

What took them to the Onyx Club from Buffalo in 1936 was a song Smith had written called *Ise a-Muggin'*, and the intervention of saxophonist Dick Stabile, who persuaded an agent to hear the band and the number. The agent booked the group into the Onyx immediately.

"I didn't get the amplifier until I was in the Onyx," Smith said. "There was a girl from Chicago, a classical violinist, who was working for a company trying to sell electrical violins. She came to the Onyx and got me to try one. I fell in love with it, because Jonah and Cozy Cole were playing awful loud in those days and I used to have to hug the mike. But when I got this thing, I said to myself, 'Oh, oh, this is it, man!'

"There isn't very much difference between it and playing the violin close up to a good mike. A classical violinist wouldn't use it, because he couldn't get the complete violin tone, but I think a jazzman should use it. You can relax more, because you don't have to press so hard on your strings and your chin, and you can develop more of a technique with your bow and your fingers. You can phrase better than with the ordinary violin, where you have to phrase with your fingers, *and* your bow, *and* your chin. It's much easier with the electric violin, but if you hit a bad note—it's hit! People talk about the long tradition back of the violin, but there was a long tradition back of the horse-and-buggy, too. It's the same with the guitar. Before, you couldn't really hear the guitar. Now look how the boys have advanced. And you can hear them! I imagine you'd hear more swing violinists if violinists would pick up the electrical violin or just use the violin amplifier with a pick-up. All the hoe-down boys in California use them, but a player like Eddie South never did. You do get just a slight metallic tone, but you have to learn how to tune up that amplifier to make it sound like a violin. It's a very good sound for jazz in my opinion. If Ray Nance and I record together, he and I are going to use the same amplifier, so we'll have the same balance. We've tried it, and he's in love with it. He could have benefited from it in Duke's band."

The Stuff Smith band was a tremendous success at the Onyx Club on 52nd Street. The music was always exciting, particularly when Smith and Jonah Jones were backed by Clyde Hart and Cozy Cole. To this was added a full measure of entertainment as the violinist indulged his impish wit. Fritz

Stuff Smith's Band. L. to R.: George Clark (tenor saxophone), Jimmy Sherman (piano), Al Williams (alto saxophone), "a hell of a clarinet player," Buster Nash (drums), Smith, Jonah Jones (trumpet), Sylvester Turpin (bass), Lee Hilliard (trumpet), Gus Wilson (trombone).

L. to R.: Herbie Cowans, George Clark, Jonah Jones, Sam Allen, Stuff Smith, Bernard Addison, John Brown.

Kreisler became a friend and frequent visitor, each musician finding much to admire in the other's playing. "Man, when Fritz played," Smith told the *Melody Maker*'s Max Jones in London, "that violin was barking. That big sound is what you want. I'm never going to be satisfied until I get it."

Records and wide publicity led to a call to make a movie in Hollywood, where the little band also proved a great hit at the Famous Door. "We were packing 'em in there," Smith said, "and the people just wouldn't release us, so we had to stay out there another six or seven months. We returned to New York and then had to go back again to the Famous Door, where we stayed about a year. Same problem. We finally left the job without giving any notice or anything, and got thrown out of the union before we came back to New York. It looked like the head of the union was never going to let me back in, until I sent my wife down there, and she was crying, telling him we were poor, had no money left for food, and please let her husband back in the union. So finally he did."

Jonah Jones and Cozy Cole joined Cab Calloway, and in 1943, after the death of Fats Waller, Smith took over leadership of Waller's band with Sammy Benskin on piano. They went out to Hollywood, where the violinist caught pneumonia. Eventually, he returned to Chicago and his sister to recuperate. There he formed another brilliant group, this time a trio with Jimmy Jones on piano and John Levy on bass. They went to New York and played the Onyx for six months. Then Jones left, to go with Sarah Vaughan, and Levy to go with George Shearing.

"In their places," Smith said, "I got Lloyd Trotman and Erroll Garner. When Garner left, I got Billy Taylor. When Billy left, I said, 'I'm going back to Chicago and sit out.' I sat around in Chicago several years, playing sometimes, but not with a regular group. I had a restaurant, too, where we served nothing but chitterlings, pig feet, fried chicken and barbecue. Then I decided I had better come into New York again, but somehow or other I just couldn't get my hands on the men I wanted for a trio or quartet. When my sister on the Coast got sick, I drove out and stayed there until 1964. I had a little group from time to time and used to do a lot of single work. It wasn't too rough. I like California for living, but not for working. It makes you real lazy, and you never feel like dressing up. You rarely see a guy walking around and looking real sharp in the daytime. They're lazy in their music, too. Their ideas are mostly what New York did ten years ago, and they love those cowboys and cowboy tunes. There are exceptions, of course, like Gerald Wilson, but he's not a Californian. He's got about the best thing out there.

"After I made the album with Ella Fitzgerald singing Duke Ellington, Norman Granz had me make one with the Oscar Peterson Trio. Then he said, 'Stuff, how would you like to go to Europe?' I had just had an operation and was feeling up to par, so that was fine with me, but unfortunately I got sick in Brussels. The trouble with me and my liver was that I just couldn't stand food when I was drinking. I used to float the Normandie, and when I quit drinking it just turned over on its side. So I thought I'd better start drinking to raise it up again, and I started, but this time I was the one to turn over. I guess I had had my share.''

When Smith came into New York to work with Joe Bushkin at the Embers in 1964, he set about organizing a ''nice little quartet'' to play at the World's Fair. The men he wanted were Charlie Fox on piano (''played with me in St. Louis, and he's original''), Lloyd Trotman on bass, and Denzil Best on drums (''plays smooth and has good ideas''). The gig didn't materialize, so Smith, cheerful and indomitable, went back to the Coast until Timme Rosenkrantz and Europe beckoned once more.

Stuff Smith told about the ups and downs of his career, his illnesses and operations, without a word of complaint. On the contrary, some of his gravest statements were accompanied by amused chuckles. But it was about the violin—and it was always the ''violin,'' never the ''fiddle''—that he talked with the utmost animation and ardor.

''There's one thing about the violin I'll tell you,'' he said. ''You can swing more on a violin than on any instrument ever made. You can play two strings all the time if you want, or, with the hair on top, you can play all four strings at once. You've got all those octaves on the violin, from D to altissimo D, 'way up there, a bigger range than the clarinet's. Once you perfect the knowledge of where jazz will sound good, you stay there, in that position, which is easy for you. After all these years, I've found out that I can get better jazz from the end of my bow than from the base of it. It leaves you with a free arm, and you can slur like a trombone, play staccato like a trumpet, or moan like a tenor. So you have all this to your advantage, but only experience will show you where to put it.

''There haven't been too many violinists who swing, and I'll tell you why. There's a wall between some of those classically trained musicians and jazz. Most violinists can only play what they see. I never took too many lessons and I played violin the way I felt I should play it. And that's another thing the violin will do for you, more than any other instrument: it will give you a pair of the strongest ears in the world. When you know if you're playing flat or sharp, you've got it made.''

Stuff Smith, who was credited with perfect pitch, had been named the ''Palpitatin' Paganini,'' and his music ''barrelhouse'' and ''demoniac,'' but the best summing-up was quoted by John S. Wilson in a *New York Times* article. It came from Jo Jones, who described him as "the cat that took the apron strings off the fiddle."

(1965)

Stuff Smith died 25 September, 1965.

COZY COLE

DRUMS

William "Cozy" Cole, the oldest of four boys, was born in East Orange, New Jersey, in 1909. His mother died while he was still in grade school and his family—the father, boys and a daughter—moved to the paternal grandmother's home in Atlantic Highlands, a seashore resort near Asbury Park. Two brothers, Jay and Ted, became pianists, while Herbert, who remained in the Asbury Park area became a drummer. The sister, who graduated from Wilberforce University, became a teacher and retired in 1972.

"Atlantic Highlands is about fifteen miles from Long Branch, where Sonny Greer was born," Cole said. "He used to come to our little town and play, the only colored guy in a white group that did all the gigs along that shore. All of us kids used to go to see Sonny, and I must say that he was the inspiration that made me take up the drums. Count Basie, who was from Red Bank, not far away, used to come around, too, and we'd hear him playing piano in neighbors' homes.

"I got my nickname on the football field, where the fellows called me 'Colesy' until they shortened it to 'Cozy'. My father died while I was a junior in high school, and after I graduated I went to New York City, where I had an uncle with a barbershop. I worked for him, and as a shipping clerk. I got different odd jobs around.

"My grandmother worked hard to raise us five children, but all of us worked, especially after school closed, to help send our sister through school. I went to Wilberforce for a couple of years myself, but I wasn't too interested in studies then. I just wanted to play drums, and that went back to high school, where I used to make drumsticks in manual training classes.

"I used to be a tap-dancer, back when they had chorus boys as well as chorus girls! Derby Wilson and I had an act together, and he's quite well known today. In those days, you could see kids out there dancing on all the street corners in Harlem. The Charleston was going on good then, and everybody I saw dancing it seemed able to out-dance me. Because everybody could do it, this trade seemed too easy, so I thought I would *learn* something you couldn't just pick up. I mean, something you would have stamped in your mind.

"The father of a pal of mine in Atlantic Highlands was a musician, a cello player who belonged to the Clef Club in New York. When I asked him who he thought was a good drum teacher, he recommended me to Charlie Brooks, the pit drummer at the old Lincoln Theatre at 135th Street and Lenox Avenue. I studied with him for a couple of years, and then I started playing for little house parties. Then, after Wilberforce, I started studying vibraphone with Milton Schlesinger on 48th Street. He used to do all the Lucky Strike programs then. I also studied vibes later with Freddie Albright, but I never got much opportunity to play them. The fact is, I never lost an opportunity to study! I studied with Billy Gladstone, the drummer at Radio City Music Hall for a while. Around 1940, I studied tympany with Saul Goodman of the New York Philharmonic, who enrolled me in Juilliard Conservatory, where I studied piano, tympany, theory, harmony and drums. I did it out of interest, to know the drums good, and because I knew you really had to know all this if you were going to be a top-notch artist in the business, to do all the shows, to do anything and everything.

"About my first real band job was with Wilbur Sweatman, but it lasted only two weeks because I couldn't read fast enough then. Sweatman fired me because I got all out of time and mixed up the chorus girls.

"I joined the union around 1928, and I was so glad I did. I used to go around the Rhythm Club and the Band Box, and hang out with the musicians—just look at them, you know. I hadn't really started playing then, but I'd see Hawk (Coleman Hawkins), Buster Bailey, and all those guys with Fletcher Henderson, and I'd think that was great. Mornings at the Band Box, I'd see Jack and Charlie Teagarden, Tommy and Jimmy Dorsey, big-time musicians coming up. Anyway, the guys got to know me and know that I played drums. One day, Jelly Roll Morton was looking for a drummer for a record date.

" 'Well, there's a drummer over there,' somebody told him. 'Get him.'

"Now I'd never played with anybody like that in my life, but here comes Jelly Roll Morton asking me to play drums for him. God! Jelly Roll Morton! He was big then. There was nobody else around, so I went and made the

Cozy Cole

date with him at Victor in 1930, and I was very happy about it. It was my first time in a record studio.

"Three or four months after that, I was sitting in at a little dancing school on 125th Street, between Eighth and St. Nicholas Avenue—the Dreamland, if I'm not mistaken. The band that was playing there was leaving, and the owner was moving the school across the street to a new place named the Primrose. He came up to me and asked, 'Would you like to bring a band over to my new place?' I'd never had a band of my own, didn't know the first thing about hiring guys, but I put a band together.

"Everybody in it was older than I was. Cy St. Clair for one, the bass player who had been with Charlie Johnson. Jack Celestian played piano and Charlie Courcy was on trumpet. Joe Thomas, Walter 'Foots' Thomas's brother, was on tenor, and that wasn't the same Joe who was with Jimmie Lunceford later. They were more experienced than I was, and when they weren't telling *me* how to play drums, I was asking them what they wanted. But I used to call rehearsals, and Walter 'Foots' Thomas would bring arrangements down. He hadn't been arranging for Cab long, and he used to rehearse them with our band to get all the wrong notes corrected before Cab's band played them at the old Cotton Club uptown.

"After a year or more at the Primrose, Edgar Battle came after me. He was straw boss of Blanche Calloway's band, and he was revamping it then. Some of Andy Kirk's men went with her, and Battle got Clyde Hart, Joe Keyes, Booker Pittman and Ben Webster from Kansas City, and brought them to Philadelphia in 1931.

"I was with Blanche about two-and-a-half years. She was quite a girl, had a good personality, and looked exactly like Cab. She was the only sister I ever knew he had. It was a nice little band and, for the time, we thought it was great. It was good experience for me, and I was still playing for people to dance. Clyde Hart made most of the arrangements (years later, he made a couple for me when we were recording for Continental), and Edgar Battle made some. Clyde and Ben Webster were already playing good then, and Clyde stayed on with Blanche when I left.

"I came back to New York and joined Benny Carter at Connie's Inn just about the time they changed the name to the Harlem Club. A little later it was the Ubangi Club! This band of Benny's was the one that opened up the Apollo Theatre for vaudeville. First, we played in the pit; then we went up on stage after the acts were finished. Of course, I had to have two sets of drums for that. It was a first-class band. I remember that Teddy Wilson was in it. Keg Johnson and Big Green were the trombones. Johnny Russell was on tenor, Lawrence Lucie on guitar, and the trumpets were Bill Coleman, Bill Dillard and Lincoln Mills. All the musicians loved to work with

Benny. When Blanche Calloway's band came to town, I invited Clyde Hart and the others to come down and hear us. We had an arrangement on *Blue Lou* that I thought was the greatest thing I'd ever played. We loved to go to work and just play that music. In fact, it was one of the most musical bands I've ever been with.

"I don't know how interested in the band Benny really was, but sometimes he'd lay off ten weeks at a time, and you couldn't keep men together like that. They had to eat, and they'd go off one by one. Yet some of them, me included, would quit a job to join Benny. But then you'd grow a little sceptical wondering how long he was going to keep *this* band together. Late in 1934, Teddy Wilson and I joined Willie Bryant, who was working steady at the Savoy. Edgar Battle was already there, playing trumpet in the section, taking solos, and arranging. He was a good musician. Later, he was featured as a soloist in *George White's Scandals,* where they gave him the nickname of 'Puddinghead.' Willie's was another good band. We played the Apollo, too, and made records.

"It was when we played the Vendome in Buffalo that I met Stuff Smith and Jonah Jones. We were all staying in the Vendome Hotel, and the club was right downstairs. In the afternoons, Stuff would come by with his fiddle, and jam. He liked my playing. I thought then, and still do, that Stuff was the greatest violinist I'd ever heard. We were there about a month— a big band with a chorus line, and an NBC wire out of the club.

"In 1936, we heard that Stuff Smith and Jonah went to New York, and had this hit number, *I'se a-Muggin',* on 52nd Street. After they'd been there about a year, Stuff approached me. His drummer, Johnny Washington, wanted to go back home, so I joined him at the Onyx Club and was with him for about three years. We had some great times together.

"We were working at the Merry-Go-Round over in Newark when Walter 'Foots' Thomas talked me into joining Cab Calloway's band. 'What the devil, Cozy,' he said, 'it's a good job, and more stable than Stuff's, I imagine!' Well, namewise there were only two colored bands then: Duke's and Cab's. Jimmie Lunceford came up a little later, and Don Redman and others had nice names, but they weren't *big* like Duke's and Cab's. 'We'll be in the Cotton Club six months of the year,' 'Foots' continued, 'and then we'll be out on the road playing theatres. It's a good job!'

"I had about six months at the Cotton Club, and then it closed, that same year. So I got only one semester! But during that time I got acquainted with a lot of performers. After the place closed, we stayed on the road a lot, mostly playing theatres as 'Foots' had said. It was the best band of Cab's career. He had men like Chu Berry, Hilton Jefferson, Milt Hinton, Tyree Glenn and Jonah Jones. I stayed with him up to 1942, when John Ham-

Stuff Smith's group. L. to R.: Mack Walker, Bobby Bennett, Smith, Jonah Jones, Clyde Hart, Cozy Cole.

mond sent for me and asked if I'd join Raymond Scott and be among the first colored musicians to go to CBS. Emmett Berry was on trumpet, George Johnson on clarinet, and Billy Taylor on bass. Mel Powell or Sanford Gold was playing piano, and sometimes Raymond Scott did. When I left, I took Specs Powell up there, because Raymond wanted another colored drummer, and Specs has been at CBS ever since! He has a good musical background, and I understand he studied piano for six years.

"John Hammond was the instigator of that job situation, and in 1944 he approached me about joining the show, *Carmen Jones,* a Billy Rose version of Bizet's *Carmen.* Robert Russell Bennett conducted the big, sixty-piece band, and they needed a drummer for the pit and to do a seven-minute performance on stage, playing for the dancers with a full set of drums. Billy Rose asked John if he thought I'd be able to handle the music in the pit, because he knew a lot of jazz drummers couldn't read well in those days.

"I was going to Juilliard at the time, working with the orchestra and foreign conductors, and I had had experience doing the Frank Sinatra, Perry Como and Dorothy Collins shows, but I had never played any semi-operas before. So the day of the rehearsal came, and there were all these great fiddle players from the Philharmonic Symphony, and this great conductor, Robert Russell Bennett, and me, down there in the pit—and I have to play hand cymbals!

"When you get into that pit, drums aren't just something to beat on. You really have to *know.* I was glad then that I'd never lost a chance to study. The teachers at Juilliard always told me that the notes are the same, regardless of whether they're in symphony, jazz or whatever. If you can read, and have confidence in yourself, plus experience, you don't have too much to worry about. Anyway, we rehearsed, and Bennett liked me, and the assistant conductor, Joseph Littauer, liked me, and I just made it. Then I became the first dance drummer up to that date to do two Broadway shows at the same time, to be featured in both, and to have his name on the playbills.

"The Broadway Theatre is at 53rd and Broadway, and that's where *Carmen Jones* was. The Ziegfeld Theatre was right down the street at 54th and Sixth. *Seven Lively Arts* was playing there, and Billy Rose produced both shows. Benny Goodman had the first ten weeks at the Ziegfeld, but the show wasn't a smash hit like *Carmen Jones.* Benny had other commitments, and Billy Rose auditioned several five-piece bands, but he wasn't satisfied.

" 'Cozy, bring a five-piece band over and take Benny's place,' he said. 'We've got seven more weeks to go.'

"I reminded him that I was in the pit and on the stage at the Broadway.

" 'Don't worry about it,' he said. 'I'll fix the times so that you can come over and do it.'

"We followed Bert Lahr and Bea Lillie, and we played *Hallelujah* and *Stomping at the Savoy* in a six-minute presentation. Then I hurried back to the Broadway! In my group were Don Byas on tenor, Billy Taylor on piano, the other Billy Taylor on bass, and Tiny Grimes on guitar. All of them were working 52nd Street at the time.

"After *Carmen Jones* closed, I went to the Paramount Theatre with Benny Goodman. I had been playing eight shows a week at the Broadway. Now I suddenly found myself playing eight shows a day, using the high-hat cymbal, and swinging four to the bar on the bass drum. We'd do all Benny's feature numbers with the big band and with the trio. We'd play until the picture came on (*Road to Utopia* with Bing Crosby, Dorothy Lamour and Bob Hope), and then as soon as it was over, ninety minutes later, we're right back on, seven days a week! We were in that theatre eleven to twelve hours a day. My ankle swelled up and I had to tape it up. The change was just too sudden, but after a couple of weeks I was all right.

"I did a lot of freelancing and recording around New York after that, and then in 1949 I went with Louis Armstrong when the doctor ordered Big Sid Catlett to stop playing. In the band when I joined were Earl Hines, Jack Teagarden, Barney Bigard and Arvell Shaw, with Velma Middleton as vocalist. I always liked to sit and listen to Dixieland music, but I'd never really played it until I began freelancing. With Louis, it was nearly all Dixieland and those Dixieland tunes, and I was glad I'd got acquainted with them. They're difficult if you don't know them. There are certain breaks you have to know, passages that have to be played just the same way, and so on. Of course, you can put your own feeling into some of those things, but they have to be almost identical each time in order to stay with the group. If it's played right, it will swing, and what Louis had was a good, swinging Dixieland band. All those guys could swing, and when Jack Teagarden left we picked Trummy Young up in Honolulu.

"I began to get tired of the road, and in 1953 (or maybe '54?) Louis and Benny Goodman did a tour together. Gene Krupa and I had first heard each other at a battle of music in Springfield, Massachusetts, when he was with Mal Hallett and I was with Blanche Calloway. He was with Benny during this tour, and he and I began putting our little heads together. We conceived the idea of setting up a drum school. Our lawyers thought it would be a good deal. So I left Louis, and Gene and I opened this school. It ran from 1954 to 1960, and it was very successful. Most of that time, I was working at the Metropole on Seventh Avenue in New York. We had excellent teachers at the school, but regardless of how good they were, a lot of the students wanted Gene or me to teach them. Gene was working fairly regularly with his quartet, and I was out of town sometimes, but I was there most of the time until I had that hit record, *Topsy*. So now both of us were often away, and we just had to dissolve the school. It was too bad.

"A young girl and a guy came in the Metropole one night when Red Allen and I had the band there. We used to break it up with *Caravan,* and this kid, who was very high, said to me afterwards:

" 'Cozy, I'm in love with this girl. I want you to record *Caravan* for me, and because I'm in love I'm going to call the label Love.'

" 'Okay,' I said, humoring him, 'but Duke Ellington did *Caravan,* and who can do it better than him? You stop in another time and I'll have a number for you.'

"A couple of nights later, there he was again, but I still thought he was jiving. I was doubling on the Arthur Godfrey Show at the time, and I asked Dick Hyman, who was guest conductor, what he thought of slowing Edgar Battle's *Topsy* down and making a drum feature of it. He liked the idea, so when the young fellow came back, we had a number for him, one we planned to do in two parts for a single.

"I told this guy, Alan Hartwell, what we wanted to do, how we would do it, and what it would cost. He said okay to everything and came up with the money. He wasn't kidding. I got the guys out of the Arthur Godfrey band. Dick Hyman wrote the arrangements, and I had Burt Farber go back into the control room and balance it right. A session is three hours, but we had the whole thing finished in an hour. We had so much time left, I told Hartwell to send out for a quart of scotch and a quart of gin, so we could have a little taste while we listened to the playbacks. The record was timed right, and it took off natural. It had a good beat, it wasn't too fast, and the kids could dance to it. We dubbed my voice in after the session, and that was the idea of Hopewell's girl friend. That record must have made a lot of money, and I did get one check out of it for a nice amount.

"*Topsy* was in 1958, and then I got my own group—George Kelly on tenor, Ivan Rolle on bass, George Hunt out of Buffalo on trumpet, and my brother Jay on piano. In 1962, we went to Africa for the State Department, with a six-piece show added to the band. We were there five months, in fifteen countries and about ninety-five cities. I kept the group until 1966. Then I freelanced again until I joined Jonah Jones in '68.

"We'd been friends ever since I met him in Buffalo when I was with Willie Bryant, and we'd been together with Stuff Smith and Cab Calloway. Jonah was working in Cleveland when his drummer, Sol Hall, got sick. Jonah called me in Columbus and asked if I'd come and finish the engagement. They had another booking in Indianapolis, and I went on there, because Sol had to go into hospital. When Sol passed, I just kept on with Jonah.

"I often think about the ingredients I'd like to have in a small group. Some of that John Kirby co-ordination, because Charlie Shavers, Russell Procope and Buster Bailey were *together*. Some of that good old Jimmie Lunceford two-beat funk, along with some four-beat funk. And a little Benny Goodman in there, too. (Remember *Rollin'?*) Get that incorporated in a five- or six-piece band, and get it to swing, so that you can pat your foot to it . . . Not too much Dixieland, not too many mutes, not too much nothin' . . . ! You don't want it burdened down with too much schmaltz, you don't want it too loud, and you don't want it pounding. You want it so that it swings, and sounds good, with good melodic lines. If you could put that together, I think you could go in there and make some money."

Looking back over his long and successful career, Cole recognized Sonny Greer and Chick Webb as his major influences, but he expressed special admiration for the work of Gene Krupa with Benny Goodman, Jo Jones with Count Basie, Jimmy Crawford with Jimmie Lunceford, Dave Tough with Woody Herman, and George Stafford ("first with the high-hat") with Charlie Johnson. His own solid beat was long proverbial, and his press-roll was always a special source of wonder to musicians. Paul Whiteman referred to him in 1938 as "the greatest press-roll drummer in the world." The following year, writing in *Bandstand,* Dave Tough said: "One of the greatest things in modern drumming is Cozy's roll, which goes on for a half-hour or more, building steadily all the time."

(1972)

DUD BASCOMB

TRUMPET

Dud Bascomb is probably best known for his muted trumpet playing on Erskine Hawkins records. He is unlike the usual underrated jazz musician in that he gives no indication of considering himself unjustly neglected.

Obviously amused by much that makes others excited, he states facts with a quiet confidence, but without complaint about his present lot or his long career in music. He is slow to criticize, and when he does it is without rancor. Perhaps he is supported in his philosophical attitude by the esteem of his professional colleagues.

In a *Down Beat* story (17 June, 1965), Dizzy Gillespie told Dan Morgenstern that Bascomb was one of the most underrated musicians he knew. "He's beautiful," he said. "A lot of the harmonies that Clifford Brown used to play remind me of Bascomb." Others often speak of him as a player who should have had a permanent place with Duke Ellington.

He was born in Birmingham, Alabama, the smallest of ten children. His mother played piano, and his father played drums in little pick-up groups around the city, but the biggest musical influence was his oldest brother, Arthur.

"He was a great blues pianist and we all played piano after him," Bascomb said. "He went to Chicago later on, and he used to play house parties there. He died about five years ago. I played good blues piano, too, and I still like to play when I come across a good instrument, but I knew my hands were small and that I wouldn't be able to play all the things I wanted to play, so I switched to trumpet. A lot of the ideas in Avery Parrish's *After Hours* came from me. My brother used to call it *Mississippi Blues,* and practically everything in it was his. Avery was a very good jazz pianist, but not a blues pianist. He liked the way I played blues and took a lot of things from me."

Bascomb began playing trumpet at Lincoln Grammar School in Birmingham. Eventually, he went to the senior high school on the campus of Alabama State Teachers College in order to be near his brother, Paul, who was completing his education there. He also wanted to hear the college band, which had already acquired a considerable reputation, and it was there he first met Erskine Hawkins. After a year and a half, he traveled north in 1934, playing dances as a member of the 'Bama State Collegians' band.

"When we played in Louisiana, in Mobile and all those places," he said, "we were supposed to be paying for our tuition, but when we came east in the summer the school put us on a salary of twelve dollars and fifty cents a week. They paid our transport and hotels, but they took the money when we played dances and it went towards our schooling in the winter.

"We all decided to quit school when we got to New York! We played at the Harlem Opera House, a few doors east of the Apollo, and ran into a guy by the name of Feets Edson. He started looking out for us. He went and got overcoats for us from the pawnshop, and so on. We were all young. I was the youngest, just going on eighteen. When Sammy Lowe joined later, he was two years younger. He was from Birmingham, too, and he had been in my school band, but he came to us from Tennessee State.

"We got forty bucks a week at the Harlem Opera House and we were all very excited. We laid around the Woodside Hotel waiting for Edson to get us dates. We played the Academy of Music on 14th Street downtown, the Brooklyn Fox Folly, and a few places upstate. Then we went into the Apollo, playing the show and a specialty, and getting union scale. From there we went to the Ubangi Club, where we had quite a run. In 1937, we went downtown to the Harlem Uproar House. Hazel Scott was doing a single there in the bar part, and I remember being told she was only fourteen.

"It wasn't a big place, and we were still playing loud the way we did down south. We were really a dance band then. Avery Parrish did all the arrangements until Sammy Lowe came into the band. Avery liked Sy Oliver's arrangements for Jimmie Lunceford, so a lot of ours were in that pattern. Lunceford's was the band I liked, too. Later on, we had three top-notch arrangers when Bill Johnson began to help out. He had been to a conservatory out in Illinois. Sammy Lowe picked up arranging around Birmingham, and he kept after it till he got to be a top man, but he was never taught. Avery picked it up the same way, and being a piano player he had a mind for chords.

"We went down south again on one-nighters with Feets Edson, but when we came back to New York we figured we would have to do a little better than we had been doing, and we started to work up at the Savoy every chance we could get. Mr. Buchanan was getting big there then, and Moe Gale thought our band pretty good when he heard it, so he signed Erskine up. We were still using the name, 'Bama State Collegians, but we realized we would have to have a front man. We had been using J.B. Sims as director (he had been my teacher in high school). He wore tails and sang pretty well, like Cab Calloway, and that was what the people went for. Now Erskine was elected as our leader.

"He was one of the best first trumpet players I ever played under. He also played trombone, tenor and drums, and quite well. He never got credit for his lead, because they had him play solos. I must have been about fourteen or fifteen when I first met him, and I know what happened to him at 'Bama State, where we were both copying Louis Armstrong solos verbatim, like those on *Chinatown* and *Shine*. That was what Erskine was doing all through the South—playing like Louis. He had no time to think of doing something for himself before he was drawn out front. He was at the Apollo when Louis came back from Europe, and Louis stood on the

Dud Bascomb. In background: Kelly Martin, drums; Bobby Johnson, trumpet.

stage to hear him hit those C's and make F on *Shine*. So his own individuality never came out, although his gifts were more those of a studio musician. He could play all the way up to altissimo C, and that's kind of hard!

"Louis was my only influence, and I never forget hearing the whole Earl Hines trumpet section play his *Chinatown* in four-part harmony when they came through Birmingham once. But after Louis, I think I was my own man. I got on the plunger through numbers like *Ring Dem Bells,* which we used to play like Duke. Avery Parrish copied it off the record. At that time, everybody in the South wanted to hear that number, and I think every band down there had an arrangement on it. I didn't particularly like the plunger sound, but the public did. And I didn't like using the mute with it because of the feedback. Two musicians who I feel use the plunger very well are Money Johnson and Elmer Crumbley."

Moe Gale succeeded in getting the Hawkins band a recording contract on Vocalion and a number of dates in New Jersey, but his main interest at that time was Chick Webb. When Webb died, Bascomb remembered, Gale asked musicians which band he should build as its replacement— Teddy Hill's or Erskine Hawkins'? The consensus of opinion was that the latter's had the most to offer, and Gale went to work. The band became a great favorite at the Savoy, and after a long series of successful records on Bluebird it was promoted to the major label, Victor.

"I think we were tops then among the colored people," Bascomb said. "Every now and then we would play a country club with a white audience, but most of the time we played for Negro audiences. The money was big on one-nighters down south. When I left in 1944, we were getting something like $1700 a night, seven nights a week. We used to outdraw Count Basie, and I remember we once played to fifteen thousand people in a big Kansas City auditorium. In Norfolk, we used to play double dances—let everybody out after one dance, and then play another. We were drawing that well. Other bands drew in the South, but we played simpler music. We could even draw the coalminers, because they could understand what we were playing. We had talked that out in our conferences. We had decided that the more simply we recorded the better it would be for us. We had guys who played more horn than you heard on records. I think we could run over those horns as fast as anybody, because we had the know-how, but we'd stick to the same solos at dances as on the records. Of course, we would run into guys who wanted to jam, and we would get together in hotel rooms. Budd Johnson and my brother Paul used to sit down every time we'd meet up with Earl Hines.

"Paul was one of the originators of the band. When he was still a junior in college, he had gone with C. S. Belton's band from Florida. Belton was supposed to be like the Duke Ellington of the South, and he had a very good band of seventeen or eighteen men. I think their home was Palatka, but they'd work West Palm Beach and play ballrooms as far up as Cincinnati. Bill Johnson, the guy who wrote *Tuxedo Junction,* came out of that band. Erskine Hawkins and Julian Dash have their names on the number, too, but the last chorus was mine. We weren't even expecting it to hit, because we'd made other things that day which we thought sounded better—*Hot Platter, Gin Mill Special, Cherry* and *Weddin' Blues.*

"Haywood Henry, who played clarinet and baritone, had been in the 'Bama State band, but he came to New York before we did to work in a church on 131st and Seventh that had a big jazz and singing thing going. He was playing at the Arcadia in Leon Englund's band with Dicky Wells and Kaiser Marshall, and he joined us again when things began to go pretty good. Bobby Smith came in from the Sunset Royals just before I left. He took Bill Johnson's place and wrote *Tippin' In,* which put a little fire into Erskine again. He's out in Los Angeles now, I hear, playing in some club. Bill Johnson went to work in Canada for Joe Glaser, and died of lung cancer four or five years ago.

"What happened to Avery Parrish? Following the success of *After Hours,* he decided to stay in California and work on his own. He began to get some nice stakes out there, around $750 as a single in nightclubs. The way I heard it, a friend of his came by the club, a young kid, and they decided to go in the bar and get a few drinks. One of the ruffians there came up and wanted to pick at the boy, and Avery took it up. When he turned around to take a drink, he had forgotten about it, and then this guy hit him across the head with a bar stool. It crushed his skull in and a piece of his brain was damaged. When I went to see him in hospital, they had cut it off, but it seemed to be a part he needed. His hands were paralyzed, but he strengthened them by exercises—squeezing a board, and so on— and he did make another record of *After Hours.* He started working in restaurants, washing dishes in the kitchen, and things like that. He was still living with his mother in New York when he went to a place on 127th one night. He was drinking, and he fell down a flight of stairs and hit the same spot again, and died. He was still making good money from *After Hours* and he'd just had a check for eight hundred dollars."

The fact that the band experienced relatively little trouble in the South was due, Bascomb explained, to the fact that most of its members had been brought up there and knew the ways of the region. In the early days, too, it was almost entirely a teetotal band.

"There were some incidents, of course," Bascomb continued. "During the war, Moe Gale decided to send us in cars instead of by train. There was a rubber shortage and tires were bad. We had pulled out of Macon, Georgia, when one of the tires blew. Erskine went on ahead to try to find a couple of spares, and we sat on the highway from 9 o'clock in the morning until about 3 the next night. Now, there was a sheriff who kept passing us in his car, keeping an eye on us. About the third time he came by, he had a soldier with him, and he came over and said:

" 'You all been sitting out here all day, and you can't be up to no good.'

"We had a driver with us who had never been down south before, a big fellow, six-foot tall, 220 pounds. He'd been teasing a lot the whole trip about the way they treated us. 'Hey, get up off that stool, boy!' he'd say, when we went into a restaurant to eat. Well, about 1 o'clock this morning, when everybody was trying to sleep, the valet started fooling around, shining his flashlamp in everybody's face. 'Go on away!' the driver said. 'Don't do that again!' A little later, it was the sheriff who was shining a light in his face, and he woke up cursing.

" 'Didn't I tell you not to do that, you . . . . er?'

" 'What did you say, boy? Get out of that car,' said the sheriff. And as soon as he got out, he hit him on the head, so that the blood flew like an oil well, and he fell over in the ditch. Then the sheriff made us all get out of the car, but the soldier cooled him down, and he didn't do anything else."

When Dud Bascomb left the Erskine Hawkins band in 1944, it was with very considerable regret.

"I really didn't want to leave," he said, "because Erskine and I were very close. Every time I would ask for a raise, he would give it to me, so I had no kick coming. But Paul and Erskine didn't get along so well, and when Paul left he went to my wife and talked to her to talk me into leaving and getting a combo together with him. Because I was satisfied, I was set on staying where I was, but after a year or so I saw Paul wasn't doing so well, and I felt I had to try to help him. So I came out, and bought a lot of arrangements, and we went down to 52nd Street. We had seven pieces —four rhythm and Rudy Williams, who had left the Sultans. Monte Kay booked us in there. Paul did most of the hiring, but I remember we had Snags Allen on guitar. (He does a lot of recording downtown now.) At different times, we had Nick Fenton and Teddy Sturges on bass, and we had several pianists. Rudy was a good musician, but he would get nervous if he looked out the front door and saw Charlie Parker sitting across the street in his shirtsleeves, listening to him.

" 'God, if that man's gonna come in here he's gonna . . .' he'd begin.

" 'I'm not gonna let him play,' I'd say, because it never was good policy to let another musician come and embarrass one in your band. But he got in there somehow once, borrowed a coat from somebody, and when I came down the stairs they were into *Cherokee* and Rudy was having a fit. Rudy was advanced, too, and Charlie liked to hear him play *Cherokee,* but he just wanted to get in there and play it *for* him.

"We had a nice little group, but it wasn't as good as the six pieces Red Norvo had there. Being a musician, I knew that! I'd been in the night before we opened, and I knew what was going on."

After 52nd Street, Moe Gale got the brothers engagements with a fifteen-piece band, which they kept together for three years.

"We'd run into bands like Lucky Millinder's at the Savoy and get arrangements of their best tunes by Bill Doggett and Buster Harding," Bascomb continued. "Andy Gibson was doing a lot of arranging then, too, but to my mind the best arrangement he ever did was of *When Irish Eyes Are Smiling* for Teddy Hill's band. It was terrific, and we used to hate to hear them start it out. We knew what they were going to do to us when they played that one! It was an up-tempo thing, and in the last chorus Al Killian would come over the ensemble playing an octave higher. I think that was the first band Al played with in New York.

"We played St. Louis, Buffalo, and about fourteen weeks for U.S.O. The band didn't sound bad, and we played one date with Billy Eckstine up at the Golden Gate. Some of the people in the band were Kenny Dorham, Clyde Bernhardt, Steve Pulliam, Al McKibbon and Sonny Payne. I think the first time Sonny ever worked a theatre was when we went into the Apollo. There were a lot of Paul's friends in the band, because he goes mostly by friendship. Charlie Parker would sell him a lot of stuff, which we were not going to use, because I was standing in front of the band and knowing the people didn't want it, not back in those days. I've still got some of it home. But when it comes to playing the horn, Paul *plays.* He's been working in Chicago with an organ for some time, now.

"Things began to get rough for big bands and we weren't doing too well. Louis Jordan had come out with a small band, and everybody began to talk about small bands in the different offices, and say they couldn't do anything with the big bands. When the union stepped in and said the agents couldn't have more than 10 percent, it became impossible for the agents to spend the kind of money they had been doing to get network time and publicity for the big bands."

The Bascombs' band broke up in 1947 and the trumpet player joined Duke Ellington.

"He sent for me," Bascomb recalled, "and asked what I was doing. 'Nothing,' I said. Then he asked me what I would have to get, and I said around one-hundred seventy-five dollars. So he said, 'I'll send you a

Dud Bascomb at the Savoy Ballroom.

Marquee at the Savoy Ballroom.

ticket,' and I joined him in Chicago at the Civic Auditorium, and found myself playing first trumpet parts that night. I don't think I took anyone's place. He had a whole load of trumpet players when I got there: Ray Nance, Shelton Hemphill, Taft Jordan, Francis Williams and Shorty Baker.

"I played the last eight bars of solo trumpet on the record of *Women*, but I was supposed to have been showcased on one number. I didn't feel I could do a good job on it, because I didn't like it. I used to be the same way in Erskine's band. If I didn't like a tune, I wouldn't record it. And I'm still like that. Tyree Glenn was featured on this particular number when Duke recorded it in Los Angeles. On the older things, like *Black and Tan Fantasy*, Ray Nance had seniority and took care of the plunger solos, but Duke wanted me to record *East St. Louis Toodle-oo* before I left.

"When Taft Jordan left, Duke said I was to take his solos, but there were others in the band who were ready to fight for them. Duke is a very nice fellow, and he didn't want to hurt anyone's feelings, but he asked me why I didn't play them. I told him that I just didn't feel like fighting over them. It wasn't a band like Erskine's, where a guy would turn round and say, 'No, man, I think you ought to have this solo.' In Duke's band, every man was fighting for himself.

"I finally left because my wife was ill. I thought she had appendicitis, but it turned out to be pleurisy. Duke called me again for a concert in Ithaca. All the trumpet players had left except Shelton Hemphill. 'I'm going to charter a plane for you and Ray Nance,' he said, 'because I want you to be here.' So Ray and I went off to Ithaca in a seven-seater. I stayed for quite a while then. I remember we did four weeks at the Paramount, but I quit again when the band was getting ready to be out of New York for almost a year.

"I went into Tyler's Chicken Shack, about a mile and a half out of Rahway, New Jersey, and I stayed there about four years with a quintet. I had Lou Donaldson on saxophone and Harold Austin on drums. When I had to do some one-nighters and theatres, I put Ike Quebec in there. It was just a chicken shack with a show in the back—shake dancer, m.c., and everything. Everybody would come out there and jam, guys like Milt Jackson and Sonny Stitt, because it was only twenty-five miles from New York, and it was the kind of place I like to play in. The lady who owned it was killed turning into the place. She forgot to look up and a truck was right there, and that was the end of Tyler's Chicken Shack. It used to be packed every night.

"After that, I started doing one-nighters for Universal Attractions, and they kept me busy until 1961, although I didn't have a record going for me. I made an album for Savoy in 1960 with nine pieces and arrangements by Sammy Lowe, but they still haven't put it out. Taft Jordan, Seldon Powell, Sam Taylor and Arthur Clarke were on the dates.

"Jazz did not go on those one-nighters. I cannot remember one time when it was really accepted. Everything was very confused then, in 1960–61. Half the people wanted jazz and half wanted rock 'n' roll. When we played jazz, the agency would get a bad report, so we had to turn around and play rock 'n' roll. A lot of kids would walk in, say, 'Oh, man, they're playing jazz,' and walk out. So we'd give them a big beat. We had Skeeter Best on guitar, and he'd let the guitar ring, and they liked that. We even got fired off one job in Jersey for playing jazz. I had Lou Donaldson, Sam Jones (bass), Elmo Hope (piano) and Arthur Taylor (drums). The owner of the joint said jazz brought in beer drinkers, and he wanted whiskey drinkers. This night, while I was in the telephone booth, Lou and Sam Jones went into *The Song Is You* at up-tempo, and that did it. The man paid us off.

"I decided to quit and go into recording about that time. I didn't do badly. Sometimes I did two dates a day. It was mostly background work for groups like the Shirelles. Lammar Wright and I made that *Twist and Shout* with the Isley Brothers. We did *It's a Man's World* with James Brown, and that was a hit, a monster. Sammy Lowe arranged it, and he was a big moneymaker in rock 'n' roll records. There was a sort of clique making most of them. They very seldom called an outsider unless they got stuck. Sammy Lowe liked Ernie Royal, and liked him before I came into the field, so it got to be either Ernie or me for him."

During this time, Bascomb played club dates and led bands for Dinah Washington, Wynonie Harns, Arthur Prysock, Eddie Vinson and Sam Cooke, but that kind of work fell off until almost his entire livelihood depended on recording. It was when he went to Japan with Sam Taylor that he really enjoyed himself, because then he could play the way he wanted to play.

"That started in 1963," he continued, "and I've been three times already. Sam takes a pianist and a drummer, and augments with Japanese musicians. He has taken Sol Hall and Earl Williams twice each on drums, and on piano he has had Al Williams and Bill Black. We played mostly concerts, just one or two clubs. We stayed six weeks once, another time ten, and the last time five. Sam Taylor is a big draw there, second to Sammy Davis. It's the ballads he plays. He plays them slow, so they can understand them. They may have a few kids who understand jazz, but it's the older people who pack the halls. Sam has a lot of gimmicks, and a tendency to make F's and G's on the ends of his ballads like Louis Armstrong."

Recorded evidence of Bascomb's artistic career is, unfortunately, far from plentiful. There are recordings by his big band and small group on obscure labels like De Luxe, Alert and Sonora, and there are the more widely circulated Bluebird and Victor records with Erskine Hawkins. In his reliable *Discographie Critique,* Hugues Panassié credits Bascomb with (unless otherwise noted) the first trumpet solo on each of the following titles: *Weary Blues, Easy Rider* (second trumpet solo), *Swing Out* (after the Erskine Hawkins introduction), *Raid the Joint, Swingin' on Lenox Avenue, Hot Platter* (second trumpet solo), *Weddin' Blues, Gin Mill Special, Tuxedo Junction* (second trumpet solo), *Uptown Shuffle, Midnight Stroll, Norfolk Ferry, Uncle Bud, Shipyard Ramble* (second trumpet solo), *Bicycle Bounce* and *Bear Mash Blues* (second trumpet solo).

(1967)

Dud Bascomb died 25 December, 1972.

HAYWOOD HENRY

SAXOPHONES, CLARINET AND FLUTE

When Haywood Henry was heard around the country with Earl Hines in 1969, he was a new name and a new star to many people. Those, however, who remembered the Erskine Hawkins band in its heyday, when Henry was featured on clarinet, tenor and baritone, were not unfamiliar with his talents. In the interim, spent mostly in the New York recording field, he had become proficient on the other instruments of the saxophone family, as well as on flute and piccolo.

He was born in Birmingham, Alabama, in 1919, and there was always music in the house where he was raised. His mother played piano, and his sister was an accomplished musician who played organ in the Sixteenth Street Baptist Church, had a radio program, and taught many of the city's pianists and organists. Henry was always interested in music, and early developed an ability to play little themes on a ten-cent flute, but tuition conflicted with sport and other youthful activities. It was not until he was in Lincoln Junior High, where his sister taught, that he took up clarinet. He could not read, but his quick ear enabled him to pass muster in a band of nearly fifty pieces that included Dud Bascomb, Sammy Lowe and Lee Stanfield, three of his future colleagues with Erskine Hawkins.

When he went to Industrial High School, the instructor told him he would put him in the band if he could play a part in an overture. Henry, always resourceful, took the part home, had his sister play it in single lines on piano, and performed it next day from memory. The upperclassmen, who included Jimmy Mitchell and Paul Bascomb, helped the juniors, and Henry was also much inspired by Delmas Means, one of the best clarinetists he ever heard.

"He never left Birmingham," he recalled. "He just played clarinet for a hobby, and didn't even play dances. At that time, if you played only clarinet, you had a hard time getting in a band, because everyone wanted saxophone. He had a Boehm system clarinet, and all of us in the school band were playing Albert. I remember very vividly when I'd go by his house and watch him practice, how he'd run through keys in the instruction book like it was nothing—C-sharp didn't mean any more than C-natural. And he had a beautiful velvet tone. He used to tell me sound was the main thing.

"I learned to read while I was in high school, but I played all the first year by just listening. If I had a cadenza to make, I'd follow the notes and phrase in the way I thought was nice rhythmically. I always knew what you were supposed to do with a bar, but I couldn't break it down into fractions to give the notes their proper value. One of my closest friends was Richard Clarke, a very fine trumpet player, and the brother of Pete and Babe Clarke. We were sitting in church one day, and he was kidding me. 'Can you read?' he asked. 'Oh, yes,' I answered, 'I can read.' 'No,' he said, 'you've been faking in the band all the time.' Right there in church, he made it all very simple to me. He had a very good way of explaining what I hadn't been able to understand when others told it to me in technical terms.

"Soon after that we organized a junior band called the Moonlight Serenaders—all teenagers—and we played dances. This was when I got a tenor sax. We were ten pieces, and we were competition for some of the other bands around. Dud and Paul Bascomb had a band at one time. Erskine Hawkins, Bob Range and Captain (Ed) Sims went to a school on the hill called Tuggle Institute, and they were competition for our group. Erskine was always a tremendous trumpet player. He was playing F's and G's when he was fifteen or sixteen. We'd listen to records and copy things like

Haywood Henry.

Ellington's *Ring Dem Bells* and *Rockin' in Rhythm,* and try to improvise on them.

"In 1930, I went to Alabama State in Montgomery. Professor Trenton had come to Birmingham to get some of the best high school musicians to join the Alabama State College Band, which was going to the Elks' convention in Detroit. So I came out of high school, and with Erskine Hawkins, Dud Bascomb, Bob Range and Ed Sims went down to Alabama State for three or four days' rehearsing with the band. It wasn't a jazz band. We were about thirty pieces, playing marches, but we injected jazz into them. We marched by *Tiger Rag,* and we marched by *Dinah,* and we were quite a sensation doing things that they do at football games now. We were nothing but teenagers, but we won second place out of around thirty bands. A band of about 140 pieces, the Eighth Illinois from Chicago, I think, was first."

The young musicians who wanted to go to Alabama State were offered scholarships on their return from Detroit. Henry was also a good football player, and he went in on a joint football-and-music scholarship. Paul Bascomb was already there, and they had an excellent teacher in Professor Willis Lawrence James, who was an authority on Negro spirituals. There were soon three capable arrangers on the campus. One Henry remembered in particular was H.O. Thompson, a brilliant trombonist. He arranged a ballad interpretation of *When Our Work Is Through* for five trombones playing in harmony, this at a time when the trombone trios of the Ellington and Redman bands were still regarded as innovative.

There were three dance bands on the campus: the 'Bama State Collegians, the 'Bama State Revelers, and the 'Bama State Cavaliers. When the college year ended in the summer, the best men from all three were amalgamated in the Greater 'Bama State Collegians, and the band went on tour through the Mid-West as far as Chicago. The purpose of the tour was to raise funds and publicize the college. One result was that when young musicians finished high school, they wanted to go to Alabama State. Among those Henry remembered as being attracted in this way were Reuben Phillips, Joe Newman and Matthew Gee.

Henry not only made a name for himself at the college as a musician, but also on the football team and, in his last year, as a record-breaking member of the track team. Music, however, was by now his major concern, although his career took an odd course. He was invited to join a religious organization led by an outstanding evangelist with whom he had once played at his Birmingham Baptist church. Henry went on tour as the only reed player in a group of musicians that gave recitals consisting of "hymns, Bach, Mozart and things like Massenet's *Elegie.*" Having arrived in New York, Henry sat in one night with Kaiser Marshall at the Renaissance ballroom, which later led to his joining for some months a band under the leadership of Marshall and Leon Englund at the Empire ballroom.

During this period, the 'Bama State Collegians came north and played at the Harlem Opera House. They were a sensation with their novelty numbers, and with a compilation in which they imitated the themes of all the leading bands—Duke Ellington's, Don Redman's, Earl Hines's, Cab Calloway's, Guy Lombardo's, etc. Their success was such that they decided not to go back to college, and in due course Erskine Hawkins became leader in place of J.B. Sims, a clarinetist who sang like Cab Calloway. When the job at the Empire ended, Henry rejoined his old colleagues for, as he thought, a couple of weeks. Soon recognized as one of the band's most valuable soloists, he stayed twenty years!

"Barney Bigard was my model from the first," he remembered, speaking warmly. "I loved his sound and the way he flowed on clarinet. What he played always made a lot of sense, and he always told a story. Another of my favorite clarinet players in later years was Prince Robinson. I never heard people talk about his clarinet much, because he was more noted for tenor sax (just as I am now for baritone). I used to hear him play clarinet with Sam the Man Taylor in the '40s and early '50s, when they were working a job out on Long Island."

Henry's primary instrument in the section was the tenor, but when it was stolen one night he started playing tenor parts on the baritone, which he had used before only occasionally. The effect of the baritone in a section that had previously consisted of two altos and two tenors pleased the other musicians very much. "Boy, that sounds better!" Henry remembered their saying.

"I really don't know how I learned to transpose," he said, "but I could always do it, as fast as I could read straight, so that was no problem. Because I didn't want to carry two big horns around, I forgot about the tenor for a time. Then, too, I had always admired Harry Carney, and I liked the sound of the baritone. After Paul Bascomb left, Julian Dash came in the band, and most of the solos and praises continued to go to the tenor, although I felt I could play the same thing on baritone. One of the reasons why it didn't bother me was because I always wanted to play different instruments, and playing just one would have bored me to tears. I still like the baritone, but I don't always like the way it is handled as a result of bad writing in bad arrangements. It's a difficult instrument that requires strength. You've got to fill it, and you've got to hit the notes. You can't 'skate' as you can on alto and tenor. But during World War II I went back to tenor, to avoid carrying that heavy baritone! When we were at the

The Erskine Hawkins band in 1936, with Avery Parrish at the piano, and Haywood Henry extreme right.

Lincoln Hotel in the '40s, I was playing tenor, although Mrs. Kramer, the owner, used to like to hear me play all the sweet things on clarinet."

Most of the arrangements in the Hawkins book, apart from the many "heads," were written by Bill Johnson and Sammy Lowe, but a third writer Henry spoke of with special affection and respect was pianist Avery Parrish.

"I don't like to throw the word 'genius' about too often," he said, "but of all the musicians I've been around, I think Avery was one who deserved it. He grew up around the piano. His mother taught him and his brother Curley. Curley was a fine pianist, too, but he didn't play like Avery. The very first gig I made was with Curley, on clarinet, for forty-five cents. The next one, I made five dollars.

"Avery never studied arranging, but he could sit down and write like he was writing a letter. He could compose on the spot, too. He didn't have to resort to taking someone else's number to arrange. Any type of thing you wanted, he could do it. He knew the voicing of instruments, and he did most of the arrangements for the band that we didn't record, I guess because he didn't care about the money angle. He was a timid type of person, and he didn't push himself. We had to force him to play *After Hours.*

"He arranged things like *Miss Hallelujah Brown,* and backgrounds for vocals by Ida James, but he didn't get credit for them. When we played theaters, we had a big symphonic introduction that was all his idea. I remember we were coming from Philadelphia to open at the Apollo, and we were discussing what we were going to play. We used to bribe him— take him a bottle of gin—and he'd say, 'Well, I'll fix something for you.' This particular night, he sat in the back of the bus and wrote this opening for us.

"He wasn't a big drinker, but he loved to see other people happy. When we were working a club in California, Hoagy Carmichael used to come by every night to hear him play. When we got ready to come back across the country, Carmichael told Avery he wanted him to stay and be featured in his club. He offered him a very nice salary, I believe, so Avery stayed and worked in his club. Now we used to live on Fifth Street in Los Angeles, and one side of the street was very nice, but the other was like a bucket of blood. The story as I heard it was that Avery was sitting at a bar with a friend when a fellow started arguing with this friend. 'Why don't you leave the guy alone?' Avery asked. As he turned back to the bar, this ruffian, who he'd never seen before in his life, hit him in the head. And that was how he lost his faculties."

The Erskine Hawkins band was involved in many battles of music, but foremost in Henry's mind was the encounter with Ellington.

"Jimmy Blanton was playing bass with Duke at that time," he recalled, "and we all knew him from school days when he was in the band Sammy Lowe had at Tennessee State. He was really pulling for us on the bandstand, and we played well the first couple of sets, while Duke was mostly playing slow numbers like *Mood Indigo* and *Solitude.* Then one of Duke's trumpets said, 'Okay, Duke, let's go to town!' They went into *St. Louis Blues* and, when Tricky Sam (Nanton) got to the mike, they opened up with both barrels. The people were in hysterics, and we knew we didn't have a chance. But we were all thrilled afterwards when Duke complimented us on how well we had played, and said he hadn't expected us to give him such a run for his money.

"Playing against Lunceford was another big occasion, but that was in our backyard, at the Savoy ballroom, and we had a lot of crowd-pleasing things that would give us the edge. When people were dancing, Lunceford would drop 'way down with his mutes, and the people at the back couldn't hear the pulse. We knew that, and we'd keep our horns open."

"Dud Bascomb and Avery Parrish were crazy about Jimmie Lunceford's band, but I was always an Ellington man. One of the high points in my career was working in Harry Carney's place at the Hurricane on Broadway, and I was on the road two weeks with Duke when Harry's brother was sick. It was not hard for me, because I had known the arrangements since I was a kid. I love Harry Carney's playing, but I never consciously tried to imitate him. I couldn't help imitating Barney Bigard, because that was the only kind of clarinet that appealed to me.

"There were only three bands that stole the show from us at the Savoy —Duke's, Lionel Hampton's and Bunny Berigan's. Bunny took us by surprise. Usually, we'd prepare in advance by rehearsing or working over one of their specialties, just to make it more exciting. We didn't prepare for Bunny because we thought we had him. But Buddy Rich and Georgie Auld were with him, and the house came down! We had a number with a *Rhapsody in Blue* ending, and when our drummer's foot pedal broke we sounded so horrible after Buddy Rich had got through. As for Bunny, I've no doubt he was the best white trumpet player. And something else—he sounded like himself!

"As a rule, however, we could take care of any competition in the Home of Happy Feet. If a band came in with better arrangements, we'd beat them with showmanship. If they played fast, we would beat them with tempos. Sometimes the crowd up there wanted exhibitions, but more often they just wanted to swing all night long."

From 1938 until it closed, the Hawkins band was one of the great favorites at the Savoy, and was for years virtually the house band. The musicians were able to live at home most of the year, and the band personnel was relatively stable.

"Everyone knew everyone in the band, because we all stayed together so many years," Henry said. "You had your set of followers, your friends. I know some nights at the Savoy I knew ninety percent of the people there. It was a very warm thing."

By the time Henry finally left, the band had been reduced to nine pieces. An opportunity occurred to tour with Roy Hamilton in a small group, which enabled him to see old friends. More important, by the mid-'50s, he was beginning to be involved more and more in the developing field of rhythm-and-blues recording. At that time, written arrangements were uncommon, and it was up to the musicians to create appropriate backgrounds and atmosphere in the studio.

"It was rather easy to me," Henry pointed out, "because I used to set a lot of riffs in Erskine's band behind the soloists. But I'd been with him so long that I really didn't know how to go about getting work. When the recording people found out I could sight read, transpose, and play doubles, I began to get a lot of calls."

Like many other veterans of the big bands, Henry also had a fling at Dixieland around this time. He went to Boston for a couple of months with a group led by drummer Tommy Benford, worked at Jimmy Ryan's with Danny Barker, and was frequently at the Central Plaza in New York with musicians like Red Allen and Charlie Shavers. Later, he fronted an entertaining trio at the Garden Café with Sonny Greer on drums, and first Eddie Wilcox and then Ray Tunia on piano. He had not been really familiar with the Dixieland idiom and repertoire, but his knowledge of the great early clarinetists enabled him to cope with the requirements. His versatility was also called upon in 1963 when, with Dud Bascomb, pianist Sammy Benskin and drummer Herbie Lovelle, he played alto and baritone saxophones, bass clarinet and clarinet in the off-Broadway production of *Cindy*.

Recording in all kinds of contexts in New York was a challenge, but Henry was also conscious of its anonymity. "You do the work, but you don't get the credit," he said. "Even your relatives don't know you're on the record. You tell them you worked with James Brown or Frank Sinatra, and they look at you kind of funny and say, 'Well, what were you doing? Where? I can't hear you.' "

When Earl Hines re-organized his group in 1969, he wanted a multi-instrumentalist and Henry's ability pleased him. The pianist had always delighted in presenting a varied program, and in any one evening the listener was now likely to hear clarinet (on *Sweet Lorraine, Summertime, Caravan* and *Melodica Blues*), soprano (on *Exodus, Flakey* and *It's Magic*), baritone (on *Undecided, C.C. Rider* and *Every Day*), flute (on *The Girl from Ipanema, Tangerine, Misty* and *Theme from the Barefoot Contessa*), and piccolo (on *The Shadow of Your Smile*). That Henry played all those instruments well was impressive in itself, but more important was the fact that with Hines he was restored to the public prominence he had so long merited.

(1970)

SAMMY LOWE

TRUMPET AND ARRANGER

"I guess you could say I came from a musical family. My sister plays piano. My brother plays woodwinds, saxophone, etc. My father, who was a carpenter, fooled around on guitar and piano for a hobby. My mother was a housewife, and she didn't sing or anything, but she loved music. As for me, I've never done *anything* but this music bit, apart from a couple of weeks long ago when I worked for a boy delivering lunches to some barbers. My father always used to say that he didn't want me to work hard like he did, because he worked *really* hard.

"When I was in high school in Birmingham, Alabama, there was a trombone player named George Hudson teaching the band. He went to Oberlin or some place up there. (This wasn't the same Hudson as the one who had a band in St. Louis, although he came from Birmingham, too.) One day, it was raining and lightning and thundering, and all the kids were blowing their horns like mad. 'Quiet, everybody!' Hudson said, and then he proceeded to teach us chords—the major chord, the seventh, and so forth. To me, it was fantastic, and I started fooling around on the piano, and got into writing that way.

"But before that, when I was in grammar school, I had played trumpet in a band called the Black and Tan Syncopators. Oh, those names! That was the thing in those days. Then, when I was fourteen, Paul Bascomb got me to go with Jean Calloway's band for a year. She was no relation, but the placards capitalized on Cab's name. You could see 'Calloway' two blocks away, but you had to get up close to see 'Jean.' She had a sister called Harriet, and she was an ex-Cotton Club chorus girl, as I remember. She would stand out front and look good, and wave the baton, and sing a couple of numbers. It wasn't an organized band. Paul Bascomb and Buddy Howard got the best musicians available at that time, some from Montgomery, some from a band in Birmingham called the Society Troubadours, and some from Paul's own band. You can get confused about Paul, but the way I remember it, he was going to school; then he quit; and then he went back again. In between, he had a band. But there we were, going to play an engagement with a 'star,' and we didn't have one number the whole group knew. That was something!

"The first night we played was in Kenosha, Wisconsin, in a beautiful ballroom. We arrived late, and when we walked in the place was packed. The people started applauding, and that was a thrill for me. We got on the bandstand and said, 'Now, what are we going to play?' Anyway, we sounded so bad, it was horrible.

"Billy Shaw, the guy that became a big booker, was the road manager. Al Travis was the guy who had sent for us, and when we had a meeting next day he wanted to send us home. He was the spitting image of Edward G. Robinson, and he acted that way. I always thought maybe the cat was a gangster, because this was 1933 and gangster days in Chicago.

"Billy wouldn't hear of sending us home. 'No, I'm told these kids can play,' he said. And 'kids' was right, because I think Paul Bascomb was the oldest, and he couldn't have been much over twenty. Buddy Howard *might* have been the oldest, but we never did find out his age. He was a trombone player who could play with his foot, and all that. We had a drummer called Mutt who could sing *Minnie the Moocher,* and you could hear him three blocks away. We rehearsed for two weeks and then went out on tour. We started packing 'em in on the strength of the Calloway name. We could really upset the crowds.

"During this time, Eddie Tompkins, who played with Jimmie Lunceford, joined the band. We got along fine together. One day he showed me a letter from Billy (Willie) Smith telling him, 'Man, come on to New York. We're making as much as fourteen dollars a night!' With Jean Calloway, we made twenty-one dollars a week if we worked seven days, eighteen if we worked six, and fifteen if we worked less than that. It sounds terrible now, but it went a long way then, when a hotel cost only three or four dollars a week, and for dinner you spent only a quarter or fifty cents.

"Before we finally left Jean and went back to Birmingham, Paul decided to quit. He had a valid reason—to get more money—but he quit in Hannibal, Missouri, when there was snow on the ground, and we hadn't enough money to get home. His brother Dud and I were just kids, and we had to stick with him, but we prevailed upon him to call 'em up and tell 'em we'd come back to the band. Two days later, they sent a car for us. You have to look on a map to find where Hannibal is! If he had quit in St. Louis or Chicago, that would have been different.

"When we got back home in the summer, *we had been north*. You don't have any idea what that means down south. You've been north and you've come back a success! Well, we'd worked long enough to get a couple of suits. Earl Hines had been through Birmingham, and we had bell-bottom trousers like he had been wearing!

"Big Jack Morrison, who later became Erskine Hawkins' drummer, had a job down in Montgomery, playing for a walkathon. There was a vogue for them then. The people would just keep walking and dancing, and we'd keep playing. I think most people have a sadistic side. I mean, you take the lions and Christians in Rome, and people going to bullfights. They want to see blood. These kids would be walking around until they'd get exhausted and fall, and then their partner would be trying to pick them up, and they'd be struggling and falling all over the floor.

"We played there that summer, and then I went back and finished high school. I toured with Fess Whatley in the summer of 1934. His band was better organized than many I've seen in New York. You made time with him. There was no excuse for being late. That kind of training sticks, and in all the years I was with Erskine Hawkins I was only late twice. In those days, the bands I worked in split up the money and paid off right after the dance, but with Fess you'd go home, because you knew you could go by the next day and find your money ready in an envelope, with everything detailed on the outside. We traveled in two Cadillacs—he always hired Cadillacs. I was the only student in the band. The rest were schoolteachers and old fellows, like twenty-eight or twenty-nine years old.

"Down south, they had a thing where they'd skip the top students in a class, and I got out of high school when I was fifteen, skipping a couple of grades. I got a scholarship to Tennessee State College. The reason I got it, I think, was because President Hale decided he would start a band. The 'Bama State Collegians were known all over the south at this time, and he thought a band would help make his school better known. I had wanted to go to 'Bama State myself, but my brother prevented that, and we had a good deal going at Tennessee State. All we had to do was play twice a week in the dining room, and that paid for our tuition. When we played at week-ends, we pocketed the money.

"In the summer before I went there, in '35, I toured with the Tennessee State Collegians. I was a soloist with them and Fess Whatley. My idol was Louis Armstrong. This was before Roy Eldridge, the next big influence. We weren't acquainted with King Oliver, the guy that influenced Louis. That was another bag of peanuts. All the records we had were with Louis Armstrong. When we were in our early days at high school, Dud Bascomb and I would walk two or three miles to hear a record like his *Shine* or *West End Blues*. When I first met Louis, he asked me what instrument I played, and I told him trumpet.

" 'Yeah?' he said, grinning. 'You look just like Joe Smith.'

"I did most of the arranging at Tennessee State. That was the way I got the scholarship, to arrange and direct the band. From the time George Hudson showed me the chords, I was writing something every day and night—trial, hit and error. I took orchestrations and spread 'em out on the bed to see what each instrument was doing. With Jean Calloway, I had a showcase, and I must say that in those days the fellows were very cooperative. If it was wrong, they'd try to work it out. When I was with Fess Whatley, he told me to write, and paid me for it, something like two dollars an arrangement. I thought I'd get some formal training at Tennessee State, but I soon found out that I knew more about writing arrangements than the instructors. I have to give credit to Duke Ellington here. I idolized him. Every record of his I could buy, I copied it off. I think he was years before his time. To this day, I don't always know what he's doing. It's hard to pin him down, because he's so unorthodox. I bought every book on arranging, theory and harmony I could find, but I just couldn't find reasons or explanations for a lot of the things he was doing.

"After I'd been at Tennessee State five months, I got a telegram from Paul Bascomb: 'Come right to New York to join 'Bama State.' No amount was mentioned, but it turned out to be fourteen dollars. I quit school. I'm *gone*, you know . . .

"The band was incorporated, and they put Erskine Hawkins out front at that time, and I took his place in the first trumpet chair. When I looked at the book, I felt like going back home. Because they had high notes like D on up to F and G written on the paper! That was another reason for me to go into the arranging bit, to get those notes down out of the sky. There were some real lip-beaters in there. Avery Parrish was a piano player, and he had a tendency to write what he played, and sometimes that became too difficult and too high. Bill Johnson was the one with formal training. He'd been to Marquette University, and we were quite tight when it came to arranging. He paid me a compliment one day, 'You've got some of the darnedest ideas I've ever heard. They're terrific.' Then he'd show me what I was doing wrong! In fact, he was like a teacher, and I hadn't any qualms about going to him when I had any questions. I just wish when I wrote my first composition for the school band, somebody had been around to say, 'Look, here's what you're supposed to do now.' Going by trial and error may result in originality, but what would take me a year to discover by reading books and talking to guys could have been taught me so much more quickly and easily. On the other hand, I hear guys that have had all kinds of training, and they always follow a set pattern, and I think that's unfortunate. I could pick up a piece of music and read it off, like singing solfeggio. I've met some very learned musicians who can't do that, and it amazes me that they can't. I think it's something they ought to be able to do. I've never had perfect pitch, however, and I have an excuse for that. None of the pianos we ran into on the road were in tune, so I could never make that true A. So long as I can make what you call relative pitch, I'm somewhere near.

"I guess there are disadvantages to composing on piano, but it wouldn't be that way with me, because I can't play the piano. I can hit the chords and take it step by step, but I can't actually play it. From personal observation, beginning with Avery Parrish, I've noticed that piano players write a lot that is easy on the piano, but very hard for the horns. Back in high school, our instructor would have eighty kids to teach, and he would take fellows like Dud Bascomb and me and have us help teach the others. So that was where I got to know the positions on the trombone, the fingering on saxophone, the limitations of the clarinet, and so on.

"The 'Bama State Collegians became the 'Bama State Collegians with Erskine Hawkins right after I joined. Then it was Erskine Hawkins and the 'Bama State Collegians, and finally we were Erskine Hawkins and His Orchestra. Billy Daniels was the band singer when I got there, and we all had to chip in to pay him, because when people hired us, they didn't hire the singers. Singers in those days were added attractions. The band was *it*.

"High-note trumpet stuff was very popular at that time. Louis Armstrong really started it, but Erskine excited the people in New York when he came here. On *Shine,* Louis would usually make ten high C's and high F's, where Erskine used to make a hundred high F's down south. They had played the Harlem Opera House before I joined, and there he would play a hundred high C's and make high F, while the band counted them aloud. It was an absolute sensation. So Erskine had the potential to become a legend so far as trumpet playing was concerned. At 'Bama State, I was told, you could hear Dud and Erskine practicing their trumpets day and night. What now happened to Erskine happened to so many others, movie stars, and all of them. When we hit it big, and he started making all that money, he never

Sammy Lowe.

Erskine Hawkins.

touched his horn until he hit the stage, and that meant he was playing the same thing over and over. Actually, most of his things were written. We had a format: first chorus was melody followed by some solos, and when we got ready to go out we'd have an ensemble chorus, and then maybe a modulation, and Erskine would come in and hit the high notes, semi-ad lib, while we shouted on down.

"Of course, you could tear your lip out playing a place like the Apollo. The band would play an introduction in the pit, the girls would dance, the comedians would come on, and then maybe there would be a dance act before we went upstairs, on the stage, to play a band specialty. When you got through with that after an hour and a half, you had worked. We did it four times a day, and after we got very popular, after *Tuxedo Junction,* we did as high as six or seven shows a day.

"I stopped taking solos in the band because Dud Bascomb was a man I dug the most. He was never aggressive, and by being aggressive I mean parlaying your talents commercial-wise, getting a press agent, or something like that. That's where white musicians forged ahead and made more money. The public certainly knew Dud during the days of the big bands, because wherever Erskine played they heard Dud's lyrical type of trumpet, too. There was a marvelous trumpet player, a boy by the name of Clifford Brown, who died before his time in an automobile wreck. I still hold and maintain that he was motivated by Dud Bascomb.

"I knew the guys in the band all dug Dud, too, and so did Erskine. Because of that, they gave Dud the solos and used Erskine for his high notes. I suspect we did Erskine a disservice and that we should have given him more solos, but nearly all the bands stuck to certain guys for certain things at that time.

" 'Man, you're making all these arrangements,' Paul Bascomb told me once, 'why don't you give yourself a solo?'

" 'We've got Dud, and Erskine can play the high notes.'

" 'No,' he said, 'how do you know that there are not people who'd dig *you?'*

"I thought about that, but didn't do anything about it. Years later, I realized he was right. Regardless of how good a guy is, another can come along, and maybe he's got something the people want to hear. But the way bands were geared then, one guy played all the first trumpet parts, and the first trumpets had the name for reading. Now it is reversed, and any time somebody *can't* read it makes news. Then, all the bands had guys who weren't so hot on reading. I'll go further and say most bands had four or five well-rounded musicians, and the rest of them weren't so good—to put it nicely—as they should have been.

"You really had to be on the ball to play shows in theatres, though, what with all the new acts coming in and everything. The bands used to pride themselves on who could play the show the best. Jimmie Lunceford was known, by and large, to have the best show band. At least, the chorus girls liked his band best, because it would put fire and enthusiasm into their numbers. We admired Lunceford's band very much, and our early records show it, but we developed our own thing. We always had a good relationship with that band whenever we ran into it. I think it's a known fact that Duke Ellington's band was the worst in that area, because the guys didn't care about the show. They cared nothing about anything but playing their band speciality! When we were getting ready to go into the Apollo, we would rehearse for hours, and we would always have a soft-shoe number ready, just in case the chorus girls needed it. It would be arranged, with solos and everything, just like a band number.

"Let's see . . . I joined the band in February, 1936, and our first engagement was for two days in Newburgh, New York, and we made nine dollars apiece according to my diary. (You must remember that when I played in Birmingham, the highest I made was maybe four dollars, so now I said to myself, 'This is *it!*') Then we proceeded to lay off from February until the fall, eight months. But we rehearsed every day, and we played gigs every now and then, just enough to keep the hotel man happy. The reason a lot of bands managed to exist in those days was a Mr. Collins, who had a kind of private restaurant in his apartment on 126th Street and Seventh Avenue. You could always eat there, and he would hold you on the books for *years*. Believe me, a lot of musicians, dancers and show people were indebted to that man for keeping 'em going. I remember guys from Eddie Mallory's band there, and from Andy Kirk's. It couldn't possibly have paid off for Mr. Collins, because so many guys never paid him. Dud and I did, and I'm so glad we did, because he died shortly afterwards. When he got sick, his wife came around trying to collect some of the money people owed him, and she didn't collect very much.

"In October, 1936, we went into the Harlem Uproar House on 50th Street, at the old Roseland, downstairs in the basement. The club was a sensation, and we stayed there until we got on our feet. It was hard, though. We hit at 7 o'clock and played till 4 in the morning. Hazel Scott worked in the lounge. The room wasn't too big, but big enough to have a full show.

"Then we went with Moe Gale's agency, and he sent us on tour with Stepin Fetchit. That's when I found out the value of a name in show business. We would stop the show, and then he would come on. To my way of thinking, he didn't have very much of an act, but he would tear up the show, too. 'We're going to make it hot for him,' we used to say, 'before he gets on stage.'

"When we played Memphis, Tennessee, people were coming from all around. They loved Stepin Fetchit, especially the whites, and we were playing white theatres mostly. Every night, we would lock up the show and think we were making it so hot for him. We did so well, broke all records, and got a return engagement, because a lot of people had been unable to get to hear us. Stepin was having trouble with the theatre manager—about more money, I expect—and after an argument he decided he wouldn't appear. So they put up a big sign saying the entire show would be presented, but without him. And didn't *nobody* come! 'They loved us last week,' we said. 'Why don't they come back to see us?' Then it dawned on me: when the public pay their money to see somebody else, it doesn't matter how good *you* are, you're just part of the background.

"After that tour for Moe Gale, we went into the Savoy ballroom as one of the house bands, along with Chick Webb. We had recorded previously for Vocalion, but now Gale got us a contract with RCA Victor on the Bluebird label. (Incidentally, when we made *Big John's Special,* Dud Bascomb had had to go home, so I played the solo.) *Swinging in Harlem* and *Raid the Joint* were two of my early arrangements.*

"The big one for the band, of course, was *Tuxedo Junction,* and that's when Erskine Hawkins was kind of downed by the critics. They dug Dud and Paul Bascomb, and Julian Dash, but they were always down on him. They didn't realize that the reason the band was in New York in the first place was because of his high notes, which excited the public. You can talk about artistic endeavor all you want, but America is a commercial country where people go for materialistic things, and you don't make any money if they don't recognize you. The critics might accuse Erskine of exhibitionism, but I didn't see 'em jumping on Tommy Stevenson and Paul Webster when they made all the high notes with Jimmie Lunceford, nor on Ernie Royal and Cat Anderson with Lionel Hampton.

"Erskine Hawkins was and is a *nice* guy, and although the criticism was severe, I don't mean it hurt him that much. He was one of the most fortunate bandleaders in the business, because he had a bunch of fellows that needed nobody to tell 'em what to do. They did what they were supposed to do, and we didn't have the fights other bands had. Even though most of us were in the business for kicks, we wanted to make a living, so we had to lean towards commercialism quite a bit.

"Our best things didn't reach the records. We never knew what we were going to record. We'd take our books down to the studio, and we'd want to play something we dug, but Moe Gale would say no, and suggest something else. Sometimes he had discussed the selections with Erskine,

---

*A list of Lowe's arrangements for the band follows this interview.-S.D.

or had made notes about what he heard at the Savoy. I had made an arrangement on Cole Porter's *All the Things You Are,* and people whose judgment I respected told me they thought it was terrific. We were playing in Washington, and when musicians are around, you know, bands would lay their best things on. Dizzy Gillespie was there that night, and he asked who arranged *All the Things You Are.* He came over, shook my hand, and told me how good he thought it was. Then when we were playing in Denver, Duke Ellington was in town, and Sweet Pea (Billy Strayhorn) and Louis Bellson told me they thought it was a great arrangement. So . . . we never recorded anything like that, and there were the same kind of limitations on what we broadcasted. Unfortunately, we lost a trunkful of music —lost it, or somebody stole it—from downstairs at the Savoy, so that music is gone, because I had no scores on it.

"It was when we were at the Lincoln Hotel that I first started using a copyist. We would make the arrangements, come to work at 7, and he'd pick them up. When we finished at 2 o'clock, he'd be back with all the parts, and we'd have a rehearsal. It was not until Leroy Kirkland came in, playing guitar and arranging, that I began to be paid for arrangements at a set figure. He was a good business man. Avery Parrish and I had been making them, and every now and then Erskine would give us some money. Of course, I was doing all right with him. I got the highest salary in the band, plus a sizeable amount for royalties on my original tunes that he recorded. When I got into the record business later, Leroy gave me some very good advice: 'Charge these people some money, or they don't respect you.'

"I think I used to get twenty-five dollars for pop tunes when we were broadcasting. I'm quite sure most of the arrangers with the big bands would tell you that none of them really got paid what they were worth. Not that you got angry about it, because you were doing it partly for kicks, and you'd got those fellows who were going to play it. The bandleader was figuring that you were with the band, so anything you wrote you got a chance to hear.

"We played all around the U.S., went to Mexico and Canada, and turned down two chances to go to Europe with a show. We were all young and single, and there was nothing we wanted more than to get to England and France, but Moe Gale was a booker of bands, and I'm sure he had his mind on the transportation costs. Put the boys on a bus, and they can ride and make all this money here while they're hot! It had gotten so practically every record we made was a hit. We outdrew Count Basie, and we outdrew most of the bands till Buddy Johnson came along. Buddy packed 'em in for years, and he's not supposed to be swept under the rug the way he is in some books I've seen.

"When be-bop came in, that didn't hurt us. What hurt us was what they called 'Rhythm and Blues.' It had been labeled 'Race Music' by some of the record companies before. Jimmy Witherspoon and guys like that came along, singing the blues with small combos. I soon noticed the difference on the juke boxes. Along with Bill Johnson, Avery Parrish and Julian Dash, I'd written a lot of originals for Erskine. At the time *Holiday for Strings* was big, I wrote *Holiday for Swing,* and when I got a check for that I didn't believe it. In fact, I'd been getting eight or nine hundred dollars every three months for royalties, but now I began to notice a difference. That was when the band started to slip, too, and it wasn't happening only to us. It was happening to all the bands, and it happened overnight. Joe Liggins and the Honeydrippers, Louis Jordan and His Tympany Five—they were drawing twice as many people as most big bands could.

"In my opinion, it was because their music was simpler, more basic. It appealed to black people in the big urban districts at a time when be-bop was trying to do its thing. The big bands had gotten bigger and bigger— we had five trumpets, four trombones, six saxophones, and four rhythm —and the arrangers were having a ball! It was all getting too complicated. I'm glad some of the things I wrote then didn't get on records, because they were just over-arranged. I think it was time for a change, anyway. It couldn't go on forever.

"I think what killed be-bop, of course, was that it stopped people from dancing. When we were playing the Regal in Chicago, I went by to hear Dizzy Gillespie's big band at a ballroom. Everything was at up tempo, and they were just doing their thing. When I looked around, I saw that *nobody* was dancing. A few people were standing around the bandstand. What the band was doing should have been at a concert, where the people were sitting down.

"Erskine cut down to a small group: Bobby Smith, who replaced Bill Johnson, on alto; Julian Dash on tenor; Erskine and me on trumpet; Freddie Washington (a man, not the woman of the same name) on piano; Lee Stanfield on bass; and Bill English on drums. I finally quit in 1955. We'd been in Canada, and I found we had a month of one-nighters ahead down in the West Virginia mountains, and I just felt I couldn't make that scene. By then we were traveling in cars, too. I had gotten married, and I had a son, and what with the expenses on the road, I just wasn't making it.

"I started gigging around New York, and at first my main source of work was with Reuben Phillips' band at the Apollo. Rock and rhythm-and-blues groups were coming in there, and I'd be doing two or three arrangements for them overnight. When I brought them in next day and passed them out to the band, the band would play them—*one, two, three*—easy, just like that, and all the kids would be surprised and say, 'Wow!' Then word leaked downtown. Earle Warren told a guy named Buck Ram about me. He had the Platters, and he wanted an arranger who didn't ridicule what his singers were doing. The first thing I did for them, *My Prayer,* sold three million records. It was made with six pieces: piano, guitar, bass, drums, Count Hastings on tenor, and Earle Warren on baritone. It was a very simple arrangement, but then people started calling me up. I told Reuben Phillips to hold the spot open for me at the Apollo, but I never did return."

From 1957 onwards, Sammy Lowe pursued an energetic career in the popular recording field. Open-minded and intelligent, he was able to adjust to its vagaries and demands very successfully, but that is another story.

(1972)

Arrangements by Sammy Lowe recorded by Erskine Hawkins:

VOCALION
1936 Without a Shadow of a Doubt
      Swinging in Harlem
1937 Dear Old Southland
      I'll See You in My Dreams
1938 Let Me Day Dream
      Lost in the Shuffle

BLUEBIRD
1938 Rockin' Rollers' Jubilee
      Weary Blues
      Do You Wanna Jump, Children?
      Easy Rider
1939 Let the Punishment Fit the
         Crime
      Raid the Joint
      No Soap
      Hot Platter
      Gin Mill Special
      You Can't Escape from Me
      Satan Does the Rhumba
      Baltimore Bounce
      Fine and Mellow
      Saboo
1940 Midnight Stroll
      Gabriel Meets the Duke
      Too Many Dreams
      Junction Blues
      Sweet Georgia Brown

Ashes in the Tray
After Hours (last chorus)
Norfolk Ferry
Nona
I Know a Secret
Tonight You Belong to Me
1941 No Use Squawkin'
      Blackout
      I Love You Truly
      Shipyard Ramble
      So Long, Shorty
      I'm in a Lowdown Groove
      Someone's Rockin' My Dream
         Boat
      I Don't Want to Walk Without
         You
1942 Don't Cry, Baby
      Bicycle Bounce
      Bear Mash Blues
      Knock Me a Kiss

VICTOR
1945 Drifting Along
      Prove It By the Things You Do
      Holiday for Swing
1946 That Wonderful, Worrisome
         Feeling
      I've Got a Right to Cry
      Sammy's Nightmare

Somebody Loves Me
I Had a Good Cry
1947 My Baby Didn't Even Say
       Goodbye to Me
Ain't I Lovin' You
Fool That I Am
I'm So Doggone Melancholy
Big Fat Sam
1948 Cornbread
Cold Hearted Woman
1949 It's Divine, So Divine
Miss Eva
St. Louis Blues
Careless Love
Memphis Blues

Aunt Hagar's Blues
Beale Street Blues
John Henry Blues

CORAL
1950 So Long, Goodbye Blues

KING
1952 Down Home Jump
Fair Weather Friend
The Way You Look Tonight
1953 Double Shot

STANG
1971 It Feels So Good

The extent of this list indicates what a great contribution Sammy Lowe made to the Erskine Hawkins band. It also suggests that he has never had due recognition from jazz critics and historians.

ANDY GIBSON

TRUMPET AND ARRANGER

Recognition outside the profession came late to jazz arrangers. In the heyday of the big bands, the soloists were carefully identified and appraised, but the men who provided the settings in which these soloists performed were as often as not ignored. Duke Ellington, Don Redman, Benny Carter, Fletcher Henderson and Sy Oliver formed a kind of hierarchy whose work it was almost obligatory to recognize and acclaim, but there were many other talented writers and arrangers whose achievements were only erratically chronicled.

In this category were Jimmy Mundy, Mary Lou Williams, Horace Henderson, Eddie Sauter, Dean Kincaide, Edgar Sampson and, because of the closeness of his partnership with Ellington, Billy Strayhorn. They rightly became famous, but credit was by no means automatic when their works were performed publicly or on records.

Others, less fortunate, never won from the public the reputation for writing that they deserved, and in this category might be mentioned Billy Moore, Fred Norman, Charlie Dixon, Budd Johnson, Alex Hill, Buster Harding, Sammy Lowe, Buck Clayton and Eddie Durham. Even so, most or all of these names were vaguely known to the average enthusiast of the '50s, jazz having been much more thoroughly documented since the Swing Era.

Nevertheless, there was an item in Leonard Feather's *Encyclopedia Yearbook* for 1956 which must have been a surprise to many. In its "Musicians' Musicians" poll, the late Lester Young nominated as his preferred arranger a musician who, at that time, had not been granted an individual entry in either of the standard jazz reference books by Panassié or Feather. The musician was Andy Gibson.

Gibson was very well known among musicians and almost every adult Jazzman spoke of him with admiring respect. It never seemed to have occurred to him to court publicity. All the bandleaders likely to employ his talents knew of him and knew where to find him, so what other publicity did he need? When I first attempted to obtain information from him about his career, he was highly skeptical. Who would be interested in it? He was just an arranger.

As it happened, he was an arranger who had made contributions of great worth to the books of some of the most successful big bands.

Andy Gibson was born in Zanesville, Ohio, on November 6th, 1913. He was first taught violin, but he took up trumpet when he was fourteen. In 1931, he joined the Cumberland Bell Hops, a band led by Don Redman's brother, Louis. The following year found him with Zack Whyte's Beau Brummels, a group which at the time included Sy Oliver and Al Sears. Oliver was then already writing in the style that was to make Jimmie Lunceford's band famous, and Gibson insists he never afterwards heard Oliver's creations interpreted so well as they were by the Beau Brummels. I thought this might be a case of memories being enhanced by time, and later I queried it with Oliver.

"Well, yes, I think that was so," he said. "In that band we were more or less playing for the love of it, and I just about knew how each of the guys breathed!" And he went on to explain how in the Lunceford perfor-

Andy Gibson.

mances there was sometimes an element of virtuosity which didn't accord with his overall conception.

Gibson himself began to write while with Whyte. His first number was *Beau Brummel,* which Count Basie recorded with a little modification a decade later.

His next band was McKinney's Cotton Pickers, the trumpet section of which then consisted of Gibson, Roy Eldridge and Buddy Lee. Lee he recalled as a fine high-note specialist. Of his own playing, he said:

"I was a good 'part' man, and I took the growl solos."

He joined Blanche Calloway in 1937 and went on to Willie Bryant the following year. Later, while with Lucky Millinder, he finally quit blowing to concentrate on arranging. He spent two months with Duke Ellington—"I wrote some parts!"—and then began preparing a book for Harry James before the latter left Benny Goodman. When James introduced his own band in January, 1939, it played Gibson's arrangements of *King Porter Stomp, Sweet Georgia Brown, I Found a New Baby, Fannie Mae, Two O'Clock Jump, My Buddy, Willow Weep for Me, Avalon, Exactly Like You, Indiana* and *'T'ain't What You Do.*

He was also by now writing for Count Basie and among his many contributions to that leader's library were *Shorty George, Jump for Me, The Apple Jump, I Left My Baby, Between the Devil and the Deep Blue Sea, Hollywood Jump, Someday Sweetheart, Tickle Toe, Louisiana, Let Me See, The World Is Mad* and *It's Torture.*

This was a period of flourishing big bands and Gibson's services were soon so much in demand that he found himself under considerable pressure. By this time, he was aware of Basie's habits of remodeling and reducing arrangements to the shape and size he wanted. Dicky Wells remembers how Gibson brought in an arrangement one night on paper the size of a postcard with instructions to the band to "turn it over when you get to letter B." Basie was out having a taste at that moment and, when he came back to the stand, the band was playing it. He liked it, voiced his approval and asked what it was. When he saw the size of it, he said, "Man, this one must be on the house!"

During 1940, Cab Calloway had one of the best bands of his career, and Gibson wrote more than a dozen arrangements for it, among them being *Come On with the Come On, Hep Cat's Love Song, Special Delivery, Silly Old Moon, Are You Hep to the Jive?, Geechy Joe, Ebony Silhouette, Jonah Joins the Cab, Willow Weep for Me* and *A Ghost of a Chance.* The last four were showcases for Milt Hinton, Jonah Jones, Hilton Jefferson and Chu Berry respectively, and they revealed a skill in providing appropriate backgrounds to individual talents probably only excelled by Ellington's. *Ebony Silhouette* was a particularly imaginative and unusual presentation of the bass, plucked and bowed. Yet on more commercial pieces like *Hep Cat's Love Song*, the dynamic and textural contrasts are just as obviously the work of an accomplished and conscientious craftsman.

The bulk of his scores went into Charlie Barnet's book between 1941 and 1946. Gibson arranged all kinds of material—ballads, standards and originals—and he also re-worked such Ellington successes as *Harlem Speaks, Things Ain't What They Used to Be* and *Just a-Sittin' and a-Rockin'*. Barnet's well-known penchant for Ellington's sound and style made Gibson very valuable to him. Among the more than forty titles he arranged during this phase were *Murder at Peyton Hall, Mother Fuzzy, I Like to Riff, Smiles, Shady Lady, Oh, Miss Jaxon, Washington Whirligig, The Victory Walk, The Great Lie, Mellow Mood, Andy's Boogie, No Pad to Be Had, Atlantic Jump, Juice Head Blues, Jubilee Jump, Bunny* and the 1946 versions of *Charleston Alley, Rockin' in Rhythm, Southern Fried* and *Little John Ordinary. Budandy* was written in collaboration with Budd Johnson and the Apollo record of it featured exciting solo work by Clark Terry and Jimmy Nottingham.

In the army during 1943–45, Gibson played trumpet again, this time as leader of a nine-piece band while stationed near Stoke-on-Trent, England. Following the Normandy invasion, he went all over Europe in General Patton's army. When he returned to the U.S.A., he made straight for California and rejoined Barnet.

From 1947 onwards, he was mostly active in New York as a free-lance arranger, writing for Ralph Marterie, Buddy Morrow and Patti Page among others. He had a big success with *The Hucklebuck* in 1949 and became a member of ASCAP that year. In 1954, he took a post as composer and staff arranger with King Records. Four years later he was appointed that company's New York a. and r. man, in which role he brought tact, patience and good humor to the complexities of rock 'n' roll and the contemporary pop song.

In the autumn of 1959, this writer was commissioned to produce an album of "mainstream" jazz for the RCA Camden label. After a deal of involved arithmetic, it became apparent that it was possible with the funds available, by using a sextet on one session, to have a fifteen-piece band on the other.

Gibson had just orchestrated a couple of numbers by Johnny Hodges and Mercer Ellington for the latter's first Coral album *(Stepping into Swing Society)*. They were *Ruint* and *Broadway Babe,* and the former especially had impressed me. It had a typically lyrical Hodges theme and Gibson had dressed it in rich, smoldering colors worthy of Duke Ellington himself. So it was not long before I was asking if he would write for my proposed fifteen-piece band and direct it on the session. He agreed to do so.

Experience and inexperience then sat down to consult on the personnel of the band. I had fairly definite ideas on the soloists I wanted, if available at the time of recording, and I was determined to have Jimmie Crawford and Milt Hinton in the rhythm section. It became a little like a friendly game of chess.

"Very well," Gibson would say. "If you have so-and-so, you must let me have what's-his-name."

Then I would make suggestions regarding musicians who were not necessarily going to solo.

"He's a good man," Gibson would counter, "but he wouldn't give me the section sound I want."

Under these circumstances, Leslie Johnakins, of whom I had never previously heard, was enlisted. A member of Machito's band, he took care of the baritone sax chair with distinction. Prince Robinson, an old friend of Gibson's and absent too long from jazz recording, was brought in for the clarinet solo and to give the sax section the benefit of his full tenor sound.

In the end the personnel was decided and all the men notified.

Having again indicated my preferences as regards soloists, I now requested of Gibson just one blues composition, so arranged and routined that its performance would occupy one whole side of the album. I had often heard from big bands long performances of the kind I had in mind, and I wanted to see if it was possible to capture in the studio the atmosphere of elation and abandon that additional length seemed often to foster. Gibson took this news in good part. He began work that night.

As the appointed day, December 1st, drew near, I would call anxiously for progress reports. I was always reassured, but the shape of things to come was only partially revealed. On November 30th there was a crisis, a change of a key, and a headache for copyist Dave McRae.

Next day, at 1 p.m., the company, minus one, was assembled in Victor's Studio A. A half-hour later, there was still one musician missing, a famous trumpet player who had promised to make the date "as a favor" to Gibson. By now we were telephoning around town to locate him. We were unsuccessful. He never showed up, never explained his absence, and never apologized for it. Critic Dan Morgenstern volunteered to go forth in search of another trumpet. He eventually trapped Willie Cook on the steps of the Alvin Hotel and reached the studio with him about 2:30, when the session really began, an hour and a half late.

Meanwhile, Dave McRae had completed the parts in the studio and the sections had rehearsed some ensemble passages. Eli Robinson had been handed the first trombone part and Vic Dickenson and Dicky Wells, sitting either side of him, were wearing noticeably benign expressions. Gibson had been issuing instructions with composure, although he afterwards admitted that the delay and confusion had made him more than a little nervous.

There was a rather ragged run-through for timing, some reorganization of the routine, and then we were making the first take. Emmett Berry, it was decided, should not only play the open solo as planned, but also the muted one originally allotted the missing "star." He rose to the occasion splendidly. There was no doubt in my mind that both of his solos were superior to anything the absentee could have achieved. The big question was how Paul Gonsalves would fare in the final stormy choruses, for he had both to relate to the ensembles and improvise a story at the same time. He found the answer and rode on through triumphantly.

They made one more take and time was up—four o'clock. Crawford, who had been driving everyone with his drums and war cries, had put a stick through a tom-tom on the last beat of the very last bar—a final, exultant *wham!*

"So we made it, you see," said Dicky Wells, very cool.

"Andy knows how to write that stuff," said Eli Robinson.

"What are you going to call it?" asked Kenny Burrell.

"Blueprint," said Gibson, "a kind of a design for what ought to be."

Under ideal conditions, and subsequent to a number of rehearsals, the performance of *Blueprint* might obviously have had more polish, but then it might have lacked some of the freshness and enthusiasm given it by musicians who seemed almost to relish the challenge of the racing clock.

Apart from its unusual length, the overall conception was typical of what might be called the Gibson method. Because he was writing for fifteen men, he didn't think in terms of complexity and heavy ensemble effects. Nor did he introduce soloists for relief, but rather the other way round. More often than not, he wrote to enhance the soloist's improvisation.

Basie's famous *Tickle Toe* offers an example of this. Lester Young had the original idea and Gibson wrote the sketch around it in the band bus en route to the next engagement. The Basie group was used sparingly, but to maximum effect. Here were the spaciousness, the freedom and the climate, all within a band context, that Young loved. Gibson's similar success in establishing a thoroughly sympathetic orchestral atmosphere for Roy Eldridge should also be noted in *The Great Lie* by Charlie Barnet's band. It was the same with the Calloway showcases mentioned earlier. The soloist painted the picture and the orchestra supplied a frame that was appropriate and in perfect taste, a frame that subtly emphasized what the soloist did without drawing attention away from him.

There was a constant concern for timbre, for mellow textures, and for sensitivity in dynamics, which made any question about which other arranger Gibson preferred a little superfluous.

"Duke above all," he answered immediately.

"And then?"

"Then Sy Oliver . . . Billy Moore . . . Billy Strayhorn. . . . and Neal Hefti."

Of the many Ellington creations he esteemed, Gibson mentioned first *Jack the Bear,* and then *Cottontail, Harlem Airshaft* and *I Got It Bad.*

"Don't forget *Ebony Rhapsody,*" he added. "That was well and effectively written, and I learned a lot from it."

Apart from the reservations referred to earlier concerning the Zack Whyte performances, he admired the Lunceford versions of Sy Oliver's *For Dancers Only* and *Dream of You.* Like Oliver, he had a special regard for Billy Moore, whose *Slow Burn* (recorded by the Sy Oliver band) had much of the rich, warm coloring that he himself favored. Other arrangements by Moore that he particularly liked were *I'm in an Awful Mood, Belgium Stomp* and *What's Your Story, Morning Glory,* as recorded by the Lunceford orchestra. By Billy Strayhorn, he named *Take the "A" Train* and *Chelsea Bridge,* as recorded by Duke's band; and by Neal Hefti, *Sure Thing* and *Plymouth Rock,* as recorded by Count Basie.

Of his own arrangements, his favorites were *Tickle Toe, Louisiana,* and *The World Is Mad* for Count Basie, and *Bunny* for Charlie Barnet. Some of his best work, he felt, was done for Lucky Millinder at a time when Millinder's band was the rage of Harlem. Unfortunately, the band did not record in that period.

Gibson naturally regretted the decline of the big bands, but he was not pessimistic about their future. Dancing was too basic a human activity to be more than temporarily out of fashion, and the size and instrumentation of the big bands were not accidental. From the point of view of tonal density and color, the big bands gave the arranger a very flexible instrument with which to work, and Gibson suspected they lost popularity when too much emphasis was laid on power and complexity, on blasting for its own sake. Simplicity and mellow sounds were just as important to him, for contrast—light and shade—was a cardinal virtue in his arranging gospel. He used mutes like Ellington, not merely because he admired and understood Ellington's methods, but because they presented him with such an obvious extension of his tonal palette. However original the ideas, their expression in a low monotone or unvaried shout was to be avoided. He granted that much of Kenton's music was "great for musicians," but he felt that to communicate with the public more attention had to be paid to its melodic and rhythmic aspects.

(1960)

Andy Gibson died 10 February, 1961.

FRED NORMAN

TROMBONE AND ARRANGER

"My mother played piano and organ in what I guess you'd call a Holy Rollers' church back in Leesburg, Florida, where I was born in 1910. Music stuck with me as I grew up through elementary and high school. Then they sent me away to a semi-private high school of the American Missionary Association. I started to learn about musical instruments there and to play in the band. The *writing* of the music, and how they got it to sound good, always fascinated me, and I began to probe into it.

"I had learned how to pick a little bit at the piano—chords and things —but I didn't get any formal training until I got into this band and took up the trombone in 1927. The bandmaster taught us how to read, and all that kind of stuff. It was a marching band, and we used to tour the state to raise money for the school. We got to be pretty good for that era, although the famous band that came out of the South was the Jenkins Orphanage Band. They were all kids in it, all black, all playing brass instruments, and they were swinging like crazy then. Everybody loved to hear them, and they had a guy on trombone called Briscoe who used to break it up. I suppose he turned professional, but I never did hear of him again.

"The first job where I got paid anything was with Bubber Applewhite and His Florida Troubadours in 1927. E.V. Perry, the trumpet player, was in that band, and he really taught me how to count time right in a dance band. We played dances through the state and had a lot of experiences, but it didn't last long. Applewhite was an older man and we were just a bunch of kids, but collegiate bands were popular then. The best one in that section was from Atlanta University. Alonzo Ross had another band I remember. Edmond Hall was in it and they came out of Miami.

"In the summer, some of the school-teachers would come north, and they would sort of sponsor any of us kids who wanted to go, and keep an eye on us for our parents. That was how I came to go to Washington, and I finished high school there at Dunbar. I had to take several different jobs, and at one time I was a bus boy. When I got to my first year in college at Howard, there was another good instructor in the music department, and I had more valuable, formal training from him.

"I got to hear bands like Claude Hopkins's, Duke Ellington's, Benny Carter's and Fletcher Henderson's in Washington. Other bands came out of the South like Johnson's Happy Pals, the Hardy Brothers, and Hartley Toots, and they played almost nothing but one-nighters. But they all came through, and I used to hang in those ballrooms and backstage at the Howard Theatre. Then I got to play well enough to join Duke Eglin first, and Booker Coleman's Bellhops a little later. Coleman was a great pianist in those days, and Tyree Glenn followed me in his band. Jimmy Mundy was around Washington then, before he got his break with Earl Hines. There was a good college band on the campus, and altogether musical activity was very good in the city.

"During the period when I began to play pretty well, I got the quirk of writing. I'd never had any training in arranging, and there weren't many books available then, so I used to go to the Library of Congress and sit and study the books on music they had there. The librarian got to know me so well, he would let me take books out, and that wasn't supposed to be —ever! But I was determined to learn how to get at this thing!

"When Fletcher Henderson came through, I'd be there with my little arrangements. One of the first times I saw Smack (Henderson) was in the Lincoln Colonnades in about 1930. He had Claude Jones, Russell Smith, Bobby Stark, Coleman Hawkins and Kaiser Marshall in the band, and John Kirby had just joined him. I remember bringing them a thing called *Goofer Dust Rag*. What a title! And, you know, the guys played it! 'Let's see what you've got,' they said, and then they just ran through it like glue. There was nothing in it really, but Hawkins said, 'Man, keep on trying. You'll make it.' They weren't so much older than me, but they'd had a lot more experience.

"The black bands in those days used to play for white audiences as well as black. Even when I was in the Applewhite band in Florida, we played a lot of white parties. In fact, they wanted the 'Negro music.' Bands like Johnson's Happy Pals, which toured through the South, used to play all the big resorts in the Carolinas.

"When the bands hit Washington, it would be either to play at the Howard Theatre for a week or to do a one-nighter in the Lincoln Colonnades. That was a ballroom in the basement of the Lincoln Theatre, a movie theatre on U Street. Later on, there was a ballroom in a big new building, the Masonic Hall. When Cab Calloway played there, I was playing in a band organized for his brother, Elmer Calloway. Elmer didn't play anything, but the promotor wanted to capitalize on the name. It was a good band based in Washington, although some of the musicians were imported from Baltimore. None of them was well known, but one of the trumpet players is big in the Latin field in New York now.

"We played in the Prudhomme Club in the black section of Washington, around 11th on U Street. A lot of white people came from downtown, and the idea was to have like a Cotton Club in Washington. We were there a couple of seasons, and that's where I first started to make arrangements I felt were pretty good. I got to the point where I didn't have to use a piano, and that was amazing to me. I'll never forget how I went home one night right after work, worked all day on *Penthouse Serenade,* and brought it into the band that night. As they played it, I put my horn down and listened. There were no mistakes in it, and I had done it all without a piano! Oh, yes, I was amazed!

"Elmer Calloway's band went to New York to play in a band contest at the Savoy. On the way, we got out of the bus and were kidding around when a car hit Elmer. So we had to go on and do the date without him. Luckily, Cab Calloway was in the Cotton Club, right down the street from the Savoy, and he brought his bass player and came and fronted our band. We went over great, and then went back to Washington.

"When the band broke up, I came back to New York with a drummer named Percy Johnson. He was an older man who played drums standing up. We drove up to New York in his car to the band contest at the Savoy the following year. Tommy Ladnier, the trumpet player, was a big friend of Percy's. They'd been to Europe together in Sam Wooding's band. Tommy was a regular, good guy, and a good musician. I think he was with Fletcher Henderson then. Anyway, after getting to New York, I played gigs in dancing schools and kept on writing.

"When Claude Hopkins played at the Howard, I always used to bring him my little arrangements. His guitarist, Joe Jones, was like a straw boss, and he took some of my things to New York and put them on the air. I remember that *Ain't Gonna Give Nobody None of My Jelly Roll* was a pretty good one. Then they would send me a little money. And once, when they came through, they had only one trombone—Ferdinand Arbello. They had no second parts, but I wanted to get in that band so bad, and they took me one night. I couldn't fake well enough. That was a strong band! Claude said, 'Keep writing, you know, and keep on your horn. When we add another trombone, you might be in.'

"I used to write an arrangement every week for them when I got to New York, and when they went out on tour, they put on a second trombone and took me. I had to write the parts, of course, and learn the book. Claude Hopkins has been a friend ever since, one of my best friends, right on down the years.

"I think the office that booked him then was Rockwell O'Keefe. They booked many other bands, black and white, and it seemed that the office was supplying them with arrangements written by specially hired arrangers. They needed someone to sit in an office and grind out the scores. They offered me the job, but I turned it down, because I wanted to go on the road and play. I often wonder about that, about what different direction my life might have taken.

"Somebody else who encouraged me in Washington was Benny Carter. He'd look at what I had written and say, 'Well, you have to keep on trying. If you ever come to New York, just let me know if there's anything I can do to help you.' I remember him bringing his advanced arrangements to Claude Hopkins when we were playing in Roseland. We had a little trouble with them! He was always 'way ahead, 'way out front with his ideas. Of course, Don Redman had set standards, first with Fletcher Henderson, then with McKinney's Cotton Pickers. The guys were so steeped in the Redman tradition when Benny went out to Detroit to join McKinney's band that they kept saying, 'I don't know. Don didn't do it that way!' But Benny got his thing going. There was another guy in that band who was fantastic and never got much credit—John Nesbitt. I knew him, and I have a feeling Don and Benny both learned a lot from him. He was a trumpet player, a great, wonderful guy, but too modest.

"Claude Hopkins was known for his dance band, and he could really turn people on in the ballroom. He didn't have great, flashy arrangements, but everything was soft, cool and swinging. There were good men in his band, and Pete Jacobs, the drummer, was perfect for it. In the reed section, he had Edmond Hall and Gene Johnson, and Bobby Sands was a very good tenor player. On trumpet he had Ovie Alston, Sylvester Lewis and Albert Snaer. Leo 'Snub' Mosley worked for us for a long time, and he was a hell of a trombone player. We picked him up in Cleveland, Ohio, and we played the Regal in Chicago with him right away. He was fantastic, and we used to feature him on his slide saxophone as the Man with the Funny Horn. He really had a lot to offer, and when he came out of that Alphonso Trent's band, I remember asking, 'Where has this guy been all these years?'

"We didn't have much luck with records. *Mush Mouth,* I think, was Jimmy Mundy's arrangement, and *Mad Moments* was Claude's. He didn't write much then, but mostly things like *Canadian Capers* and *Three Little Words* that featured his piano. A lot of things were head arrangements, like that *Washington Squabble,* which we used in a movie with Nancy Carroll. *King Porter Stomp* and *Church Street Sobbing Blues* were mine. Albert Snaer, from New Orleans, wrote *Zozoi,* and I did the arrangement.

"The Hopkins band was a consistent success through most of the '30s. We used to play in Roseland in New York, and then hit the road in the summer. We'd go up through New England, into the Chicago section, and then down to Kansas City, but never much further west than that. The only time the band went to the Deep South was when I left it—in Richmond, Virginia—and then they went on into Florida.

"When we went into the Cotton Club, there was a big change in personnel, because we thought we had to have better musicians. At different times, we had Hilton Jefferson on first alto, and Russell Smith from Fletcher Henderson's band on lead trumpet. Henry Wells and I were the trombones. Joe Thomas, Jabbo Smith and Vic Dickenson came in for a time, and Chauncey Haughton was there after Ed Hall left.

"I was the arranger and a section man in the band, not a soloist, although I used to take a solo on *Church Street Sobbing Blues.* To fill out the program, I did one or two vocal things, like an act, when we were playing theatres. My biggest one was *The Preacher and the Bear,* an imitation of Bert Williams' routine. It was issued on an album in Europe (Polydor 423269), which also has me doing *Lazy Bones* in the same vein. But most of the singing was done by Orlando Robeson and Ovie Alston. After Orlando left, we had Baby White as vocalist.

"I had got sick when I left Claude in 1938, but I had already decided to leave, because the band was continually on the road. Besides arranging for the band, I had been doing some ghost writing for other arrangers who were so busy they couldn't handle it all. The band business was beginning to go down then. You'd go out on a few dates, and the expenses were eating up the salary. Claude couldn't go back into Roseland—I believe he had broken with them—and the Cotton Club had folded.

"I stopped playing completely, and I wasn't really sorry. I wasn't any great shakes as an instrumentalist. I could have made it, I suppose, by joining other bands, but I wanted to write, and now I began writing like crazy. It was always my big aim. I think it was the same with Andy Gibson, a trumpet player originally, who wrote so many fine things for Charlie Barnet and other bands. And also with Buster Harding, a fantastic writer, who worked as a pianist, and then as a free-lance arranger.

L. to R.: Fred Norman, Floyd "Stump" Brady, Vic Dickenson.

Claude Hopkins's band. L. to R.: front, Abie Baker, Gene Johnson, Shirley Clay, Jabbo Smith, Vic Dickenson, Baby White (on piano), Ben Smith, Joe Jones; back, Bobby Sands, Chauncey Haughton, Fred Norman, Lincoln Mills, Pete Jacobs. Hopkins at the keyboard.

"The first thing I wrote now was for Benny Goodman—*Smoke House*. The most successful thing to earn me money through the years was *Boulder Buff* for Glenn Miller. He had gone to college in Boulder, Colorado, and the football team there was called the Buffs. Some others I wrote for Miller were not recorded. I did some more for Benny Goodman when he went in the Waldorf the first time, before Fletcher Henderson began to write for him all the time. I was writing for Teddy Powell's band then, and Benny came in the Famous Door one night when they were working there. 'Who wrote that *Charleston?*' he asked. They told him and he sent for me. Wowee! I was very excited, for he was 'King' at that time.

"After that I went into commercial radio. Al Goodman had what they called the Million Dollar Band on NBC—something like forty guys—and he conducted for Gladys Swarthout, James Melton, and people like that. Every week they had a different guest star. Whenever the guest was black, like Fats Waller or Duke, I would be assigned to do their shots. I had to go up to Duke's apartment to take down his routine, but all he said was, 'Go ahead and fix it. Put yourself in there.' He was coming in alone, just as Fats did, and I had to write the backgrounds for their solos.

"I learned about string writing when Dave Rubinoff was big on Eddie Cantor's program. He had heard some of the things I had done for Claude Hopkins, and he was getting ready to organize a jazz band. He sent for me and Horace Henderson, and he had some of his staff writers write for it, too. I guess he wanted to get some of that 'Negro' feeling in his music! He liked what I did, and one day he said, 'I'm going to give you a shot at my radio program.'

"That scared me to death, until he took me to his office and let me study scores by other arrangers. When you're new to writing for strings, you've got to learn about the character of the instruments, and what they're capable of, or the arrangement doesn't come off. I learned about the *natural* ratio, as you would hear them on the concert stage without any amplification. I already knew that if I was going to make a career as an arranger I had to go into other areas than those I had come up in. Years later, when I went to Mercury, they didn't have anyone to write for strings, and Clyde Otis asked me, 'How do you write for these things so that they will *sound?*' I told him what I considered the correct ratio in writing for a small group, about the possibilities of double stops, and how far you could go. That had something to do with my getting a job there!

"In 1944, I opened my own office. I had really gone commercial by then, and I had been on staff at CBS. When Sy Oliver went into the service, I got a call from Tommy Dorsey as arranger. I was with him about a year, and made two trips out to the Coast with him. Hugo Winterhalter was also with him, and he and I worked together when Tommy did a movie with Esther Williams and Van Johnson. Nelson Riddle was in the band, playing trombone and also writing.

"From Tommy, I went to Charlie Spivak, and after that I didn't join any more bands. I'd been working for Raymond Scott, too, when he had his experimental jazz band, but now—in the late '40s—I began working right across the board for record companies, mostly with singers. I was with M-G-M while Frank Walker was there, and I did records with Leslie Uggams, Diahann Carroll and Billy Eckstine. Then in 1958 I got into Mercury, where Clyde Otis was director, and I did some things with Dinah Washington and Brook Benton. When Dinah went to Roulette, I went, too. Mercury had been so hot, and everything they did seemed to be a hit, but now everybody cut out and they lost Dinah, Sarah Vaughan and Brook Benton.

"Dinah Washington was fantastic, the greatest person I've ever worked for. She amazed me at one of our first sessions by making a number in one take. She didn't want to go back and do it again. 'That's it!' she said. 'I know.' Another time, when we were making that album, *Back to the Blues,* she was singing that song, *You've Been a Good Old Wagon.* Oh, she was going, singing like crazy, and it was getting so long. 'Jeez,' I said to myself, 'There's got to be an end!' And I cut the band.

" 'What the . . . ?' she shouted, exploding.

"The final version was five minutes long anyway.

"Another time, the Roulette people had scheduled a date for her to record in Los Angeles, but they hadn't decided on any of the material. So Henry Glover and I flew out to see what she wanted to do. She was working in Las Vegas and Henry called her from the airport.

" 'Dinah, we're in Los Angeles.'

" 'What the hell you doing in Los Angeles? I'm in Las Vegas!'

"So we went to Vegas, had a conference, and decided on the tunes. I had to write all the music in about ten days. We got everything organized, and a band of fine L.A. musicians, but she jumped the date and we had to do the whole thing in New York! She was making so much money for the company then, and they were just recording all the time.

"She had her group with her when we were out there another time, and they recorded just as though they were in a club. They put the tape on and just let it roll. I wish I could remember the names of the fellows on that date, but the company never released it.

"A lot of people thought she was a tough customer, but I never found her so. I remember going to Detroit when she was married to the football player. We had a record date coming up and we had to discuss the music, but she had a restaurant then, and she'd spend days in it, supervising, and handling the cash register. She wasn't thinking about music at all! I was staying at her house, and I tried to prevail upon her: 'Now when are we going to sit down and work out the sound you want?'

" 'Oh, don't worry about that,' she said. 'You go on back to New York, and I'll pick the tunes.'

"She made the date, and my next project was to fix arrangements for a big band for a concert she was planning in Chicago. But she died before it could happen.'

"Another singer who really surprised me was Sarah Vaughan. I had done the arrangements for one of her dates, and Clyde Otis was the a. and r. man. There was one tune she didn't like the changes in, so she sat down at the piano and played it just the way she wanted it, and it was great. She was another who would make a number in one take if she wanted to.

"How do I hear the bands today? In the early days with Claude Hopkins, we had only three saxes and the music moved much more. To me, Stan Kenton's music doesn't move and doesn't swing. Well, Basie, he still swings and always has. I caught a record by Buddy Rich on the air the other day, and there was so much happening I couldn't hear the theme. The arrangers went so far out, there was nothing the people could put their feet down to. I think that partly explains the acceptance of rock 'n' roll and the heavy beat. Maybe some of it was interesting, but most of it was old-timey to me. What would happen, I wonder, if *Blood, Sweat and Tears,* for example, could add a few instruments? The kids hear old things now and think they're good. They are good, too. They could really go for something like boogie woogie. The reason they like ragtime is because it's so percussive. I wish it were possible, but I don't see big bands coming back. People don't want to dance. They don't want to get out on the floor. 'What's a ballroom?' they ask."

(1971)

HOWARD JOHNSON

ALTO SAXOPHONE

"My father played piccolo in a Knights of Pythias band, and he had a bunch of instruments around the home—banjos, tipples, mandolins. All us kids used to pick on those things. There were twelve of us, but to my recollection only eight survived.

"My older brother, Walter Johnson, was quite famous up in Boston, where I was born. He played piano and did all the society work. He went to Chicago in 1925 or 1926, and played in the Vendome Theatre. They liked him because he could read so well, and they had a lot of different shows to play there. Earl Hines, who was much younger, replaced him later.

"Walter was about twenty years older than me, and he left home when I was in high school and just beginning to play—fife, in a fife-and-drum corps. A lady used to teach the kids how to play, and we'd march up and down the street.

"I got my first saxophone from another brother, Bobby Johnson, who was playing banjo professionally. When he started making some money, he bought himself an alto saxophone, but he couldn't get the knack of it. He was eight years older than me, and he used to practice about once a week and then lay it aside. I used to sneak it out sometimes when he was away. One day he came home and saw me playing it, and I was frightened. I thought my big brother was going to bawl me out, but he didn't.

" 'Keep it,' he said. 'Take it whenever you want.'

"I discovered the basic fingering was just like the fife, so I could find what I wanted and play a song on it. He had had trouble breathing into it, but I had the natural breathing, and I was entranced by the sound of it. When he left Boston, he left the saxophone behind, and it became my instrument. I had no professional tuition, no particular teacher, no formal teaching, but I got books and studied. Jerome (Don) Pasquall was going to the New England Conservatory at the time, and he used to help me. There were several of us just beginning down there—Johnny Hodges, Buster Toliver, and George Matthews, who played violin as well as saxophone, and later worked with Noble Sissle. We'd ask Don questions. Charlie Holmes and Harry Carney came up a little later. When you're young, it makes a lot of difference if you are a year or two older.

"My main influence on alto saxophone was a fellow named Brownie, who used to play with George Tynes. Tynes had a big band that played all the dances in Boston. Brownie was the hottest thing around, and we all used to marvel at his playing—Hodges, Carney, all of us. He was a big, husky black fellow, but I can't think of his full name. He worked at the union in New York for a time, too.

"Sidney Bechet came to Boston in a show. Now when a show comes to a small town, you know, *everybody* goes to see it, and when we were exposed to Bechet he became our idol, especially Johnny Hodges's. He was crazy about Bechet, and that was where much of his style came from. Bechet's execution was impressive in those days, and he also had more soul on saxophone than anyone. When, during the '30s, people said his style and broad vibrato were old-fashioned, it may have been because what Johnny had since done with the style made Bechet's sound poor in comparison. But Bechet was a *great* influence.

"I had been playing saxophone a few months before Johnny, but I didn't know him well, although he lived just around the corner from me. We went to different schools, and I knew him by sight. He had a couple of young friends—Joe James, whose brother played saxophone, and 'Apple' Diggs, whose brother was a drummer. I knew Little Apple, and he came to me one day and said Johnny Hodges wanted to see me.

" 'What about?'

" 'Come on around. He said something about a saxophone.'

" 'He's got a saxophone?'

" 'Yeah, he wants you to look at it.'

"So I went around to his house on Hammond Street, and he had this little turned-up soprano, one of those shaped like an alto. I played some scales on it, and that was what he wanted to know. And that was the extent of my contact with him at that time.

"Johnny picked up very fast. He was a couple of years older than me, and in six months he was playing for Bechet. He was into the big world, but I was still in the little world. I could read, but he never bothered then. He used to hang out nights, while I was more or less a home boy. He was playing up there with a pianist named Dan Carey, a fine player who looked like Fats Waller. He played in all weird keys to fit anything, and Johnny's experience playing in those keys gave him a lot of schooling and experience. And Johnny was very creative in his style.

"When I was in my last grade in high school, my mother wanted me to finish, but I got a couple of gigs. After I got through playing them, it was hard for me to go to school next day! As a matter of fact, I lost interest in school. All I wanted to do was practice. Then Joe Steele, the pianist, came back to Boston on a vacation.

"He'd been playing *Rhapsody in Blue* in a show called *Rhapsody in Black*. They couldn't find anybody in New York to play it, but up in Boston most of the fellows could read very well. I don't know why that was, or why it was easier to get tuition. It must have been the way we were oriented. A lot of musicians went to the New England Conservatory, and there was no race problem there at that time. Everybody used to study and practice reading. It was all we had to do! I don't know why fellows from other parts didn't learn to read so well, unless they had more natural talent and just started blowing. We'd buy sheet music and learn how to transpose. I could play off a violin part before I ever saw an alto saxophone part. The trumpet players who were around, like Wendell Culley, did the same. So when it came to playing from regular parts, we already knew how to transpose.

"When Joe Steele's show closed, he had a chance to take a band into the Bamboo Inn at 138th Street in New York. (It's had a number of different names, and it's now the Dawn Casino.) He asked me if I wanted to come over. I had made up my mind to go to New York anyway, because Johnny Hodges, Harry Carney and Charlie Holmes had already left, but by the time I got there a month later the job had fallen through, and Joe Steele was with somebody else.

"I did a few dates with Freddy White, his brother Carl, and some fellows from the Clef Club on Long Island. I was lucky to get with them, because they were getting top money—about forty dollars when the figure was between twelve and fifteen in big bands. But I didn't like their kind of music. It was too dull, and I wanted to get with a swinging band.

"About this time, in 1928, Benny Carter had been out on the road with Horace Henderson's band, and Horace quit as it came back into New York. Benny took it over, and because he was going to front the band, he wanted someone to play the first alto chair. Somebody told him about me, that I could read, and by then he was already writing arrangements. I stayed with him about six months, and we went into the Arcadia Ballroom. We didn't have too much work, but we had a lot of fun rehearsing. In those days the rehearsing went on longer than the actual jobs. We would rehearse for five or six weeks and the job would last two or three. That's the way it was.

"I wasn't making much money, but I enjoyed being with that group. Benny was marvelous even then. He played the lead when he picked up

At Jackie Robinson's estate in Connecticut, June 23, 1963. Front row: Wendell Marshall, Seldon Powell, Zoot Sims, Howard Johnson, Jerone Richardson. In background: Herbie Lovelle, drums; Quentin Jackson, Britt Woodman, trombones; Clark Terry, Taft Jordan, trumpets.

the saxophone, but most of the time I played it. And it was great experience. Benny's band never caught on too well. We played beautiful music, and the musicians loved it, but it didn't seem to move the public enough, so the spots we could play were limited. At that time they wanted black musicians to 'get hot', and nearly all the bands had gimmicks of one kind or another. They were entertainers more than musicians, and we were not entertainers. That's why, I guess, the band didn't catch on.

"Then the chance of a steady job came up when Billy Cato was taking a band into one of those ten-cents-a-dance places, the Broadway Danceland at about 53rd Street. I was with him about two years, and later we went to the Rose Danceland on 125th Street. Harold Blanchard was on alto and Johnny Russell on tenor when we started, and both of them played violin. I still had a soprano saxophone then, and we got some beautiful blends. I liked the soprano very much, and used it quite a lot, but when it was stolen I never got another, and stayed with the alto. When we were at the Rose, we had Bobby Cheek on trumpet, but then a variety show came to the Apollo, and Johnny 'Bugs' was in it—Johnny 'Bugs' Hamilton, who later played with Fats Waller. After they got through, he came to our place once or twice and asked if he could sit in with us. He played so good then, very vibrantly, high and everything—great. We were going into the Savoy, so he joined us. Some people had the wrong idea about him. He was never a real alcoholic—just wild. Before he passed, he was very straight.

"Joe Britton, the trombone player, was in that band, too, and Cato himself also played trombone. Clarence Johnson was on piano, and William McIlvaine (he's a bartender now) on drums. Lee Blair played guitar and did arrangements. I wrote a couple, too. We mostly used stocks, and we'd take them and change them around, jump from one part to another, and make a 'head' of the stock. It was a good band, and we used to have nice effects with the fellows playing their violins. Besides his tenor, Johnny Russell also played nice clarinet. I played clarinet, too, but only as a double.

"After Cato, I had a brief association with James P. Johnson. He had the band in a show Miller and Lyles were trying to revive—the old group that had had the success with *Shuffle Along*. I forget the name of this one, but it was a flop, ran a week on Broadway some place.

"Then I worked with Elmer Snowden at Smalls's for a good run. He had a real splendid band then. After that, in 1932, I went with Benny Carter again, and was with him until I went into the Savoy with Teddy Hill in '34. Benny had been trying to get that job at the Savoy, but something fell through, so Chu Berry and I left and went in there with Teddy.

"I thought Teddy's was a very good band, but somehow we never seemed to get much of a reputation. I've noticed when people write about the Savoy they often don't mention Teddy Hill's band at all. It's a funny thing, because we were there so long, till 1940, and there were always good musicians in the band, like Roy Eldridge, Dicky Wells, Bill Coleman, Frank Newton, Cecil Scott, Bob Carroll and Chu Berry. I was playing lead all the time, and I was the alto soloist. Chu and I were featured on *Deep Forest,* Earl Hines's theme. We had our own arrangement on it, and we got to be known for that.

"The fellows in the band considered Teddy a good business man, because he kept us working. He was a good-looking fellow, and he used to get up there and wave a long stick. I think some people resented that. He had played tenor saxophone with Luis Russell until Greely Walton took his place. Then he got an alto and played it in this band, but after a while he put it down and just waved the stick.

"Around 1937 Dizzy Gillespie came to New York and put in his card for transfer down at the union. At that time I think you had to wait about three months after you asked for a transfer. You could play gigs while you waited, but you couldn't take a steady engagement. Dizzy came to the Savoy and sat in once or twice about the time we were getting ready to go to Europe. Frank Newton and Cecil Scott didn't want to go, I think because they were not satisfied with the money. So Teddy got Dizzy, who was glad to go, because he could play out of town. He was playing rather like Roy Eldridge then, but very fast, and with something of his own. Europe was just great, and I was on one of those fine sessions with Dicky Wells while we were in Paris.

"No, Teddy Hill never toured down South, although we opened up the Harlem Square in Miami and stayed there three months in, I think, 1936. This was after we had been in Connie's Inn on 131st Street. We also used to go on the theatre tour that they called 'round the world'—to the Earle in Philadelphia, the Royal in Baltimore, the Howard in Washington, and then back to the Apollo in Harlem.

"The band broke up after the World's Fair in 1940, and then I went to the Renaissance with Vernon Andrade's band for the better part of that year and all of the next. After that I worked with Claude Hopkins. It was another one of those things where we rehearsed for longer than the engagement. It's amazing now to stop and think of all those groups I spent more time rehearsing with than in actual playing. It broke up a lot of families in those days, too. I was a bachelor, and it was much harder for fellows who had to make money for wives and children.

"I did quite a bit of work as an arranger—all sorts of things, but mostly reproducing stuff somebody else had done for other big bands, and few originals. That's something I regret, because it would have been just as easy to compose something of my own. A lot of the 'originals' of the Swing Era were just heads a whole group had made up. Somebody would be brash enough to put his name on the 'composition' and copyright it. I didn't have that kind of ingenuity. *Everybody* was playing *Christopher Columbus,* for example, and it was like common property then.

"During the '30s, I got my nickname—'Swan.' Everybody seemed to have a nickname in those days. I guess I was called that because I had a long neck. Although I always had a good appetite, I stayed thin, and they used to call me 'Crane' and 'Pelican', too.

"I was in the Navy from 1942 until 27 December, 1945, in a navy band, and we were fortunate enough to be stationed down at Pier 92 in the heart of Manhattan. We played all the marches, and we had a swing band to entertain the fellows. We were on a couple of ships they had there till May, 1945. Then there was a violent upheaval and all of us who hadn't done duty overseas were shipped out to Guam, where we stayed for the last six months of the war.

"When I came back, I joined Harry Dial down at Smalls's for about a year. Hilton Jefferson had been there before me, and Harry was looking for somebody. I was really enjoying myself at that stage. I had come out of the service with a lot of money and I was cabareting. Smalls's was a cabaret anyway, and that was the life I loved.

"One night, my night off, I went up to the place that used to be the Cotton Club. I think they had renamed it the Club Sudan. Billy Eckstine had the band there and Dizzy Gillespie was sitting in. He came over to my table, and when he got ready to go back, he said, 'If you have time, come on down tomorrow.' He was putting a big band of his own together.

"The next morning, I was kind of hung over from the night before, and I forgot all about it, but Dizzy called me and had Walter Fuller come by and get me. So then I was with Dizzy from 1946 to 1948, and it was a rewarding experience, because I was in that *new* group, playing stuff that was very interesting and exciting.* I was playing first chair alto, playing what somebody had written, and I more or less had to get in the spirit of what they were doing. Sonny Stitt had the alto solos at first, and John Brown took them after he left. We played dances, theatres and everything, and I think we went on the road in a package with Ella Fitzgerald.

---

*Recordings by this band, as well as by Teddy Hill's, can be heard in an album entitled *Dizzy Gillespie,* RCA LPV-530. Others by Gillespie's band are in *The Be-Bop Era,* RCA LPV-519.

"What was the reaction of dancers to our music? Well, in those days there was a kind of hiatus or something in dancing. For two or three years people weren't dancing. They'd still turn out, listen, stand around and applaud, and try to pretend they dug it. I think they appreciated the artistry of fellows like Charlie Parker and Dizzy, because marvelous technique was involved. But the music wasn't really danceable. Be-bop didn't have any beat, or anything to make people want to try to dance to it. There was very little dancing until Fats Domino brought back the beat again.

"After Dizzy, I went to the Hartnett School of Music on the G.I. Bill and stayed there for about three years. I completed the Schillinger course. Aside from the history part, I did not get too much from it. If you know conventional harmony, you don't need a lot of that kind of schooling. It's a mathematical approach to music, and very good, but if you mix the two you find there is a little conflict. Since the government was paying for it, I figured I'd learn it. Meanwhile, I was just gigging, until I went to Alaska in 1953.

"A singer and entertainer named Tommy Roberts called me. His wife played good piano, and I had rehearsed with them and a drummer, but when the time came to go to Alaska, I didn't want to go, so they took another saxophone player. They were doing very well in Anchorage until the saxophone player got sick, and then they wanted me to come right away. I wasn't doing anything, so when they sent the fare and money in advance, I flew up there and stayed four months. From Anchorage, we went to Fairbanks, where it was very, very cold—fifty-three degrees below. You've never seen such weather! You'd look out the window and see this mist, like a cloud. There was no other way I would ever have got up there, but now I have been in every state in the Union.

"Ever since then I have been gigging around New York. In 1956, I started working a day job in the mail room of the Great American Insurance Company. Charlie Holmes got that for me. Later on I went with Merrill, Lynch. Without a day job, there just wouldn't have been enough work. And as I look back, there never was enough work, not even in what we call 'the good old days'. Some musicians have studio jobs of one kind or another today, and they're making very good money, but for every one who is doing well there are ten or twenty who are not.

"I got a chance to play in a good big band again in 1972, when a group of his contemporaries was organized for Benny Carter to front in the Newport Jazz Festival in New York. We didn't have much time to rehearse, but people seemed to like the band, and it was a happy reunion for all the fellows in it. I have been invited to play in the 1973 festival, too."

(1973)

CHARLIE HOLMES

ALTO SAXOPHONE

"I had an older brother who used to go to dances, and one night he came home talking about some kid playing saxophone.

" 'Oh, this kid can play,' he said.

" 'Yeah?' I said. 'Who is he?'

" 'Johnny Hodges.'

"I was about ten then, and I'd never heard of a saxophone, but Johnny's name just spread all over Boston. When I eventually heard him at another dance, I was amazed. I sat right up in front of the hall all night long, like he was God. That was 'way back, when he was nothing but a kid, about thirteen years old, but he was blowing that saxophone *then* as well as he played it all down through the years. I've never known anybody in my life just pick up an instrument and play it the way he did. I mean he was playing it—he wasn't just playing *with* it! And he didn't know a note as big as a house, but he had a hell of an ear. After dances, we'd go to them little house-rent parties, where they'd have somebody playing the piano in F sharp or B natural. That's all they'd play, on all the black notes, you know. And Johnny would take his horn out, without knowing about the keys, and just blow in any key.

"There was some music in his family, but they were not schooled musicians. He was just a natural musician, and I recognized that in him the first time I heard him. I thought he was the greatest thing in the world. Man, I admired him! Every time he played a dance, I would be there. He's always been my idol.

"There's a funny story about when he was starting out. He was always very cocky, and he sent word around to Howard Johnson that he wanted to show him something on the saxophone. The Johnsons lived around the corner from him on Shumant Avenue, and everybody in the family was a trained musician. Bobby Johnson, who played guitar and banjorine, had bought a saxophone, but he didn't work on it, and he gave it to Howard, who did. Now Johnny, who didn't know A from B on the saxophone, *he* wants to show Howard something. Of course, he wanted Howard to show him something, and Howard obliged.

249

"After hearing Johnny, I wanted a saxophone in the worst way, but my daddy wasn't *thinking* about buying me one. He'd paid a lot of money for a piano, and it just stood there, for nobody in the family played it. Back in those days, he wasn't making a big salary. He had a family of fourteen kids, and I wanted a saxophone! They cost about seventy-five dollars then, and that was a lot of money to throw away on top of that piano just standing there. But I just had to have a saxophone! That's all there was to it.

"A doctor around Boston, Dr. Holmes (no relation), got all the kids together for a brass band, and said he would furnish the instruments if they promised to stay with the band. Buster Toliver, a great musician, went to Dr. Holmes and got a clarinet. Harry Carney and I went together, and Harry got a clarinet, but he gave me an oboe.

" 'Oboe?' I said. 'What is that?'

" 'That's all we got left—an oboe and a flute.'

"I didn't want no flute! And I didn't know what an oboe was.

" 'Well, I want a saxophone,' I said.

" 'I'll tell you what,' he said, 'we'll give you the oboe and in a year's time, if you show any progress whatsoever, we'll get the saxophone.'

"That sounded good, and I took the oboe home, even though I didn't know how to put the thing together. I found a teacher and paid him three dollars for a half-hour lesson. I was real serious, and I studied this oboe. I tried to make it sound like a saxophone! I got in the regular school band, and when the year was up I went to Dr. Holmes.

" 'I played this oboe for a year. Now I want a saxophone.'

" 'You know, Charlie,' he said, 'you've made so much progress on the oboe, we think we'll keep you on that.'

"I have never been hurt so much in all my life. I was ready to pass out. I had concentrated, studied hard, trying to learn music, blowing the oboe and imagining I was playing saxophone.

" 'Well, if that's the way it's going to be,' I said, 'you take the oboe back. I'm through.'

"When I went into high school, some kid told the leader of the school symphony that I played oboe. They sent me to the principal's office and gave me a con job: 'We need you in the school orchestra, and it will help you with your studying.' So here I was with an oboe again, in the school symphony. For three years, doing my homework, this, that and the other, my marks were great. Beautiful marks, man! So in the summer of the third year my daddy decided to buy me a saxophone.

"It was a Thursday—I'll never forget—and I knew where kids used to have little dances, with a fellow playing piano. I walked in, took out my horn, and started playing. That's the way we used to do, the way Johnny

Hodges had done. Everybody was astonished. 'Gee,' they said. 'you sound just like Johnny.' Well, who else would I sound like?

"The first thing I knew, a man offered me a gig for five dollars the next Friday night. I could only play in a couple of keys, but this guy could only play in E flat and B flat himself. That was all right with me, because E flat was always easy. So we made this dance, and my name began getting around town, and different guys were putting their little bands together then. We were playing a dance over in Cambridge one night, when Johnny Hodges walked in. He didn't know me, but I knew him, and I was glad to see him. He was about three years older than me, and he said, 'All right, boy, get up from there!'

"To me, he was king, so all I said was, 'Here, play the horn!' and handed him mine. Man, he got to tooting on that horn, and when he got through I got up and played what I knew. I noticed that during the first number I played he turned around and gave me a look. Of course, I sounded just like him. We became good friends from then on—never any clashes or anything like that.

"Howard Johnson was on the same kick, but he got away from it. He can play anything. He can play that be-bop, and everything else. He even plays that West Indian music. You name it, he can play it. Sit him in the pit and he can read *fast*. He's a very good musician. He used to play lead, but he was never a leader and never aggressive. Anytime we were going on a gig together, he wouldn't play solos unless I told him to. You had to make him play solos. As a musician, he's in a class with Benny Carter. He has his funny ways, too, like anybody else. Like Johnny. The world took to Johnny, accepted him. He was arrogant in a way, but he was still a *quiet* person. He had what you would call self-reliance or something, and he always believed he was the best in the world. Maybe I shouldn't say that though.

"When I went to New York the first time, it was on a visit with Harry Carney—and here we are, still visiting, forty-three years later! I met Johnny again the first night. He was working at the Savoy ballroom with Chick Webb. 'When you get time,' he told me, 'you go to Smalls's Paradise and hear the greatest alto saxophone player in the world.'

" '*You* are the greatest,' I said.

" 'No, you go to Smalls's and hear the greatest. His name is Benny Carter.'

"I had never heard of Benny then, but he was working with Charlie Johnson. Harry Carney and I went down to Smalls's, like two farmers, you know. We walked up to the bandstand and we knew one of the fellows, the tenor player, Benny Waters.'

" 'Hi, Benny!' we said.

" 'Hi,' said all three saxophone players. Besides Benny Carter, the third one was Ben Whittet, who also played clarinet. Benny Waters introduced us to all the musicians, and we had a big time there that night, we two kids from Boston.

"But Benny Carter didn't play much and he didn't impress me, so I went back to Johnny Hodges and told him so.

" 'Yeah?' he said. 'That cat can play. He's the greatest.'

"Later on, he and Benny hooked up at a bar down on 129th Street, and I never heard such saxophone playing in my life. That's when I said, 'Benny's the king!' And with all Johnny's popularity and everything, and much as I admired him, Benny's still the king on saxophone to me. Of course, his style is different, but I don't know how to explain the difference.

"The next night after that, they had a South Sea Isles Ball up at the Savoy. It was a big affair and they were hiring another band to play for an hour intermission, and a violin player named Ellsworth Reynolds needed two saxophones for it. Somebody told him about the two fellows from Boston. The only thing was he needed an alto and a tenor, and both Harry and I played alto. I'd never touched a tenor in my life. In fact, I was very shy about playing, period. But Elmer Williams in Chick Webb's band said he'd lend me a tenor. So we got up there and made the gig. I thought it was terrible. What did I know about tenor? On top of that, it was a Buffet tenor and had some funny fingering on it, but what we did must have pleased somebody.

"Johnny took us around, and we went to a cutting contest, a saxophone players get-together at Mexico's. Greely Walton was playing tenor when we walked in, and after him Coleman Hawkins played. Nobody else would play tenor after Hawk, and I couldn't blame 'em. So Johnny took out his alto and gave it to Harry. 'Come on, show 'em what you can do!' He was schooling Harry, and Harry played, and sounded good. Then he said to Johnny, 'Make Charlie play.'

" 'Are you kidding?' I said. I was scared to death just being in New York. But they happened to play *Sweet Georgia Brown,* a number I knew and could swing, and after I got through swinging they were whooping and hollering in there.

" 'Here's a kid come here who can outswing Johnny Hodges,' said Chick Webb, and after that he was talking my name up all over New York City. As a result, I worked at the Lenox Club about two weeks, and then I went to work down at the Club Alabam on Broadway with Billy Fowler's band. That was big-time stuff at the Club Alabam, and I worked there till the place closed. I was in my last year at high school, but I didn't see no need in going back. I was seventeen and picking up more money than I ever dreamed of, because I had hardly worked professionally in Boston at all—just kid affairs.

"After Billy Fowler, I went to work in a Brooklyn nightclub six nights a week with a fellow named Cohen, a trumpet player with a small group, and no big names. Harry Carney and I were still rooming together, and I was traveling between Brooklyn and New York every night when he went with Duke Ellington. Then a fellow named Lew Henry offered me a job at the Savoy, and I asked Harry what he thought about that.

" 'Well, I tell you, Charlie,' he said, 'you stay in Brooklyn the rest of your life, and who will know about your being out there? You work in the Savoy, and somebody can see you.'

"So I went in the Savoy for three months with Lew Henry, and in that time my popularity with musicians grew a lot. I think it was the night after we closed at the Savoy that I was up at the Band Box when a call came for a saxophone at the Nest Club on 133rd Street. A little fellow named George Howe had the band, and Luis Russell was playing piano in it. I didn't know any of them, but we got to playing and it sounded good. They said the job was mine if I wanted it, and I thought that was beautiful, but one thing about it wasn't so good. We'd start playing about eleven o'clock at night and the sun would be high in the heavens when we came out of there. We didn't make much salary, but big-time gangsters would come in there after three in the morning, and we made quite a bit of money with tips.

"Johnny Hodges and I had both been rehearsing with Chick Webb's band, but Chick wasn't working much, although we did go up to New England with him for ten days. So then Johnny went into the Cotton Club with Duke, and after I had been in the Nest a week they fired George Howe and made Luis Russell the leader. I stuck with Russell from then on, and we had quite a few years together.

"We went in the Saratoga Club across from the Savoy on 140th Street. Caspar Holstein owned it, and it was a nice-sized room, but it didn't do too much business. We stayed there about two years and a half, and they were the happiest days of my life. Everybody was young, and none of us was married. It was a different type of music to me altogether. They were all from New Orleans—Luis, Pops Foster, Albert Nicholas, Red Allen, Paul Barbarin. They'd been playing that stuff for years, and it was born in them. We had a whole lot of heads, but a good bit of the music was written out, too. We'd get together, play it like it was written, and then somebody would set a riff, change it half-way through the chorus, and before you knew it we had got another tune.

"Johnny Hodges used to come down and sit in for me sometimes at the

Saratoga, and once, when his first wife was having a baby and he had to go to hospital, he asked me to do the broadcast for him from the Cotton Club. So I went up there, and sat in with the band, and on one number Duke turned to me and said, 'You got it!' So I played it. The next day I was walking down the street with Johnny and Don Kirkpatrick, the piano player in Chick Webb's band, who was married to Johnny's sister.

" 'Caught the program last night and you sounded very good,' Kirkpatrick said to Johnny.

" 'That wasn't me,' Johnny said. 'That was Charlie!'

"We got a big kick out of that.

"Luis Russell was the nicest guy in the world, the kindest, and very easy-going. But, you know, they say nice people don't get nowhere. When Louis Armstrong came from Chicago to work a two-day engagement at the Savoy, he had no band, nothing. We were working at the Savoy when they hired him as an attraction, and Luis Russell told Charlie Buchanan, who ran the place, that he knew all Louis' numbers. So they put Louis with Russell's band. Meanwhile, Russell had written out little things Pops (Armstrong) had been playing, so on the very first night Pops broke up the place. Naturally, he would. The next day, they had us down in the studio recording some of those old numbers with him. Russell's group knew those numbers, what they call Dixieland today, because they had been brought up on them and we were playing them all the time. We had also recorded with King Oliver. It was his date, but he didn't play on it, because he had no chops. Those were some of my first recordings.

"Later, of course, Louis Armstrong fronted the Russell band, and I stayed with it till 1940. They were still doing great when I left in Chicago to come back to New York. They were going out on one-nighters again, and I went in the opposite direction. Louis looked around, they told me, and asked, 'Where's Pickles?' That's what he used to call me—just a nickname.

"I had had enough of it. I didn't like working in that band then. It was okay when it was Russell's, but it had become very commercial, and there was always this one and that one telling you what to do. It was just a job —no satisfaction, no kicks. Well, you have to be careful what you say when it comes to naming people!

"I did a little short thing in New York with Bobby Burnett, the trumpet player. He had some money and wanted to be a bandleader. He could play, and he and Leonard Feather were working together, and he got a few engagements, but nothing happened. There were some trying days then until I went with Cootie Williams.

"I stayed with Cootie till 1945, and that was real kicks. I've never in all

Luis Russell's reeds: front, Albert Nicholas, Charlie Holmes; back, Pete Clarke, Bingie Madison.

my life played with such a bad band that sounded so good. There were
more people in there who couldn't read a note as big as a house, and they
had no more conception of music than the man in the moon, but they
could play, and they could swing, and it sounded good. They went up to
the Savoy and ran Duke Ellington out of there one night! That was Cootie's
greatest triumph. And Eddie Vinson tooted up there, tooted over Johnny
Hodges, and said, 'I am the king!'

"I was there before Eddie, but I never played any solos. When I went
in, I told Cootie I didn't want no solos, because I had got so sick of them
with Armstrong's band, which was a loud-playing band. They had me
sitting right in front of the drum, and I was damned near tone deaf sitting
there. Then having to jump up and run to play solos was too much.
Between Big Sid Catlett whaling that drum and the brass section—well,
Pops could top it all, and he liked everything loud. That's all right, but a
saxophone should sound like a saxophone.

"Cootie didn't care when I didn't want solos, because he had got this
boy from Texas, Eddie 'Cleanhead' Vinson, who could play solos and sing
the blues, too. He was the success of the band, definitely. I thought he was
the greatest blues singer in the world, but he was a nut. Any time a man
gets in a cab in Los Angeles, has it driven to 'Frisco, runs in the stage door,
tells the manager he's got a cab outside to be taken care of . . . That
manager went out, thinking he might have to pay sixty cents or a dollar,
and found he had a 450-mile bill to pay!

"Next, I went on a six-month U.S.O. tour of the Far East with Jesse
Stone. It was a great trip, but I wouldn't want to make another. They
briefed us, told us what we were going to go through, and we were
accorded the best of everything that they had. They told us we would eat
Spam until it came out of our ears, and we did that, too. I never had had
a desire to go to China and Asia. I wanted to go to Europe, but I just never
had an offer, and it's too late now.

"Back in New York in 1947, John Kirby came by my house, and asked
if I could open up with him the following Monday at the Brown Derby in
Washington. It was summertime, and I didn't have a gig, period.

" 'I don't see no reason why not,' I said.

" 'We hit at 8 o'clock,' he said.

" 'Ain't we having no rehearsal?'

" 'Ah . . . hit at 8 o'clock. Do you need any money to get down there?'

"We met in a hotel—John, Billy Kyle, Bill Beason, Jerry Blake and a
trumpet player we used to call Mino, who's dead now. We sat around and
then went and opened up on the job. I was scared. They had a big, old,

raggedy book that looked like they had been turning the music over with their feet. Both Jerry Blake and I were new, and the first number didn't sound too good. We played another, and when we did *Sunny Side of the Street* I stood up and played a little solo. The people applauded, and when we finished the set Kirby threw his arm around my neck and said, 'That was beautiful. You got a raise comin'. Come on, let's have a drink!' So he got a fifth of whiskey right there in the club for fifteen dollars, which he could have got at a liquor store next door for three. Jerry Blake wasn't drinking, so five of us drank up this fifth, pouring it out in water glasses. After the next set, when I'd played a solo on something else, the same thing happened. 'You got another raise comin',' he said, and he got another fifth. Every time we came off, he got a bottle of whiskey. When we did the last set, Mino went to stand up to play his solo, and I had to grab him to keep him from falling off the stand. I couldn't attempt to get up to play mine, because I was so drunk. That was my first night with Kirby!

"Come the next night, he asked if I wanted to draw any money. I didn't, but he insisted I draw something, and I said to give me ten dollars.

" 'What are you going to do with ten dollars?' he asked. 'Here, take a hundred!'

"Before that, any time I worked with a group I'd had to fight and struggle to get money. Now, by Thursday, I'd had my whole salary, and Kirby was still giving me money. If I'd worked for him long enough, I would have been rich. He was always great with his money, and he'd give it to his band until he ran short and was broke. Nothing was too good for his band, even when we were in Chicago and he had a suite at the Sherman Hotel—and another uptown in another hotel—and couldn't pay the rent.

"I remember when he called a rehearsal in Milwaukee. We were working behind a bar and living in a hotel upstairs. He called the rehearsal for two o'clock in the afternoon. They were so elated with the band that they hadn't taken the whiskey off the bar. So everybody got a glass, and ice, and poured himself a big drink. We sat around, drinking and talking, drinking and talking, and nobody took his horn out or anything. After a while, somebody said, 'I'm going upstairs to bed.' That was the end of the rehearsal! Another day, when the boss came in and found everybody with a glass in his hand, Kirby just looked at him and said, 'This is on *you.*'

"Billy Kyle was the main thing there at that time, the one who really made things interesting. Kirby was a nice person, but funny in his ways, really funny, and the most unusual man I ever worked for. He could be very biggety on the job, too. After we'd been laying off in Chicago, we

John Kirby's band. L. to R.: Charlie Holmes, Sidney Catlett, Charlie Shavers, Billy Kyle, John Kirby, Buster Bailey.

were booked into a hotel in St. Louis, and because the man wouldn't serve him a drink at the bar, he was going to pull the band out the first night.

" 'Now, wait a minute!' I said. 'We just got through laying off four weeks.'

"My biggest trouble all through the years has been that I am retiring. I always shy back. I haven't made a record since 1952, when I did the date for King with Al Sears. A lot of people thought it was Johnny Hodges playing, because it was his band. I never cared about making records when I was with Pops and different ones. I never had no trouble with it, but I never liked it. So I'd avoid it. See, I'm a funny type of person. I like to play where people are dancing. I was supposed to work at the Famous Door or one of those 52nd Street joints during the war. Red Allen was there, and they gave me a big introduction, and I was supposed to show up the following week as the attraction. It was the kind of place where the people come in, buy a drink, and just sit there digging you. You're on display, and when I'm standing up there for that sort of playing, I'm sort of tense. So I always steered away from that, and I didn't want to be a leader. I liked to play where people were dancing and not paying attention to you. Lately, as you know, everything is presentation in these bars and places. So far as recording is concerned, I've been working days, and the only playing I've done has been on club dates, Fridays, Saturdays and Sundays."*

(1970)

*In 1972, Charlie Holmes was persuaded by his friend Clyde Bernhardt to take his horn to a recording studio again. The entertaining results are available in Europe on an album entitled *Blues and Jazz from Harlem,* Saydisc 228.

BENNY GOODMAN

BANDLEADER [CLARINET]

"My interest in classical music has heightened a bit in the last six or seven years. I think that's shown in the work I've done. Last year, for instance, we gave a concert tour with a program that consisted first of jazz and then, in the second half, of classical music. This fall, I'll play quite a few concerts with symphony orchestras, and I'll also be doing the same kind of program as last year.

"Audiences in America hear so much music nowadays that they're sophisticated enough to accept a program like that, and some of the jazz being played now is more difficult to listen to than classical music. One of the remarks I've often heard is, "Well, *I* liked it. I don't know about anybody else." I think a lot of today's jazz fans like to hear some classical music, and we do this sort of thing as part of a series, so that they come to the concert knowing exactly what they're going to hear.

"If I can generalize, and I think one has to in this case, then I think all kinds of music—not only jazz—are going through an experimental phase. There are a lot of far-out pieces to play in classical music! Eventually, it will all tighten up and the best of what they're experimenting with will be used to make something altogether more concise. For instance, a classical composer, writing a piece that's thirty to forty minutes long with a lot of interpolations, may decide he can say it all in five or six minutes.

"Where the length of jazz improvisation is concerned, I think it's completely up to the leader or the performer. If the soloist plays seven or eight choruses and they're all interesting enough to stay, that's up to him. If the audience feels the same way about his 'editing'—good. Of course, there's no problem editing with tape. One of the first records where that principle was involved was in the Carnegie Hall package. I think the jam session was twice as long in the original. We decided, as I remember, that everybody had said what they had to say in the solos as left on the record. In the studio today, if it doesn't go right from this point, you pick it up from there and splice the tapes together. They're even doing that with symphonies. But on the three-minute records, if there was a mistake it had to be done over again.

"Much the same applies on the job as on the record. You can start editing right there, or in rehearsal you can say four choruses is enough, or fourteen. There is often an over-abundance in jazz improvisations, but the same goes for the *Mozart Clarinet Quintet.* There are repeats in all the movements, but you can get the gist of it without playing all those repeats. I think what we're trying to say is that there should be more editing in public appearances by jazz musicians, but it really is up to the individual. It's like a play with a lot of talking. If you can cut out some of the talk and get the point over with simple sentences instead of four paragraphs, then to my mind it's always better.

"At one time we were thinking of a dancing audience and arrangements were planned for the three-minute record. On some of them, you wanted to go further but couldn't. Then came the great release of tape and the long-playing record. A case in point was *Sing, Sing, Sing,* which we did many years ago. Even on the original twelve-inch record, which ran eight minutes, we were limited. We eventually extended it, but the kind of over-indulgence tape makes possible reflects, I think, on your in-person performances, too. It's not hard to do, you know, and it's very easy to get into the habit, and then to assume it's correct. There were some pieces like *Sing, Sing, Sing* that needed a certain amount of length to be effective, but there are far more that don't need it! I think I've over-indulged in this respect many times.

"When people were dancing, you couldn't play one piece for ten minutes. I don't know whether they would have left the floor, but you had to give them a variety of tempos and tunes. Usually, you'd play five or six numbers in a set and each one would be about three minutes. Some of those arrangements Mary Lou Williams wrote, for instance, you would want to play longer than three minutes, and the dancers would want you to, too. Since then, everything has become 'concert,' a listening thing.

"It's true there were all those big bands in the '30s, but in those days you had to wait for a record release. Compare that with the number of records now, and albums, not 78s. I suppose you might say there is a bigger audience sitting at home today, or tonight, but I wouldn't say that the clubs are not doing well. A lot of things enter into a club doing well or not doing well. Some people know how to run them and some do not. There are even a lot of dancehalls—and I think of many we played in years ago—doing well right now. The people on the periphery, who opened up just to cash in on a boom—they're not doing well. They really had nothing to offer.

"Regardless of what they say, a lot of bands have gone into the concert field, and they're trying to do something in the style of a time that doesn't exist anymore. If you wanted to book Heifetz or Rubinstein for fifty weeks,

where would they play? It could be done, but they'd have to play in a lot
of outlandish places, which is what many of the bands do now. Much of
the music that has entered the concert field is not being handled as concert
business, except at certain times, in the summer, at jazz festivals, and so
on. A lot of colleges have begun to book jazz attractions as well."

"Influences? When I was a kid, we used to dig up records in the record
shops. I remember the Isham Jones band, Paul Whiteman's, Ted Fiorito's
and Roger Wolfe Kahn's. Bix Beiderbecke, Red Nichols and Louis Armstrong were all making records. I became a professional pretty early, but
the clarinets I heard were Jimmie Noone, Leon Roppolo, Johnny Dodds
and Volly de Faut. I never heard Leon in person, but Volly used to play
with Muggsy Spanier at that time. When I was about eight, I used to like
Ted Lewis, and eventually I wound up playing clarinet for him. Jimmy
Dorsey did, too. Some of the bands used to come to the Trianon ballroom
and play promotions at big stores in Chicago. The Middle West was quite
hot for music in those days. There were plenty of nightclubs and a lot of
action. All of this was influential.

"I loved Jimmie Noone's clarinet playing. He was an excellent clarinet
player, period. I remember his *Four or Five Times, Sweet Lorraine* and
I Know That You Know. He played Albert system and so did I at the
beginning. I was about sixteen when I changed to Boehm. I think I'd have
to say that the Boehm system is superior, but what is strange about the
clarinet is how, with all the technical advancements, there were certain
areas where it retrogressed as compared with the Albert system. There
were things about the Albert that are still missing. The advancements and
ease of the Boehm produced certain difficulties—articulated notes and so
forth. Any clarinet player will understand this. Something was lost.

"There are no clarinet players anymore, are there? Actually, there are
more clarinet players than there've ever been, in school bands and orchestras, but not in jazz. I really don't know why that is, unless the instrument
won't make as much racket as they want to hear nowadays. After the flute,
maybe it will be the turn of the oboe to come by!

"To me, the idea of merging jazz and classical music has always seemed
one of the most difficult things in the world. You might get something good,
but you would probably destroy the character of both. I think concert
orchestras have such a different idea of time that they *must* play differently. They wouldn't sound well if their playing was *too* relaxed, but
subconsciously there has, I believe, been a great change in the attitude of
concert musicians in the last twenty years, towards a more relaxed way
of playing. A lot of them have been influenced by jazz musicians, and

Benny Goodman, Chick Webb and Joe Bushkin, 1937.

many of them—especially on woodwinds—know about all the jazz trumpet and clarinet players. Then, too, a lot of the best musicians in New York are always making records with singers. Whether they like it or not, I don't know, but they must get a feeling and be influenced in some way.

"I have always felt that the older jazz bands had a more exact way of playing, that fitted closer to a jazz style than much of the new music does. Of course, you have a terrific type of player now, one with all the technical qualifications. In a way, the new generation of jazz musicians consists of a different kind of man.

"I still go out to hear jazz, but in New York everything seems to start so late, and one of the problems today is bad microphone technique. Some musicians get so close to the mike that you don't hear the real quality of their instrument. I've sometimes found the music so loud and overbearing that I've been driven out of the place. I really cannot listen long to a man with strong lungs blowing his brains out that way. Maybe the public likes it. There are times when you need enhancement of the sound, I know, but not distortion.

"Folk music isn't a new problem. It has always been here, of course, but we only used to hear it in Wheeling, West Virginia, and places like that. If we played a one-nighter there, or in some of the smaller towns, that's all you were going to hear when you turned the radio on until you shut it off. If it can sell down there, the record companies decided, it can sell all over the rest of the world! There used to be race records and race labels, but then they found that what was a hit in Savannah could be sold all over the world, too. Folk singing has always been popular. Jimmie Rodgers sold millions of Victor records. If someone like that came up now, they would promote six other Jimmie Rodgerses on six other labels. It was true once of jazz and swing, too, but there were different locales for different music then. Jazz is bigger in one sense than ever—in terms of the number of albums that come out every week. Some of the people who talk about music in the old days just like to talk about it. If there were something to listen to, they wouldn't go. The people who come and are a part of it are the ones who count."

(1963)

LIONEL HAMPTON

BANDLEADER [DRUMS AND VIBRAHARP]

Lionel Hampton was born in Louisville, Kentucky. His father, Charles Hampton, who had shown promise as singer and pianist, was killed in action during World War I. His mother took him to live with her parents, Richard and Lavinia Morgan, in Birmingham. Later, the family moved to Chicago, but his grandmother, distressed by school conditions, sent him to Holy Rosary Academy in Kenosha, Wisconsin. He played drums there in a fife-drum-and-bugle band, and received strict tuition in the correct handling of the sticks from the Dominican sister who acted as instructor. From Kenosha, he went to St. Monica's school in Chicago, and in that city he was soon attracted to the band organized by a famous black newspaper, the *Chicago Defender's Newsboy Band.* Tutored by the celebrated Major N. Clark Smith, he played drums in the marching band and tympani in the concert orchestra. When he reached St. Elizabeth's High School, he was given the responsibility of drumming the students to roll call and classes.

It has often been claimed that, whenever he was missing from school at this time, he was to be found at the Vendome Theatre, listening to Erskine Tate's band. His big thrill in it was certainly Jimmy Bertrand. who played xylophone and chimes, had lights in his drums that flashed on and off, and threw his sticks in the air and caught them while playing. Hampton was fourteen when his grandparents surprised him with a present—his own set of drums, complete with lights. Not long after that, he left home with a traveling band.

"We were just a bunch of kids from Chicago when I went out with Detroit Shannon," he recalled. "I'd go with any band as long as I could play drums. Maybe it was Hastings, Nebraska, where we got stranded, but I wouldn't have cared if it had been Albuquerque, New Mexico. Les Hite, who was several years older than me, was playing saxophone in that band. He went to Los Angeles, got him a band, and sent for me in 1927. I had

Lionel Hampton.

an aunt living out there who had a very good job in one of the picture studios, so I had a crutch to lean on.

"Les Hite had a little bad luck with his band, so he and I went over to Vernon Elkins's band. From there we went to Paul Howard's Quality Serenaders, and it was with them I recorded for the first time. There were a lot of bands with funny names like that out there then, and they had a lot of the New Orleans influence. Minor Hall, the brother of Tubby Hall, was playing drums. Bill Johnson and his brother Dink were there, and they were from New Orleans, too. And there was one of the finest bass players I ever heard. He played all low notes on his bass, and he played the prettiest changes. He died of T.B. He was named Mr. Williams, and he played with the Spikes Brothers band. I worked with them on a couple of gigs, and also with Curtis Mosby and His Blue Blowers. Mosby was a drummer, and I used to jive him up, so that I'd get the gig. 'You get your stick, man,' I'd say. 'You ought to be directing. Let me play the drums!'

"They had bands all over town. All of 'em worked, and they made good money. We'd get thirty or forty dollars a week, and pick up as much as that again on tips. It was the Gold Coast, and people flocked to hear the band. There was a lot of activity, a lot of sportin' life, you understand? The big sport of the night was who put the most in the kitty. They had fancy entertainers, and we'd play for the people to dance. We'd take a piano and go round the floor. Being the drummer, my job was to help push the piano —and watch the pianist to see he didn't palm the money on us. They had great singers, too, in those days. They sang everything from classics to blues, and every one of them had a parody on a song.

"Gambling was a great influence out there, and when the big gamblers came in, the girls would always sing for them. They were guys who would like to sit up and get high, and we'd have a big kitty for them with a light flickering in it, and they'd throw silver dollars into it. There were a lot of racehorses and races out there, and then there was the moving picture industry. The big stars would come down and frequent places like the Cotton Club with its big show and 'copper-colored' chorus girls. Producers named Bloomfield and Greeley used to come out to stage the shows and do the dances. Eddie Rochester was one of the comedians there, and he did a song called *Waitin' for Jane,* dancing with a broom. People would throw him money, and he'd go around sweeping it off the floor with his broom.

"Les Hite had got his band together and pulled me in. Lawrence Brown played trombone, and a boy who died, Rostelle Reese, was on trumpet, one of the best I ever heard. We had twelve pieces and auditioned for Frank Sebastian's place, where one band had previously been playing for about ten years. Everybody in our band could read, and we had been listening to records by McKinney's Cotton Pickers and Duke Ellington, and we had a terrific repertory. 'I've got Louis Armstrong coming out,' Sebastian told us, 'so you all can be the band to back him up.'

"But before Louis, Duke Ellington came out to Hollywood to make the picture, *Check and Double Check,* with Amos 'n' Andy. When Sebastian heard Duke's band, he said, 'Damn, they ain't no good! They're copying all my band's arrangements. Why don't they get some music?'

"Of course, we had copied all Duke's things off the records by ear. *Birmingham Breakdown* was our favorite, but we were also playing *East St. Louis Toodle-oo* and *Black Beauty.* We had all McKinney's arrangements down, too. Remember the one on *Cherry?* And *If I Could Be with You* which Fathead (George Thomas), a great singer, sang on the record? I think Les Hite sang it with us. I well remember Cuba Austin's drumming, too. Oh, McKinney's was a *heavy* influence. They were something else.

"When Louis came to California in 1930 to play with us, it was such a happy day for me. Playing with him was a revelation, and he always encouraged me. I was appointed librarian to look after his music. We were supposed to start work at eight o'clock, but I'd be there at six, shining up my cymbals and all like that. I didn't have a vibraharp then, but I had a little set of orchestra bells. Les Hite only let me play 'em on one piece, a jazz chorus on *Song of the Islands,* when I would play the solo Louis had played on his record. That knocked him out, and he said to me, 'When I sing, you play behind me like that.'

"I had a ball playing behind him, and that's where I really got my roots. Of course, Coleman Hawkins was a great favorite of mine, too. And I could play all of Earl Hines's solos. At one time, I was the only kid in the country who could play his *Deep Forest.* Men like that inspired guys who wanted to be musicians.

"When we went to the studio to record with Louis, we saw the vibes standing in the corner. He asked me if I knew anything about that instrument. 'Well, you know, I've been playing the bells behind you,' I answered, 'and it's got the same keyboard, only bigger.' So Louis said, 'Play some behind me!' And that's how I first started playing vibes. For Lawrence Brown and me, that session brought what you might call overnight fame. *Confessin', If I Could Be with You, I'm a Ding Dong Daddy,* and *I'm in the Market for You*—we ought to listen to those records more, because they really sound good.

"Of course, you'd hear sloppy sax sections in those days, because saxophone players hadn't learned to play together—not until Fletcher Henderson and Don Redman started smoothing 'em out. Fletcher had the best musicians. But Louis was the first one to give backgrounds to *soloists.*

Lionel Hampton, Louis Armstrong and Lawrence Brown.

He'd have the saxophone play his favorite riff, and then you'd hear him say, 'Give me the mute. Watch that chord there, baby! Give me some grits!'

"We were on the air one night, and he said, 'Look out, man, we're gonna open up with *Dumas*. I feel good tonight, and if I'm going well, Hamp, you sit on those cowbells with me, and I'll play another chorus.' Well, man, I was sitting on those cowbells, and Louis played about ninety-nine choruses on *I'm a Ding Dong Daddy from Dumas*.

"Every musician that could get to the Cotton Club in Culver City was there. They were walking off their jobs to hear Louis play, and the place was packed. Musicians were pushing people off the dance floor, so they could get close to hear him, and he was making breaks from high C up to high G. There was a little seat down by my drums, where two people could sit, and guys were offering me anything to sit there, to be close to him. He kept me right in the middle, and I had his replacement handkerchiefs on the drum. And, do you know, cats used to take his old handkerchiefs away as souvenirs. They knew he was a great man, and he influenced everybody.

"Louis was out there nine months, and while I was with him I met Gladys Riddle, who later became my wife. She was a modiste, and she bought me a little set of vibes. She knew what Louis thought of my playing. 'You set those things up,' she told me, 'and you play 'em!' At night, when I got through playing, I'd take those vibes down, take 'em home, put 'em up in my living room, and practice all day long. That was how I really learned to play 'em. She made me do it, even on the days when I didn't want to practice at all. It was Gladys, too, who had me go to school and learn. She had me take piano, harmony and counterpoint, to learn the chords. I went to the University of Southern California for about eighteen months, and I learned a whole lot, learned how to put chords together. What I'm using now, I learned then. But when I played vibes in the band, the guys kept saying, 'Oh, man, cut that out!' Finally, I got mad and quit, because vibes was what I wanted to play.

"I got together a little band of my own and started working up and down the Coast—Seattle, Washington, Vancouver. Before Count Basie's band became permanent, some of his guys weren't doing anything around Kansas City. I sent for and got Herschel Evans. Buck Clayton was already out there, and together we consolidated the band, and went back into the Cotton Club. It was a good group, and I guess it lasted six or seven months. Besides Herschel and Buck, there were Teddy Buckner (trumpet), Johnny Miller (bass), Caughey Roberts (saxophone and clarinet), and I think we had Henry Prince for a time before he died. He was a great piano player, played beautiful chords.

"After that job, Buck took part of the band his way and Herschel went with me. We went out on the road, traveling in three cars. Ernie Lewis was the piano player then, and he drove one. Herschel was a revelation to me. He had so much rhythm, so much drive, so much know-how. He played good all the time. I'd stop playing myself just to listen to him. Then Basie sent for him to go back to K.C., and Gladys's mother kept saying, 'You've got to come home, or you're likely to starve to death.' We had an agent who went in front and, even when we'd got the job ourselves, he'd collect the money and go on home with it. So I came off the road and got a job at the Paradise nightclub.

"It was on Sixth and Main in Los Angeles, and all the sailors were coming in there to get the last beer before they took the train down to Long Beach, about twenty-two miles away. They'd buy a pitcher of beer for a quarter, a glass for a nickel, or a big mug for fifteen cents. There was sawdust on the floor and we got three dollars and fifty cents a night. We did business, and the second week the guy raised the salaries to five dollars.

"People started coming from all over, just like a wave, and one night I heard all this clarinet playing, looked around, and there was Benny Goodman. The next night, Teddy Wilson and Gene Krupa came down. This was when they asked me to play a recording session for Victor with the Trio, making it the Quartet. We did *Dinah* and *Moonglow,* and after that the man at the Paradise took the sawdust off the floor, put white tablecloths on the tables, and charged people a buck to get in. He transferred a license from another place he owned, put up a bar, and started selling hard drinks. His waitresses had been wearing just anything, but now he dressed 'em up, put 'em in short outfits like miniskirts. He added a chef and started selling hot beef sandwiches. The place would hold about five hundred people and it was loaded every night. People fought to get in there, and the man raised my salary 'way up. He knew I was on my way then. All Hollywood used to be out there, and we really had a good nine-piece band. Teddy Buckner and Tyree Glenn were in the brass section, and when I played vibes Tyree doubled on drums. It was Tyree who answered the 'phone when Benny Goodman called.

" 'Hey, Hamp, Benny Goodman wants to talk to you!'

" 'Oh, man, go get lost!' I said, not believing him.

"Finally, Gladys picked up the 'phone.

" 'It really is Benny,' she said.

" 'I want you to come back right away,' Benny said, 'to be on my Camel cigarette program, and to work with the trio and the quartet.'

" 'I can't come unless Gladys comes.'

" 'Well, bring her, too.'

" 'She's gotta be everywhere I'll be . . .'

" 'She will be. You bring her back. Y'all fly, or come on the train, or whatever you want to do.'

" 'No, we'll drive back,' Gladys decided. She had a white Chevrolet, and we had a little trailer to put my drums and vibes in, and we drove across country to New York. We got married in Yuma, Arizona, on our way back to join Benny. He had me play *Dinah* on the Camel program, and we broke it up.

"It was a great experience playing with Benny. The quartet consisting of him, Teddy Wilson, Gene Krupa and myself ushered in a new era for show business. Before that, there were no black and white people playing together. They just had those Uncle Tom stereotypes for us, Stepin Fetchit parts, but nothing much to do. Benny pushed for me to star, and this was before Jackie Robinson and the Brooklyn Dodgers. Benny took us all over the country, all over the South, and insisted we stay in the same hotel. The applause in Texas was as long and loud as any I ever heard in my life. In Dallas, we stayed only one day with the group, because my wife's home was about fifty miles away in Denison, and her father wanted us to stay with them. So we used to drive down every day. That was the origin of the title, *Denison Swing,* and later of *Rock Hill Special.* Rock Hill was the Harlem of Denison.

"But we did get in trouble in Dallas, because Teddy Wilson and I were drinking water out of the 'white' drinking water faucet. Benny called up and got the Chief of Police, and Marcus of Nieman-Marcus, one of the leaders in the town, came down.

" 'Boys,' they said, 'you ain't got nothin' to worry about!' Even the cop who had stopped us agreed, and it ended up very happy with us drinking out of all the drinking water places!

"Yes, Benny was exceptional among white musicians. When he heard Johnny Dodds and Jimmie Noone play, he felt it, and he idolized those guys. When Charlie Christian and I would play and get into a terrific groove, you could see tears come into his eyes. He had that soul, that feeling, and he wasn't doing it just for money. Right here, in New York, I heard him cussed out once.

" 'What're you doing with those niggers in your band?'

" 'You say that again,' Benny answered, 'and I'll take this clarinet and hit you in the head with it.'

"We'd travel a lot on trains in those days, and Benny would have Drawing Room A, and Gladys and I would be in Drawing Room B. Outside of girl singers, she was the only woman to travel with the band, and she had the character to carry the situation.

"That was a great band in 1937 when you first heard it. The Fletcher

Henderson arrangements were very, very important. If a guy missed one note, or Fletcher said he wasn't playing it right, Benny would fire him right away—saxophone, trumpet, anything—and get someone else. You had to play Fletcher Henderson like Fletcher Henderson wanted. I got a chance to study some of his arrangements, and I guess some were as good as Bach fugues, the way he put them together. *Sometimes I'm Happy* is a classic, it's put together so well. You had to be relaxed playing his music. For instance, all the horns had to be *there* at the same time, like a guy making a chord on the piano. You just had to be at the right place at the right time. I also used to like to hear his *Get Happy,* and *Down South Camp Meeting,* and *Sugar Foot Stomp.* When I was with Louis, we used to play a piece called *Poor Little Rich Girl,* and Louis used to make all those fantastic breaks in there. Benny had an arrangement on it, too, and I liked to hear him do those breaks. It took a good musician with imagination to play that type of music.

"When Charlie Christian joined us, we played a lot of stuff that never was recorded. Some of the things we played on steady gigs were just terrific. Goodman's group was really the front door to modern changes in music. We used a lot of whole-tone chords, and we were just kidding around doing 'em. It was easy. Then I really enjoyed playing with Dave Tough. He had the same thing I was talking about. He could be playing drums and crying. 'Man,' he'd say, 'your playing just fills me up.' He had a unique gift, and he was one of the swingingest cats who ever played drums.

"In 1937, Eli Oberstein, who was recording director at RCA Victor, came and told me that any time I wanted to record, I had an open invitation. He wanted me to record with all different types of musicians, so whenever I came into New York I'd call him.

" 'You want me to record?'

" 'Yeah, come on down.'

"By 1941, I'd made about ninety sides for them with the cream of the profession. On trumpet, I had cats like Cootie Williams, Harry James, Ziggy Elman, Jonah Jones, Walter Fuller, Mouse Randolph, Rex Stewart, Dizzy Gillespie and Red Allen. For reeds, I had Johnny Hodges, Benny Carter, Buster Bailey, Herschel Evans, Budd Johnson, Omer Simeon, Eddie Barefield, Chu Berry, Coleman Hawkins, Harry Carney, Ben Webster, Earl Bostic and Marshall Royal. In the rhythm sections, were Jess Stacy, Gene Krupa, Clyde Hart, Johnny Miller, Cozy Cole, Sonny Greer, Billy Kyle, John Kirby, Jo Jones, Alvin Burroughs, Milt Hinton, Charlie Christian, Artie Bernstein, Sidney Catlett, Al Casey, Freddie Green, Joe Sullivan, Zutty Singleton, Nat Cole, Oscar Moore, Marlowe Morris, Hayes Alvis, Sir

Lionel Hampton and his band, with Billy Mackel at extreme left and Milt Buckner behind him. (1950)

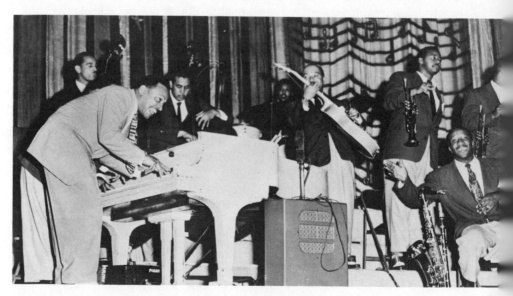

Lionel Hampton at the piano; Charles Harris and Charles Mingus, basses; Earl Walker, drums; Billy Mackel, guitar; Jimmy Nottingham and Duke Garrette, trumpets; Johnny Sparrow, tenor saxophone. (1947.)

Charles Thompson and Irving Ashby. Besides all these, I used a lot of fine musicians out of the Benny Goodman band.

"After I had been with Benny four years, he took sick, and the doctor told him to stop playing for a while. And so, with his blessing, I went and got my own big band. Joe Glaser financed me and was my first booker. Marshall Royal helped me put it together. We had his brother Ernie and Karl George on trumpet, and we picked up Joe Newman later in Alabama. Jack McVea was playing baritone, and Cat Anderson came in for quite a while. I picked up Milt Buckner in Detroit. Ray Perry played violin and alto; Illinois Jacquet and Dexter Gordon played tenor; and Irving Ashby was on guitar. Lee Young was on drums, but he didn't stay long, because Shadow Wilson came in, and he was very good. On trombone we had one of the greatest players *nobody* ever did write about—Fred Beckett. Joe Glaser found him in Kansas City, called me, and said, 'I'm going to send you a trombone player.' And he took him off the bandstand, practically kidnapped him, and sent him out to me in Los Angeles. 'This is the greatest trombone player in the world,' Joe said, and he was never so right in all his life, because Beckett certainly was that. He just didn't live long enough to get due recognition. Then Wild Bill Davis used to arrange for me, and at that time he was playing guitar, not organ.

"Joe Glaser told me about a friend of his, Joe Sherman, who had a girl who worked in the washroom of his club. They couldn't keep her in the washroom, because she was always trying to sing with the band. Walter Fuller had about six pieces there with Mouse (Alvin Burroughs) on drums. Mouse was a great time drummer. They took me down there and told this girl, 'Now I want you to sing for this orchestra leader.' She sang a couple of blues numbers and sounded good, so I said, 'I'm playing at the Regal Theatre. Come on out and sing with me tomorrow.'

"Joe Sherman brought her out, and she got up and sang *Evil Gal Blues,* and, boy, she broke it up! Hre real name was Ruth Jones, but I asked her if she would mind if I changed it.

" 'I don't care what you call me, so long as you give me a job!'

" 'Okay, you're hired. From now on you're Dinah Washington.'

"I don't know why that name came to me, but that's the way it was, and she took it, and became famous with it. After that, the guy who was doorman at the Regal said, 'I didn't know you wanted a singer. I sing. Give me a chance!' So I told him he could sing on the next show, and he sang *Every Day,* and that was Joe Williams. But he wanted to be a ballad singer with the band, and I didn't need that then.

"A lot of people came up through my band, and when they're interviewed they skip over that fact, but, you know, when I picked them up they often didn't have any hope at all. They all got a living and a chance. I didn't hold them back, but I was strict and I disciplined them. I see so many write-ups where they pass over that experience.

"During the '40s, it was the hottest band in the country. We broke every record. We'd open up at nine o'clock and hit the first intermission at twelve! I had six trumpets, four trombones, five reeds, piano, guitar, two basses, two drummers. We had to have two drummers, because we'd wear one drummer out.

"A lot of guys who weren't known then came up through my band. I brought Charlie Mingus out of Los Angeles. We had Wendell Marshall, who used to play with Duke, from St. Louis. We had Morris Lane, a terrific tenor man, Johnny Griffin, Benny Golson, Earl Bostic (he did a lot of arrangements for me), Arnett Cobb, Herbie Fields, Snooky Young, Joe Wilder, Al Grey, Britt Woodman, Sweet Daddy Cleveland, Booty Wood, Al Hayse (a good arranger and a wonderful trombone player), Benny Bailey, Quincy Jones, Wes Montgomery, Monk Montgomery, Art Farmer, Betty 'Bebop' Carter, and so many more. Bobby Plater, a great saxophone player, was with me a long time, and Billy Mackel, the guitar player, is *still* swinging with me. The band was like a Who's Who. Another wonderful trumpet player I had was Duke Garrette. For some reason or other, he went back to the Navy, and they made him a Chief Petty Officer, gave him back all the pay he had lost while he was out. He was one of the greatest plunger and hat men I've ever known. Man, he could do more different things with a hat! He would practice all day long, which is something you don't see with bands anymore. And, oh, how old Duke could lead a section!

"During the '40s, I wanted to add some fiddles, but Joe Glaser said no. Then I heard a white boy playing organ in a Harlem bar. His name was Doug Duke, and he had the top part of his instrument fixed up for another manual, and he could get all kinds of weird sounds out of it. I got him to come down when I was playing the Apollo Theatre. 'What is this?' Joe Glaser wanted to know. 'You'll spoil what you've got.' But in the middle of the show I introduced Doug playing things like *Where or When, There'll Never Be Another You* and *Solitude*. The people just tore the house up! They wouldn't let us off the stage, and we stayed on for hours. A whole lot of other people started playing organ after that.

"Roy Johnson came in the band around 1948. He'd been an insurance broker in Kansas City. He played good bass, but he played soft. 'You ought to get something to bring the bass out a little,' I told him. 'These horns are too heavy for you. You play good things, and I can hear 'em, but the people can't.'

" 'I was thinking the same thing,' he said. 'Before we came up here, I was in a jam session, and a guy came in with a thing like a ukulele, but it was a bass, and it just cut through everything. The other guys on the session put him out, told him, "Don't be bringing that old loud thing in here!" But I've got his card, because he wanted to see you.'

"So when we were playing a matinée dance at the Shriners Auditorium in Los Angeles, the guy came by with this thing. 'If you'll use it,' he said, 'I can get an electronic company in Santa Ana to make it for me, and you can have a piece of it.'

"I was just about to make a tour through Arizona, New Mexico, Texas and into Oklahoma—all country where they played Western music. Man. when we opened up with that bass, cats came from everywhere. 'What is that?' they wanted to know. 'Where can I get one?' I had that boy's address and by the time we got to Oklahoma he had orders for three or four hundred. I think he went on a percentage with the Fender people, and later they sold it to CBS. I never took any part of it, but he always gave me a bass any time I wanted one.

"When I first started my band in the early '40s, we played in the South a lot, because at that time one-nighters in the South were the most flourishing happening for the big bands. Earl Hines is right when he says the people in the bands were the 'first freedom riders.' The black experience in music was a matter of heartaches, going hungry and even being beaten. Many a night, when we'd played in places like Waco, Texas, or Shreveport, Louisiana, we'd have to go to the bus station if we wanted anything to eat when we got through. And there they would close up the 'colored section'. Maybe, if we went behind to the kitchen, some old dishwasher with dirty hands might give us a sandwich. In the South, we couldn't go into a decent rest room. This was all a part of jazz then. It got you emotional, and the next night it all came out in your playing.

"I think jazz is more a question of experience than of environment. Whites can play jazz—especially the technical parts. That's why this little white kid, Gary Keller, who's with me now, amazes me. He plays more like a black kid, and the reason is that when he was coming up he played all the old records by people like Chu Berry, Herschel Evans and Lester Young. He told me the way they played sometimes made him cry.

"Most kids talk about John Coltrane, but Trane was very confused. I remember once when I opened at the Apollo Theatre, and it was packed, Coltrane was on the bill, playing all those little things he played, and he got hung up on a passage, and he kept playing that passage for half an hour. When I looked around, everybody was out of the theatre.

"I remember when he first came to play with me in the late '40s. He'd come up from North Carolina with a little band, and he, Jimmy Heath and Red Garland used to come to a little play room we had at the Earle Theatre in Philly. There was a piano and a set of drums, and we would have jam sessions. A lot of the kids didn't know the right chords, and I'd sit back there and teach 'em, like that D Minor part in *How High the Moon.* Coltrane had an alto sax then, and he was an ambitious guy. I used him on stage a couple of times when my saxophone players were late, and I encouraged him to play tenor, just as I did Illinois Jacquet, Dexter Gordon and Johnny Griffin. 'You have a very unusual technique,' I told him. 'Why don't you play tenor?'

"So long as you go along with progress, that's what makes you *move.* I hope some day I can bring something else to music. The vibes was unique, the organ, the Fender bass . . . But a lot of the things they're doing in music now, we did 'em before. I know this boogaloo beat. I played that a long time ago. There isn't too much new under the sun. They talk about the back beat and rock 'n' roll. We had that eight-beat thing going, what they used to call boogie woogie, when Milt Buckner was in the band. We had riffs, but we weren't aiming at commercial things like they do now in music. We didn't have a name for it, but when I came back from Europe in '53, and heard about this new thing called rock 'n' roll, I found it was something we'd been playing for quite a while. For boogie woogie, you need a piano player who can really play that bass. I still keep it in all my shows, and it still breaks it up.

"For several years now, I've operated with a smaller group, the Inner Circle, because we play a lot of country clubs and places like that, but I still put together a big band for special occasions, as we did at Newport in 1967 and 1972."

Proud as Lionel Hampton may well be of his career in music, he also has a remarkable and unusual record as a fund-raiser for charities. The Lionel Hampton Development Corporation has been responsible for an ambitious project providing much-needed accomodation for low and moderate income families between 130th and 132nd Streets in Harlem. He also hopes to build a university in the same area, where black youngsters can obtain education to fit them for careers in the professions— including music.

(1972)

BILLY
MACKEL

GUITAR

For three decades, with only occasional absences, Billy Mackel has been a vital element of Lionel Hampton's band, as indispensable in his way as Freddie Green to Count Basie, with the difference that he is also an accomplished soloist, and is extensively featured as such. Quiet, modest and genial, he has undoubtedly been one of the most *consistently* underrated musicians in jazz history, and this despite his manifest authority as an accompanist and his ability as an imaginative, swinging improviser.

"I was born in Baltimore on December 28th, 1912," he said. "My parents were not musical, and I started off in music playing the ukulele, which was very popular at the time. I progressed so fast that one Christmas my mother made me a present of a banjo. It was a big surprise to me, and for a time I used to tune and play it like a ukulele. That same Christmas, a fellow in my class at school got a saxophone and started taking lessons on it. Every time I'd go by his house, he'd have his sheet music up, playing popular songs. So I took lessons, too, and soon I could play the chords while he played the melody. As a result of this, we were able to form a little band at high school. His name was Glenford Henderson, and he became something of a professional musician, but he stayed around Baltimore, gigging, and never traveled.

"We played a couple of public dances for the teachers' association, and somebody who was at one of them told the leader of a big band in Baltimore about me. As I was coming out of high school one day, a fellow came up and said, 'Percy Glascoe has sent me, and he wants you to come to one of his rehearsals.' I was so surprised, and at first I thought he was kidding, but finally he convinced me. So I went to the rehearsal and Glascoe liked what I did. He asked me if I would join his ten-piece band.

"I could read quite well by then, and we mostly played stock arrangements. At that time, in the '30s, people were dancing, and most of our jobs were dances. On banjo, of course, I mostly played rhythm. When the guitar started to get popular, I had to carry both the guitar and the banjo to the job, because there were only a few pieces I could play on guitar.

279

The banjo was like security, but I think the rhythm guitar blended better with the bass fiddle. The bands mostly had tubas when banjos were used, but when the tuba players started switching to bass fiddles, the banjos didn't blend so well.

"I stayed with Glascoe about a year, and then began to work in the cabaret section of Baltimore, what they used to call The Block. It was similar to Bourbon Street in New Orleans. They had dancing girls and everything, and there were clubs on both sides of the street for three blocks. The girls were the main attraction, and the music was there as an accompaniment. Mostly it was played by combos of five or six pieces. It was good experience for me, but there wasn't much outlet for the musicians.

"I don't recall any well-known musicians working there then, but there were a lot of good ones who left Baltimore. Chauncey Haughton, who played clarinet and alto saxophone, worked with Claude Hopkins, Fletcher Henderson, Chick Webb and Duke Ellington. Then there was Wallace Jones, who also went with Ellington. A neighbor of mine, in the same block, was Bill Kenny of the Ink Spots. Chick Webb was from Baltimore, but he left early and I never knew him.

"The Block is still going with much the same policy. There are no places where name groups can play, although there are some where the band is the feature. The Left Bank Jazz Society brings in name groups, but only on Sunday afternoons.

"I played The Block for about a year, until 1942, when I went to the Club Orleans, which had entertainers and singers, but where the band got a chance to play. It was an altogether different feeling. We had six pieces, including a trumpet player named Roy McCoy who went with Lionel Hampton before I did. Our piano player was Don Abney, who later toured in *Jazz at the Philharmonic* as accompanist for Ella Fitzgerald. They were the two most prominent musicians in the group, which never had a name. We were just a bunch of fellows who played at the Club Orleans. I was there about two years.

"World War II was on at this time, and there was a Coast Guard station near Baltimore. There were a lot of good musicians in the Coast Guard band, such as Benny Goodman's brother, Irving, who played trumpet. Some nights they would come and sit in with us, and I think he was the one who told Lionel Hampton about me. Roy McCoy was with Lionel then, and he came by my house one afternoon in 1944 and told me Lionel wanted me to come down to the Royal Theatre that day and sit in with the band. That's what I did, and I've been with Lionel most of the time ever since. He and I get along fine, and I enjoy playing with him.

Billy Mackel.

"The fellow who turned the guitar around, for me, was Charlie Christian. When he started playing the amplified instrument, it put the guitar in another perspective, and gave it an individuality it didn't have as a rhythm instrument. Anyone who was interested in guitar work then was affected by Charlie Christian.

"I don't remember what numbers I was first featured on with Lionel, but he used to start passing out solos in no set routine right in the middle of an arrangement.

"It was one of the best bands he ever had. Milt Buckner was on piano then, and his way of playing was his original idea, and strong, and it couldn't be duplicated after he left. Freddy Radcliffe was playing drums. The bass player, Charlie Harris, joined at the same time as I did. He had been playing in another combo on The Block. Later on, he went with Nat Cole. The reed section had Earl Bostic and Gus Evans on alto, Arnett Cobb and Freddy Simmons on tenor, and Charlie Fowlkes on baritone. The trumpets were Cat Anderson, Lammar Wright, Jr., Joe Morris and Dave Page. The trombones were Fred Beckett, Al Hayse (he's still in Detroit, but after we had that bus accident in 1955, the doctor advised him not to travel anymore), and Booty Wood.

"When you've been working with someone so long, you can almost anticipate what he is going to do before it happens. The instrumentation of the bands Lionel has had in recent years has often changed, but the character of the music remains much the same. The girl playing organ in the group the other night was Bu Pleasant. I think she came from Texas. I know she worked with Arnett Cobb for quite a while. The trombone player was her brother, and I guess you don't often see a guy using a plunger with a valve trombone. The straw boss was Charles McLinton, the tall fellow who played tenor, and the bass player was Eustace Guillmet. Lionel certainly finds musicians, and always has. They keep popping up.

"Since Charlie Christian, there have been many good guitar players, but the one I really liked was Wes Montgomery. I met him in the '40s when he was still living in Indianapolis, and we became friends. He was playing then the same way as when he passed away, because his style was his own invention and a unique way of playing. I like Kenny Burrell and George Benson, but I only heard Django Reinhardt on records, and never with an amplifier.

"The average guitar player is crazy about the natural guitar sound, but he keeps juggling about with amplifiers until he finds one that suits him. The sound depends very much on what the individual wants. One wants a mellow sound, another wants that high, harsher sound. Most use a pick, but Wes Montgomery always played with his fingers. Then again, the type of guitar makes a lot of difference. It seems to me that the little, thin-bodied guitars they use now produce a shriller sound than the conventional kind. The guitar I've been using for fifteen years has the regular, standard body with an 'f' hole. With some of the smaller models, where the body is solid wood, what you hear is just the amplifier. The hollow bodies do have an effect on the sound, even though it is coming through the amplifier. But still the sound really depends on what the individual likes.

"I hope I can keep going, because I still have plenty of enthusiasm for music. The road doesn't bother me. It gets into you. The business of packing and unpacking your bags, for instance, becomes a regular routine that you hardly notice. You do it automatically without thinking. Of course, it is easy to get confused and not remember what city you're in, or what your room number is, when you keep waking up in different hotels every day.

"As long as I've been with him, Lionel Hampton has always treated me the same way, as a gentleman, and I've had respect for him as a gentleman, and we've never had any conflicts at all. As for his musicianship, I just conclude he is a genius. He has an unceasing inventive ability, and I think he is inspired by his own ability. He has a way of getting what he wants from his musicians, and he has a kind of rhythmic force that must be a matter of heritage. He has always emphasized the beat, and he had that strong back beat going when I first joined him."

(1972)

BENNIE MORTON

TROMBONE

Bennie Morton, who was born in New York in 1907, has had a long and distinguished career in jazz. From 1924 onwards, he played in the bands of Billy Fowler, Fletcher Henderson, Chick Webb, Don Redman, Count Basie, Joe Sullivan, Teddy Wilson and Raymond Scott. After forming his own band in 1944, he worked for fifteen years in the pit bands of some twenty Broadway musicals, as well as at Radio City Music Hall. He began freelancing in the late '50s, playing in a variety of contexts with such musicians as Henry Allen, Red Richards, Wild Bill Davison and Bobby Hackett. In 1973, he took Vic Dickenson's place with the World's Greatest Jazz Band.

A consistent, disciplined, dignified and widely respected musician, Morton referred with some amusement to an assertion by Dicky Wells, his onetime colleague in the Basie band:

"So Dicky says I play more like Jimmy Harrison than anyone else today! Well, I think I have more of it *left* than anyone else. I've retained more from that period. I don't have enough knowledge of Jack Teagarden's background before he came to New York to know how much Jimmy influenced him, except that I know both Jack and Jimmy idolized Louis Armstrong. So each took from the same source much that they said on trombone. The problem with Jimmy was that he didn't live long enough to say all he had to say.

"I knew him very well. He wasn't hard-living. He didn't live the pace, say, Lips Page or Charlie Green did. He may not have looked after himself as he should, but he wasn't a big drinker. He loved to eat and cook. If he cooked a pan of biscuits, he might eat them all. He was a man whose stomach wasn't the strongest, and that was against him, but he was six-foot-one or -two, and he looked as though he had been on a football team! Now, I think weaker people generally give themselves more care, because they are weak, whereas strong people neglect themselves, because they don't feel so much and overcome ailments more quickly.

"As a person, Jimmy was one of the most likeable you could ever meet. He could keep a band in the right frame of mind just by his humor and talk, because he reminded us of Bert Williams, the great comic. He had the same kind of big voice, and he enjoyed imitating Williams. In the band, he could be playing while the rest of us were roaring with laughter. He might play a half-chorus and then say something that would knock me out —and leave the rhythm section playing by itself!

"You have to have a special kind of personality to get away with that. Actually, it didn't disturb the band, but pushed it on. And he had a quality, a drive, that meant a lot to bands like Charlie Johnson's and Fletcher Henderson's. He did for them what Bill Harris later did for Woody Herman. Many musicians can play, but they don't have this particular thing that stirs the others. We all had some of it in Fletcher's band then, because when a fellow played he gave all he had in front of Jimmy. Following him, you had better come up with something! And when you followed Joe

Smith, Coleman Hawkins and Buster Bailey, you had to show that you had something to say on trombone, too. You had to make your own self interesting to the listeners. Of course, in jazz you play the way you feel at the time, but with taste and with relation to the arrangement and what has gone before you.

"For his time, Harrison was ahead of the others in regard to jazz. He played more jazz, in one sense of the word, than Charlie Green, but Charlie was a great blues artist. He played the blues so well you *had* to listen.

"There are no records I know of that do Jimmy Harrison justice, that show what the man meant to any hall in which he played. Only short solos were recorded in those days, but at night, when he was playing live, he might take five or six choruses. A lot of people didn't have that kind of endurance, didn't have so much to say, but he was doing it and exciting audiences. The records don't show that unfortunately.

"He and Hawk (Coleman Hawkins) were room-mates, and Hawk liked him because Jimmy gave him inspiration. He was a kind of pacemaker. Jimmy gave him more incentive than most people, and they had something in common. Jimmy could give him the kind of stimulation he wanted. Others played well but didn't move him.

"Jimmy had soul and drive, and everybody was crazy about him. He had the warmth of a good Baptist preacher, and he made other people happy. And it all came out in his music.

"He died in 1931, and I wish he had lived, to see what his place would have been in these times. I came up behind him and what I heard undoubtedly influenced me, but there were trombones before him that influenced me too, and you never know where your imagination has been developed. You accumulate from the people you hear, and express something of your own. Copying in those days was taboo. You could be *influenced*—but you didn't copy. It was a time of real musical individualism in jazz.

"As long as I can remember, I was impressed by the trombone, and certainly from the age of eight. By the time I was ten, I was very well aware of the instrument. One reason was Lieutenant Simpson, a trombone player who led the 369th Regiment Band right on my street. Arthur Pryor was the great American trombone soloist then, and Simpson was called the *Black Pryor*. (Race at that time was black or white.) Simpson was quite a musician. He had played in minstrel shows, circuses, and everything, and he arrived in New York as a composer, conductor and authority on trombone to take Jim Europe's place with the band. My mother tried to engage him as a teacher for me, but he was too busy for that kind of work.

"My mother played piano and could sing. She taught me my first notes.

Bennie Morton, 1973.

The man who started me on trombone was Rohmie Jones, who graduated from the Jenkins Orphanage Band. A lot of great talent came from there. He played piano, bass horn, trombone, everything. After I got to be with Fletcher Henderson, I continued to study with different people.

"Another who came before Jimmy Harrison with me—and Jimmy was nearly seven years my senior—was 'Dope' Andrews. I don't know what his first name was, but the nickname didn't have the significance we might give it now. It had to do with his sleepy-looking eyes. The first time I heard him, he was with Mamie Smith, and he was making those bugle-call breaks. He played more jazz than 'most anybody I ever heard, and he was manipulating that trombone—I mean, *really* moving over it! He was an excellent musician, and he also played in the military band Simpson directed. I went to their Sunday afternoon concerts, and sometimes the two of them would tackle duets. They had ten trombones in the band, and some of them were just trombone players, but these two could play equal to any we have today. The interesting thing about Andrews is that his nephew doesn't remember him for the musician he was, and the nephew is a great trumpet player—Charlie Shavers.

"The big man on trumpet when Dope was playing, before I or the rest of the country was aware of Louis Armstrong, was Johnny Dunn, but Dope wasn't influenced or slowed down by Dunn's style. He was playing *himself*. He had a good musical background, and he knew he could do that much on trombone. It was fortunate I heard him. Of maybe fifty trombone players I heard in brass bands around—we had plenty of them—he was the one man who stood out. 'That's the way I would like to play trombone,' I said to myself.

"Despite Simpson's reputation as a musician, I much preferred Dope. Simpson was brassier, but I didn't particularly go for that. If he was playing an obbligato against fifty pieces, he had something that would cut through, and you'd catch it plain. But it wasn't the best quality and, for myself, I'll always sacrifice attention for quality. Of course, if I'd worked only as a jazz player, I probably wouldn't be in business today. A lot of good musicians gave up for one reason or another. You heard me the other night at Eddie Condon's club. I went from there to a nineteen-piece band—half strings —accompanying Sarah Vaughan, and we finished about 4 o'clock Saturday night. The next day, I was playing the show at Radio City Music Hall without rehearsal, in an orchestra of fifty to sixty pieces with four trombones. You have to go right in. The fellows alongside guide you as much as they can, alert you to what's going to happen, but they can never stop playing completely to do it.

"Playing in the pit for a show that has a long run can indeed get monotonous, but a lot depends on a man's temper, and what he's doing with himself musically. It's not a complete outlet, and I'd still be tinkering with my horn in the daytime, if only to develop or maintain the type of skill needed to play the show's book. Then you also have to be able to play up to the standard of the fellows who are still playing outside. That's where jazz really has to be a *natural* part of you. If it's not, you're liable to get into a rut.

"Long before I was ten, even when I was in my mother's arms, the music of my church was sinking in, harmonically and rhythmically. The rhythm of the church singing had that beat people try to acquire today for different reasons. What offends me is the people who are running to record companies and publishers with hymns and religious music, saying, 'You can make money off of this. Let's use it!' Some of them may have sung and performed in the church in years gone by when they were kids, and some still have a spiritual feeling, but I don't appreciate what they're doing. It's like jazzing the national anthem. One person who always presented it the way she would have done in her own church was Mahalia Jackson. But there's a group now that has taken the music of people who were worshipping God and have tried to make a new kind of Tin Pan Alley with it. I don't think it's necessary, and I blame the directors of the companies who have encouraged it. There are plenty of other tunes to do. You've got to be open-minded, but by the standards of my church, that sort of thing is forbidden. There are other churches, other races and other denominations, and they're not taking *their* religious songs and making a mockery of them.

"I must admit I was shook up when I first heard the way Louis Armstrong played *When the Saints Go Marching In*. He was my idol. Why did he have to do that? I was born in New York and didn't know about the New Orleans tradition, about those long processions walking at a solemn pace to the cemeteries, and then coming back at a faster clip with *The Saints* played the way we sometimes hear it now. Louis grew up in that.

"You run into a problem when you try to decide what jazz is, where it came from, and who it belongs to. Now I can go past small buildings, store-front churches, on my way home at 12 o'clock at night, and the people are shouting in there. There may be only a handful of them, but if you are measuring swing, they're out-swinging all the bands we got. First one gal tells the good story; then they go into song; and then it gets to a pitch where it looks like they're dancing. They say it isn't dancing, but spiritually they are satisfied. They come out, go home, go to sleep, get up, and go to work. This is a church set up by these people so they can say what they want to say. There's probably another one a few doors down. In ten blocks, you can maybe find five of them.

"One of the evils in our business has been the operators who have preferred musicians not to be too strict, because so long as you don't toe the mark, you can't hold *them* to the mark either! Then, too, some people think it's big to be late. It's important; you make an entrance; you get attention. The customers and the boss, they're all waiting, and then you come in . . . big deal! When you arrive an hour late, they know when you arrive all right.

"In Fletcher Henderson's days, the way we traveled had a lot to do with whether we got to the job on time or at all. We traveled in separate automobiles. Not everybody had one. In the early years, there were four regular car owners: Fletcher, Russell Smith, Joe Smith and Kaiser Marshall. Don Redman sometimes had a car. Coleman Hawkins came along later with his, and he was a speed man. But Fletcher was the fastest driver, and he belonged on the Indianapolis Speedway! Because he was the fastest, he would linger longer in a town, and anything might happen. He would start late, and he might have the key players in his car, so those who got there earlier couldn't get started. Maybe he was speeding and a cop took him back twenty miles to a judge, and he came in an hour or so late. Charlie Dixon, the guitar player and arranger, was the straw boss—and a worrier. He'd be pulling his hair out, and then Fletcher would walk in like nothing had happened. He had no agent to answer to, only a fellow named Fishman, who went ahead like a traveling salesman, and got rich hustling on five-per-cent commission. Fletcher did what he did because he was a big man, and carefree, and he survived until big business and a lot more bands came into the picture. If anybody lost money on a date, he'd come back and make it up to the guy by an adjustment of price. Usually, they'd make more money with Fletcher than they would with other attractions.

"Twenty-five years ago, big bands would play four or five hours a night, and play hard, so you couldn't expect a man to play solos and all the leads, too. I played lead with Basie, but when I was with Henderson it depended on who the other trombone was. Claude Jones and I would split the lead. That would come about when a man had the ability to play both, but I played more of the jazz than Claude. On the two albums I made with Dicky Wells, you had a fine musician in George Matthews, who could play the leads so that Dicky and Vic Dickenson were fresh enough to give their all in the solos.

"Jimmy Harrison had something everybody was crazy about. He had a lot of curiosity, and he found out what made music and other things in the world tick. There are some people like him, who, when you call their names, everybody begins to smile. You take Vic Dickenson, for example.

"Vic is good company, and he entertains well, and it doesn't stop when he goes on the bandstand. He says the right thing at the right time. Some might say it's cute, or brilliant thinking, but it's humorous, and it still says something. I would say that today, in 1962, Vic has more to say on the trombone than anybody I know. He says it like the headlines in a paper. He doesn't have to take the whole column to say it. What kind of message do you get if you're in his company? If there are five other people there, and Vic is talking, they're enjoying Vic, and he's got 'em laughing. He gets musicians laughing when he plays, yet he's serious, and he can say the most serious things with a touch of humor. That's why he has been re-corded two thousand times, and I and others twenty times. And, of course, with all that recording you can't help but notice how many different colors he has on the trombone, and how many different things he has to say. He can change course, play a ballad, a waltz, anything, and it's still jazz, with humor, and in good taste. There's no accident about it. He's a very good musician and he knows music. There's an excellent foundation beneath the carefree attitude. You know somebody else in this country who could always deliver a serious thought with a touch of humor? Will Rogers. Vic Dickenson is the Will Rogers of the trombone.

"I want to say something about sound. Some people often find the kind of sound that is called 'small' very attractive. Rough sounds seem loud, and smooth sounds seem soft. Compared to the general level of trombone playing in the '20s and '30s, the whole business has smoothed out since. A gimmick may command attention, get a guy a job, and that more or less forces another to copy the gimmick. But a big tone doesn't have to be lush and it doesn't have to be ragged. It's true what Trummy Young told you about Louis Armstrong. He may be playing softly, but his is still a big tone. The same with Coleman Hawkins. At one time, I was playing a small trombone, but later I played the biggest of any fellow playing in a dance band. An 8½" bell is very different from a 6" or a 6½", so my sound may have seemed 'smaller' with Henderson than with Basie.

"The action of the trombone, in general, is clumsier than that of other instruments, so in order to play it well, to match the kind of skills of those playing trumpet, clarinet, saxophone and other horns, the trombone player has to double his efforts to be in their class. And physically, it takes a hell of a lot, which is why some trombone players feel they need a little nip to help them along, to make them forget the hassles. One or two Seven Up's is my limit! But the drinkers have something in common. When they finish the night, they leave the bar arm in arm, and the fellow that gets the call for a gig next day is naturally the one you were drinking with last night.

"Fifty years ago, the trombone was in much the same position as the bass—boom, boom, boom, boom!—but now it runs as rapidly as anything else. Some of those manipulating the trombone today have, you might say,

Fletcher Henderson, Ben Webster and other distinguished musicians at a fancy dress party.

Fletcher Henderson, his Packard and friends. Unidentified saxophonist from The Buffalodians; Harold Arlen; Henderson (at the wheel); Bobby Stark; Lois Deppe (waving hat); Will Marion Cook (standing); Rex Stewart.

gone beyond the demand to a pinnacle they have set up for themselves as the objective. This is the Jet Age and we are all affected by it! I don't think the character of the instrument really lends itself to playing as rapidly as some are doing, but this is a matter of the soloist, the virtuoso, the exhibitionist. Yet the general run of arrangements any trombone is required to play today does demand an awful lot of him, especially as compared with days far back. Of course, some musicians have said, 'This is my trademark, and I have to stick to it.' With others, the experience of having to make a living has led to compromise. But if you came on the scene when jazz was being played, and you could play it, and because of your age you *were* playing it, and the chips fell in such a way that there were enough jobs and opportunities—then you don't know much about compromising. However, over a period of twenty years, playing with many different groups, you learn how to adjust to many different styles. In Fletcher's best days, he was earning and paying three times as much as most bands. This meant that he could always have his choice of men, and replace those who didn't measure up. I was in and out of that band three times myself, and I had to *play* to keep the job.

"Musicianship and adapting yourself to fit a situation is a subject in itself. I remember when we made those Keynote records with the trombone 'choir': Bill Harris, Vic Dickenson, Claude Jones and myself. 'So what?' the jazz people say right away when they see a title like *Where or When*. But we had fellows there who could interpret any tune given us, and we knew we had to play it with a lift. All the same, you can't expect a man to interpret or get the heat up on *Where or When* the same as on *King Porter Stomp*. We had all had experience and knew the importance of connecting with the arrangements. It used to be more than a matter of running up and down the chords, and then leaving the band to pick up and get out as best it could.

"There are a lot of mistaken ideas in circulation today. People talk as though improvisation were something peculiar to jazz. Many musicians improvise. Gypsies do, and so do symphony musicians when they're warming up before a concert. Jazz musicians improvise, but few musicians play jazz."

(1962)

QUENTIN JACKSON

TROMBONE

"My mother used to get a magazine every month called *Etude,* and she played the music in it for her own amusement. Every time she played, I'd crawl up on the piano stool after her and play. That began when I was four years old, but my parents didn't let me have piano lessons until I was six. By that time, I didn't want to play those simple exercises, which sounded like nothing to me. I had perfect pitch, and I wanted to play what *I* wanted to play. The teacher played through my lessons and, although I wouldn't practice, when she came back the next week I'd play the right notes. She could tell I hadn't practiced, because I'd be using my own fingering. I formed a dislike for piano while I was still taking lessons.

"Springfield, where I was born in 1909, was a city of about sixty thousand people, and great artists came to Memorial Hall there. My mother took me to all the symphonies, and I heard Caruso, Galli-Curci, Fritz Kreisler and Paderewski. I loved it. The first opera I ever saw was *Aida.* I didn't know what they were singing, but the music fascinated me and woke up my imagination. I could see things when I heard music: situations, people, things. I was always told that I should write, and when I was with McKinney's Cotton Pickers later, I used to sit at the piano sometimes and play.

" 'Why don't you put that down?' they'd ask.

" 'Naw, it was nothing,' I'd answer. I just loved to listen and execute. Don Redman and Benny Carter used to give me the devil all the time, because I would play for my own amusement and not put it down on paper. I always felt that other people would not understand or appreciate what I was doing.

"I had a job lighting gas lamps when I was twelve years old. I had seventy-five of them, and besides lighting them I had to clean them. I used to ride a bicycle round the streets to them. One day I passed a music store and saw a violin in the window. Because of my experience of the symphonies, the violin was a beautiful instrument to me. Now I always used to give my mother my paycheck when I got it, and she was standing on the corner waiting for me, but I slipped around in the arcade to the music store, and bought that violin. She tried to get mad at me, but she had to laugh, because it amused her that I had done this and come home without a penny.

"I started taking lessons with a German fellow, and I had first-chair experience in the junior high school symphony. I not only liked the violin very much, but the organ, too. I used to sing in the church choir, and I sat right beside the console. It fascinated me. I knew the music was the same as piano, only you had three staffs, one for each hand and one for your feet. So I asked the reverend if I could come after school and practice on the organ. He agreed, because by then everybody knew about my musical background. I've always been very observant, and I knew about the different sounds you could get from different combinations of stops— sounds to fit your mood. I took a buddy along to pump the organ, as I had done when I was a kid. I got so I played for church services every Sunday. I remember the choir used to have a hymn, *Holy, Holy, Holy,* that they sang as they were marching up the aisle. When they began, I would play with a soft combination of stops. As they got closer, I'd make it a little louder, add another stop and open the swell pedal a little more. I loved the sound of the instrument, and still do, but I can't stand the Hammond. It sounds so mechanical to me, whereas a pipe organ sounds alive.

"Claude Jones, the trombone player, married my sister in 1927, and he was playing with the Synco Septet. To me, he was the greatest, and he played beautiful melody in a style like Miff Mole's. 'There are very few good trombone players,' he used to tell me, 'and there's going to be a field for them. With your background, you should take up this instrument.'

"I was working for an undertaker in 1929, and he had a brass trombone and played in the Elks band. I asked him about this trombone, because some guys near home had a nine-piece band and needed a trombone in it. Jazz orchestrations at that time were made for ten pieces—two trumpets, trombone, three saxophones, piano, banjo, tuba and drums. That was the standard. The undertaker showed me how to put my mouth to the instrument, how to hit the notes, and the seven positions. Trombone parts were written simple in those days, not nearly so complicated as they are now. I would see B flat, C, or B natural on down in these positions, and I'd remember where I found the note. So I started playing in this little band right away.

"Gerald Hobson, the drummer, came from New York to visit his father, who was a big lawyer in Columbus, Ohio, forty-four miles from Springfield. Gerald played for a while in our little band until he went to Cincinnati to join Wesley Helvey's Troubadours. I was singing at that time, too, and Gerald always used to say, 'You have a nice voice and a nice musical background, so I'm going to look out for you!' He told Helvey about me, and in August, 1929, Helvey called and asked if I would like to join his band. And when could I leave? I could leave the next day. I already belonged to the little local union—dues seventy-five cents a quarter—and now I went to a pawnshop and bought myself a trombone of my own for six dollars. You should have seen it! When we got to Buffalo, the guys made me buy another.

"On New Year's Day, 1930, I took Stump Brady's place in Zack Whyte's band. Stump was joining Andy Kirk. Buddy Lee, the trumpet player, came with me from Helvey at the same time. Sy Oliver and Henry Savage were the other trumpets, and I was the only trombone. Earl Tribble and Clarence Paige were the altos; Fred Jackson was on tenor; Herman Chittison was on piano; Montgomery Morrison on bass; Charles Alexander, out of Louisville, on banjo and guitar; and William Benton on drums. By the standards of the time, it was a mediocre band, but it got better. I stayed with Zack the whole of 1930, but I didn't make much money. In fact, at one time I was *very* hungry, in Cincinnati, seventy-four miles from Springfield, but I wouldn't write my dad, because he would have made me come home.

"George Thomas, the singer with McKinney's Cotton Pickers, was killed in an automobile accident in November. Joe Smith was driving, and they were juiced. I was playing with Zack in Wheeling, West Virginia, at the time. I knew all the guys in McKinney's band, because the band had originated in my hometown as the Synco Septet. They were John Nesbitt (trumpet), Claude Jones (trombone), Wesley Stewart (tenor and violin), Milt Senior (alto), Todd Rhodes (piano), Dave Wilborn (banjo) and—after Bill McKinney decided to concentrate on the business side—Cuba Austin (drums). They used to play a beach place every summer, and Jean Goldkette heard them up there and wanted to enlarge the group and make it the house band at the Graystone, a million-dollar ballroom he had just built in Detroit. He had his own very popular band, but now he sent to New York to get Don Redman from Fletcher Henderson to come out and build McKinney's band. Don was already an important figure. He had made *Sugar Foot Stomp* and those things before Fletcher himself was writing, and he wrote for Paul Whiteman when Tommy and Jimmy Dorsey were in his band.

"McKinney had heard me sing and wanted me to take George Thomas' place as singer, and play trombone as well. I had a strong tenor voice at that time. There were no microphones, and you had to open your mouth and sing. Miss Gillette, the director of music in my junior high school, used to take me home to teach me reading, voice, and everything. She thought I was going to be another Caruso!

"I joined McKinney's band on 7 December, 1930, and stayed till May,

1932. Ed Cuffee took all the trombone solos. Don Redman left in August, 1931, to get his own band together in New York. When Rex Stewart and Benny Carter joined McKinney's, it was Benny who took Don's place. Goldkette had moved out by this time, after a dispute about money, and Charlie Horvath, one of the Graystone managers, took over booking the band.

"One of the first arrangements Don Redman did for McKinney's was *Shim-Me-Sha Wabble* in 1928, and that sounds almost modern to me right now. But some of his best arrangements were the simple ones. He used to say, 'This is just a little something to get by . . .' And it would be simply beautiful. He was never the type of guy to push himself out front. He's a gentleman, a man, yet an ordinary guy, and the most wonderful fellow I've ever been around in my life. He gave me my nickname, 'Butter', when I joined McKinney, because I was kind of chubby then. He never has changed. He's been the same ever since I've known him. He's a small-town guy, too, from Piedmont, West Virginia. He went to Storer College in Harpers Ferry, a college that had to close about three years ago, because their last enrollment was only eighty-five students.

"When I was coming up, Jimmy Harrison and Claude Jones were great influences among us. Charlie Green, too, and he was the greatest blues trombone player I ever heard. Charlie was a good reader and everything, and he could play a beautiful waltz. When he first left Fletcher, they got Jimmy Harrison in his place, but Jimmy couldn't read so well then, and they fired him and got Charlie back. Later on, Charlie left and they got Jimmy again! Charlie Irvis was with Duke Ellington before Tricky Sam Nanton, and they say he played just like Tricky. I never heard him. Another one who was good they called Slats, and he was with Chick Webb when he had eight pieces, including Johnny Hodges. He played similar to Jimmy Harrison. Of course, I listened to Tommy Dorsey a lot, because he could play a melody and really make you feel it.

"When I left McKinney's, I was supposed to join Fletcher Henderson. Rex Stewart had already left, and Buddy Lee had come back to us from Don Redman's band. Rex called me and said Fletcher wanted me to join him. Benny Carter, Hilton Jefferson, Billy Taylor and I all quit together, and went to New York, where I ran into Don Redman again on Seventh Avenue.

" 'What're you doing here?' he wanted to know.

" 'I'm supposed to go with Fletcher.'

" 'You don't want to go with him. He's not doing much. You come down with us. You *know* us!'

"I said okay, because I would rather go with him. While I waited on Fred Robinson to leave, I worked with Cab Calloway a week at the Cotton Club, doubling at the Lafayette Theatre. Cab wanted me to join his band, but in 1932 it sounded so bad. He had only had it two years. He offered me ninety dollars a week, but I went down to Connie's Inn with Don for sixty-six. I wanted to play good music, and Don's was a wonderful band.

"I remember when Duke first came out with *Solitude*. We were playing at the Harlem Opera House. Ed Inge used to rehearse the band for shows if Don wasn't there, although Don would always rehearse new arrangements. This day I remember, while Inge was rehearsing the show, Don went upstairs, and by the time we finished he came down with an arrangement on *Solitude*. He just tore the manuscript and gave each guy his part. That sort of thing's still happening now. NBC and people like that, when they want something real quick, at the last minute, they call him. And, of course, he does all Pearl Bailey's stuff.

"I was with Don from 1932 to 1940. We did good business up until about 1938, and then it began to get tough. Don had been the first to have three trombones, at the end of 1931, and right after he got 'em Duke went to California and picked up Lawrence Brown to join Juan Tizol and Tricky Sam, so that he had three, too. With me were Claude Jones and Bennie Morton, but after Claude went back to Fletcher Henderson, Gene Simon came in.

"I joined Cab Calloway in 1940. He'd been after me twice before. From the viewpoint of business and discipline, it was good, and I was with him over eight years. During this time, around 1943, Cab had the best band he ever had. The trumpets were Russell Smith, Lammar Wright, Shad Collins and Jonah Jones. Russell was strictly a legitimate trumpet player, not a swing man, and he played a terrific lead. Cab used to give him the first on pretty melodies. On swing things, Lammar or Shad would have it. We had *four* trombones: Keg Johnson, Tyree Glenn, Claude Jones and myself. The saxophone section was great: Hilton Jefferson was on first alto; Andrew Brown, a good section man, played second alto and first clarinet; Walter 'Foots' Thomas and Chu Berry were the tenors; and Al Gibson came in later on baritone. The rhythm section, with Benny Paine on piano, Danny Barker on guitar, Milt Hinton on bass, and Cozy Cole on drums, was also strong. It was a *very* good band, and we had good arrangers in Buster Harding and Andy Gibson. Walter Thomas also did some of the writing, and so did Elton Hill later. As for the singing . . .

"You know, I've heard Cab Calloway settle down and really sing sometimes. I've heard him stop hollering and sing *good*. He was funny about his band. Every year, we got a whole month's vacation with a hundred dollars a week. He started that in '43, when he didn't have a lot of work either.

"When his band broke up in 1948, I fooled around New York for a while. Duke had asked me to join the band before he went to Europe that year, and I took Claude Jones's place in October—for eleven years. Before Tyree Glenn joined, Wilbur De Paris had been responsible for the Tricky Sam plunger work, and it had been all right, but not exactly the way Duke wanted it. Tyree really got the style down. We were playing at the Blue Note in Chicago when he decided he wanted to come home and see his family. He told Duke I would play the plunger solos and, sure enough, when I went to work the next night, there were the mute and plunger by my chair.

" 'What the . . .?' I began.

" 'Tyree says you can play it,' Duke said.

"I found out afterwards he had told Duke, 'Butter can play anything!' Well, we had been good friends since about 1934, when he was with Tommy Miles's band out of Washington. I used to show him a lot of things when he came to New York. This particular night, Duke even called numbers like *Turquoise Cloud* and *Transbluency* on me. I knew them because I'd heard every note Tyree played, so I didn't have to look at the parts. But it was a scuffle at first.

"The plunger is not only something you have to learn, but you've got to know how to characterize Duke's music, how to portray the moods of the different things he writes. You've got to know wnat it's about to get the picture. That's the reason not everyone can go in that band and play successfully. You can be a good musician all you want, but if you don't have imagination, you have no business there. You've *got* to have imagination.

"Duke always had a good trombone section, even when he had three totally different, terrific musicians like Tricky Sam, Lawrence Brown and Juan Tizol. When I was there with Britt Woodman and Juan Tizol—and later John Sanders—he worked the trombone section to death. He'd sit us right in front of the piano, and he'd listen to us all the time. When I first joined, he also had a terrific section of five trumpets—Al Killian, Francis Williams, Shorty Baker, Shelton Hemphill and Ray Nance. They had a very good section sound. Killian played most of the first, and Francis Williams played some, but Shorty played a lot more than people knew about. He has a lot of feeling, a lot of art in his playing.

"When I left Duke in 1959, it was to go with Quincy Jones in the show, *Free and Easy.* It was a take-off from *St. Louis Woman,* and Sammy Davis was supposed to join it. I thought it would mean I would not have to go on the road and do one-nighters anymore, and that I could stay in New York and get recording dates, because I knew a lot of contractors. But the show fell through. Quincy wanted to keep the band, and because he's such a wonderful guy we all agreed to stay with him. We toured Europe, and I liked that. We did a couple of months in Sweden and toured all the folk parks. We settled in Paris for a few weeks, and then traveled around.

"When we came back, we went into Birdland, but then Quincy had nothing else coming up. Soon after that, when Count Basie was going into Birdland, Al Grey broke his ankle, and I went down and took his place.

" 'Gee,' Basie said, 'that's the sound I've been listening for!' He had a fit, you know.

"After that, I made the music for a picture with Quincy, and was around New York until one night when Britt Woodman and I were sitting up talking in my room. The telephone rang, and it was Basie's man, Snodgrass.

" 'Can you make it?'

" 'Yeah.'

" 'You got fifteen minutes!'

" 'What'm I gonna wear?'

" 'Anything brown.'

"I had a brown suit and put it on. They were playing over at Fort Dix, New Jersey.

" 'It's nice working in the band again,' I told Basie. 'Al'll be back tomorrow night?'

" 'No, he won't,' he said. 'He won't be back tomorrow night, nor the next night, nor the next night. This is your gig so long as you want it!'

"We came back to New York and Snodgrass got me a uniform. I've been with Basie since 19 January, 1961. This was the fifth time Basie was after me. He wanted me to take Dan Minor's place 'way back. And he wanted me to take Bill Hughes's place once when he left. When Al Grey left this time, I *did* take somebody's place in the band. I have a few first parts to play, too, although I never played first in other bands. I get tired of one-nighters, though, because I seem to have been doing them ever since I left home. The longest I've been in one place since 1929 is sixteen weeks. There's a certain goal I'm trying to reach financially, and when I reach that I'm going to quit one-nighters. I want to get a bass and play that!

"I started fooling with bass when Billy Taylor and I were in McKinney's band in 1931. Then, when I was with Don Redman, I got to fooling with Bob Ysaguirre's bass. In Calloway's band, Milt Hinton and I used to do a duet together. And I played bass in Duke's band once or twice when Wendell Marshall or Jimmy Woode couldn't make it for one reason or another.

"My biggest kicks? I had a lot of wonderful kicks with Don Redman, but I had more kicks musically with Ellington than with any other band. To me, his is the greatest music that's ever been written. He plays the things he

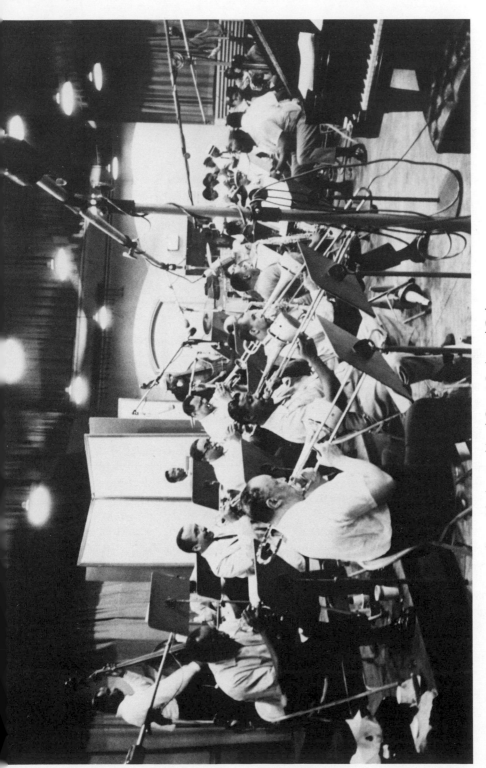

Quentin Jackson (nearest camera) recording with the combined Count Basie and Duke Ellington bands, 1961.

figures the public will go for right now, but he kept over three hundred arrangements in the book. In the course of a year, we would only play about a hundred of them. Some of the others had been recorded, but never released.

"On the other hand, not since the Calloway days have I been in a band that plays and swings with the consistency of this one of Basie's."

(1962)

VIC DICKENSON

TROMBONE

Vic Dickenson is not a little unusual in his love and knowledge of melodies, and in a mind which inclines to original tempos and treatment for them. "He knows about a million numbers," his friend Dicky Wells once said, "and he always likes to play melodies."

"That's partly true," Dickenson said when reminded of that statement. "I like to play the melody and I want it still to be heard, but I like to re-phrase it and bring out something fresh in it, as though I were talking or singing to someone. I don't want to play it as written, because there's usually something square in it. Now, Johnny Hodges, he plays melody, but he makes such *beautiful* melody because he plays it in his own way. He's one of the best soloists I know. You've got to feel it, and Johnny does. He's the greatest alto, I think. Bechet had a lot of what Johnny has, but it wasn't as smooth and tender. He played with more drive and was rougher."

Vic Dickenson was born in Xenia, Ohio, in a musical milieu. There was an organ in the house, but he never, he noted with sadness, heard his mother play it. His father played a little violin—"folk music, you might call it"—and his own first instrument was harmonica. "I could play things like *There's No Place Like Home,*" he said, "but I couldn't play them well."

His brother was supposed to be taking trombone lessons, but he failed to give much time to the horn, which lay about the house, neglected. The time came when the principal at young Vic's school decided to form a band and asked all the children who had instruments to bring them. Vic told him he had a trombone home but didn't know anything about it. "Bring it on in anyhow," said the principal, who had formerly been a trombone player.

He showed Vic positions by the solfeggio method and left him to find where they were in every key by himself. "I had been something of a singer when I was a kid, and that was the way the singing teacher had taught us, so it wasn't too hard to understand," he said. "But it takes time to learn trombone. It's the brass horn most like the violin and it's a matter of position rather than valve. You just have to learn to feel it, so you won't play this note too flat or too sharp. I used to copy records at first and I loved Mamie Smith's Jazz Hounds, but then I got tired of hearing the trombone and wanted to play like the other instruments. The singing and the words meant nothing to me; it was the horns and the melodies that I heard. The trombone's part was too limited and I learned what everybody played on the records, the saxes and clarinets, too."

Dickenson's father was a contracting plasterer and his two sons were learning the trade in Columbus when Vic met with a serious accident. "I had a heavy hod full of mortar on my shoulder and a rung of a ladder broke," he explained. "I was bent back double and never could lift anything heavy after that, so I had to quit hard, physical work."

Vic and his brother, Carlos, who played clarinet and alto, joined Roy Brown's band in Columbus. A cousin, also a plasterer, was playing piano in it, but only in F sharp. "And I could play very good in F Sharp," Vic claimed. This was his first band and after that he and his brother were in another local group, the Night Owls. Work and money were not plentiful around Columbus, however, and eventually Carlos joined a band from Cleveland while Vic went off to another led by Don Phillips in Madison, Wisconsin.

"I was up there until I was fired because I couldn't read," he recalled. " 'Play the C scale,' the leader said one day. I didn't know the C scale from any other, because I was just playing from doh-ray-mi-fah, but I could pick up the horn and play anything I heard on it. It was just like singing to me. I was fired without being given any notice or transportation back, and that made me mad. I had to play piano and sing to make enough money to get out of town.

"After that experience, I learned to read and to arrange by myself, from books and by asking questions. That would be about 1926. I found that to play melody on a trombone you had to transpose pieces to a brighter key than the one they were originally written in. I'd heard Claude Jones with the Synco Septet by this time—he was with McKinney's Cotton Pickers later—and been very impressed. He didn't play the instrument like a trombone. He played all over it. Then I heard Jimmy Harrison with Fletcher Henderson's band, which was popular around that time—1926–29. I also used to buy all the Gennett records by Ladd's Black Aces and I liked the way Miff Mole played melody, rather than the old way that sounded like a dying cow in a thunderstorm. The trombone was late developing as compared with the other horns. Jimmy Harrison and Jack Teagarden both sounded like Louis Armstrong and they influenced me because they were playing the way I had wanted to play before I heard them."

While he was still studying, Dickenson went to Kentucky for a period and then to Cincinnati, where he took J.C. Higginbotham's place with Helvey's Troubadours. "We were troubadours all right," he remarked. "We went all around!" Then he went back to Madison and a band which contained Reunald Jones and some of the musicians he had previously worked with, but this time they were fronted by Leonard Gay.

On his return to Columbus in 1929, he joined Speed Webb's band for a little over a year. "It was a very good band," he said. "Webb had Roy Eldridge, who used to come down from Detroit with his brother, and Teddy Wilson and his brother. Teddy was crazy about Earl Hines and was playing beautifully even then. Seven guys arranged in that band, including Teddy's brother, Gus, and every week we had seven new arrangements. Of course, we played everything in the way of dance music in those days —waltzes, pop songs, everything. I did some arranging, but I didn't bother with it much because I found it held me up in my playing. I'd be thinking about the other horns and get mixed up. I wouldn't want to get into it now unless I stopped playing. I imagine that was how it was with Sy Oliver. It's not the same for a piano player, because he's got everything there. Playing a horn is a different thing.

"Sy Oliver was in Zack Whyte's band, which Roy Eldridge and I joined in Cincinnati. Several guys left Speed Webb because there was no work. Zack was playing walkathons. That was what they were called, but people just danced, for hours and hours and hours. It was like polesitting, to see how long they could do it. We'd play for a time and then another band would take over. After we'd been to the Savoy in New York, we went out on a five-band tour with Bennie Moten, Blanche Calloway, Andy Kirk, and Chick Webb. We played all around and the tour broke up in Cincinnati. The guys weren't making so much, but the ballrooms used to be jammed and the promoters made money. That was how the Kansas City guys came to know about me. When Bennie Moten's band was splitting up, they sent for me. So I went out there and played with Thamon Hayes for a while. Harlan Leonard was in that band and later he took it over. I left after a few months, but went back the following year.

"This time we had a booker and we went down the Missouri on a boat, up the Mississippi and on to Peoria, Illinois. From there we went to Chicago, where a lot of negotiating went on, but not much happened. Eventually I got a wire from Blanche Calloway and I joined her band. Cab Calloway was famous then and besides Blanche there was a Ruth Calloway and several other Calloways trying to cash in on the name, but so far as I know Blanche was the only other one to have a good band, with people like Ben Webster in it. On the records, she did a lot of singing, but we played plenty of dance music, too, and with her I started to come east more often. I was with her from 1933 to 1936, when I joined Claude Hopkins. Jabbo Smith was in that band. Stump Brady and I took the trombone solos, but Stump wanted to play like Tommy Dorsey then."

After a spell with Benny Carter in 1939, Dickenson joined the flourishing Count Basie band in 1940. "All the musicians knew me," he remembered, "but it wasn't until I was with Basie that the writers and people seemed to become aware of me. Dicky Wells and Dan Minor were in the section. We went all around and being with Basie was a big help to me. Dicky and I played the jazz solos and we had many a nice drink together. There were two or three numbers on which we both used to solo.

"When I left Basie in 1941, I worked with Sidney Bechet. He and I got on fine together, personally and musically. He had a style of his own and you had to know it. He just didn't like trumpet players. He said they got in his way.

"The next job was with Frankie Newton, the trumpet player. I was down at Café Society when Frankie's contract ran out and the guy there hired Eddie Heywood's trio. After about one night of the trio, he called me to see if I wanted to come down and play with Eddie. So I said, 'Sure,' and I was the first horn Eddie had. Then he got a saxophone and a trumpet, and that went on for two or three years and was quite popular. After playing the Downtown Café, we went to California, came back and played the Uptown Café Society as well as 52nd Street. We did some recording and people still talk to me about *You Made Me Love You.*

"I got very sick when I was out on the Coast again in 1947. I had a lot of trouble with an abscessed ulcer and I had to hang around a long while and have a second operation. In the meantime, I formed my own band and it was pretty nice, though the fellows in it were not well known."

When he returned East, Dickenson "played around Boston for a long, long time—about eight years." He went into the Savoy there with Edmond

Vic Dickenson and Charlie Shavers.

Hall and stayed on as a kind of house trombonist until the manager opened his own club downtown. Dickenson took over there with his friend, Buster Bailey, and stayed on to play first with the McPartlands and then with Bobby Hackett. After working in New York with Hackett, he went back to Boston and George Wein's Mahoghany Hall. Wein's appreciation of the trombonist's talent subsequently led to appearances at Newport, in Belgium, Germany and Japan. In 1957, he returned to New York and once more took J.C. Higginbotham's chair, this time with Red Allen and Buster Bailey at the Metropole.

With Red Richards, the story comes more up to date. "I'd known Red since the early '30s, when we both lived in Harlem," Dickenson said. "He would go out and play piano as a single, but he and I used to sit down and talk about getting a group together and the Saints and Sinners really began about 1960, and that became the main thing."

Vic Dickenson is a musician of considerable and varied experience, as these notes may have indicated, but he still has a number of unresolved ambitions.

"I always wanted to record with my brother, Carlos," he said, "but he died this year. He played alto and clarinet very well and he was due to retire from the mail service in 1964, and then I thought it would be easy to get him to come and make a record with me, if only someone would have backed me.

"I would like to make an album that was really my own, one where I picked the men. Every time I've made a record, someone else has picked for me. I'd like seven or eight pieces and if I chose them I would get real co-operation. I have some beautiful numbers of my own, too, that I want to record, but I want my own date—and royalties. I never have had any royalties on any records. When I was in Japan and Australia, people were always asking where they could get my records. Sometimes I wonder whether companies wait until musicians die before they re-issue records, so that they won't have to pay royalties.

"One of my numbers was recorded in 1956—*What Have You Done with the Key to My Heart?*—but it was issued in Europe only. It was a good album, made with Budd Johnson (one of the greatest), André Persiany and Taft Jordan. Some of my numbers like that could use a good singer. You know who I would like to record with—the Mills Brothers! As I said, I always have liked melodies."

(1964)

DOC CHEATHAM

TRUMPET

Adolphus "Doc" Cheatham was born in Nashville in 1905. His father had played mandolin at one time, and he had an aunt who taught voice at Tuskegee Institute, but he recalled no other musically inclined individuals in the family background.

"A little church down there in Nashville organized a boy's band," he began. "They took up donations from the neighborhood to buy used instruments for kids who were interested. I wanted a saxophone, but they gave me a cornet, and I started playing it before I had any lessons. The teacher was well qualified, and I think we had only to pay a quarter a lesson. My father later bought me a soprano saxophone, and I liked that. To me, it seemed to finger something like a trumpet, and I didn't have any difficulty at all.

"When I was about fourteen, I went down to Atlanta, which is my mother's home. She had a twin who married a Chinese, and he had a laundry down there. I worked for him in the summer. He taught me how to wrap parcels and make change. It was pretty unusual to be allowed near the cash register in a Chinese laundry! I had my cornet with me, and I got to play with Eddie Heywood's father in an old, makeshift theatre called the 91. He was a heck of a piano player, and you can hear a lot of him in what his son does today. Even that strong bass Eddie played on *Begin the Beguine* reminded me of his old man, and I told him so. Eddie, Sr., played all the shows, all the acts, and we just had a ball!

"I had a good ear and got some reading experience in the pit at the Bijou Theatre in Nashville, where I played the shows that came down on the circuit. That's where I heard all the singers, including Ethel Waters, and played for them. I don't think Ma Rainey was as talented as Bessie Smith, and her voice wasn't as big as Bessie's, although I don't think Bessie had a very large voice, either. Clara Smith had a stronger voice than Bessie. Ma Rainey was not a real, loud-singing type, and Bessie had a more musical voice for singing blues, but Clara shouted and was louder than all of 'em. Everybody liked her, and she was more popular than Bessie at that time. She would pack that theatre. She was a rough, mean-looking girl, and she'd come into rehearsal cussing everybody out. The class of people who

Doc Cheatham.

came to that theatre liked that! The acts in those days would play a month at a theatre, and not get any sleep. Then they'd get on a train, travel to the next town, and go straight to the theatre before they even got their room. That was the routine. We'd be sitting there rehearsing, and they'd come in, mean and evil, cussing everybody out right off the bat. They didn't want to hear from nothin'! That's the way it was.

"While I was in Nashville, I met Jimmie Lunceford, Willie Smith and those guys when they were still at Fisk University. Willie Smith was some player! You don't hear lead players with distinct personalities like that anymore. It's a matter of slam, bam, you take it now! Everybody's expected to be able to play everything. I wasn't around Willie much, but there always seemed to be something on his mind, something worrying him.

"I went to Louisville and worked in a roadhouse there during vacations, but when I really left home for the first time it was in *Sunshine Sammy's Revue,* playing saxophone in Marion Hardy and Charlie Turner's band. Hardy played clarinet and alto saxophone. He was a good musician and he had a nice band for a long time. The show broke up in Chicago, where I joined Al Wynn's band, a regular, Dixieland-type combination. While I was with Wynn, he had a record date with Ma Rainey, and he set it up for me to play soprano on it. I remember that very well. Ma was a homely woman, not rough at all. I don't think she'd gotten to the point then where she'd be nasty to musicians.

"Dreamland, the place where Wynn was working, didn't do too much business, and closed down. I had started playing cornet again in his band, and I noticed that people seemed to like it better than my saxophone. I was listening to everybody all the time, and making progress on the cornet. The first trumpet player I liked was Louis Panico! Of course, what he was doing was a lot of funny stuff. Then came Johnny Dunn, and I liked the first recording of his I heard. After that, I saw Joe Smith and heard him play, and he made a big impression on me. These guys just knocked me out one after the other, but I don't think I would have continued on cornet if I hadn't heard Louis Armstrong. At that time, I liked tenor saxophone so much, and although it wasn't so advanced, there were a few guys playing it, like Barney Bigard . . . I thought he was the greatest tenor player I ever heard in my life! I hadn't heard Coleman Hawkins then. On alto, it was Darnell Howard for me.

"After hearing Louis Armstrong, Joe Oliver and all those trumpet players from Louisiana in Chicago, I saw something very different and interesting in the trumpet. I decided that it was *the* instrument, and I just forgot saxophone altogether. I even substituted for Louis Armstrong a couple of times at the Vendome. But my trumpet style didn't come from just one player. I had too many influences, and I liked the ones who could play lead trumpet. In fact, I wanted to be a good lead trumpet myself, and that threw me off a little bit.

"In Chicago, I had to buckle down and learn to read. I had a lot of help. Erskine Tate's brother, James, who played second trumpet in the Vendome band, was very kind, and he showed me a lot of things. Jerry Blake, the clarinet player, and I worked together just like a team, and somebody sent us tickets to join Bobby Lee's Cotton Pickers—a ten-piece band—at the Cinderella Inn in Philadelphia. We didn't get paid the first week, and when the place closed down we went to a theatre in Atlantic City, and got stranded there. I got a job pushing chairs on the boardwalk and working in a hotel. Then I met some musicians and was offered a job with Charlie Johnson's band at the Paradise. He had about ten pieces, too, but when they brought on a new show and found I couldn't really read, they let me out.

"I remember playing at the Pearl Theatre in Philly with Wilbur DeParis around this time, but then Jerry Blake and I went to New York and joined Lew Henry, a trombone player who had a band and was quite popular. We played the Keith Circuit theatres in a show with different acts, and sometimes Lt. Tim Brymn—a veteran or something—used to direct the band. That didn't last long, either, and then I worked with Chick Webb before he went to the Savoy. That's when I first met Johnny Hodges and Freddy Jenkins. They were both in the band, and gigging around, playing different dances. Johnny was playing the same way then. He always played the same. Chick liked me very much, and I thought he was some character, a fine fellow.

"Then Sam Wooding came along. He was a more established leader than Chick, and he took Jerry Blake and me to Europe in May, 1928. Tommy Ladnier, the trumpet player, was my roommate over there, and he was a wonderful guy, full of jokes all the time. He kept the band in good spirits. He was not too much interested in reading, and he was certainly not a *fast* reader. I played lead and did quite a lot of the solo work, too. They worked me pretty hard in that band. We went straight to Germany, and stayed there a long time. Then we went to Spain and France, and all through the Balkans, but for some reason they wouldn't let Sam take the band into England at that time. I was thrilled with Europe, and really didn't notice any discrimination at all.

"When I came back from Europe in 1930, I joined Marion Hardy's Alabamians at the Savoy in New York. It was a very entertaining band, and most of the guys were western musicians. Eddie Mallory was the best known. After a year with them, I went to McKinney's Cotton Pickers.

"They were making changes about that time, and Benny Carter and I went in practically together. Joe Smith was already there, and then Rex Stewart came in. Mr. Quentin Jackson was there, and that trombone player I liked so much, Ed Cuffee. Besides Benny Carter and Prince Robinson, there was Jimmy Dudley, a very fine alto player. In the rhythm section were Billy Taylor, Dave Wilborn, Cuba Austin and a big fellow on piano who died not long afterwards. The Graystone in Detroit was the home base, but we traveled a lot on the worst buses anyone could find. Sometimes the bus would break down before we could get out of Detroit. Even the stage we were on broke down one time. You had to be young and have a certain temperament for that kind of life. We just looked forward all the time to getting on the bandstand and blowing.

"I played lead and some of the solos. When Joe Smith left, I took most of his solos. I knew his brother, Pops Smith, very well. He didn't play what you'd call a swinging trumpet. He was very well schooled, and he played what he saw, and he played it *right*. He was strictly legitimate. When Louis Armstrong was in Fletcher Henderson's band, he had played some lead, too, and he had played with a different swing. I don't think Coleman Hawkins ever forgot that.

"McKinney's was the best band I'd been in up to now. I only recorded with them once, because they had a system. They would take a nucleus only to record in Camden or New York, and pick up other men in New York. I guess they did that to save money.

"After about a year with them, I got a call to join Cab Calloway. I think Walter Thomas was responsible for that. He had heard me somewhere, and I was beginning to get a bit of a reputation as a lead trumpet. Lammar Wright had been there a long time, but Wendell Culley and Reuben Reeves, the other two trumpets, left right away. Then Swayzee ('King' Edwin Swayzee) came in. He was originally from Little Rock, and most of the time he had been with different road shows. He was a very good trumpet player, but he was not known enough when he joined Cab, and he died in 1935 before he could really make a name for himself. He had a good sound, and he wrote very well, too. I remember him writing some arrangements for Cab. He was not an alcoholic, just a moderate drinker, but he had something like uremic poisoning.

"Irving Randolph took his place, and he could always play. He had studied a lot, and he played *everything,* especially good New Orleans music. He was tops in that. He had a good conception, and I could never understand how he could give up music, but I think it was just that he got tired and wanted to be more with his family.

Doc Cheatham, saxophone, with Pearl High School Orchestra. Jerry Blake, clarinet, in front.

Doc Cheatham, trumpet, at Dreamland Cafe, Chicago, 1926, with L. to R.: Gerald Reeves, trombone; Joe Duff, drums; Bill Woods, piano (at one time with Bessie Smith); Count Turner, banjo; "Fat Man" Turner, bass; Warner Seals, tenor saxophone; Jerry Blake, alto saxophone.

Bobby Lee's Cotton Pickers at Sea Girt Inn, New Jersey, 1927. Lincoln Mills, trumpet; Juan Tizol, trombone; Doc Cheatham, trumpet.

Jimmy Crawford, drums, 1958. In background: Doc Cheatham, Buster Bailey, Coleman Hawkins, Juanita Hall, Claude Hopkins, George Duvivier.

"I liked Cab. I think he was one of the best leaders. The money was always right there on time, no matter what. From 1932 on, the band started swinging and kept getting better. He brought in artists like Chu Berry, Ben Webster, Jonah Jones, Shad Collins, Milt Hinton, Hilton Jefferson, Cozy Cole, and all those guys, and made a great band. I played lead all the time until 1939, when we were playing at the Cotton Club and I got a very bad case of 'flu. That led to a real breakdown, and I went back to Nashville for a while. Later in the year, I joined Teddy Wilson's band in New York.

"Teddy and Buster Harding were doing most of the arranging. They had a way of writing for the trumpets so that I played an octave lower than the first trumpet, so the lead was doubled. With the two trombones, they got a very nice sound, good and strong. Shorty Baker and Karl George were the other two trumpets. We played the Golden Gate ballroom uptown, and it was a very clean band, but it didn't last too long. I don't know what happened, but I heard too many tales. All of a sudden, Teddy just gave it up and the band broke up.

"Joe Watts had a place in New London, Connecticut, and I played up there with Wayman Carver and Cliff Jackson. We had five pieces, and I stayed up there until I joined Benny Carter in 1941. I was also rehearsing with Fletcher Henderson for the Savoy around that time, but something happened and we didn't make it. Then I joined Eddie Heywood at Café Society and was with him over a year. That little group he had then was really terrific. I always remember one night when there was a heckler in the club, and Eddie got into a fight. Al Lucas, the bass player, flew off the stand like an airplane, right into the middle of it. Of course, Eddie was more exposed, because he had his piano right out on the floor, but the whole band soon got involved. So much was happening back in those days! The only reason I left Eddie was because I had another sort of breakdown. I was in hospital a week in Tennessee, and they said I was just run down —too much going too fast! I never was a very strong person, and when I was young I was very thin. Traveling on the road a lot, and just living on sandwiches, was more than I could take. But some guys seem to get fat on it. They can eat a hamburger and go for twenty-four hours.

"I knew I wasn't strong enough then to go back in a big band, so I opened a studio and started teaching. I had a lot of Latin students, and sometimes there'd be a need for a trumpet player, and I began to get a few gigs that way. I began playing in Marcelino Guerra's band, and in Machito's, going from one to the other, and I liked it for a while. It was easy playing for me, and I was building myself back up again. The music was very easy to play at that time—light, simple, requiring no force—but they began to swing after a while, and you have to be strong to play in a Latin band now. After the period when the rhumba was popular, the music merged more with jazz, and Perez Prado had a lot to do with that.

"Prado was and is a great man, an individual with a talent different from anyone else. I played in his band for about three months, and it was a hard band to play in. He didn't care about any limitations. He'd write in one octave and then tell you to play it an octave higher. Paul Webster and I worked for him on a tour of South America, and he was crazy about Paul. He had written something he didn't think Paul could make, and one night down in Uruguay he called Paul out and tested him. Paul played that thing, went up so high, and played so long and beautiful up there, that Perez Prado just fell out on the floor! He couldn't believe it.

"Prado was a Cuban, and he started his band in Mexico. He wrote most of the arrangements himself, and he liked the idea of the American influence. He didn't like Latin trumpet playing, but wanted it on the jazz side, and that was why he hired us. At this time (1957–60), I was also doing a lot of dates and recording with Wilbur DeParis. (You could always get away from a Latin band. They're always nice like that—let you out, and you can come back.)

"Sidney DeParis was a great trumpet player, but several years younger than Wilbur, although he didn't look it towards the end. When their father died, Wilbur had promised to look after him, and he was always the boss. Sidney had to get permission to do this or that, and I don't think he cared too much for that.

"So I was doubling in Latin and Dixieland, playing with all kinds of bands, with Sammy Price, Herbie Mann and Benny Goodman, here, in Europe and in Africa. I didn't ever have one bit of trouble with Benny. I rehearsed with him a lot, but I never heard him fire anyone, or tell musicians he couldn't use them. They just didn't come back. Whatever he did, he did it very quietly. I thought he was very nice, a fine man.

"After that period, I joined Ricardo Ray's band for about four years. We played clubs and ballrooms around New York, and went to Puerto Rico and South American countries. There are a lot of Spanish places all over New York, Brooklyn and Long Island—they've got a thousand of them! It was always dancing, and we had two trumpets, piano, bass, two drummers and two singers who sometimes doubled. We recorded for Roulette and United Artists, and I did a lot more with other little Latin bands. I'd have ad-lib solos to play, and most of the time only two chords to improvise on. That's very, very hard, but you get used to it, and it comes out all right. Around 1945, when I had the studio, I wrote a small book trying to explain improvisation, and the use of the ear. I had some demonstration choruses written up, and it went like hot cakes when it was published in London. It wasn't a whole lot of *études,* not just a book to make some money. Most of the 'method' books are all alike.

"When Dizzy Gillespie first came out with his be-bop trumpet, I didn't like it at all. It sounded to me like it was absolutely nothing. He had to develop that tone in order to play like that. It took me a long time to understand, but if you hear anything long enough it begins to make some sense. One result of bop was a split in the listening people, and I don't know that it really helped any. There used to be a tremendous following, but what with this kind of rock, that kind of rock, jazz, bop, progressive, big bands and everything, the people are all divided. You notice the split even more in Japan. Dixieland is practically gone in New York City now. You can go to clubs here and see people sitting up listening to this new music, and they say it's great, but they *can't* understand it. I think the musicians who work together may understand what each other is doing, but I know it took me a long time to understand what Ornette Coleman was up to.

"It was all right putting jazz in the concert hall, but it was *absolutely* wrong taking it out of the dancehall. You play in a different way when people are dancing. The people who go to Roseland, for example, want to do the cha-cha-cha and dances like that. Basie and Harry James have drawn big crowds on one-nighters, and they might be able to work a whole week there, but there would have to be a small Latin combo as well.

"I played up at the Concord in the Catskills with Machito for several years. He started with the full band, and he wouldn't reduce it under ten pieces for anybody. The people up there were mostly Jewish, not Latin, but they loved the band. Latin music has retained its popularity with dancers, but the jazz people have lost it. People stopped dancing to jazz and sat down listening to it. Of course, when the cha-cha-cha came in, it was a new thing, a new craze, and very easy for people to do, almost like when the Charleston came in. And they're still doing the Charleston up there in the mountains! You play the Charleston and *everybody* is out dancing. It's still very popular, and Machito would play it. After all, Mario Bauza and quite a few Americans were in the band. Once a week, we'd play out by the pool, mostly cha-cha-chas and meringues, but when we played the Charleston everybody would be jumping up and down.

"I'd agree that Basie's is probably the best jazz group for dancing today, but you put it up against Machito's at a place like the New York Casino and it wouldn't stand a chance, because Basie cannot play a meringue or a cha-cha-cha. But Machito can turn right around and bring out a nice American arrangement, too. All those places in the Catskills have instructors, and every day they're teaching the people how to do the Latin dances, and when the people have learned they naturally want the music to go with the steps. Even in Harlem, the kids like the Latin dances. There are a lot of places in Queens where Americans go to dances, and they all have Latin bands. The Latin people don't go there. They're very funny. They like to dance in a neighborhood place, where they feel at home.

"What else is there for Americans to dance to now, apart from rock 'n' roll? They don't play fox-trots. I don't think bands like they used to have at the Savoy could make it today. I attended a dance at the Renaissance ballroom where they had a good American band and Ricardo Ray's. The first band was playing good stocks and arrangements like Basie's, but the people didn't get out on the floor and dance until Ray began playing. And that was in Harlem!

"I've been very lucky. I've played with some fine bands, but I've never worked with Duke Ellington, and I wanted to so badly at one time. Juan Tizol was a good friend of mine, and once, when they were playing in Brooklyn, he told me they needed a trumpet player. He took me over there to see Duke. Duke was in his dressing room, but he didn't have anything at all to say about the job, and I had felt that was why Tizol had taken me. I just sat there while Duke got dressed, and he passed a remark every now and then, but nothing about the job. I wanted to play in that band so bad, and I felt I could have done a good job in it. When Artie Whetsol died, I felt it was *my* band, and I wanted to get in there. So that was one of my major disappointments, and I felt foolish just sitting there in that dressing room.

"I'm not the type of fellow to ask for a job, to come right out and say, 'I hear you want a trumpet player.' I prefer someone to *want me*. Eddie Heywood came to me and said, 'Doc, I like the way you play. You want to come with me?' That was it! That's how I like it to be. And that was why I worked with Maynard Ferguson's band once in London. He was so nice. I didn't ask for any money, and maybe I should have, but he made me feel so good, and I played with him on the whole *Top Brass* tour of Europe in 1967. Benny Morton and I were featured with the same rhythm section as Clark Terry and Bob Brookmeyer, and then we joined Maynard in the last set. We really enjoyed that."

A quiet, dignified and courteous man, Doc Cheatham looks every inch the professional when he takes the stand to blow his trumpet in different contexts around New York. The correct, precise way he handles his instrument is immediately indicative of someone intent on giving his best, and his best—among the handful of trumpet-playing survivors from the Swing Era—remains extremely impressive. As the foregoing must have made clear, he is an unusually versatile musician, one capable of playing pretty and sweet with Benny Goodman at the Rainbow Grill, and of storming out with a high-flying lead in last choruses by the group of Basie alumni Earle Warren presents in college auditoriums.

(1972)

EDDIE HEYWOOD

PIANO

"Some of Fletcher Henderson's musicians knew my father very well, and Don Redman was a particular friend of his. They used to kid me, saying that I played well, but that they thought my old man was better! He had gone to the Boston Conservatory of Music as a young man, but he didn't stay as long as he should. His father wanted him to stay and study more, but he came to Atlanta, met my mother, got married, and that was the end of that.

"They had five kids, but I was the only one to become a musician. I would say that I owe everything to my father, who taught me. He was a very fine musician, and besides playing piano he was an excellent trumpeter. He could play saxophone well enough to play first in any band, but as a soloist he was better on trumpet. He was pit conductor at the 81 Theatre in Atlanta, and he stayed in that city with his family except when he went on tour with the great vaudeville team of Butterbeans and Susie.

"All the performers who played the vaudeville circuit, the Lafayette in New York (before the Apollo) and so on, would wait until they got to Atlanta to have him write their act. He was that good. What used to fascinate me was that he could be playing and listening to what was going on on stage, and writing their act more or less at the same time. I can write and arrange, but I've never seen anyone else able to do that, to play and never cross them up on stage, and still concentrate on writing something else altogether in between. His penmanship for writing manuscript was excellent, too; it looked exactly as though it was printed.

"What sort of piano did he play? Well, he came along at the time of the great jazz pianists like James P. Johnson, and there were times when he played like them. There was one thing I'm sure I got directly from my father. He was capable of playing a melody so great, and then he'd put all those other things in between. His style wasn't like mine. I can stretch a tenth, but that's all. He had large hands and could go beyond that. He really came along at the time when tenths were the vogue, and he played a lot of them in his interpretations, but in his melodic lines he was ahead of his time. I remember that that was what Don Redman always used to say to me: 'He's so far ahead of his time! Why doesn't he come to New York?'

"Don used to come down there in the old days when he had a band, and Fletcher Henderson never used to come through there without seeing my father. They'd hear him, too, when he went to New York to record with Butterbeans and Susie, but they could never persuade him to stay. I believe he would have done it if my mother had consented, but she had a happy home, and kids to bring up.

"He started teaching me at the age of five, when I learned to play a hymn. At fourteen I was playing in the 81 when he went on tour with Butterbeans and Susie. Having been in the theatre all my life, under him, I had some knowledge of how to play an act. As a matter of fact, I had the distinction of playing for Bessie Smith. I used to see her when I was a tiny kid, but now vaudeville was beginning to go down, theatres were closing, and she was not carrying a pianist around with her. She knew me anyway, because I'd met everyone in the theatre who was playing that circuit.

"I was in the 81 about two years. The man who owned it held on as long as he could with vaudeville, but then he saw it was no use. He had to go the way everything else was going. It was all talkies, talkies, talkies . . .

"While I was still at the public school, I played in the Clark University band led by Wayman Carver. It was a good band, and he was a fine musician. He was playing alto then, not flute. I didn't see him again until I went to New York in my early twenties.

"I left Atlanta when I was seventeen and went to Dallas. I had a gig one night in a roadhouse, a log-cabin-type of place, and who should walk in there but John Hammond. He was a youngster then, and just starting to go around and listen. We had drums, saxophone and guitar, and we didn't exactly bowl him over, but I guess he thought I had something, because he didn't forget me.

"After that I went with Clarence Love's band for a couple of years. There was nobody well known in it, but I would say it was the best band I ever worked in. The musicians played wonderfully together, and were great overall so far as tone and everything were concerned. That was when I found out that stocks could sound very well if they were played well. One man who did a lot of them that I remember was Frank Skinner.

"The band went to New York in 1937 to work with the guy who used to sing with Claude Hopkins—Orlando Robeson—but we weren't pleased, and the band went back to Dallas. When Love took it out on the road again, I stayed and organized a little band there in the town. My father had already taught me how to arrange, and I wanted to try something on my own.

"After a while I decided to go to New York, and I was playing in a place one night where Benny Carter used to come. He heard me and hired me. It was a wonderful thing, because I knew of him, had heard him play on records, and respected him as a really first-class musician. I fell right in with him, with his style, because he would sometimes play those rich ballads, and they were the type of music I had been playing with the other band. My good friend Tyree Glenn was in the band, and all the time I was there Benny seemed to lean towards him. Tyree was ill one night and another guy sitting up there, just playing in the band, stood up. I had never heard him take a solo, but now I was astonished. This man can play this much trombone? It was Vic Dickenson.

"Next I went with Zutty Singleton's group at the Vanguard—Zutty on drums and Albert Nicholas on clarinet. I don't know just what really happened, but there was friction. My style wasn't knocking Zutty out, and he, after all, was the boss! But I didn't leave the Vanguard, because Max Gordon was bringing in three youngsters who had worked for him before —Betty Comden, Adolph Green and Judy Holliday. They had arrangements in which every note meant something to their mood, and I was fortunate in having read music since I was a kid. So Max hired me to play for them.

"Then I went to the Three Deuces on 52nd Street where Georgie Auld was the main attraction. He had that big sound, but I didn't regard him as a copy of Hawkins any more than Ben Webster was. He played *himself*. I was happy enough there, but John Hammond came and asked if I would like to work for Barney Josephson at Café Society Downtown. When Barney told me to organize a band, I knew exactly the men I wanted.

"Vic Dickenson had been working with Frank Newton down there, and I wanted him. I remembered a trumpet player who had stood up and played just eight great bars in the middle of *I've Got the World on a String* when Cab Calloway had been appearing at the theatre in Atlanta, and I found him—Doc Cheatham. There was an alto player I'd heard at this time, playing with another man right down the street—Lem Davis. I listened to all these guys play, and a lot of friends of mine couldn't understand how come they didn't get these jobs, but I was hiring men I knew were going to be able to blend with each other. Looking back now, I can see that I had a success with that little band because I hired men who had the same kind of *feel* I had. There must be some sort of communication, something clicking, even in a regular orchestra personnel, if it's going to sound well, and not stiff. That applied to Benny Carter, whose musicians weren't always *all* of the kind he needed for his music. Even though he was capable of playing anything he wanted to play on his horn, basically he was a melodic player, and in order to play his music right you had to feel that type of thing. I did, and he saw to it that I had some solos.

"I organized my group in the last part of 1943, and we stayed together until 1947. It clicked right away, and I did all the writing for it. When Doc Cheatham became ill, I had to hire Emmett Berry, who was a wonderful trumpet player, but he didn't fit like Doc. His way of playing was a little too harsh. Of course, I would do some little things, but I had the band playing melody, and I wasn't really playing. If I may say so, I was really swinging on that date I made with Coleman Hawkins for Signature in 1943.

"During this period, the success we had led to my working too hard. Besides playing, and writing arrangements for my own little band, I played and wrote arrangements for some of Billie Holiday's dates. I recorded with Ella Fitzgerald and did the arrangements. Jack Kapp had me record with Bing Crosby, and with the Andrews Sisters, and do arrangements. It was too much. My health went bad in 1947, and the main place it was settling was in my hands!

"The doctor I had was a bone specialist and he discovered that I had what he called, in layman's terms, an occupational disease. He said it was plain fatigue like a soldier gets who's been in the line too long, and the hands had just gone. Both hands were put in casts that I could take off only twenty minutes a day, and they stayed in these casts for eight months. Sure I was frightened, and I used to cry like a little baby. The doctor knew what was going to happen, that strength would return. But my hands shrank, and they were small anyway. I couldn't even stretch an octave. It became a mental thing with me, and what saved me was my wife. We had married in 1947, just before I became ill, and it was the best thing that ever happened to me.

"I tried to come back in the '50s, but 'out of sight out of mind' is a very true saying. I wasn't doing anything and I was treated real bad by the agencies. Singers started to unfold and the big offices lost interest in instrumental acts. Joe Glaser was great for booking, but he didn't seem to have the kind of rooms that suited me, and I went in places that were wrong. Then I got a job at the Embers, and I must say they weren't nice to me at all. I had to open and close, open and close, but my wife said, 'Just keep right on playing!' Joe Bushkin was the star at that time, but as I began to get better I became the star, and people kept coming in asking what time Eddie Heywood was going on. But then I still wasn't happy.

" 'Eddie,' my wife said to me one day, 'do you remember when you were in Hollywood what Cole Porter told you?'

"I had had a big hit in 1944 with my interpretation of his *Begin the Beguine,* and what he said was: 'Listen, any time someone can play something so different in the left hand as you do, without hurting the composer's work in the right hand, that someone is a born composer.'

" 'Why don't you write?' my wife wanted to know.

" 'I'm a performing artist . . .'

" 'Well, you know what *he* said!'

" "I started to write. First there was *Land of Dreams* with Hugo Winterhalter. Then I wrote *Canadian Sunset,* a big one, and it was funny how that came about. I happened to be playing in Quebec City, and I couldn't speak French, and there was very little communication between the audience and me. I always used to think the people could speak English, but just refused to, or something. Quebec was very quaint and peaceful, and I walked around every day, looking at this and that, including a sunset. One night I went home, and sat right up in bed and wrote *Canadian Sunset,* with no piano. It sold a million and was voted the outstanding song of 1956.

"The next one was a sleeper, *Soft Summer Breeze.* I was making an album for Mercury and decided to put this little song in, and it was this that sold the album. They had to take it out of the album and put it on a single, and it became a hit.

"The music business was getting so bad. Everything was noise. I decided to quit, and I just went up in the country. We could live off the royalties. What helped me make up my mind was the memory of my father leaving home to go on the road with Butterbeans and Susie. There were material things for us kids at home, but we didn't have *him.*

"My boys were growing up, and when I came home I found it was normal for the older one to ask his mother for anything he wanted, because, you know, she had become the father *and* the mother. Who needs this? I thought. I got a little tired of it. So I stayed home, up in Martha's Vineyard, for ten years.

Eddie Heywood's band: L. to R.: Lem Davis, Jack "The Bear" Parker, Eddie Heywood, Doc Cheatham, Vic Dickenson, Al Lucas.

"I listened to other artists, and became convinced that what has hurt jazz as a whole is that the youngsters don't have any respect for the forerunners. When I came in, I had a chance to meet Fats Waller and, in his declining years, James P. Johnson. It was an honor for me, and I was happy. If there was anything I was doing wrong, they would tell me. Teddy Wilson had come along just before me, and he brought something fresh to jazz, but I think the main reason he was capable of doing that was because he had great respect for his peers and those before him.

"To get back into high gear, I think the youngsters must learn to respect the elders. Of course, if they get some respect, the elders must go along with some of the new chord progressions the youngsters have. Then the youngsters have to have the basic foundation the others had, to build on and add to. Otherwise, everyone is just running around in circles.

"One of my sons is twenty-two, the other sixteen, and, yes, they're going to be musicians. They like the new music, but they have respect for the older kinds, too. One of them was playing something by Burt Bacharach today, and he said to me, 'I like this song, but I don't like this change here.' I laughed, because it proved to me he had his own inventive ideas.

"While I was off the scene, I wrote this *Martha's Vineyard Suite*. It has four parts—*Spring, Summer, Fall* and *Winter*—and it reverts back to *Spring*. I played it for the first time up there at a public concert, a hospital benefit that raised eighteen thousand dollars. I wasn't thinking about dollars and cents, but I was very happy with the audience, how attentive it was, and how I was received. Now, when I opened here at the Cookery (Barney Josephson's New York restaurant) the other night, I hadn't gotten used to the instrument, or anything like that, but it was a wonderful feeling when I started on the piano and the audience—young and old—began to applaud. That's one thing *Canadian Sunset* has done for me. It has stayed so strong over the years that the youngsters have heard and know it. One of them told me he had never heard anyone play with so many different moods, nor anyone play so soft and still hold the audience.

"I'd like to go out now and play solo concerts. I believe in my heart that I could have done that at the time I made *Begin the Beguine*. I was known as a jazz player, and jazz will always be my love, but whether it comes from me or someone else, there has to be a new approach and something fresh."

(1972)

ROGER RAMIREZ

PIANO AND ORGAN

Roger Ramirez or "Ram," as he is known to his friends and familiars, was brought up in the San Juan Hill section of New York, along with musicians like Benny Carter and Russell Procope. He lived in the house where Thelonious Monk later lived and his piano tuition began when he was eight years old. Something of a child prodigy, he was in the union when he was thirteen and playing dances not so long after that with an amateur band called the Louisiana Stompers.

"The first jazz records I heard were by Louis Armstrong and Earl Hines," he said. "I'll never forget *Save It, Pretty Mama*. Hines and Fats Waller were my first influences."

After working with Sid Catlett in Rex Stewart's band at the old Empire ballroom, with the Spirits of Rhythm and then Willie Bryant, he took off for Europe in 1937 as a member of Bobby Martin's band, which also included Kaiser Marshall, Johnny Russell and Glyn Pacque. He stayed on after the band broke up and was in Switzerland when World War II began. He made the journey home from Geneva in 1940 via Bordeaux, blacked-out Paris and Holland. After refusing a number of lucrative jobs there, he left Rotterdam just a short while before the city was bombed by the Germans. His ship took eight or nine days to get through the English Channel because of minefields. "It was," he confessed, "a little nerve-wracking."

He played for a while in Ella Fitzgerald's band, for about a year with Charlie Barnet, and then for two years with John Kirby. He very much enjoyed this last little group—and Charlie Shavers' arrangements—and recalled an occasion at the Aquarium when Dizzy Gillespie and Charlie Parker auditioned but didn't satisfy Kirby. He left Kirby in 1945 on the Coast and came back to 52nd Street, where he joined Sid Catlett's group at the Down Beat. This included Miles Davis and Lockjaw Davis, and they played opposite the Al Casey Trio. Big bands were beginning to fade and Ramirez remarked the success of the Nat Cole and Art Tatum trios. After acting as musical director and a fourth of a piano quartet for a French puppet show at *La Vie en Rose*, he increasingly appeared as a single or with a trio.

In 1953, he was working at the Senator Hotel on the boardwalk in Atlantic City. After the job, he would go over to where Wild Bill Davis was playing.

"That was where it happened," Ramirez said. "I had never heard an organ sound so good, and it inspired me. Bill's rocking beat appealed to me at that time of the morning! It was kind of a fight after the piano, but I was soon working really hard on the organ. I had been at Wells's in Harlem with a trio and had returned as a solo pianist. The third time, I appeared as an organist! Wild Bill began at Wells's, too, and I remember jamming there once on piano with him on organ. To this day, Joe Wells will say, 'I wish you and Bill Davis and Bill Doggett would chip in and buy a new organ for me, because you all learned on mine!'

"I think Wild Bill really began it all, although styles have changed. Bill plays more of a band style and that's still good for me. Latterly, there's been more of a pianistic approach. Jimmy Smith has done something for the modern school. He's very fast, has a beautiful technique and tremendous drive, but it's a different technique and approach to Bill's. Of course, the swell pedal is the soul of the instrument. No matter how hard you hit an organ, if your pedal isn't in position you hear nothing—you don't hear what you put into it. It isn't a percussive sound, anyway, but nowadays they're using the pedal to punch more than before. Bill had that technique, but he didn't use it as much as the younger organists are doing. Then they've not worked in large groups as Bill and I have, so they don't have that band feeling.

"That affects piano today, too. It's an unfortunate thing, but young guys have few chances of playing either in large groups or really on their own. Maybe I'm old style, but I believe if you're going to play alone you've got to play the bass of the piano. The piano's a magnificent instrument, but many bop players were only using half of it, because they had never been through the school where they had to play two hands and that bass. Sometimes, I'll play the same thing one of these younger cats has played, and add a bass, and they'll say to me, 'Gee, where did you get that sound?' Very few pianists can play without bass and drums and sound interesting. Fats Waller could. Garner can, and Duke, and Earl Hines, and the Lion. Billy Taylor can, too, because he knows all schools of piano playing. And Tatum could, of course.

"One thing Tatum used to tell me was, 'You have to have a variation in tempo.' Maybe you bring it up a little, or maybe you accentuate it a bit more, but when you accentuate it there's a tendency to bring it down. No one has really perfect tempo. One might be at your pulsation, but your normality might not be mine. One person's natural *andante* might be a strain on the emotions of someone else.

"I set up my standards by Tatum. I thought there was no one like him. I still do as a matter of fact. He liked to play old pianos. They were a challenge to him, to make them really come out. He used to idolize a pianist by the name of Lee Sims, who was what you might call an impressionist. Tatum himself was an entertainer, like the Lion and Luckey Roberts, only he belonged a decade later. He could imitate a nickelodeon piano, or any pianist, such as Earl Hines, just as Sid Catlett could imitate all drummers."

Ramirez has played in all kinds of places these last few years: uptown at Branker's, Minton's and The Shalimar, and downtown in clubs, hotels and restaurants. As this was written, he was playing piano again at Cheers on 41st Street. He had his fingers back ("The different touch can bother you after organ.") and sounded the complete pianist. Seldom fazed by the most outlandish request, the richness and variety of his music, whether on organ or piano, was decidedly impressive. He played show tunes and ballads in an ornate yet highly musical manner that was wholly appropriate to the cocktail hour; but he would swing, too, and madly, with the kind of possession that often seizes Hines, where man, hands and instrument lose individual identity and are absolutely one.

Sooner or later, someone always asked for *Lover Man,* and he would give it the definitive treatment. The number's world-wide success has not, however, been an unmixed blessing to him. In her book, Billie Holiday said, "Ram Ramirez gets all the credit for *Lover Man,* but that's only part of the story." Many people have read into this and the preceding paragraphs an implication hurtful to him. In fact, he had the melody before lyricist Jimmy Davis came into the picture, and the song was not written for Billie. Ramirez holds the certificate of copyright registration issued by the Library of Congress on May 3rd, 1941, over three years before Billie recorded it. The certificate shows Roger Ramirez as responsible for the music and Davis for the words.

"Willie Dukes," Ramirez said, "was the first to sing *Lover Man.* He was with Dizzy and Bird at The Onyx and he sang with great conviction in Billie's style. Eddie Heywood recorded it first, with Doc Cheatham, for Commodore. Then he made it again for Decca and it had *Begin the Beguine* on the back, and that meant a lot. It was later that Billie's version became the big one."

Other examples of Ram's compositional talents to be heard on records

Roger Ramirez.

are *Mad about You* (Helen Humes on Mercury and Ike Quebec on Blue Note), *I Just Refuse to Sing the Blues* (Helen Humes on Mercury) and *It's Better to Wait for Love* (Louis Jordan with Nelson Riddle on Decca). In preparation was a suite, *The Hills of New York*.

"Why not?" he asked. "I was raised on San Juan Hill, I live on Murray Hill, I know about Sugar Hill, and. . . ."

(1961)

NAT PIERCE

PIANO AND ARRANGER

I

"There's a kind of feeling that happens when a band's swinging which is hard to explain, but it's one of the greatest feelings known to man so far as I'm concerned."

After many years of professional music-making, the essence of Nat Pierce's credo was in those words. Considerable experience of the "business" hadn't diminished his appreciation of the first principles of jazz, and he thought beyond the fleeting successes of the moment.

"It seems to me," he said, "that with all the different fads, types and new names that come up every year, there's still something basic going on all the time underneath. I think they try to pull the music forward too fast. They say jazz is a young art, but it's really not *that* young. There are guys who have been in it for a long time, professional jazzmen like Coleman Hawkins. He has been nothing else but a *jazz* tenor player for more than thirty years. There are other musicians who dabble in jazz, but who make most of their money in studio bands or on gigs that are not strictly jazz. Coleman Hawkins, you *know,* is going to play *nothing* but jazz, and it is men like him and Duke Ellington and Louis Armstrong who really give us our criteria.

"The young guys have almost no idea of what went on before Charlie

Parker. They don't realize how he got all his things together, how much hard work there was, how many heartaches, how many times he was told to go home and forget it. They want to show up and win a poll in six months or whatever, and if they make one record date, then that's supposed to ensure their career for the next ten years. It ain't quite like that! They don't realize that Coltrane and guys like him, who are supposed to be *avant-garde,* played with Johnny Hodges, with rock 'n' roll bands, with Dizzy Gillespie and so on. Coltrane has a foundation and knows just exactly what he wants to do. If he makes a mistake, it's more often than not due to exuberance, because he's trying too hard.''

Pierce is no elder statesman himself, but he hit the scene in time to gain big-band experience. It is the possession or lack of this experience that makes for a major jazz division in our time. He maintains that opportunities for younger men to get it still exist.

"But they don't want it. They should learn to play with somebody else, to read music as a member of a section. The sounds they get from their instruments are not band sounds—they are solo sounds. You couldn't have five Coltranes in a sax section. Two altos, two tenors and a baritone with that kind of sound wouldn't add up. Similarly, if you had four Miles Davises in a trumpet section, it would no longer be a trumpet section. Miles has tailored his music to his certain type of sound, and it fits him fine; but guys like Roy Eldridge, Emmett Berry, Shorty Baker and Clark Terry get a note on the trumpet that sings out at you—pow!—and you can hear that thing. Even Dizzy does that, but you couldn't make up a band out of these new people today, because they wouldn't be interested in having only little eight-bar solo bits.

"Where guys live together, drink together, and go on one-nighters together, they may even hate each other, but they *play* together. The reason so many big-band records today don't sound good and don't swing is because they are studio outfits without the time to build up that *rapport.* Stereo hasn't helped, because of the way they split up the rhythm section in the studio. But shakes, trills, matching vibratos—all those things come out right through working together. One guy knows that this other guy is going to play flat on this note, so he tries to pull up on his. It's automatic, a kind of compensation. There's more than one way to swing, of course, but there does seem to be a kind of heartbeat or pulse that is almost completely lacking in jazz today. I was very fortunate to play on a few record dates with the original Count Basie rhythm section. They had a kind of throb going, no one instrument louder than another, so it was like a real section. The key man was Walter Page. They would get behind soloists and give each one a different sound, and there was attention to dynamics in a way not known now.''

As a leader himself, and as a pianist and an arranger, Pierce had good cause to study and appreciate the role of the bandleader in a group's success.

"A bandleader," he said, "has to know how to get that band across to the people out there, and it's not a matter of funny hats and flowery speeches. I learned from watching those I worked for. They're like supersalesmen, but each works differently. Of course, the guys you hire have to have respect for you, unless you can give them fabulous salaries. But a lot of guys who lead groups are not bandleaders.

"Now, Duke Ellington is a professional bandleader. There's no possible way in life he's going to play piano for anyone else. He's out there, and he has a theatrical feeling that's part of show business. Basie is a bandleader of a different class, because he's very shy, but he knows how to control the men without creating any scenes. He may have learned some of this from Duke, too. Guys like Shorty Baker told me how they would rehearse a piece and maybe not play it for six months, and the guy who was featured in it would get juiced or do some stupid thing, and then Duke would call on him to play that piece. It wasn't a question of playing it from his chair in the trumpet section, but down to the mike he must come, and he hadn't seen the piece in six months and then had only played it three times. The others would be playing from their parts, but he was out there mumbling and stumbling, trying to get the piece together, and maybe there'd be a call, 'Take another one!' I've seen Basie do that a lot of times, even up at the theatre. A guy would start moaning and groaning, and maybe get a little stoned, and—boom!—the first number, there he was, out there, on his own. And Basie would be there, tinkling gently away at the piano, apparently unaware of anyone's discomfort!

"Woody Herman's band was another kind of operation. When it was playing its worst, he would be the happiest, because he knew he couldn't do anything about it. We'd be doing one-nighters and he's out there shaking hands with the people, operating in a different kind of way. Some guys in the band, like myself, might want him to do something about it, to make changes. 'Be patient,' he would say, 'there's plenty of time. It doesn't happen overnight.' Now when the band started to get good—and he had some excellent bands while I was there—then he'd get tough, and want morè, because he saw it approaching how it could really sound, and he wanted to hurry it along. Those guys have patience. It's a protective thing, too, because you could get an ulcer in ten minutes worrying about everything."

One of the leaders Pierce worked for was Larry Clinton, and he retains great respect for him as a leader and musician. At that time, Woody

Herman had his Second Herd and records like *Lemon Drop* and *Early Autumn* were being issued.

"We flipped," Pierce recalled. "Boy, these were the greatest! Larry would come up to the room and we would play him the records. Now I also had a Capitol record of *Prelude to a Kiss* by Benny Carter's big band, which was horribly out of tune, but it was a good record. Larry would listen to a Herman record and say, 'Yes, it sounds good, but it's cold. Let's listen to that Benny Carter record again.' We'd say, 'Yes, it sounds great, but it's horribly out of tune.' He'd say, 'Forget about how out of tune it is. Listen to what's coming out of the record: the warmth, and the guys are molding and singing those parts rather than just playing them and hitting them on the head.' Everybody thought he was a square, but meanwhile he knew exactly what he was talking about. Everything he ever did came out professionally, even if you might say mechanically, but when he started to talk that way I changed my ideas about him."

The dedicated jazzman that Nat Pierce is made a reluctant entry into music. When he was about eight he began to take piano lessons. "My mother forced them down my throat for three years, because evidently her mother had done the same thing to her." He griped about the nature of his tuition until his teacher bought a couple of Fats Waller piano books, which he supplemented with others of boogie woogie by Pete Johnson and Mary Lou Williams. "I felt that if I had to take lessons for three years I wanted to play something I could enjoy, but by the time I was twelve, and nothing was happening, I said, 'Later with the piano—forget it!' "

Circumstances, however, led to his entry into the high-school dance band and then to tuition with a pianist who demonstrated secondhand instruments at the Stark Piano Warehouse. "He was an old drinking buddy of George Gershwin's," Pierce recalled, "and every week he would write out one chorus of a tune, and show me the chords and what notes were in each chord. He would show me Teddy Wilson runs, too, and he could play stride, and to me he was hot. All the other guys were going to another fellow who had more Teddy Wilson and Art Tatum runs, but he gave them the technique, the series of runs, with the result that whenever they came to, say, an A^7 or D^7 chord in a song, they would put in this particular run. So all those guys were coathangers who sounded the same, and people began to say I sounded different, because I tried to play a piece as a whole rather than just taking one chord and embellishing that."

The war was at its height and, about six months before graduation from high school, credits were made up and kids encouraged to get a job if they could. Pierce got one in the Silver Dollar, a bar in downtown Boston, where he played from noon to one o'clock at night, a half-hour on, a

Nat Pierce.

half-hour off, with an hour for supper, seven nights a week. It was good basic experience, playing with singers and all kinds of instrumentalists. This went on for a year, during which he first tried his hand at arranging. "I didn't know what I was doing, but I said, 'Hell, I'll find out!' Because I didn't know anything about transposition, the first arrangement I wrote had everybody in the same key and it sounded atonal already!

"Later, I moved into another group led by Charles Hooks, the trumpet player, with Sam Margolis and Marquis Foster. Charlie seemed like a master musician to us. He had a fabulous range and had turned down offers from Duke, Basie and Lunceford. He didn't want to leave town, but I think he's in Detroit now. When big-time musicians came in, it would be a matter of, 'Who is this local guy here?', but Charlie would play their stuff right back at them, higher, louder and faster. On a summer's day, you could hear him two blocks away, screaming above the traffic. Ask Roy Eldridge about him. He came in when he was with Krupa, and Dizzy Gillespie when he was with Earl or Eckstine. Charlie had such an ear and such knowledge of music! He was the kind of guy who wrote out the piano parts, ten notes, one for each finger, beautiful manuscripts. And his wife sang like Billie Holiday. I owe a lot to him.*

"There was plenty of money, life and music in Boston then, and I used to hear all the traveling big bands, including the second- and third-class ones that played at the Tick Tock Club. There was another little band up there—Jeremy Freeman's—with Lloyd Trotman, Ray Perry, Joe Perry, Bay Perry and a pianist, Charlie Cox. I took lessons from him, block chords and so on, and you can pick up little things like that which you can't always put together until you know more, but you retain them. I took a kind of half-course at the conservatory during the war, too, but there were too many girls enrolled and it was too slow; so after six months I said, 'To hell with it! I can learn more on the street.'"

Eventually, he left Boston with a band which broke up and dumped him in New York. "Fifty-Second Street was swinging then and there were a lot of musicians in the hotel I stayed at. They were almost junkies, but not quite, give or take a few guys that went over the hump. I knew about it, but I never got into that. At first, I used to go down to these guys' pads and try to figure out what they were doing. It was dark, the windows closed, the curtains drawn, and they're playing like Charlie Parker or Lester Young. They were all out of their nuts. At night, we'd go to 52nd Street and sit on the steps of a brownstone across from where Lester was playing. The door would be open and we'd sit there for hours and just listen. We'd

---

*Hooks can be heard on King records made by Todd Rhodes in 1952–53.

move down a couple of clubs to where Art Tatum or Dizzy was playing. The White Rose was on the corner, where everyone used to hang out, and drinks were like twenty-five cents. So I was just sitting around, not even sweating out my union card. I went up to a studio one day where a band was rehearsing for a U.S.O. tour of Japan. They needed a piano player— 'Okay, come with us to Japan.' "

Six months later, back from the Far East, Pierce joined Ray Borden's band in Boston. He went out with Larry Clinton in 1948, took over leadership of the Borden band, toured again with Clinton, and then put together his own group which included Lenny Johnson, Charlie Mariano and Teddi King. He joined Woody Herman in the fall of 1951 and stayed with him until the summer of 1955, a very important phase in his career. After that he went to New York, which became his base for free-lance operations as pianist, arranger and composer. He played in all kinds of groups, made trips abroad, led his own big bands at the Savoy and Birdland, and, of course, recorded extensively. Anyone who has heard his *The Ballad of Jazz Street,* as orchestrated for full band and played by his rehearsal group, will know that the entire scope of his artistic ability has not yet been publicly heard. Some record company could profitably rectify this situation.

"It's a game of chance around here now, a gamble," he said of the current scene, "and you depend very much on your friends, to a degree where you know so-and-so will hire you if he gets a job, and you'll hire him if you get one, back and forth, until you build up a little network. There's no substitute for money with the landlord, but I've always tried to smile my way through the slow periods. Something goes on. The 'phone always rings."

(1961)

II

Nat Pierce became a professional musician in 1943, but his background in jazz extends beyond that, because of his very considerable knowledge of its recorded history. Although he is what might be termed a young veteran, his interest in all the music's many aspects is unflagging. He takes his phonograph on the road with him, listens to records whenever possible, and visits clubs to hear all kinds of musicians in person. Moreover, his position as Woody Herman's pianist and chief arranger gave him special insight into the problems of the big band, and a special position for viewing the world of jazz at large.

He had come off the road early in the morning. The Herman band was recording for Columbia that night, and leaving for Europe the following day. Meantime, relaxed and seemingly under no pressure, he found the opportunity for a leisurely discussion which began with consideration of the material to be recorded that night: a collection of songs associated with Al Jolson.

"The companies like to have a general idea, a premise, of why an album is to be recorded," he said. "Like all songs by the Beatles—*Woody Plays the Beatles,* or something like that. It was different with 78s, when they just went in and covered the pop tunes of the day and maybe got away with an instrumental or two. Today, it's all albums. Once in a while they take a single out of an album, but there's not too much to eat behind the single, because other groups on the label, rock-'n'-rollers and folksingers, get the bulk of the exploitation.

"The day when the big band instrumental like *Woodchoppers' Ball* or *Tuxedo Junction* could become a hit with the public is probably gone. The Tijuana Brass is not a big band, but why shouldn't a big band make it like that? We've been trying to figure it out for a long time. With the help of record companies, we decide we should try this or that, but eventually we all go back to making our own kind of music, just as Duke Ellington did with *Concert in the Virgin Islands.*

"The Tijuana Brass is verging on the rock 'n' roll bit. They have the guitars there, and that heavy bass drum beat. Now the kids might go for that bass guitar effect in Gerald Wilson's *When I'm Feeling Kinda Blue,* but after my experience on a whole lot of college dates, I really don't know.

"Sometimes, they get so brave in those colleges that they put a rock 'n' roll group opposite us. We start off, play about an hour, try every possible thing that can be done, and nobody comes on the dance floor. We make our concessions with numbers like *Watermelon Man* and *Do Anything You Wanna.* Then the group comes on at the other end of the hall with its electric thing, the amplifiers blasting away, and the floor vibrating. They love that, and they all start dancing. When we come back again, we save about ten couples, and by the end of the night we'll have a few more. I presume it's the same with Duke, Basie and Harry James.

"The best way we've discovered to drag those kids off their chairs is with ballads. They don't move if we play the accepted Lanin-type tempo, unless it is in straight eighth notes. We even have a couple of arrangements that start out with straight eighth notes and go into regular swing in the middle—and the kids are *hung* on the floor! They don't know what to do. We think the other thing swings more, but how're we going to tell them about that and switch them over when they're bombarded by the radio day and night? The college dates are usually booked by the faculty, and they like bands. They don't realize that most of the kids do not, and that they would get along with half the money, two guitars and a bass drum.

"After two or three years in college, they go from that to the folksinging bit—Bob Dylan and so on. They all fall into that, but then some of them jump into the Dave Brubeck department. That's good, because at least they're heading in the right direction, and they'll always hear big bands accompanying singers. Some of the name singers even think they should help the cause by doing this, and it's a great thing, because otherwise we wouldn't get so much exposure."

There were exceptions to his generalizations about college kids, he pointed out, and they were the students who had been involved in stage bands at high school or college. In fact, he believed there were now more bands in operation in the U.S. than there were in the heyday of the big bands, but most of them were in schools.

"What happens to the stage-band kids after they come out of school? We get some of them. They've mostly played concerts, of course. Now there's a conception that there is a line drawn between jazz and dance music, but so far as I'm concerned there is no line. We don't play any different music at a concert than at a dance, except maybe a faster tune here and there. Nevertheless, we usually have to train those kids from the beginning, and sometimes they rebel and leave after three months to play in a quartet in their hometown. A few months later, they call up, out of a job, and want to come back; but you can't keep doing that all the time.

"I don't know why it is that there's so much sameness in the way the kids play today. You get one playing in a certain groove that is exactly the same as the next kid's that you get the next week, and they're using the same material. It used to be different in the years before Bird and Dizzy, when you'd have two main soloists playing quite differently on the same material, like Buck Clayton and Harry Edison, or Herschel Evans and Lester Young. You could always tell them apart. I don't think it is merely a matter of more schooling, because plenty of the older guys had very good schooling, too.

"The young guy tends to over-estimate himself, anyway. He wants to play on every number, but maybe he isn't the great soloist he thinks he is. You can't give just everybody a shot at the ball, because the quality level might drop, and it might be kind of empty when one particular fellow came in, although he might be a good friend and a good section musician. How're you going to explain, 'This is not your meat,' to someone who is sure it is?

"Another thing: if you went down to the corner and bought ten of those

Blue Note albums which have long jam-session pieces on them, and picked out all those which had a blues in F on them, and listened to all the trumpet and tenor solos on them, it would be very, very difficult to distinguish between those soloists unless you were really a student and familiar with an individual and his nuances.

"Something we'd like to have more of in Woody's band is the sense of dynamics—not from loud to louder, but from soft to loud! That's one of the factors that makes the present Basie band so great. It's really difficult to explain to a young man that there are such things as momentum and build-up in the course of a six-minute arrangement. Sometimes we just start out and go on up, and I don't understand how we do it. They have more energy than you can imagine, and it helps keep me young, just chasing around with them, because they run every place."

The question of leadership was another subject with which Pierce was much concerned.

"Some musicians are so involved in their music that they just can't see around the corner," he continued. "People say that musicians should review records, that they should be a. and r. men, and so forth, but these are outside parts of the business, and all most musicians know about is music. Projection from the bandstand to the audience is one reason why there will probably never again be bands like Duke's, Basie's or Woody's, because there are no bandleaders as such with enough training. There are hundreds of trios, quartets and sextets, all musicianly and capable. They have good arrangements and soloists, but they don't project, because no one is bothering to tell the people what they're doing. Maybe they think it is too commercial to do that? I know when this all began, when leaders ceased announcing their numbers, but the people still feel cheated.

"I recently went to hear Thad Jones and Mel Lewis. They had a great band down there at the Village Vanguard, and Thad wasn't against grabbing the microphone and telling the people what they were going to do. They had a lot of humor in the music, too, and I think that's great. Dizzy Gillespie always had that, but where are the rest of them? Where are the rest of the bandleaders who are going to take over ten years from now?

"I saw Earl Hines last spring when he was working with a trio. He told the people what he was going to do—a Fats Waller medley, a Duke Ellington tune, an Erroll Garner number—and he had them charmed completely before he hit a note on the piano. In my opinion, he's a great bandleader—not that he had a band there—but he could communicate with the audience. Duke can do that, and so can Woody. The people are on their side before a note is played, and they may play the worst. They still win. It's important if you're concerned with the state of the business, and we must be concerned, although it's nice to be idealistic, too—jazz for ever, and all that!

"There are a lot of little clubs across the country, and little groups go out and do a tour. Maybe they go from New York and back, but after their Chicago job there's no job for them in Omaha and they lay off a couple of weeks. Or they can't find a place in Kansas City. But finally they get to the Coast, and then they have to come all the way back to New York, and by the time they get back all their money is eaten up in transportation costs, and they have no work. There they are, although they have a great little band from a strictly musical point of view! One group that avoids some of these problems is Cannonball Adderley's. They work most weeks, and one reason is that he makes a very good appearance at the microphone. He can talk. I don't think it's a sin to do that. He doesn't fluff off the audience. He plays the various little hits that he's had, and he's always listening to other people's things. Maybe he can take something from some other band and utilize it in his. It helps keep the group going."

The fact that the three major bands had recently been much less dependent on vocalists than formerly was not, Pierce felt, a matter of conscious policy.

"I don't think it was planned," he said. "It just happened. If we, Duke, or Basie found somebody exceptional that could help us—and we could help him—we'd have him. But Basie has Bill Henderson now, and when Duke was in Vancouver he had Esther Marrow with him. She's a young gospel singer from Detroit, and she's very good. Woody had Joe Carroll for a time, and he has been singing more himself lately. In the past, he had many girl singers, but the economic situation is against additional vocalists. In the long run, that one salary can make a lot of difference. Moving around sixteen people, a band boy, a manager, suitcases, much equipment, and a few wives on occasion—this thing can be unbelievable. Some people even brought cats and dogs. Woody has a dog on the road quite often. It rides in the car with him. If he wants a dog along, why not? It's his life.

"I always travel with a phonograph because I regard it as part of my education. I don't hear all the records, but I hear quite a few. Then we have two or three guys who have 'deeper' records than I have, 'outside' records, some of those 'New Thing' records, and we exchange, and I listen to find out what's going on. Not that I can ever change the way I feel about music, but I want to be informed.

"A lot of things that happen are just fads, it seems to me. I wrote an arrangement for Woody in the middle '50s on *Opus de Funk* which was probably the original 'soul' arrangement for a big band. We had heard this music and been intrigued by it before it became 'soul.' Then when Horace (Silver) went on to write *The Preacher* and *Sister Sadie,* we did them as well, and a few other tunes that we never recorded. After 'soul,' there could have been some other fancy names, but now it seems to be just the New Thing.''

Like many musicians of his generation, Pierce has been baffled by the New Thing, but he has made conscientious efforts to understand it.

"I would like very much to see some of this new music written down,'' he continued, ''and have somebody else play it, somebody outside the playing circle of the New Thing. That's what we used to do when we were kids. We wrote down Charlie Parker and Dizzy Gillespie's solos, and their little heads, and we played them all and tried to find out what they were doing. You go and hear one of these groups today and they play the same song for an hour. They go off the stand, come back, and go right into it again. How do they even tell each other which song is being played? How do they call the tune? There can't be a secret there, because they don't play it behind closed doors without telling anyone about it. They make records, and there must be some things of value there, because there are . quite a few people doing it.

"I hate to say it, but if it's all going to be like that, we're going to be in tough shape ten years from now. Maybe it can be dissected down to where we get some good out of it. Through most of the U.S. and Europe you can hear Muzak-type music coming through the ceiling, and these commercial bands are playing be-bop now. Twenty-five years later, they're playing it! They wouldn't have dared to do that twenty years ago. Just like fifteen years ago they were all playing Lunceford, when they finally caught up to that! Possibly there's something in the new music that can be translated into Muzak fifteen years from now, but I think a lot more work has to be done on it. Some of it is just plain noise so far as I'm concerned, and I doubt whether there could ever be a big band playing it, because it would sound like one of those John Cage concerts.

"I know they're serious musicians and that they know about music, but they're really far out, and I wonder whether there is as big an audience for it as they claim. Jimmy Giuffre recently decided to come back 'inside' from the 'outside.' Maybe it's because he needed to make a living. In the case of a person like Coltrane, we know he can play another style if called to do so. He played on the order of Lucky Thompson in the early '40s with Dizzy Gillespie's small group, and then, slowly, for the next ten years, he broke away from it. Now, in the last six or eight months, he has really gotten into something else.

"We saw him in Chicago, at the *Down Beat* jazz festival, with Archie Shepp and Elvin Jones. I sat out there and listened to them with an open mind, but I didn't know what they were doing. I didn't have an inkling. I didn't know where they started from, where they would end, or how you would accompany something like that. It was very strange to all of us. At this point, the whole thing is based on improvisation, but they do have songs. They have titles, so there must be some semblance of a pattern, although it wouldn't seem that the pattern is repeated.

"This thing all started when Ornette Coleman appeared on the scene, and went into his 'moon' bag or whatever they call it. A lot of us went down there years ago. We listened, we looked at each other, and we listened again. We knew he was a fairly good alto player, and that there was a lot of feeling in his work. Then we started reading the magazines and the so-called critics delivered their evaluations, and it seemed that that became all they listened to. He would play out-of-tune notes and they would start talking about East Indian scales. To me, it was like a cop-out. Don Ellis, on the other hand, did go into East Indian music, and made a study of it, and I'm sure he's qualified to speak about it, whereas I wouldn't be, because I've never studied it. But to pick a guy out of the street and say he did this and that with all those long words. . . .

"Then there are the others who are doing the race department. I read that article by Archie Shepp in *Down Beat* where he was talking about paying this and that dues. Where was he before three years ago? If he was out on the street trying to play his music, someone would have known about him. Lately, he's got jobs, and he was out in San Francisco with a quartet when we were there. There was a piano player by the name of Denny Zeitlin, too, a marvelous piano player, but I defy anyone to tell you what he is playing. He plays the piano excellently from a technical point of view. We know that. But he has no form, and he just plays on and on the same way. I'm sure he has a few little melodies, but all the rest is out of Lennie Tristano, Bill Evans and Bud Powell, plus a Brazilian influence from the bossa nova guys. I don't know what he's playing, or how you can sell this thing if there's nothing you can put your finger on. After listening to a set or two, you come out with the same feeling you get from the saxophonists: each song sounds the same. I come back to that, because I don't understand how they differentiate between them. Maybe one's in six-eight, or three-four, or four-four, but when they get wound up it all sounds the same. There's no real tempo happening. You can't sit there and swing as you would if you went to hear Basie, or Jimmy Rushing, or somebody like that. The new audience just sits there, their heads in their hands, as though it were a mortuary or something. The drums overshadow everything, even when the saxophone is playing right into the microphone. It's rough on my ears. No dynamics, no microphone technique. But there's an audience for it! I've been there. I've seen it."

As an arranger and pianist, Pierce has always shown a marked affinity for the Basie approach.

"Basie's arrangers and the conception of his band, especially in the '30s, had a big influence on me," he admitted. "The band then was like an offshoot of Fletcher Henderson's or Benny Carter's, the big difference being in the rhythm section, which was so much smoother than the average at that time. The idea of riffs being something special to Kansas City is ridiculous. Fletcher's band, Don Redman's, Cab Calloway's and McKinney's Cotton Pickers—they'd all been using riffs as launching pads for individuals for years.

"Basie emphasized a simpler approach than, say, Jimmie Lunceford's, which was a complete show band. I remember one time in Symphony Hall, Boston, his four trumpet players were throwing their horns up to the ceiling. It was a big, high hall, and they'd throw them up twenty or thirty feet, pick them out of the air, and hit the next chord. I was just amazed by the whole thing. They used to do a lot of hot versions of the classics, too, and many of the arrangements were written by people nobody ever heard of then. Now they're hearing of one—Gerald Wilson. They think he's a new fellow on the scene. I'm glad it's this way, that he's getting recognition at last, even if it has taken him twenty-five years to get off the ground.

"His newest album, *Feeling Kinda Blue,* may not get five stars from jazz reviewers, but it's closer to what he's written in the past for other bands like Duke's and Basie's. It's more swing-type music, and not like those modal things that were on his first albums. Maybe it's a concession, but I don't think so.

"But we were discussing Basie, and I think the main difference between the band now and the one of the '30s is in the smoother conception today. I was talking to Basie recently about writing some things for him. He has a tempo thing in his head. It's hard to put into print, but he immediately starts popping his fingers at a tempo he likes to play. Then, thanks to Marshall Royal, his band is very well disciplined, and they can swing you out of the joint whenever they want. I heard them play a blues recently. Basie played about ten choruses in front; the band played something; Lockjaw played about twenty choruses, and it was building into a monster; and then the ensemble came in screaming, and it almost knocked me over, it was so beautiful."

Despite this deep affection for the Basie style, Pierce claims he is most influenced as an arranger by Duke Ellington.

"I can't possibly write like that," he explained, "because I don't have the musicians to play the solos. Duke's records of the last few years, if you examine them closely, have been mostly solos with backgrounds, even when it's a case of pop tunes as in *Ellington '65* and *Ellington '66*. When a tune ends up as a feature for Johnny Hodges or Lawrence Brown, quite a bit of writing is eliminated, because putting a few riffs behind a good soloist can be done very quickly.

"The problem today is the young musician who usually plays the same solo on each song. If it's a ballad, he'll go instantly into double time, without trying to fit his solo into the arrangement. If they have only eight or sixteen bars, they put in as much as they possibly can. After a few years, when perhaps they're more tired or have more sense, they'll just float through there and try to relate to what came before and what's going to come after.

"Most of the fellows in Duke's band are well past that point, and when he writes for them the arrangements are tailor-made. Our personnel changes so much that if we had a whole library of those tailor-made arrangements we'd hardly have anyone to play 'em. Next guy comes in and he has a different quality to the one that left, and that makes it kind of difficult. So far as I'm concerned, a more stable personnel would change the writing quite a bit.

"It's not usually, I agree, a good idea having all the arrangements in an album by one man, because they're often pushed together in a matter of weeks, and the band doesn't get a chance to play them beforehand. They're played in the studio, and then perhaps they're never played again. Take the music in Ellington's *All American* set. It disappeared. Nobody knows what happened, and it was a shame, because there were beautiful things in it that might have become part of his standard repertoire. The same with *Midnight in Paris,* another great album. It happens with Basie, too. I know they made that album of James Bond themes recently, but when I heard the band a couple of weeks ago they didn't play one of those arrangements. They'd just gone back to the regulars like *Shiny Stockings, Mellotone* and *Cherry Point.*

"The programs of the big bands in the '30s varied much more. I think it was Chick Webb's band that had a library of waltzes, and I believe Fletcher Henderson's did, too, because they played uptown society dances—cotillions, they called them—with white gowns and everything, and they had to have appropriate music. It wasn't a crime to play a waltz then—not just a jazz waltz, but a regular waltz with a pretty melody. Big bands have limited themselves so far as the material they play is concerned. They keep closing it up.

"But it's hard for leaders like Basie, Duke and Woody to play a whole new program, just as it's hard to build a new bandleader as an image. Those three have had bands for thirty years or more. They're household words and mostly household people come to see them, people past thirty or thirty-five, and they know what we're trying to do, but they want to hear their favorites. We all have to play staples, but we don't play *Woodchoppers' Ball* more than once or twice a night unless we're forced to."

The predicament of the leader faced with the will of an audience he has created was exemplified for Pierce by Stan Kenton, whose Neophonic orchestra he had heard rehearsing in January.

"Bill Holman," he said, "had written some beautiful music to feature Gerry Mulligan as soloist, but it is such a *large* orchestra—ten brass, four or five French horns, and all the reed men doubling on flute, piccolo, bass clarinet or contrabassoon—that it's actually in competition with the New York Philharmonic. The writers are newer, and though they do out-of-tempo things, most of the numbers are jazz-type things. They try out a lot of different things, but I don't think the rehearsals are really long enough for the musicians to get their teeth into the music and give it the best performance possible.

"Stan Kenton is an electric personality. I've known him for about twenty-six years, ever since I was a kid in Boston, where I went up and asked for some arrangements he didn't need anymore! He gave them to me. Basie also gave me some in later years when I had my own band. So did Woody. But over the years Stan's music has kept getting further and further away from actual dance music, and he has gotten more and more people in his bands. Once you build an audience for his kind of thing, you can get out on a limb, and I think this was Johnny Richards' problem, too. You get 'way out there, so far out that after a time the audience begins to drop off, but you still have some of it left. If you tried to come back, you feel you'd lose everything, so the outwards direction continues, and it becomes hard to play just a regular thing anymore. The people who are out there with you wouldn't accept it. 'What happened to him?' they'd ask one another. 'He sounds like Sammy Kaye now.' So you get out on that limb and you've got to stay there. You live or die on it."

(1966)

LAWRENCE LUCIE

GUITAR

"My father played violin, and that was my first instrument. He always had music around the house, and he taught me how to make the fingers on the violin. He was self-taught himself, but he could read ordinary pop music. A friend of his was a very good fiddler, and they played all the fiddlers' tunes like *Turkey in the Straw* together. We were living then in Emporia, Virginia, where I was born. It was a big day when the minstrel shows used to come there. They were like vaudeville shows, and all the musicians were black. (There were white minstrel shows for white communities as well.) I didn't know any of the players, but I would hang around and listen to them. Quite a few of those shows came through, but the famous ones I remember were A. G. Allen's and the Georgia Minstrels.

"I discovered that the mandolin tuned like the violin, so far as tone and strings were concerned, and when I started playing it, it put a different sound into our family band. I learned to play it from just looking at the pictures in a correspondence course I sent to Chicago for. I really learned to read music from the only music teacher in our town, an Episcopal minister, the Rev. C. E. Green. He taught me to read the notes on the piano when I was seven or eight. After taking the piano lessons, I stopped playing piano, and because I could read I became almost like the leader of our group, playing mandolin. Later on, I started playing banjo, and later still I made a guitar out of a cigar box. Although I studied the piano, I liked the strings, and I stuck with the strings all my life.

"My parents moved to New York when I was quite small, and I finished high school there. Before I started playing professionally, I worked for a fellow named Jimmy Russell in what you would call an amateur band. I learned to read stock arrangements, and I continued to study at the Brooklyn Conservatory. I also studied banjo with Luther Blake. He was an entertainer who used banjo to accompany his singing. He played from violin parts, and right away he taught me to play melody. Eventually, we began playing chords, but I always thank him for starting me off reading from violin parts. There were not too many guitar or banjo teachers at that

345

time who did much reading. They more or less played by ear or memorized the music in chords. I was still practicing banjo when they advised me at the Paramount Music School to start playing guitar, because Eddie Lang had got something going. We would hear him on the air once in a while with Paul Whiteman, and the guitar had such a fascinating sound. There was Frank Victor, too, playing with Rudy Vallee.

"The banjo carried more in dancehalls, and I think it is a more percussive instrument. It was used in all kinds of combos, and when we did houseparty gigs there might be just banjo and saxophone. The banjo would put down a lot of rhythm and still carry four-part harmony. With the right sound, I would like to see the banjo come back in bands. Men like John Trueheart and Bernard Addison used to play it with a really mellow sound, rather like electric guitar now. Of course, some banjo players sound harsh and offensive, but there are others like Elmer Snowden who *never* play too loud. In the hands of a good player, the banjo is still a great instrument. When I first came on the scene, the big bands didn't have guitars, but they did have great banjo players. It was always an inspiration for me to go to the Savoy and listen to John Trueheart with Chick Webb, or Elmer Snowden, or Benny James, or Bernard Addison. Those were the ones I really idolized. Snowden was the leader of his band, so he played melody and lead, but Trueheart was a rhythm man.

"I used to go to the Savoy all the time, and the first guitar player I ever heard play a single-string solo was Eddie Durham, when he came there with Bennie Moton's band around 1932. He had one of those National guitars with a resonator inside it, and it sounded loud and rather metallic although there was no electrical amplification. Eddie played very good solos on it, and he played trombone, too, just as he did with Jimmie Lunceford later. Count Basie was playing piano in that band, and he was very popular even then. Everybody crowded around, and the musicians expected him to take those little solos. When I first went to Kansas City with Fletcher Henderson, we went to the Sunset, and the people crowded around his piano there, too. He was a very rhythmic pianist, and he played the light sound, and the public liked him very much.

"The first real professional job I played was with June Clark's band in 1931. Even before I joined the union, I used to hang out at the Rhythm Club to listen to Jelly Roll Morton and all of them talking and playing. I was set on becoming a musician. Two days after I had joined the union, I ran into Benny James, who was what we called a big-time banjo player. He was then with Mills Blue Rhythm Band, when it was first organized by Willie Lynch, the drummer.

"'Do you want a job?' Benny asked.

"'Yeah,' I said, although I was a little afraid, because I had had no professional experience before.

"'Okay, go see June Clark!'

"So I went down and started working for June Clark at Hogan's Dancing School on 14th Street. I learned to fake tunes, and play tunes from memory. You really got plenty of practice there, and I continued to study as well. Musicians didn't really like to work in a dancing school, because it was continuous playing, but if they were out of work and needing money, they would go there. The rhythm section usually stayed on, but the horn players would come and go. June Clark was terrific then, a very good trumpet player, and a great friend of Louis Armstrong. Teddy McRae, Rudy Powell and Howard Johnson were some of the saxophone players who worked there. Lloyd Phillips, who later was Pearl Bailey's accompanist, played there, and he was a wonderful pianist.

"It was good experience for me, and great ear training, because you had to play in all keys. We had to start off with good rhythm right away, on the first and second beats, because people were dancing. It had to be swinging and it developed you as a rhythm man, because you had to start and stop, start and stop, always with a good tempo. The dances were short, for it was just one or two pennies a dance, so you would play just one chorus, stop, and start another. Each time you started again, the customer had to pay more money. It was a school for musicians as well as dancers! I must have been there a couple of years, and for about three years I had a summer job in a hotel out at Southold on Long Island with Lorenzo Caldwell, a violinist and a very good arranger. He was an excellent musician, and he fascinated me, because I was always trying to learn. He didn't buy the music our quartet played, but he would sit down and write the music of all the pop songs right from the radio. Within the course of a day, he would have three or four songs written down with beautiful harmony. He had absolute pitch, and I learned so much from him. Eventually, he went back to Philadelphia. He was a well-schooled musician who knew the symphonies and could play the classics. After the Civil War, European musicians had come over here as teachers, and there were a lot of well-trained black musicians like him around who had learned from them and those they taught.

"Today, kids seem to have the idea that older people don't know, don't have anything to offer. I often play old records with kids, and then I point out that this musician playing twenty years ago played better than the modern musician they keep talking about now. I play Red Allen's records to them, and Red usually had a very strong sound on trumpet. Then I show how the newer men may play a lot of notes but don't have the power. To me, too, it is obvious that this pianist they are always listening to—I won't call his name—plays so well because he listened to older players. Young people think they are going 'on their own', and a lot of them were doing very well, especially with pop music and rock 'n' roll that was very easy to play. There was so much money, and they got a little bit off the track, but they are coming back now. Everyone has to lean on someone else, and they have to listen to what went before.

"The pianist with Lorenzo Caldwell was Charles Everett Ford, a good musician who was studying the classics with Dr. Nathaniel Depp, but he could also play jazz. Hampton Institute got this job for him with us at the hotel. He was brought up in northern Virginia and he was an expert swimmer. He taught us all, and after about a couple of months we would swim right across Peconic Bay. We had to play for dinner, but only about four hours altogether each day, and the rest of the time we were on the beach. It was like a vacation. I kept on practicing and studying until I finally had a chance to audition for a name band.

"I got my first big break from Duke Ellington. I always give him credit for being a great guy and a person true to his word. A friend of mine, who didn't know much about music but thought I played well, arranged for me to audition for Duke. I know this started everything for me, so far as being a success before the public. I had an appointment at Duke's house, and I was playing all the modern chords like he was—fifth chords, ninth chords, major seventh chords—because I had really studied guitar.

"'This is great', he said. 'I haven't heard guitar like this before. You certainly have talent. I'll tell you what I'm going to do. When someone needs a guitar player, I'll be sure to recommend you.'

"I was very pleased, but I wondered if he meant it. About six months later, I went home and my wife was all excited. 'Duke Ellington has been here,' she said. 'He said he was going to give you a break if he ever had the chance. Well, Fred Guy got hurt, and he wants you to come and play with him.'

"Then it was my turn to get excited. I went up to the Cotton Club that night and sat down with his band, and started looking around. He had some music, but not too much. The band was on the air every night, and here all of a sudden I'd got a chance to play in it! I must have been tense, but I knew I could play, because I used to go to nightspots and jam every night. Most of the fellows in the band, like Johnny Hodges, were smiling and were very nice to me. They figured if Duke had asked me to play, I must be good. Then Duke surprised me and gave me a solo on *Tiger Rag,* on the air. It was one of the fastest numbers, and exciting to play, and everything came down all right, although nobody had heard guitar played on *that* tune. Duke was laughing, because he knew I was a little nervous. In fact, everybody was laughing, and I guess I was the only serious one, but I knew that number and had played it as a solo many times. When they played *Sweet Georgia Brown,* Duke took the introduction and I had a chorus on that, too. So it was easy, because I had been listening to most of the songs they played. I did all right that night, and the eight days I was there before Fred Guy came back.

"When I went down to the Rhythm Club, everybody was so surprised. 'Why did they hire this kid?' they were asking one another. 'Here's Benny James! Here's Elmer Snowden!' Then they came to me. 'How did you get that break?' they wanted to know. 'You're so young, and we've been around so long!' I never told them how it happened, that Duke wanted a guitar player, and most of them were still playing banjo. Years later, after Fred Guy had left, Duke offered me a job with the band, but by then my own group was going well and I didn't want to break it up.

"The next call I got after that was from Benny Carter. The time I worked with Duke made people know I could play, and Benny was looking for anything new. I was one of the first to play rhythm guitar in a band uptown —and read. Benny's band was playing the Lafayette Theatre when I joined it. I was greeted with all this music, and all these chords, but the chords were no problem to me, because I had studied so much.

"Benny's was really an all-star band. He had all the guys I admired— Chu Berry, Hilton Jefferson, Dicky Wells, Sidney Catlett—and later Cozy Cole—Bass Hill, Shad Collins, Bill Coleman, and that very good first trumpet player who used to be with Louis Armstrong, Bill Dillard. Wayman Carver, Glyn Pacque and Big Green were also in the band when I joined. They used to rehearse for the fun of it.

"We were playing at Connie's Inn, that was later known as the Ubangi Club, and doubling at the Lafayette. We were the first band to play in the Apollo Theatre when it opened up in 1934, and the Apollo became like a school for musicians. Benny was musical director and we were playing in the pit. They asked what we should use for the theme song, and he said, *'I May Be Wrong, But I Think You're Wonderful.'* It has been the theme song there ever since.

"The theatre's first show would be around eleven in the morning, and we would play at the club until three at night. We'd get pretty tired, but we were all young with a lot of energy, and staying up nights didn't mean anything. We could never get more than four or five hours sleep after work, but we used to take a cot in the dressing rooms and sometimes get a couple of hours between shows. Even when I was with Louis Armstrong, years later, we would sometimes be traveling two days without sleep, except what we could catch on a train, but the work was enjoyable, so it didn't bother us.

"During one of Benny Carter's lay-offs, I worked for Dave Martin when his band was playing the show at Connie's Inn, and I also played with him at the St. George Hotel in Brooklyn a couple of times as a substitute for Eddie Gibbs. Dave was a good musician, a nice person to work for, and he had a good band.

"Rhythm became my function, and as compared with banjo I think guitar has more rhythm—if it's a straight guitar. It has a bigger, blending sound, a little more weight, and a better blend with the bass. The banjo blended very well with the tuba, and when the tuba went out the banjo went, too. Because there were no amplifiers then, when you took a guitar solo, you played it in chords, three or four notes at a time. Unless you went up to the microphone, you couldn't be heard otherwise.

"If you wanted to make it, you had to be a good rhythm man *in the section* then. I wanted to keep working, and I was happy playing rhythm. For one thing, I had listened so much to John Trueheart. I used to sit right near him all the time when he was with Chick Webb, and listen to Chick's rhythm section. Trueheart was a nice, easy-going guy, but he never got too much credit. I probably got more through going around and playing with different bands. Like Fred Guy with Duke, he was happy with just this one band, and he and Chick were buddies. He was like a straw boss, and if Chick wasn't on the stand to start the band (when Chick was ill, Bill Beason used to substitute for him) Trueheart would start it off. Chick played a lot of solo drums, and then Trueheart helped hold the rhythm section together. Because Chick had the bass and guitar going, he didn't have to play strict rhythm. That nice, right-hand stroke Trueheart had helped keep the band swinging. What a band appreciates, you know, the audience doesn't always hear.

"When the electric guitar came in, the guys who were playing it naturally got more publicity. It was a solo instrument. But a guy like Freddie Green with Count Basie liked rhythm, and felt rhythm. I still like to play rhythm, and if there are two guitars on a recording session, I usually end up playing rhythm. Most of the young guitarists don't want to play anything but lead. They are not happy playing rhythm and feel as though they are being cheated of something. I like to be in a position to hold things together.

"John Hammond was a good friend of Benny Carter, and he often used to come uptown. He loved jazz, and he always had that big smile. He liked my playing, and I understood that he recommended me to Fletcher Henderson, because while we were laying off I got a call to join Fletcher. And

Fletcher's was the only big band I didn't make an audition for! I had to for all the others, all down the line, even for Coleman Hawkins's band. In this case, I think Clarence Holiday was sick and Bernard Addison had left. They had three or four guitar players try out before I was recommended. I went in cold, joined the band upstate, in Boston or somewhere, without a rehearsal or anything. And they had a book in that band! I know the first night I was so anxious to play that I had music strewn all over the floor, and they were all laughing, because it was all mixed up. But they knew I was playing whenever I could find the right sheets.

"That was a great kick being with Fletcher Henderson's band. I played in Duke's and other fine bands, but when those guys started blowing it was some feeling! People may talk about a lack of discipline at times, but when we got on the bandstand the band had a good feeling to it, and we played. I loved Walter Johnson's playing, because you could hear the guitar with him. He was a good drummer, and I always associate his type of feeling with Jo Jones's. The band would be swinging like the house was falling down, but the guitar would cut through. They used to call Walter 'Stick and Brush', because that was what he played mostly. He used brushes a lot on the cymbal, and he was a great cymbal player, a smooth cymbal player. He had a wonderful feeling for rhythm. He could feel it if you were just a little bit off, and he would check it right away. That's a gift, and Jo Jones has it, too. I can feel it when anyone in the rhythm section is slightly off, or the tempo wavers a bit. You can learn rhythm, but if you start thinking about it too much after you learn it, you won't have a good feeling. That's why I hung around those bands with people like Snowden and Trueheart, people who *really* had rhythm. Once you learn it, you forget about this being a quarter- or an eighth-note, or whatever, and play from feeling. A note means nothing. A note is just mechanical. You look at the note, and you play what you feel. A quarter-note is about this or that, but if you count one, two, three, four, it will be stiff. Some drummers sound mechanical like a metronome. They play too perfect, and they don't give with it. But if you have a feeling for rhythm you can play with almost anyone.

"I thought Fletcher Henderson was great as a leader. He had just what Duke has, personality-wise. He enjoyed seeing the band play. When he got on the stand, he would look at everyone and smile, as if to say, 'I'm enjoying this.' The same thing when anybody took a solo. So that made everybody relax, and the band was never tight. A lot of times, when a guy came on late or some of the fellows didn't behave well, he could have been really angry and made them uncomfortable. Although he didn't like it, he didn't let them know it. But the others in the band would be mad with the guy who came in late, because it could jeopardize the job. Everybody's ready and waiting up front, wanting to get together, and there's a big crowd, and here's this guy coming late! Fletcher would put up with all of that, and keep smiling, until we were ready and he could say, 'Okay!' Five minutes later he would be telling the guy who came late to take a solo, and not long after that he would be admiring what he played. So he had become a part of the whole thing, not like a leader, but like one of the band.

"I also thought Fletcher was a very good piano player, although he didn't have a flashy style. He played in rather the same vein as Jimmy Johnson. He could read and transpose, and he had absolute pitch. He could write an arrangement in three or four hours without going near the band. In Chicago, he used to write arrangements in the hotel with no piano in the room. A lot of us were studying arranging, and we were hitting chords on the piano and making arrangements in two or three days, or a week maybe, to put in the band book. Then when we came to play them back, we didn't like them, and we had to go over them again. But Fletcher would sit down with no piano and make an arrangement overnight, and a couple of nights later you would hear Benny Goodman playing it.

"When I joined Fletcher, Coleman Hawkins had gone to Europe and Lester Young had already left. Ben Webster was there, and a couple of new guys, and nobody was really taking advantage of Fletcher's attitude. We had Russell Smith on first trumpet, Red Allen, and another great trumpet player, Mouse Randolph. Fletcher used to play his specialty, *Stealing Apples,* and then get up to direct the band while his brother, Horace, played piano. Horace had a great feeling for rhythm, too, so the rhythm section was very good. Horace liked Mouse a lot, because he was not only a fine, swing trumpet, but he read well, had a nice personality, and plenty of punch when he played lead on certain parts.

"Horace must have been the baby in the family, because there was a sister in between him and Fletcher. He had had a band of his own, but it never became famous like Fletcher's. I don't think there was jealousy between them, but I think Horace was very anxious for the band to do great things, and he was restless with certain things that went on. Fletcher was the type of person that could relax under any circumstances. I know a lot of times Horace would go after Fletcher for being so easy-going. He wanted things more organized, and he worked hard making arrangements to pull things together, to make the band stronger, because Fletcher wasn't doing too well then. We were supposed to be going into the Cotton Club, and the band was looking forward to that, but the job went to Jimmie

Lunceford. That made for hard feelings. Jimmie had a fine show band, but Fletcher's was the first *great* band, before Duke's, and he didn't get a chance to go into the Cotton Club, which was considered the Number One job at the time. Connie's Inn, where Don Redman played, was Number Two.

"Although we were happy in Fletcher Henderson's band, and the guys loved the music, and were playing so well, we were not really making top money. Red Allen and I were offered more money to go with the Blue Rhythm Band, which was Irving Mills's third band. It had been organized as a show band, as a substitute for Cab Calloway's. Now it was going into the Cotton Club, and Red and I went and talked to Fletcher. We were in Cleveland at the time, and the future was pretty uncertain. We told him how we enjoyed the band, but how here was a chance for us to make more money. Fletcher thought it was all right, so we left and went to the Cotton Club after all as members of the Blue Rhythm Band.

"Lucky Millinder had taken it over then, and there had been quite a shake-up. Lucky was not a musician, but he was a good organizer and bandleader, with a great feeling for production and what would sell to the public. He was a salesman, like Cab Calloway. He never let you down. He could direct, and he could remember the arrangements, every note, once we had rehearsed them. We didn't have as much air time as Duke and Cab, but we did very well wherever we went, including the Apollo Theatre. Chuck Richards was singing with us then, and he sounded something like Bing Crosby. He was a very good commercial singer, and a nice, clean-cut guy.

"Incidentally, I remember Chuck Richards and Billie Holiday singing with Benny Carter's band when Charlie Barnet had the idea of presenting black and white together. Benny's band (Cozy Cole was on drums) was on one side of the stage, Charlie's on the other, and after each had played everybody would play together. This was in 1934, and we did theatre dates around New York when Benny Goodman was still planning a black-and-white band to take to Europe. I was supposed to play guitar in that band, too, but the deal fell through.

"I knew Benny Goodman from when he used to play with Ben Pollack. As a kid, I used to listen to the radio so much. I'd put it on the floor and lie down beside it, and go to sleep listening to the bands. I knew all their theme songs, and I knew musicians like Benny by their sound. Later, when I got with Benny Carter and Fletcher Henderson, Benny would come up to the Ubangi Club and sit in, pick up a clarinet and play it. This was before he got his own band, but I think he had an eye for organizing one even then.

L. to R.: Lawrence Lucie, John Simmons, Velma Middleton, Prince Robinson, Bernard Flood, Carl Frye, Joe Garland, Shelton Hemphill, Rupert Cole, Frank Galbraith, Louis Armstrong and Luis Russell in foreground.

"After about a couple of years with Lucky Millinder, *his* band was not working so much, and I went back to Fletcher. He always had a job waiting. He had gone in the Grand Terrace in Chicago and had a hit record on *Christopher Columbus,* so he was able to pay more money. And Walter Johnson was back with him, too, and I always liked to work with Walter! Emmett Berry had just taken Roy Eldridge's place and Israel Crosby was on bass. After a while, we went out on the road, traveling all over, to California and everywhere. Eventually, when Fletcher was laying off, I left the band upstate at the same place where I originally joined it.

"I think I may have gone to Lucky Millinder for some dates in between, but my next big experience was with Coleman Hawkins. He had had a big, hit record on *Body and Soul,* and he was paying real money to start up his big band. So I was asked to come down and audition for him in the Roseland ballroom at the beginning of 1940. 'I want that boy there,' Coleman said after I had played, so I got with him, and we went into the Golden Gate Ballroom, and then the Savoy, where we had a battle with all the bands, and also into the Apollo.

"After that, I went with Louis Armstrong, and while we were in Mobile, Alabama, I got a call to the service. I didn't want to go before the draft board there, so I came back to New York and got a defense job. After the war, Lucky Millinder asked me back with his band, and we went in the Savoy.

"I was working on 52nd Street with my wife, Nora Lee, as vocalist, and another girl, and Lawrence Keyes (a solo pianist), when I got the idea to form a quartert. I got Claude Garvey, a fine pianist just out of the service, and Al Matthews, who had been Al Casey's bass player on 52nd Street. My wife sang, played guitar and cocktail drums, and we kept the group together for seven years. I wrote arrangements on everything in our repertoire, because I wanted a small group that could play like a big band, and for that I had to have musicians who could read. We were at George's in the Village for about three years, and we went out to the Coast every year. When I gave up the quartet, I joined Luis Russell, and I went from him to Cozy Cole. I also played with Buddy Johnson.

"The last fifteen years have been freelancing—and teaching. I wrote a couple of books for students called *Lawrence Lucie's Special Guitar Lessons.* I feel my background with the bands helped me a lot. I've been very lucky."

(1972)

AL CASEY

GUITAR

"I think interest in instruments goes in cycles," Al Casey said. "At one time there was nothing but tenors on The Street. The guitar had its day, too. You consider all the fine guitarists who were around like Oscar Moore, Jimmy Shirley, Teddy Bunn and Leonard Ware. Some of them are working in post offices now."

A couple of brilliant Prestige albums served to bring Casey temporarily out of an obscurity that is the concomitant of star-manipulation and a declining business. Fickle and wasteful as jazz fashions are, his was clearly an undiminished talent deserving of wide recognition.

He was born in Louisville, Kentucky, in 1915. Though they were older than he, he knew of Jonah Jones and Dicky Wells there, and Bob Carroll, the tenor player, was a friend of the family's. When he was five, his mother began giving him violin lessons. "But that didn't last long," he says, "because I didn't like that screeching sound, and none of that tuition stuck." The family moved to New York in 1930 where, with a cousin, he used to "fool around, playing guitar by ear." Meanwhile, two uncles and two aunts who formed a spiritual group had struck up a friendship with Fats Waller while working on *Moon River,* a nightly show over WLW, Cincinnati. One of the uncles introduced him to Fats.

"So one day," he said, "I made an appointment and went over to his house and sat down and played a little. I always could swing a bit, and Fats said, 'I'm going to put you on one of my record sessions.' I still had two years to go in high school, but when a man like that said he liked the way I played, then I really got interested in guitar. I guess I had a pretty good ear to begin with, and now my uncles sent me to the Martin Smith Music School for three years.

"When I began to record with Fats, I became even more excited about music, and I wanted to join the band. He already had a guitar player—John Smith—and during the summer he used to augment from seven pieces and go on the road through the South with a big band. I wanted to quit school and do that, but he told me, 'If you finish high school and get your diploma with decent grades, you've got a job!'

"Recording with him was a light-hearted business. The record people

Young Al Casey, 1935.

would give him all those pop tunes the other artists refused. Fats would look through the music. 'Okay,' he'd say. 'We'll try this one.' Then we'd make the record. Just like that. Sometimes we cut seven or eight numbers in three hours. That was a matter of working together. I knew what Fats was going to do, what Gene Sedric, Herman Autrey or Johnny 'Bugs' Hamilton were going to do. It's different when you go into a studio today, without rehearsal, with people you maybe never worked with before.

"In June, 1933, three weeks after graduating, I was in the bus and riding with Fats. I was seventeen and I had the luck to be in the small band that played all the big clubs, like the Yacht Club in the Chicago hotel, and I was also in the big band that toured. I made nice money and had no ties. I had a ball and it was a time I'll never forget, but Fats saw to it that I didn't go overboard. He was really like a father to me. And not only him, but the other guys kept an eye on me, too. It was Gene Sedric who took me down to the union and stood for me.

"Once I was in the band, there was the end of tuition and the beginning of experience. That was the reason I never got to be the technician I wanted to become, but Fats told me what I played swung. He wanted me to swing and tell a story. He didn't want a whole gang of notes. I was with him over a period of ten years except for the time when Teddy Wilson put a big band together. I wanted to try it—no solos, just rhythm. That was one of the best bands that ever was. It could play in tune, it could swing, and it could really play ballads.

"I used to listen to all the guitar players, but Charlie Christian was my god. He brought something new to what we were already playing. I liked Django very much, and in the early days I heard Lonnie Johnson and liked his blues style. Teddy Bunn influenced me, too. He swung! That group he was in, the Spirits of Rhythm, was the swinginest group I ever heard.

"I didn't start all the single-string stuff I do now until after Fats died. I was upset, laid off for a while, and then went down to George's Tavern, a little beer joint in the Village, and worked with Clarence Profit and a bass player for quite a while. Later on, the owner asked me to form a trio and I had Teacho Wiltshire on piano and Al Matthews on bass. I think a trio of that instrumentation has so much more to offer than piano, bass and drums. By this time, I was playing amplified guitar, but I wasn't in love with it. In fact, I had begun to play it with Fats's big band, and all I knew was that it was louder. I played with a pick-up at first and couldn't get the full guitar effect, but later I bought a whole electric outfit.

"Guitar was big then for a time, because you could work quite big rooms and be heard. There was steady work and when Teacho went into the marines I got Sammy Clanton as pianist. Sammy didn't read then, but he was wonderful, and he sang and played like Nat Cole. (He's been in Atlantic City several years and he works all the time.) That was the greatest trio I ever had. The Street started jumping and we were in the Onyx Club for eleven months. That must have been around 1942 or 1943, because we were in the midst of all those be-boppers. We stayed in the Onyx while they brought in groups like Dizzy Gillespie's, Don Byas' and Big Sid Catlett's every two weeks. After a spell in Baltimore and Washington, we came back to the Down Beat, right across the street from the Onyx. We sat in there a long time and they used to call us 'the Nat Cole group of the East Coast.'

"Then we went out to California, to a job at Randini's, but the night before we left Sammy met with an accident. I was lucky enough to get Edward 'Sharkey' Dixon in his place. He could sing, too, and we were out there nearly a year. This was the period when I twice won the *Esquire* poll, and played that famous Metropolitan Opera House jazz concert when they had Louis Armstrong, Roy Eldridge, Coleman Hawkins, Art Tatum, Sid Catlett and Billie Holiday. So I was feeling pretty happy out there then.

"When we came back to New York, Sammy Clanton rejoined and we worked around for a couple of years, but I seemed to be out of luck as regards recording. The Street was going down, too, and big bands were losing ground, so work began to be hard to find. From then on, it was all kinds of jobs, week-end gigs and so on. I remember a job in the Bronx with Doles Dickens, and we played uptown at a place called Jock's where they had pretty decent acts like Marie Bryant and Billy Daniels. I joined King Curtis for four years in 1957, and to begin with we played pure rock 'n' roll, but after a time he began to turn around a bit. Lately, I've been playing with Curley Hamner in the Bronx. I would like to have my own group again, but meantime I have to eat and support a family.

"People always ask me about my time with Fats Waller, and I do have so many funny stories, but it's more of a touching one that stays freshest in my mind. Two or three times we were in Chicago at Christmas and Fats would have an organ put in his sitting-room at the Sherman Hotel. 'Come on by when you get off work,' he'd say to musicians and entertainers. He'd be calling people to come on up to his room at 4 or 5 in the morning. He would play that organ then—carols and things like that, and not loud. He would really play, and make you cry. You ask Earl Hines about those times. He remembers, too.''

(1962)

TINY GRIMES

GUITAR

Lloyd "Tiny" Grimes, born in Newport News in 1917, began his musical career as a drummer in a high school band.

"We had a little band on the side that played dances," he recalled. "I was on my way to being a drummer and was doing pretty good until my drums got washed away in a big flood. I had been playing at a beach resort, but I didn't have any money to buy another set, so I started messing around with piano at little Saturday night parties, or wherever I happened to run across one. It wound up with me getting to play for some of those little house hops, making a couple of dollars and maybe getting a dinner. I just liked music!

"Then we got a trio together which we called Wynken, Blynken and Nod—just me and three voices. We sang the best we could, and we sang good enough to make the Major Bowes radio show. What we had was nerve! We appeared on it several times, and got to be like regulars. He thought we were a kind of boost to the other acts. I could only play in about two keys.

"We were broke when we left home and went to Washington. We worked in Alexandria for quite a while, for a dollar a night and a sandwich apiece, twenty-one dollars a week for three people! Out of that, we had to pay a fellow to take us over there, because we were living in Washington. We struggled and struggled . . . and went on to Philly.

"I didn't start playing guitar till I was very old. It must have been '37 or '38, after I hit New York. You could get a good room then for three dollars a week. Five dollars was extry! The subway was a nickel in those days. I called myself a piano player, and I used to hang out with some fellows who called themselves the Four Dots. They had tipples and guitars. Snags Allen was one of them. He's a very good man, and very much underrated. He's been with the Supremes for seven years, playing background guitar, and he never got any breaks except with Roy Eldridge a couple of times. Listen to him on that great record of Roy's, *Fish Market*. When the Dots got through playing, they'd leave their instruments around, and I used to pick up a tipple and fool with it. Basically, it was a four-string instrument like a large ukulele, but it went out of fashion. It had a helluva sound, a

360

mandolin sound. Eventually, I went to the pawnshop and got me a guitar for five dollars.

"I've learned everything I know by *myself.* No one ever learned me *nothing!* I never could read too much. The way I did my chords, I used to find sheet music with ukulele diagrams on them. I got my own little system going, found out how to make certain things, and just translated the music my way. It took a lot of practice. After I got interested in it, I used to lock myself in my room all day, every day, because there was no piano and I had nothing else to do. After three months of sitting up in that room day in and day out, I could make little gigs. Then the fellows used to say to me, 'Lay off it, man! I want to solo this time!' But I kept after it . . .

"After I'd been playing about seven months, I got with the Cats and the Fiddle. They had tipples and guitars, too—no fiddle—and they recorded a number called *Oh, I Miss You So* on Bluebird that made some noise. I stayed with them a year or two, but I wasn't really getting much experience there. I knew more than anybody else, and they were just playing to accompany their singing. We ended up in Los Angeles. They wanted me to go back to New York with them, but they were paying me so cheap, and I said, 'My fare will cost just about what I'm going to make at the Apollo theatre.' So I decided to stay out there.

"Then I met Slim and Slam. When Slim (Gaillard) went in the army, Slam (Stewart) and I teamed up. I couldn't sing or do the stuff Slim did, but I could play good enough, and we soon got a few little jobs. We used to go to an after-hours spot called Lovejoy's Big Chicken, or something like that, and Art Tatum would come in there, and we'd sit around and jam. We fell in with what *he* was doing. Now I had only been playing guitar two years, but I had quick ears, the desire to play and be in the fast crowd. We played every night, and the word got around. We weren't getting paid, but we were having fun, and the guy would give us chicken sandwiches and something to drink. First thing you know, there were large crowds. When we went outside, we saw long lines of people and a chain across the door. We never paid it any mind at first. He was making thousands of dollars off of us, and we didn't even know. We were just having fun! After a time, we said, 'Man, look at all these people in here! Do you think they have come to see us?'

"You see, at that time Tatum had been catching it pretty hard himself. There was so much in his playing that people couldn't dig, and he wasn't getting too many jobs. But then we began to become the talk of Los Angeles. A fellow at the Streets of Paris heard about us and suggested to Tatum that he form a regular trio with Slam and me, and that he would

Tiny Grimes, Slam Stewart and Art Tatum.

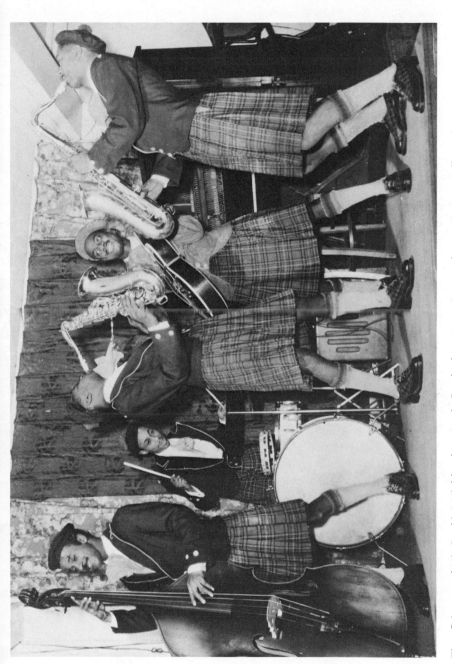

Tiny Grimes and His Rockin' Highlanders: Herb Gordy, bass; Jerry Potter, drums; George Kelly, tenor saxophone; Grimes, guitar; Joe Sewell, tenor saxophone.

pay whatever extra money was necessary. I think Tatum was to get between $150 and $175 a week.

"We never rehearsed. Everything was made up on the bandstand. Why in the world did those two guys keep *me?* I know I was the weakest thing in there, but after we started working I'd go downstairs during every intermission with my guitar and work on whatever song we'd been playing, trying to catch up with them as best I could. I did that every set, every intermission, and they would have to come and get me. I think that's the only thing that kept me with them. They knew I was trying *so* hard.

"Tatum was a lot of fun, and he could sing the blues! While he was working, he'd drink Pabst Blue Ribbon beer, but when he got through he'd drink bourbon. He was no more temperamental than the average person, but he hated people to take advantage of him because he couldn't see. He could see well enough to play bridge, holding the cards real close, and he was a helluva bridge player. Anything he did, he did well. And he never practiced, although he did have what looked like a pecan nut that he rolled in his fingers all day.

"The arguments he and Slam had were funny to me. They both had perfect pitch. You could hit on a glass, and they'd tell you what note it was, or what notes it was between. They'd get into arguments about things like that, but all in fun. Because Slam had that perfect ear, Tatum couldn't lose him. Me he could lose, but I'd catch up with 'em sooner or later! I tell you it was an honor playing with them, but playing wasn't too much enjoyment. It was a struggle, because nobody would learn me nothing, and I had to catch it as it went by, and it was so fast all the time.

"I was with them nearly three years. We went to Milwaukee, Chicago, Cleveland and 52nd Street. An agent was the cause of our breaking up in 1944. The trio was the hottest thing around, but he told Tatum he could do it all by himself, that he didn't need Slam and me. So Tatum went out on his own for quite a long time, and when he had to go back to a trio he got Everett Barksdale on guitar.

"When we broke up, I started with my own group, playing for Billie Holiday. There was no problem about jobs at that time. When I was working in the Spotlight, Charlie Parker used to come around and jam every night. He was a nice, friendly guy, so when the time came for a record date, I naturally got him. We were good friends, and he liked the way I played. Nobody understood what he was doing, but I knew, and it wasn't 'way out like these fellows are doing now. It was just a different kind of music, and he was sending a message across, but the average person couldn't dig it.

"I was at the Down Beat on 52nd Street for a year or so with Joe Springer on piano, Jimmy Butts on bass, and Eddie Nicholson on drums. We were the house band. John Hardee used to come and sit in with us, and we made some record dates together. He was from Texas, played tenor, and was in the army at the time. 'Man, when you get out of the army,' I told him, 'come on back and get a job!' He could play.

"The Street went dead around '46 or '47, and I went into Gleason's in Cleveland for two weeks—and stayed two years. We had a pretty good group there with Red Prysock on sax, Sir Charles Thompson on piano, Herb Gordy on bass and Jerry Potter on drums. I left for a couple of months, and then went back for two more years. That's where the Rocking Highlanders started.

"The idea behind that, the kilts and all, was to attract attention and make more money. We had a little show, an entertainment—dancing, singing, telling jokes, as well as playing. But we could never find the right agent. They'd sit behind the 'phone in New York and book you all over the United States. You need somebody who's interested in more than the ten per cent. It's a *surprise* if you're working somewhere to see your agent come in, as though he was protecting his interests. That seldom happens unless you've got a personal manager.

"I worked in Atlantic City every summer for a long time with these Highlanders at Weeks's Tavern. When we were not there, we were mostly on the road, although we often played the Apollo Theatre. We were there the first time with George Shearing, and another time the Cats and the Fiddle were on the same bill.

"After that, it was gigging for me, from Colorado to New England, but usually around New York. I've played with Duke Ellington on an Ed Sullivan television show, and I've been working with Earl Hines. In 1968, I went to Europe with Milt Buckner, and then again in 1970 with Jay McShann. Jay is wonderful to work with. When we were touring France, he'd get tore down on that cognac—smashed or real high, you might say. Now he is one of the few people in the world who always stays happy when he's drinking. A lot of other fellows I know get mean and violent. He can still play all right, too, except that sometimes he gets cramps in his fingers. I gave him a remedy for that—quinine. I use it myself if I get on a binge. The first time I got cramps, it scared me to death. A doctor in Atlantic City told me to take quinine tablets, and they worked. I always tell musicians who drink a lot about them. If you've got an important job to do, you can take them and be sure you'll be able to play all right.

"When I started playing, I hadn't heard of Charlie Christian. Snags Allen was my idol, and then all of a sudden here comes Christian, and he became an idol, too. After I heard him, I could forget about everybody else, guitar-wise. There were other fellows who played good hard guitar and technical stuff, but Christian was *it*. Of course, I also liked Django Reinhardt, liked him very good, although I couldn't see how he did some of the things he did with just three fingers.

"A lot of people ask me why I've always played four-string guitar, and I always tell 'em I never could afford the other two strings. I got so I could do a whole lot of jumping about, and do practically the same things as a guy with six strings. I'd done it so long, I was used to it. I tried six strings two or three times, but couldn't do myself justice. Most of the folk players, or hill-billies as they used to be called, use four strings, but they mostly tune them like a banjo. I tune mine like the first four of a six-string. I've won only one award, and you might say I've been underrated by critics who, I've been told, don't regard me as playing the full instrument."

Despite Tiny Grimes's own modesty, and despite the dubious verdicts of magazine polls, the company he has kept and the records he has made testify to the fact that he is one of the most exciting and swinging guitarists in jazz history.

(1972)

MILT HINTON

BASS

At the end of 1935, Milt Hinton was playing at the Three Deuces in Chicago with Zutty Singleton's small group when Cab Calloway came in one night. Calloway was on his way back from California, where he had just finished making a film with Al Jolson called *The Singing Kid*.

"He and the band were making a tour," Hinton recalled, "playing their way back to New York. A tour in those days could last six months. I remember that with Cab it took months to get from Chicago to New York. We played everything, all those week-end theatres, two days in Sandusky, three days somewhere else . . .

"Al Morgan, Cab's bass player, was a tremendous showman. In that movie, and in several things Cab had done before, all of the directors were looking at Morgan. Every time there was a shot of Cab Calloway, you'd see another one of Al Morgan, and Cab didn't like this too much. Fortunately, Morgan decided to stay in California after the picture was made.

"He was a big, tall guy—much taller than me, I remember, because I had to wear his uniform when I joined the band. Before I got it changed, you could just see my fingers as I tried to play the bass with his long coat on. He was quite a flashy performer and he made a big impression. He had a way of getting in front of the bass and working his right foot. I'm not taking anything away from him, but he wasn't a great musician. The notes he played weren't what I'd consider in the chord all the time. In those days, if you hit a bad note here and there, it wasn't really noted. The brass was playing so very loud, too, and the bass was often more of a visual thing. I remember when Cab was taking his bow, Al Morgan would twirl the bass in one direction for Cab to go off the stage. While the audience was applauding, he would set the bass spinning in the opposite direction to bring Cab back. Visually, he was great, and I was always thinking, 'Gee, I would like to be like this!' And I actually tried to copy him. There was a lot of clowning around while I was with Cab Calloway, and when Dizzy (Gillespie) came in later we would have the whole theatre upset with the antics we were pulling on stage. I never was able to come up to Morgan's class, but though I clowned, I would always, with a clear consicience, play the right notes. I had been to Northwestern University and had really studied music.

"This Calloway band I joined was a staid band and very disappointing to me. It was a set thing. Cab was the star, and there was nothing else but Cab the star. The men sat there and made a hundred dollars a week, which was a tremendous amount of money in the '30s, when there were no taxes to speak of. No one man made a dime more than another. There was absolutely no difference in the salaries.

"One thing I always admired about Cab was the way he took the advice of musicians he liked, or of whoever was in charge. He was not a musician himself, but Walter 'Foots' Thomas was in charge of the band when I joined, and he was a very good musician. Cab would also take the advice of Lammar Wright, Keg Johnson and Claude Jones, because he knew they were good men who had been with Fletcher Henderson or in other name bands. Ben Webster was in the band, too, and all of them were getting a hundred dollars a week, which was, on average, more than Duke (Ellington) was paying in those days. There might be exceptions, of course, but Cab's at this time was a higher paid band. If he needed a replacement, or didn't like some particular guy, or thought a musician was getting lax and he wanted to make a change, he would go and ask advice. 'Who's good? I need another bass player . . .'

"But music was secondary to Cab's act, even though there were great people like Ben Webster there. Ben was very unhappy because he had nothing to play. Claude Jones was unhappy because he had nothing to play. Keg Johnson was unhappy because he was just sitting there. Besides Keg and Claude, the third trombone was De Priest Wheeler. The three trumpets were Doc Cheatham, Mouse Randolph and Lammar Wright, all good men. The four saxes were Andrew Brown, Garvin Bushell, Ben Webster and Walter Thomas—two altos and two tenors, no baritone until Jerry Blake arrived. The rhythm section was Benny Paine on piano, Morris White on guitar, Leroy Maxey on drums, and myself.

"A change gradually came about when we went into the Cotton Club in New York, which was then where the Latin Quarter is now. I think we stayed about six months. Benny Goodman was at the Pennsylvania Hotel, and he was on the air, and everybody was singing his praises, saying he had a tremendous band. Lionel (Hampton) and Teddy (Wilson) were there, and we'd all worked together on different occasions around Chicago. Now everybody was asking for jazz, and people were interested in *playing,* and they wanted to hear musicians as well. The recording business was beginning to take on, too.

"Cab was always anti recording. He'd give the record people hell. He didn't make his reputation as a recording artist! They were always telling him, 'Too loud! Back up!' And he would bawl 'em out, and cuss 'em out, and walk out of the studio. He didn't need records to make him. He was made before records. This whole scene . . . it was very sad to see him in a record studio. It was just chaos, and he never recorded well. When he had first come into the picture, the avenue was open and he had stepped right into it. All young men are headstrong, and success is hard for young people to adjust to. He even got into big scenes with Bing Crosby, and sloughed him off a couple of times, until Bing got bigger and sloughed him off in turn.

"Yet Cab was a great business man and a good guy concerning his band. He wanted the men to play well—what *he* wanted them to play. Discipline was his main issue. He had a big show and it was going to make money for him, and it had to be disciplined. He didn't want any stars, because stars leave. When we opened at the Cotton Club, Lionel Hampton came over and told me he wanted me on a record date he had at Victor next day.

" 'Okay,' I said. 'I'm coming down.'

"Some time later, Teddy Wilson called me: 'Milt, I've got a date with Billie Holiday at Columbia. Get Ben. Come on and make it.'

"A record session then was thirty dollars, and this extra money was a godsend, but when Cab heard about it, he flipped.

" 'If I hear of you guys going out making records, making somebody else great when you're working for me—whoever makes a date is fired!' That's what he said when we went to work that night.

"He just didn't understand. This hadn't been done to him before, to his exclusive organization. I hadn't been in the band long, and was just getting to the stage where I had a couple of decent suits, and I was scared to death. But Ben Webster had quite a name by then, and he resented it deeply. He went and bawled the daylights out of Cab.

" 'What do you mean?' he demanded. 'You should be ashamed of yourself. You should be honored that you've got men in your band everybody else wants. If you do what you said, you'll be interfering with my living, and you can get yourself another saxophone player.'

"Ben was a pretty wild guy in those days. So was Cab, and he yelled. I think they went out and got loaded afterwards, but the next day Cab came to work and okayed our recording. He had changed overnight. It made me very happy, because I wasn't established in New York and wasn't in a position to quit. I had to work out a union transfer, because they wouldn't let me just walk in and go to work on the very best job in town! Cab was really very gracious to me then. He paid me three months salary and hired Elmer James to play in the band!

"Again it was a matter of his advisers, of Claude Jones and Keg Johnson saying, 'There's no finer bass player in New York than Milt. You've got plenty of money. Why let them dictate to you? You're going to open the Cotton Club and the union won't let him work. Why send him back to Chicago? What's another hundred bucks to you? Man, you *need* a good band now!'

"I went down and rehearsed with the band twice a week, and after the first month Cab let me play the broadcasts every week. Elmer James was a good bass player, but he was older, and he didn't have the fire. We were trying to make good, and I was the 'flash' as you might call it, trying to outplay everybody, to keep the impression that I was great, and live up to what Claude and Keg had said about me.

"As the record business picked up, Cab began to get arrangements to feature the band. Also, when we had to play a dance at the Cotton Club, he often wouldn't be on the bandstand—and we had nothing to play but background music.

"When Ben Webster left, Chu Berry took his place, and Chu was a real string-saver and swapper, a real changin' man. He'd go to Chick Webb and say, 'Cab's got a couple of arrangements that would sound good for your band. I'll get Cab to give you them if you'll give us one of those Benny Carter made for you.' Then he'd go to Cab and say, 'It won't cost you

Danny Barker, guitar; Milt Hinton, bass; J. C. Heard, drums.

nothin'. You've got a good band and we've got to have something to play. Chick will let you have a Benny Carter arrangement if you'll give him two of those Swayzee and Harry White arrangements.'

"Chu was very frank and forward, and Cab liked him, and would listen, and they would make the switch. Chu also sold him on the idea of getting somebody to write for the band, and he was very much responsible for our having good music in the book. Chu had the kind of confidence that made Cab listen. He had come out of Fletcher Henderson's band a star when Ben went on to Duke. A little later, Andy Gibson came in as arranger.

"Meanwhile, Doc Cheatham got sick and had to go home to Tennessee, and this young kid, John Birks 'Dizzy' Gillespie, came in, blowing like crazy. Our first recording date in 1940 was for Vocalion in Chicago, and Chu had suggested featuring Dizzy on something, so Dizzy wrote *Pickin' the Cabbage*. Hilton Jefferson was on alto, and Tyree Glenn had joined by then with his trombone and vibes, and Chu had the idea for the formation of the Cab Jivers.

" 'Look, you're only going on twice a night,' he told Cab, 'so let's have a little group, a small band out of the big band.'

"Danny Barker was in on guitar now, and Cozy Cole had taken Leroy Maxey's place. Chu was just diddling Cab into these things. Cab is the biggest man in town, he wants to feature his band, but his drummer can't play a solo. This was at a time after Chick Webb died, when he and Gene Krupa had been doing everybody down in town. And the reason Maxey couldn't play a drum solo was because Cab wouldn't let him for so many years.

"As I said, when I came in this band, I had been disappointed. The guys didn't get to play anything and they just sat there and got rich, but they didn't go out, and never walked from one club to another. Guys like Maxey, and Andy Brown, and Morris White, and De Priest Wheeler had been there so long. They came from Missouri and they wouldn't walk across the street to hear another band. The one guy that would go out with me was Ben Webster, and we're friends to this very day.

" 'Soon as we get out of the theatre,' Ben would say, 'we'll go by such-and-such a club,' depending on what town we were in. Ben would sit in with the band, and then he'd say, 'Go home and get your bass.'

"I couldn't understand those other guys being the way they were. Sure, when I came in there I played accompaniment for Cab, too, but I never let that keep me from listening to what somebody else was playing. I remember during the first couple of nights I was there, I saw a whole note and picked up my bow. 'Put that thing down,' Cab said, 'and keep playin'!' But before shows and between shows, I'd practice with my bow in the dressing room. Sometimes Ben Webster would say, 'Get your bass and we'll go down in the basement of the theatre.' Just last year, he and I made some tapes at home in my basement. They're just beautiful, and the quality's fabulous.

"Dizzy was the freshest influence that came in the band so far as I was concerned. He took up where Ben left off. He was really creative, and always anxious to be playing. He had been in Teddy Hill's band, and hadn't been able to accomplish what he wanted, so far as his chops were concerned, but he was trying all the time. We sat down, and we blew together, and went through his things, and it was very stimulating for me.

"Dizzy wasn't like some of those young fellows who felt they must not smile or let the audience know they were enjoying what they were doing. I feel that has been one of the failures in the music business. What they called 'Tomming' was often a matter of being happy and enjoying yourself, and it was all right so long as you *played.* Don't do it if you were not saying anything! We had an expression to fit certain situations: 'Tom, but play! Be sure you play something!'

"I remember one time we went through Longview, Texas. It had been the worst hole in the world. Everybody was poor, white and black. The white people who had the farms were renting them out to Negro share-croppers for a pittance. They tried to sell the land to the Negroes, because something kept oozing up out of the ground that made the cattle sick. 'The land ain't gonna be worth a damn,' they said. They didn't have the sense to know that it was oil, and they kept palming the farms off on poor Negro families. Later it came out there was a gigantic river of oil under this area, which was eighty miles wide and as many miles long. When the oil speculating companies came through, the people became rich overnight, black and white alike.

"They didn't know what to do with the money. They'd never had anything in their lives. New York clothing people were sending salesmen down, selling ten-dollar suits for three hundred dollars, and they would buy half a dozen at a time. I saw people there with four or five watches on them! Some had three or four Cadillacs. It could happen to anyone who had lived near starvation all his life and suddenly found he had ten thousand dollars a month coming in. They went crazy.

" 'Get us the greatest entertainers,' they said. 'Get us the greatest band in the world.'

" 'We've got Cab Calloway, but it will cost you ten thousand dollars for a night.'

" 'What do we care? Bring him down!'

"So we got to this place, a little dancehall, five miles out of town. I can't begin to picture how bad it was. You could probably get three hundred people in it if you squeezed 'em all together really tight. There was a little nothing of a bandstand, and we went out there from the nearest town in cabs.

"They were the white people, all in their white suits, and they'd got their girls with them, and there was liquor everywhere—flowing like the oil. They were trying to live very fast, to make up. They were not accustomed to associating with Negroes, and we were not even second-class citizens. We weren't even considered human beings. But we were entertainers, and we played.

"There was a guy with his girl at a table near the stand. The girl saw this handsome fellow, Benny Paine, sitting at the piano, and she asked him, 'You want a drink?'

" 'No, thank you,' he answered. We knew our place in this particular area!

" 'What do you mean? You're a Southerner and you don't want to drink with me?'

" 'Okay, I'll have a drink if you think I ought to.'

"So this white lady poured Benny Paine a drink while the guy was away from the table. When he came back, he said, 'What're you doin', drinkin' with my woman?' And he added some nasty remarks.

"Although a Negro was nothing, there was a law that if you hit a Negro you had to pay a three-hundred dollar fine. So now this guy went to the man who was giving the dance and said, 'I'll pay the three hundred dollars just to hit him!'

"By now the people were getting out of hand, anyway. Everybody was drunk. They were fighting one another. Some guy was dancing with the girl of someone else who didn't like it. Soon they had a general fist fight going, a mass thing on the floor. We were playing just as loud as we possibly could, and we were scared to death. Everybody carried a gun in Texas in those days. If a Negro was killed, they didn't do anything about it. They might have to pay a thousand-dollar fine, or get five years—and get out in three months—if it was an important Negro. If it was a nobody, just some ordinary guy, there was no problem at all.

" 'I guess we better stop the music for a while,' the man said, 'and you niggers better go downstairs, because these people are getting out of hand and I can't handle them.' So we hustled down into a little basement room, down a staircase—no other way out! Overhead, we could hear all this stompin' and fightin' and chairs breakin'! Every now and then somebody would shoot a pistol through the roof.

"We made trips in the '30s and '40s through these towns in Texas and all through Louisiana. The smaller the town, the more drastic the conditions. It was the same in small Florida towns. We would play a dance for white people, and they'd put a ring five feet back from the bandstand, so the people could stand but not get too close. There would be police in front of the stand, but the police didn't like us either. We were very sharp, dressed very neat, we were playing very good, and we all had money. After playing two hours, there'd be a half-hour intermission, and they'd put ropes through the hall for us to go outside. As we walked through this aisle, roped off each side, with police in front and behind, these people would be swinging at us. We'd be ducking to keep these guys from hitting us. They were showing off to their women.

"As conditions got better, and Cab made more money, he would exclude the places where we'd had trouble. We played dances in Oklahoma where there were nothing but Indians, and there were some wealthy Indians where oil had been found on their land. The problem with them was that they just couldn't drink whiskey. They would never fight with us, but they would fight among themselves. They'd have a few drinks and go completely haywire. Nobody would dance. There would just be fighting —up on the roof, or on the beams of the place—everybody swinging, literally.

"I never quit Cab. He fired me. He fired the whole band in 1951. It was the first notice I received in my whole career in the band business, and I felt deeply insulted. All he had to do was say, 'Look, you've been with me fifteen years, but I can't go any farther.' I would have been glad to shake hands and go out and find me a job. But to this day Cab's still my friend.

"I remember that every Christmas he gave us a hundred dollars and paid our fare home, wherever we lived. Jonah Jones, who was with us from 1941 to 1951, still does something like that. Christmas Day is Cab's birthday, and we'd stop working a few days before. For almost ten years, our first engagement afterwards was a New Year's Eve opening in the Panther Room at the Hotel Sherman in Chicago. During the summer, if he got tired, Cab would take a vacation, and he'd give the fellows who'd been in the band a long time their full salary for four weeks, or however long he was going to be off. The new guys, who'd only been in six months or so, would get half their salary if they promised to return, but he'd never let anybody go without giving them something."

After leaving Calloway, Hinton began to work in New York clubs, and he soon became one of the most sought after bassists in the recording field. On one occasion, he recalled with amusement, he even played with Guy Lombardo when the latter was re-recording his old hits in stereo and needed a string bass to "take the edge off the sound of the bass horn." There is probably no great name in the music business for whom Milt Hinton has not played.

(1961)

PANAMA FRANCIS

DRUMS

Panama Francis was born in Miami in 1918, on Fourth Avenue and 12th Street, which used to be known as "Old Iron Street." His mother told him that even when he was quite small he was always beating on the dining table with his spoon. By the time he was six, there was just one thing he wanted for Christmas—a drum.

"When I was eight years old," he recalled, "I became a member of a drum-and-bugle corps. All the other kids were from eleven to thirteen, and I was the littlest thing in there, but I worked my way up to where I was second drummer within a year, playing the regular, field marching drum. When I was eleven, I got a Sunday gig at the Holiness Church. We had trumpet, piano, bass and drums, and the people in the church would clap their hands and play tambourines. We used to get some good swinging rhythm there, and that's where I learned so much about what later went into rhythm and blues and rock 'n' roll. Before I was thirteen, I was playing house parties around Miami, and people used to wonder about 'this little kid fooling around with all this stuff.'

"At fourteen, I joined George Kelly's band, which started out in school. All the guys were in high school, and I was in my first year at junior high when I joined. George was a good leader, and he and all the others were older than I. In fact, I was the youngest in all the bands I played in until I joined Cab Calloway after World War II, when I found that Lammar Wright, Jr., was younger than I was.

"George Kelly's Cavaliers used to work club dates around Miami, and go as far as Fort Pierce for an overnight gig, but we would be back next day for school. Ivan Rolle, the bass player who later worked with Cozy Cole, was the conductor. He used to do an imitation of Cab Calloway, singing and dancing in front, and waving a baton just like Cab. He was known as the *Hi-de-ho King of the South!* George wrote the arrangements, and we had four brass, four reeds, and five rhythm—a bass fiddle and a tuba. George had played piano for Bessie Smith when he was twelve and still in short pants. She came to Miami with a show, and something had happened to her piano player, so they called George in. He could read and play pretty good, but later he gave up piano for saxophone. By the time he was sixteen, he was arranging very well. He had just learned from experience and by reading books like Archie Bleyer's.

"I didn't have any tuition until I came to New York. I was self-taught. There were older drummers around Miami, and bands from the North used to come down, and I would stand and watch the drummer. I always admired Chick Webb, and he was my idol.* I listened to his records and he was about the only person who really impressed me then. I tried to learn different things others were doing, but I wanted to play drums like him. He came to Florida once when I was out on the road, and when I went to New York I finally got to see him, but right after that he took sick. I don't think the records did him justice, and when I saw him I thought he was fantastic. I watched the way he handled his band, the way he stomped it off, the way he knew the arrangements—and he knew what he and everybody else was supposed to do. I've since watched other drummers who were leaders, but nobody compared with him so far as having control of the band was concerned. As soon as you walked in, you knew he was the leader. He wasn't only playing the drums. He couldn't read, but he could hear it—read their ears, the guys said—and he knew every arrangement in that book from beginning to end. He could hum every one of the arrangements, what everybody was supposed to be playing. I was glad I met him, but I was so very sorry when he passed away, because there was so much I could have learned from that fabulous man.

"For a guy playing drums to show people what he can really do, I think he needs a big band. In a way, I'm a frustrated leader, because I would have liked to have had a band like Chick did. A drummer has to have control, because the whole band relies on him. In small combos, as you often hear today, you can have weak drums and a strong bass, and the bass carries it. In the big band days, they used to say a band was no better

---

*In 1973, when the Chick Webb band was revived for the Newport Jazz Festival, Panama Francis was the drummer.

Panama Francis, 1969.

than its drummer. If the band had a weak drummer, it was a weak band; if it had a strong drummer, it was a good band. This went for Jimmie Lunceford, Tommy Dorsey, Court Basie, Benny Goodman, right straight down the line.

"Drummers have forgotten how to play the bass drum, and the bass drum is the heart of the band. It doesn't have to be overpowering, but you have to be able to control your foot. A lot of young drummers today can't play time with their foot because they can't control it. The bass drum and bass fiddle are supposed to blend, and the bass drum should reinforce the notes of the bass fiddle in a big band. This is what gives a band a beat, and you cannot go in a big band and just play cymbals and accent with your foot, because so far as the band having any *feeling* is concerned, it just won't be there. The bass fiddle cannot do it by itself. It's not a matter of what's heard, but of what's felt, and this comes from control. A lot of drummers that have reputations today, that have made big names for themselves, would never have made it in the big bands.

"We had a great love match going in hot jazz, or whatever you want to call it—between Africa and Europe. This was what made the music so great. They've lost that. It's much more European and less African. Africa was the rhythm and Europe was the chord changes, the melodic line, and what not. The change has hurt jazz very much. The avant-garde people are finding an escape. We're very prosperous, everybody's got money, and you can sell *anything*. If we had hard times again, people would not accept a lot of this stuff they're accepting today, because they *know* it isn't right, *know* there's something wrong with it. But they look around for novelty, for something different, and they buy it even if it's bad.

"Well, to go back a bit, I was with George Kelly five years. We got the bright idea of an organized band to play at football dances and different clubs because of the example of the top band around Miami, which was led by Hartley Toots. They came up and played the Apollo Theatre once, and they flunked out because they couldn't play shows, but it was a very good band for dancing in ballrooms. I'm not going to argue about whether jazz was born in New Orleans, but I would say that wherever you found a lot of Negroes you found jazz, and each city had a band that was pretty good, like Hartley Toots and the Orange Pickers, bands with fourteen to sixteen men in them. They played stocks and arrangements. They used to take the stocks, and when they got through with them they sounded like their own arrangements. I can do that myself. If the introduction isn't swinging, you have the piano player play four bars, and then go right into the reed chorus. That kind of thing. There were fellows in each band who arranged, who had learned from experience—no teachers. We had a guy named Richard Smothers, who used to write out each individual part with no key signature, but the sharps and flats were all written out. Which is something I hear is being done today. You have to know your sharps and flats!

"Then there was always one guy in the town who knew all the instruments, but you had to learn yours on your own. Mostly, you just got the rudiments, and you'd go from there. Just like with me and the drums. I picked up a pair of sticks, and whatever I heard I played. I didn't know whether it was correct, or wrong, or what, but what I heard I could execute. I never had anyone sit down and show me this was a five-stroke roll, or this was a seven-stroke roll, until I came to New York and went to a drum teacher.

"In 1938, I left George Kelly and joined a band in Tampa called Charlie Brantley's Florida Collegians—eight pieces. Lem Davis had just left them when I joined. After a couple of months, they were working only two days a week, so I wrote my father in New York, told him nothing was happening, and said I wanted to go up there.

"I arrived on August 9th, a date I'll never forget. I didn't know any of the big names. There were a few Florida musicians playing Friday and Saturday nights, but they weren't making it. On my first night in New York, I went to the Victoria Club on 141st Street, where Fred Moore was playing. In those days, club operators would hire a piano player and a drummer, and a half-hour after the club opened they would have a full band on the stand. Everybody was sitting in. I made the whole round, went to all the jam sessions. The fifth night in town, I was working, and I've been working ever since.

"I went to work at the Rosebud in Brooklyn, a non-union job. Jimmy Hamilton was on clarinet, Charlie Drayton on bass. I'd never belonged to a union, but a union guy came by and said the club had to go union and we all had to join. My father helped me get the money together, and I passed the test, and joined the union. Two weeks later I went into the Apollo Theatre with Billy Hicks and His Sizzling Six. Billy played trumpet and Joe Watts was the bass player, but Edmond Hall wasn't in the group then. We played gigs around the city until Chick Webb became sick and Bill Beason left Roy Eldridge to take his place. Roy had heard me at the Victoria and the Apollo, and he asked if I'd want to work with his band —nine pieces—at the Arcadia ballroom. I didn't know who he was at first, but when they told me Roy Eldridge I just started shaking all over. I couldn't believe it. He had his brother Joe, Franz Jackson and Prince Robinson on saxes, Clyde Hart on piano, John Collins on guitar, Ted Sturgis on bass, and Eli Robinson playing trombone. I made my first recording session with Roy, for Variety in 1939.

"One thing that he did for me, I later very much appreciated. During intermission, he made me go in the next room and practice on my practice pad. I wanted to be out there with the rest of the guys, and I was angry about it, but I respected him and practiced. He helped me, too, and showed me a lot of things about the drums, for he played very good drums himself. Don't let anybody kid you about that! He gave me my nickname, 'Panama', when I joined him. I went into rehearsal with a panama hat on, and when he couldn't remember my name, he said, 'Hey, Panama . . .' All the fellows in the band thought that was my name, and they started calling me by it, and I was too scared to tell them my real name was David.

"I went out on the road with Roy, and when we came back I got a call from Lucky Millinder. I had to compete with Shadow Wilson for the job, but I won out and went in the Savoy with Lucky. Shadow was older than I. In fact, the little trumpet player with Count Basie, Bobby Moore, and I were the youngest musicians in New York playing with big name bands. We were both twenty and everybody thought we looked alike.

"I joined Lucky Millinder in the summer of 1939 and was with him six years. I think 1943 was a peak year, when we had Freddy Webster, Dizzy Gillespie, Archie Johnson, George Stevenson, Willie Moran, Tab Smith, Sam Taylor, Ernest Purce and Bill Doggett. You couldn't wait to go on the job at the Savoy every night, because you'd know there was going to be somebody on the other bandstand blowing at you, and you were going to have to be blowing back at him. In those days, it was mostly the Savoy Sultans opposite us, with Razz Mitchell playing drums, and he was a good rhythm man. The Sultans were only eight pieces, but from the time they hit until they finished, they were swinging! They had no big stars. Rudy Williams was a youngster, and the only outstanding guy in the band. But put them all together . . . look out!

"Sunday nights they'd bring in a different band to play a battle of music with the house band. It might be Earl Hines, or Tommy Dorsey, or Harry James. Erskine Hawkins, Lucky Millinder, the Sultans, and the Sunset Royals led by Doc Wheeler (they were there a couple of years) were some of the house bands after Chick Webb died. Jay McShann came in from Kansas City with Charlie Parker, Gene Ramey and Gus Johnson. In those days, bands used to dress sharp, and these guys were a raggedy-looking bunch. They could play though!

"We looked at them over in a corner and wouldn't even speak to them. We opened up with one of our big flag-wavers, *Prelude in C Sharp Minor,* a great arrangement by Chappie Willet, to show off our musicianship. McShann opened up with *Swingin' the Blues,* and at three o'clock that morning they were still swinging! They swung us right out of the place and made us feel like a bunch of Boy Scouts that night! Yes, they really shot us down, although we could more than hold our own with other bands like Erskine Hawkins's.

"There was no band in the country that didn't play the Savoy. Would you believe that Guy Lombardo held the record for drawing the most people in that swinging joint? Some of it was due to curiosity. Then a lot of people don't know that at the Home of Happy Feet, as it was called, we had to play waltzes and *La Conga*. But although every band played the popular tunes of the day, it was primarily jazz up there. The programs changed so much more then, and you used to like to go to rehearsal— maybe three times a week—because you knew there was going to be new music coming into the book. You didn't just keep playing the same things over and over, as some bands do today.

"At the Savoy, we started at ten o'clock, and each band played three hours. We played six tunes in a half-hour set, and the leaders used to say we played two for the people and one for the band. In other words, there were two arrangements where they could dance or listen, and one arrangement for the band to get its kicks.

"Lucky was a nice guy to work for. He was a little bit eccentric. He'd stay up all night and go from one bar to another. I learned how to rehearse a band from him. He couldn't read a note, but if you gave him a bunch of guys who could read, in one week's time he'd have them sounding like a band that had been organized for a year. He could remember everything in an arrangement after it was run down once. He was a genius in that way. Of course, he always had somebody like Bill Doggett as straw boss to help on technical problems.

"After I left him, I formed my own eight-piece band and went in the Savoy for six weeks. I had Jesse Drake on trumpet and Elwyn Fraser on alto, and the group was modeled on the Savoy Sultans. I was well liked up there, but I didn't have enough name at that time, and they brought in Tab Smith and Trevor Bacon when they left Millinder.

"In 1947, I went with Willie Bryant's big band for six months, when he had Frank Galbraith on trumpet and Steve Pulliam on trombone. After that, I went with Cab Calloway for six years. I took Kansas Fields's place, and I went to South America with Cab. I was featured there, and they liked me so well that in 1953 I took my own six-piece band to Montevideo. Opening night, they had Noro Morales with a big band and a show inside the theatre, and us playing outside. You know where all the people were? Outside. We were a sensation down there—Money Johnson on trumpet, Elmer Crumbley on trombone, Babe Clark on tenor, Charlie Bateman on piano, Laverne Barker on bass.

"When Cab Calloway broke up the band in 1952, there was a lot of jazz in nightclubs, but not much money. I had a couple of kids to raise—I had married young, at nineteen—and I wanted to raise them right. So I decided to go into studio work. I remember going to a Sam 'The Man' Taylor recording session in 1954 where Leroy Holmes brought an arrangement in with the drum part written out. I had been used to running down an arrangement, listening to it, hearing what the band had to do, and then just playing. But this arrangement called for a lot of syncopation that was written out. Some arrangers think they can write a drum part, and a lot of them will disagree with me, but I'm sorry to say that if a drummer is going to sit up there and read it like it is, it's going to be stiff. He isn't going to swing. Back in the days I was talking of, they didn't even write a drum part. Take Sonny Greer with Duke's band for an example. How can a guy sit up there and play time, and catch the syncopations and what not, if he's got to keep his eye on a sheet of music? He *can't* swing. I know one thing, and it's hard to explain, but to play drums in a big band, if you *really* want to swing this band, you can't be watching music. You have to concentrate on what's going on around you.

"When the incident with Leroy Holmes happened, I felt very embarrassed, because I couldn't read the part, so the next day I went to Freddy Albright, who taught drums and vibes. I used to look at the music, but rarely know exactly how long a whole or a half note was supposed to be held. Freddy was a great teacher, and in six months he taught me how to read and decipher music. I even studied vibes and tymps. Then for a time I was really hung up. I couldn't play anything unless the music was in front of me, and I lost some of my originality. Even now, if I have a big band arrangement to play, I put the music up there. I don't look at it, but I don't feel safe unless the music's there. That after all those years of just looking at an arrangement once and getting up there and playing! In a way, it was damaging—damaging to me, anyway. Maybe with another drummer it wouldn't have harmed him, if he started out learning to read, learning movements before he started playing. Freddy taught me technical things I hadn't done, but for a time it was like a fighter who'd been a southpaw, and you turned around and made a right-hander out of him. It didn't come naturally.

"I think it was in 1953 that I was called for my first record date for Atlantic Records by Ahmet Ertegun and Jerry Wexler. Those two guys really knew that rhythm and blues, and they brought back my experience in the Holiness Church—the different rhythms and patterns. They started recording Joe Turner, LaVern Baker and Ruth Brown, and I became very proficient playing that stuff, and it looked like everything we made was a hit. But, lo and behold, everybody forgot I ever played jazz, and I was soon typed as a rock 'n' roll drummer. It got so I felt it was unfair, because that was the only thing I was allowed to do. But a while ago I was working with a young bass player, and he complimented me on the way I played.

" 'You know something?' he said. 'You do something you hardly hear now.'

" 'What's that?'

" 'You play the bass drum, and you play it just right so it doesn't overpower what I'm doing. And it feels good.'

"In a rhythm section, you've got to have three or four guys who think alike. You can't have a drummer that's just going to be crashing and dropping bombs. A primary thing that a lot of people in this business haven't paid attention to is that colored people dance to rhythm. A drummer can start playing time and people will get out there and dance. But white people dance to melody. If they don't have melody, they can't dance. So a lot of record producers don't even think about the rhythm. If the melody's there, the rhythm can go to hell.

"Then take bass solos. Listen to the records Jimmy Blanton made with Duke. There was always something going on, something feeding him, so that it didn't sound empty. Today's bass soloists get out there and the drummer has to stop playing. Or all he's doing is playing high hat. He isn't playing time on anything, and the whole insides fall out! They're not doing it right. I've been on jam sessions with Blanton, and he never turned around and said to the drummer, 'Man, you're drowning me out! Don't play your bass drum.' He was in Duke's band with Sonny Greer, and nobody played bass drum louder than Sonny.

"There are so many drummers making it today who would *never* have made it when I was coming up. Outside of the guys like Jo Jones and Jimmy Crawford, see what happens if you tell them to just sit there and play some time! You hear guys talk about Davey Tough, who couldn't play you a decent four-bar drum break, but he could thump that bass drum and swing you all night long.

"There's no place for young kids to get that kind of experience since the union stopped jam sessions. They don't have a place to get that kind of training. They don't know how to blend in a section and play in tune. And too many kids and listeners have been brainwashed by the record companies.

"Last night, I was playing on a gig with Sir Charles Thompson, the piano player. When we came off, he said to me, 'Man, you don't know what a relief it is to play with a drummer who plays time!'

(1966)

CHICK WEBB

BANDLEADER [DRUMS]

There has been talk from time to time of a movie about the life of the legendary Chick Webb, the hunchbacked drummer and bandleader who discovered Ella Fitzgerald and piloted her to fame. To those who cherish his memory, this has come as no surprise, for his was one of the most dramatic stories in the brief but lively annals of jazz. Some of these stories, like those of Buddy Bolden and Pinetop Smith, are now regarded almost as folklore, while others enjoy a vogue because of the protest and defiance they express, their heroes being revolutionaries whose memories challenge the evils of racism and exploitation and remind us of the misery of addiction.

While the names of Lester Young, Charlie Parker and Billie Holiday probably recall the jazz world of the '40s and '50s more vividly than any others, the Chick Webb story is one that, antedating theirs by a few short years, reaches its peak in the late '30s. It embodies many elements that stir the imagination and capture sympathy. There are the humble beginnings, the grievous physical handicap, an astonishing series of frustrations and contradictions, deserved and undeserved breaks, and a burst of fame before an untimely death.

At the age of nine, when he first peddled newspapers in the Baltimore streets, despite his smallness and the hump on his back, Chick was already resourceful and optimistic. He had an engaging and aggressive good humor which overcame all obstacles. Self-pity was completely foreign to him, and he was endowed with a zest for life and a sharp wit which compensated for much that nature had neglected to bestow. His first thrill was buying a set of drums with the money he earned as a newsboy, for he was drum mad always and lightning fast. His trick drumming came naturally and every day on the streets admiring onlookers threw him coins. His first real job was with the Jazzola Band and there he formed a lasting friendship with an accomplished guitarist aptly named John Trueheart. In the following years, except by illness, these two were never parted; they shared prosperity and hardship alike. They set out for New York together, still in their teens, and there with the other musician personalities of the day like Duke Ellington, Sonny Greer, Jimmy Harrison, Benny Carter and Coleman Hawkins, they took up their stand at the street "corner," talking endless shop. This was the famed Rhythm Club at 132nd Street and Seventh Avenue, for many years headquarters for job-hunting musicians in Harlem.

Webb excelled in the art of captivating an audience, and uptown musicians labelled this *spinning the Webb*. No one could match his tall tales and he was generally the unseen center of the liveliest group, all four feet of him. His chief competition was from Duke Ellington, who, with inevitable brief-case tucked under one arm, was a sure symbol of prestige to musicians looking for work. Ellington was probably the first bandleader to recognize Webb's potential and the drummer owed a job at the Black Bottom Club to his recommendation. Later on he recalled this with amusement, for otherwise he might never have come to front a band. At that point they were five: Johnny Hodges (alto saxophone), Bobby Stark (trumpet), Don Kirkpatrick, who was Hodges' brother-in-law (piano), Trueheart and Webb. None of them had any knowledge of how to present themselves to a contractor. "But we were hungry," Hodges recalled, "and Chick had to make the grade, or we wouldn't have stood to listen to him again that season." Webb became leader, *faute de mieux*.

After the Black Bottom, and with the addition of Elmer Williams (tenor saxophone) and a trombonist Johnny Hodges remembered only as "Slats," they went into the Paddock Club below Earl Carroll's Theater on 50th and Seventh Avenue. Hodges, in those days, was also the clarinetist. "I used to put my foot up on the rail in front of the stand," he said, "and play *Someday Sweetheart* in the low register every night—with a squeak every four bars!" When a fire ended that job, the group added bassist Leon Englund and went into the Savoy Ballroom opposite the Savoy Bearcats. Webb was still green enough to show surprise when it was indicated that as leader he would receive a few dollars above the scale decreed for the band. Seeing this, a member of the management took him aside, warned him not to be a "wise guy" and persuaded him to accept scale like the others.

Business chicanery upset him very little at that time, for all his attention was on the music. "The music comes first," he insisted, and there are some fantastic tales about those early days. For months on end the group endured starvation regimes. Relying on occasional gigs to pay the rent, they would hole up in one room and refuse to separate. Webb set the example, turning down jobs which called for changing the band. He tried always to hire, and hold, the finest musicians he could get, most of the best instrumentalists of the day working with him at one time or other. Fletcher Henderson, always on the look-out for talent, customarily raided his band, and although Webb complained he recognized the compliment. Paul Whiteman was another band leader who acknowledged his abilities and during 1928 and 1929 often went uptown to hear the eleven piece band he had at the Rose Danceland. Testifying to Webb's ability to spot latent talent, Dizzy Gillespie recalled that when he was working for Teddy Hill Chick sometimes let him sit in. "I was the only one he ever allowed," he remembered with satisfaction.

The great drummers of the period recognized Webb as the master and his reputation has survived undimmed in the memories of all his contemporaries. Although he was not much of a reader, he could follow a score and had such a grasp of what was played that he could often sing an arrangement through after a single airing. When a section was in trouble at rehearsal, it was customarily Webb who located the right notes. But ironically enough, real success eluded him until most of his best musicians had gravitated elsewhere to the niches fortune had reserved for them. Ultimately Johnny Hodges went with Duke Ellington; Benny Carter left to lead his own band; and Big Green and Bobby Stark went to the Henderson band.

After the Rose Danceland in 1930, Chick encountered bad luck during the tour of a vaudeville circuit. The Savoy Ballroom made him an offer again, but on condition he reduced the size of the band. When he refused, the long lay-off that resulted nearly triumphed over his courage. He could have worked with any of the great names, but by now he was committed to a band of his own. Finally at the Roseland Ballroom he got another break. He went in for a year and was a big hit, and it was sheer bad luck that he was followed by Claude Hopkins when the time came to go out on a road tour again. For Hopkins proved a lasting favorite and Chick found himself without a job for a further seventeen months.

At last, in the early '30s, his band was back on the Savoy stand again, more or less permanently now, and the personnel consisted of Pete Clark (alto and clarinet), Edgar Sampson (alto), and Elmer Williams (tenor). The trumpets were Reunald Jones, Mario Bauza (lead), and Taft Jordan. Sandy Williams was on trombone, an indispensable fixture in the band from then on. Elmer James was on bass, Joe Steele on piano, and of the original group only Trueheart remained. But not for long, sadly enough, for Trueheart developed tuberculosis. Webb and the band shouldered his hospital fees and it cost each musician two dollars a week to underwrite his fight for life. In those days that was real money, for scale at the Savoy was only thirty-five dollars, with fifty dollars for leader. Webb spent his fifteen dollars for arrangements, and in 1934 he used them to buy Ella Fitzgerald her first gown.

It was 1933 when Edgar Sampson, a skilled arranger, joined the band. The following year they recorded a number of his instrumentals, among which were *Stomping at the Savoy, Blue Lou, Don't Be That Way* and *When Dreams Come True.* Although these remained a distinguished part of Webb's repertoire, years later they were to become the virtual anthems of the Swing Era when performed by Benny Goodman's orchestra. By the time Sampson left Webb, a young arranger now known as Van Alexander was contributing the series of commercial scores which culminated in the smash hit, *A-Tisket, A-Tasket.* Significantly, in Alexander's recorded tribute to the Savoy bands *(Capitol ST 1712)* there was no mention of Sampson!

In 1936 Webb was still fighting every inch of the way. He badly needed promotion and to give it him I left the Mills office and added his band to the Bob Crosby and Mildred Bailey-Red Norvo accounts I then handled. I believed in him and in his future, but strangely enough the years that followed were more frustrating than rewarding. For from the time he became Ella Fitzgerald's legal guardian and took her into his home to live, Webb became progressively more engrossed in building everything around her, and perhaps his eyes remained closed to the extent to which the band was pushed into the background. Perhaps, too, he had a premonition his days were numbered, for he dwelt exclusively on ways and means to success. "This is it," he said. "I have a real singer now. That's what the public wants."

It was both ironic and tragic that he took this stand precisely when the standard of musicianship he had represented for so long had finally come into its own. No one could ever convince him of the Swing Era's reality. He refused to believe such popular acceptance could last. When general opinion had no effect on his outlook, I attempted to make the point by promoting a battle of music between his and Benny Goodman's band. There was some chance this kind of shock treatment might bring results, because in many respects Goodman's group was musically superior.

Goodman had never played Harlem before and his popularity had reached a peak. Mounted police were called out to ride along the sidewalks and control the crowds storming the doors of the Savoy. Webb, however, had more than enough strategy to obscure the issue, and it was in his nature to relish the challenge. He caught up the crowds in every set with a beat that rocked the ballroom from end to end, and his regular following saved the day for him. Privately, though, he acknowledged that Goodman and his musicians had excelled, but he refused to believe any

Chick Webb and Ella Fitzgerald.

longer that his own band could survive on music alone. For in those days black bands were seldom able to break out of the deliberate promotional twilight that contained them. "Benny will make it all right," Webb said. "You know it wouldn't be the same for us."

After Goodman, the next contender had logically to be Count Basie. With this battle ahead, the days of our association were clearly numbered. But Webb had incredible nerve and was not daunted. He was also loyal and, unlike his management, he refused to view this maneuver as being on Basie's behalf. He knew I was as committed to my hopes as he was to his own. He also knew that if there remained no common ground between us, it meant a parting of the ways, and this was painful. For he had the gift of attaching people to him, and we were fast friends. Even though I could not share it, I could see his point of view. He had earned the right to success with hard work and suffering. Yet it was sad that as his popularity grew his musical reputation should diminish.

The turning point for him had been the Amateur Night when Ella Fitzgerald appeared on the Apollo Theater stage and Chick recognized one of the greatest singers jazz has ever produced. Even had he remained uncompromising, it would have been almost impossible for him to maintain the band's standards with such a singer in front of it. Her exceptional gifts demanded priority. Webb had immediately grasped the full significance of her extraordinary voice and talents, forming a true estimate of her possibilities. He foresaw, as no one else did, the career which was to follow. For decades, it continued to take her from triumph to triumph in a fashion that would have surprised him not at all. In any case, he had a natural gift for nurturing talent and he relished his role as her musical guardian. He cherished many artistic personalities, but none so warmly as hers.

The night of the Basie battle Ella Fitzgerald served the band well. High excitement infected the crowds in and outside the ballroom, for the date set coincided with a Benny Goodman concert at Carnegie Hall. Many top musicians were guest artists with Goodman that night and all who could crowded into the Savoy. Even with the odds against them, Webb and the band loved to battle. They would play deceptively at first, timidly almost, until they had lulled the opposite stand into a false sense of security. Afterwards they would flagwave them down. Webb had exceptionally strong ankles and wrists and he could electrify the crowd with two thunderclaps from the bass drum as an introduction. A roar would go up before ever the band sounded a note.

This night, however, the applause was not overwhelmingly in his favor. The audience was listening to something new. Lester Young's sound was strange and enticing, Billie Holiday and Jimmy Rushing sang their songs, and Basie led a rhythm section which even Webb could not beat. It fell to Ella Fitzgerald to rally the crowd. Critics and musicians were not deceived, but she provided the camouflage from behind which the band emerged with colors still flying. From this date on their box-office potential soared. For the year or so that remained until his death on June 16, 1939, Webb's star was in the ascendant. Ella Fitzgerald's hits, like *Flat Foot Floogie* and *My Last Affair* brought enormous popularity and record crowds in top locations.

Webb had suffered for a long time from tuberculosis of the spine which he had contracted in his teens. It now grew rapidly worse and he was in constant pain. He was too devoted to the people about him to consider a lay-off for the band. Onstage he remained as impressive as ever, but after performances he often fainted. Eventually the group set off on a tour of the South, opening with a date in Washington on one of the riverboats. At the conclusion of the dance, Chick allowed himself to be driven over to Johns Hopkins Hospital in Baltimore.

"The band must not hear about this," he instructed, referring to the operation awaiting him. "It's only a check-up, and I don't want people always reading about me being sick in bed."

When it was over and the doctors had done everything possible, they warned those close to him that the end was near. Yet Webb refused to die. Day succeeded day, and his surgeon marvelled. After a week had passed and he was no better, even Webb knew the score, but his will still upheld him. "I'm sorry," he said with a last grin, "but I have to go."

Many famous people gathered in Baltimore to mourn him. His funeral was memorable, and perversely this was success beyond his dreams. Thousands lined the streets for the procession, and thousands more viewed him in the A.M.E. church where he lay. In Montgomery, Alabama, the band was playing a dance when the sad news came. Stunned, the musicians sat silent. A few moments afterwards, they rose together to play the song which best evoked for them the blithe spirit all had loved. Later, at the end of the long, sad journey to where Chick was making his last stand, Ella Fitzgerald sang it, too. Few listened unmoved as she paid final tribute with *My Buddy*.

(1963)

MILDRED BAILEY

VOCALIST

Mildred Bailey was one of the great jazz singers, a legend in her own time, and a witty woman of taste, temperament and keen appetites. Though her voice was little, she herself was big. Her weight was a burden and a humiliation over which she persistently triumphed.

To understand the artist, it is necessary to understand the woman. Her light, sweet voice was appropriate to the lovely, slender girl she had once been. It had the innocence and invulnerability of a youngster with ideals, and when this quality was brought to lyrics like those of *Squeeze Me,* there was a curious but satisfying contradiction. No other singer has had a voice quite like hers. The nearest, that of Helen Humes, is richer and more vital, though it has a similar soaring quality.

Mildred Bailey wanted to be the person who went with the voice, regardless of the incompatibility of flesh and spirit. It wasn't success she looked for in the mirror, but the inner person she constantly projected as she sang. Nor was she vain about her small feet and ankles. She was just grateful for them, and she could dance like mad with the wit and mockery of Negro dancers in the '30s. A compulsive eater, she remained more gourmet than gourmand. Yet since she was frustrated to a considerable degree in her need for life and love, and in gaining recognition for herself, eating became an instinctive method of consolation. "What's troubling you?" is a question doctors often ask of those—even children—who eat too much.

She was gay, however, and very good company. Her highly charged personality, like Dizzy Gillespie's or Louis Armstrong's, stimulated everyone. She had a fine, penetrating sense of the ridiculous, such as many jazzmen have, and her fast wit was often directed at those who stepped on her toes artistically. Always in the vanguard of those perceptive to jazz, she roused musicians and brought out the best in them. Her musical and critical tastes were highly developed and she encouraged what was good. But little that was bad escaped her, and her rages often stemmed from the poor musicianship of others.

She was born Mildred Rinker in Tekoa, Washington, where her mother, who was part Indian, saw to it that she was well acquainted with Indian songs. In later years, she referred to this musical background, and the wide range it required, as being very valuable to her subsequent career. When the family moved to Spokane, she, her three brothers and a neighbor, Bing Crosby, became very much involved with the jazz of that time and place. She married young, moved to Los Angeles and was divorced there.

In 1929, she was hired by Paul Whiteman, largely as a result of the enthusiasm of her brother Al and Bing Crosby, who were part of Whiteman's vocal trio, the Rhythm Boys. The girl singer with the big jazz group was to become a commonplace in the next decade, but one with an unmistakable jazz sound in an orchestra like Whiteman's was then distinctly novel. In this context, and on the air coast to coast, her version of one of Hoagy Carmichael's most famous songs soon won her the title of "Rockin' Chair Lady."

While with Whiteman, she met Red Norvo, a xylophone player. They left the band together and were married in 1934. Two years later, Norvo formed his own big band with Mildred as vocalist. Known as Mr. and Mrs. Swing, they were popular during the hectic years of the Swing Era, but from 1940 onwards she worked chiefly as a solo act. Though eventually divorced, they remained good friends until her death in 1951.

Continuing their estimable jazz re-issue program, Columbia released a three-volume set of Mildred Bailey's "greatest performances, 1929–1946" (C3L 22). As produced by John Hammond and Frank Driggs, the records admirably illustrate her career and art. They include her first recording, with guitarist Eddie Lang *(What Kind o' Man Is You?)*, and one of her last, with pianist Ellis Larkins *(Lover, Come Back to Me)*. In between, she is presented in settings as varied as those in which she worked publicly.

Some of the earlier material results from the popularity of Negro musical shows in the '30s, when not a few white songwriters were engaged in composing songs appropriate to Negro singers performing before predominantly white audiences. If some of the lyrics sound inappropriate to Mildred Bailey, it should be remembered that to most recording executives of the period the issue was simple: these were lyrics of jazz songs and she was a jazz singer.

Her acceptance as a jazz singer was, in fact, complete, yet she had the humility to refuse to sing at the same concert as Bessie Smith. Her attitude towards racial problems was always progressive. In her accompaniments, she normally used the best musicians available regardless of color. As early as 1935, she was recording with a thoroughly integrated group and singing at a benefit in aid of the Scottsboro Boys in Harlem's Savoy Ballroom. And

Mildred Bailey.

musicians still recall with a grin the name of one of her 1939 recording combinations: Mildred Bailey and Her Oxford Greys.

The Oxford Greys were Mary Lou Williams (piano), Floyd Smith (guitar), John Williams (bass) and Eddie Dougherty (drums), and the spare accompaniment they provided was in the best of taste. They gave her the maximum in relaxed support without seeking to draw the limelight upon themselves, and she worked over old numbers like *There'll Be Some Changes Made, Arkansas Blues* and *You Don't Know My Mind* with joyful craftsmanship.

Another session, made for the British Parlophone company by John Hammond in 1935, was of classic perfection. Her four accompanying "Alley Cats" were Johnny Hodges, Bunny Berigan, Teddy Wilson and bassist Grachan Moncur. The warmth and rapport in the four performances—*Someday Sweetheart, Squeeze Me, Honeysuckle Rose* and *Downhearted Blues*—were of a kind seldom attained. The musicians were all clearly inspired, yet she held her own with Hodges, the most lyrical of all jazz soloists.

Many other attractive recordings made with small studio groups are in the collection, among her accompanists being Coleman Hawkins, Chu Berry, Benny Goodman, Jimmy and Tommy Dorsey, Artie Shaw, Buck Clayton, Roy Eldridge, Herschel Evans, Jo Jones and Jimmie Crawford. As an inspirational source for a singer, the melodic capability of musicians of her era would seem to exceed that of their counterparts today, although the latter are perhaps seldom given comparable opportunities. On some numbers, she was accompanied by John Kirby's little band, a group often regarded at the time as too precise and too severely disciplined, but it emerges swinging and fresh-sounding here. Dave Tough's drums underline a marvelous, lightly flowing version of *From the Land of the Sky-Blue Water,* a song which may well have had a special significance for her. Also intriguing is *Hold On,* a performance on which Alec Wilder serves as arranger and director and Mitch Miller plays English horn.

A dozen or more numbers are with big bands. The recording of *Rockin' Chair* included here was made with the orchestra led by her husband, Red Norvo. Underrated by most jazz historians, this was one of the more rewarding combinations of its time. Besides Norvo's sensitive and imaginative xylophone solos, it featured subtly voiced arrangements by one of the trumpet players, Eddie Sauter. Humorous songs like *Arthur Murray Taught Me Dancing* and *Week-end of a Private Secretary* illustrate her verve and versatility, as well as public taste at the time.

Mildred Bailey and her musical personality were inimitable, and her death was a loss jazz could ill afford. From the public, she never wholly gained the recognition that was her due, but the note by Bing Crosby in the booklet accompanying the records reveals the affectionate esteem she commanded in her profession. However caustically she might speak of the world in which she lived, she had the spirit to rise above it and sing gaily up there like a skylark. Her bitterness, her burden, her cross—they were personal, and everyone in the audience had his own of one kind or another. She recognized the importance of not taking oneself too seriously and, when necessity compelled her to sing some absurd, popular song, she didn't falter. Though lyrics and melody might be of indisguisable banality, she would still phrase like the true jazz artist she was—and swing. Swinging came naturally to her.

An epitaph from George Wettling, at one time the drummer in Red Norvo's band, would probably have satisfied her as well as any:

"She was a barrelhouse gal, and she had a hell of a beat!"

(1962)

BILLIE HOLIDAY

VOCALIST

There have been many jazz tragedies involving fine musicians. Such names as Chick Webb, Jimmy Blanton, Charlie Christian, Dave Tough, Joe Smith, Bessie Smith, Eddie Costa, Chu Berry, Bunny Berigan, Wardell Gray, Herschel Evans, Lester Young and Lips Page come to mind. They all died much too soon from the artistic point of view, but they didn't make it to the fullest extent in terms of tragedy with mass appeal. Bix Beiderbecke was the first to do so, Charlie Parker the second, and Billie Holiday the third.

To those who first heard Billie Holiday in all her glory during the '30s, there was something macabre about those she attracted so strongly in her later years. These heard the decay in her wasted voice, loved it, and perhaps identified themselves with it. In a sick world with sick moral

Billie Holiday.

values, the dramatic self-destruction of a great singer overshadowed the fact of her deteriorating artistry. Conveniently, there were always near-anonymous culprits to blame. "They" did it, "they" were responsible. Who were "they"? The whites, the peddlers, the bookers, or just the ever-ubiquitous apostles of self-indulgence?

It is safe to say that Billie Holiday never realized who she was. Had she been born in other circumstances, into a different musical milieu—perhaps operatic—and been taught something of the beauties of life, how different hers might have been! Her real gift was for life itself and her temperament committed her to the farthest peaks of emotion. She sensed in jazz something bigger than all of us, the divine legacy. In jazz, she encountered joy; in men, transports of sorrow. To one of her innate generosity, limitation meant acute pain.

Her earliest records mirror her affair with jazz. Here is an inimitable, wholehearted well-being, free of the taint of disillusionment. The artistic depths she later revealed reflected the degree of her obsession, her cease-less search for the absolute.

Despite their triumphs, singers have done untold harm to jazz, but in the beginning they contributed enormously and beneficiently. The stories the blues singers had to tell, and the tones they told them in, had the hard, clean impact of Norse sagas. Their truths were dramatic enough. Having no need to color them, the singers tended towards a somewhat deadpan delivery and avoided the softly sentimental. That Billie Holiday inherited their qualities is clear enough in the offhand yet superbly resilient fashion in which she sang, on one of her earliest recordings:

> *I jumped out of the frying-pan right into the fire,*
> *Lost me a cheap man and got a no-'count liar.*

At that time (1933), the conception of the jazz singer was not very clearly developed. Ella Fitzgerald's first records were nearly two years away. George Thomas with McKinney's Cotton Pickers and Mildred Bailey with Paul Whiteman had indicated directions, but the paramount influences were, as Billie herself proclaimed, Bessie Smith and Louis Armstrong. The only purpose of the singers with the bands was to deliver the song, and they relied entirely on the words to convey its message. Men sang songs obviously written for girls, and girls songs written for men, without bothering to change nouns and pronouns, and without regard to the suitability of the sentiments they were expressing. High falsetto male voices were not unpopular, and for many, accustomed to the tradition of Irish tenors, that of Bing Crosby was at first uncomfortably masculine.

Billie Holiday was no neuter. She was young, healthy and full of animation and drive. She could phrase, push the beat, and ride out over a stormy jazz background as well as most musicians on their horns. Her "golden" years, as the notes to a three-volume Columbia set (C3L-21) quite properly intimated, were brief, but they were tremendously exciting. She had a marvelous accompanist in Teddy Wilson, and most of the best jazzmen of the day played on her records.

This period of unimpaired strength was succeeded in the '40s by one in which a more catholic development was dominated by an emphatically emotional approach, an approach which repeatedly illumined the world of heartbreak. This, in a sense, typed her, but tragedy grew burdensome at times and then the uninhibited, unalarmed Billie returned, swinging out on numbers like *What A Little Moonlight Can Do* and *Them There Eyes.*

Of course, as she found her greatest scope in "musical suffering," so suffering found great scope in her. Her art echoed every kind of intense and bitter experience to which she exposed herself. The last period was merely one of waning strength. The talent was still there, but it came out confused and, above all, weakened. There were times, however, when a breath of the old "possession" invaded her again, and the original magic overlaid and blotted out the physical deterioration. This was the case during a 1954 concert in Germany, unexpectedly presented on a United Artists album entitled *Ladylove* (UAJ 14014). Annotator Leonard Feather ascribed this to the "morale-building encouragement of European audiences" and to the fact that Billie was "lionized and feted and never Jim Crowed." Carl Drinkard's excellent piano accompaniment on the first side must have been a happy contributing factor, too. It is necessary to remember that she could always be reached by a musician who genuinely had something to say.

Though Billie Holiday has left us, she is scarcely further beyond our reach than the intangible in jazz itself. It is a cliché to say that she lives on in her records, but these mirrored her art with an astonishing and endearing candor.

(1963)

SPONTANEOUS
OPINIONS

During the early '60s, I was responsible for a quiz in *Metronome* in which three musicians were asked the same set of questions each month. They were encouraged to reply spontaneously, a fact that was explained—and emphasized—to the magazine's readers. The answers were often amusing, but on the whole surprisingly revelatory of the outlook of those who had either survived the Swing Era or were continuing its tradition.

Subsequent experiences would undoubtedly have modified some of the preferences and opinions expressed in the following selection. The period when they were solicited should, therefore, constantly be borne in mind.

That so many of the "favorite brands" named were alcoholic beverages will, it is hoped, not be misinterpreted. This was a fairly logical consequence of the fact that the quizzing was frequently done in bars after record sessions.

The days of *Metronome* were, unfortunately, numbered, and a new set of questions that had been readied for the quiz's second series was never used.

	Outside the USA, where would you prefer to live?	Apart from jazz, what is your favorite art form?	Which classical musician do you most admire?
BUSTER BAILEY (clarinet)	Paris	Opera	Verdi
COUNT BASIE (piano)	London	Movies	Leonard Bernstein
AARON BELL (bass)	Sweden	Painting	Wagner
HARRY CARNEY (reeds)	Switzerland	Photography	Koussevitsky
AL CASEY (guitar)	Sweden	Symphony	Segovia
BUCK CLAYTON (trumpet)	Paris	Painting	Mozart
COZY COLE (drums)	Zurich	Movies	Toscanini
JIMMY CRAWFORD (drums)	Scandinavia	Symphony	Beethoven
LOCKJAW DAVIS (tenor saxophone)	Hawaii	Modern painting	No interest
BUD FREEMAN (tenor saxophone)	London	Literature and theatre	Debussy
PAUL GONSALVES (tenor saxophone)	London or Paris	Portrait painting	Segovia
AL GREY (trombone)	Sweden	Photography	Stokowski
AL HALL (bass)	Tahiti	Good TV spectaculars	Prokofiev
EARL HINES (piano)	Buenos Aires	Detective movies	Leonard Bernstein
MILT HINTON (bass)	Montevideo	String ensembles	Wagner
JOHNNY HODGES (alto saxophone)	Paris	Movies	Marcel Mule
OLIVER JACKSON (drums)	Canada	Dance (all kinds)	Bach
BUDD JOHNSON (tenor saxophone)	Switzerland	Painting	Stravinsky
JONAH JONES (trumpet)	Knokke, Belgium	Photography	Stravinsky
NAT PIERCE (piano)	London	Ballet and theatre	Roger Sessions
RUSSELL PROCOPE (reeds)	Switzerland	Literature	Chopin
GENE RAMEY (bass)	Sweden	Poetry	Stravinsky
ROGER RAMIREZ (piano)	Copenhagen	Theatre	Rubinstein
PEE WEE RUSSELL (clarinet)	Paris or Rome	More jazz	Stravinsky
ZOOT SIMS (tenor saxophone)	Paris	Painting	Segovia
CLARK TERRY (trumpet)	Paris or Stockholm	Painting	Stravinsky
SIR CHARLES THOMPSON (piano)	Canada	Acting	Debussy
FRANK WESS (saxophones and flute)	Copenhagen	Dancing	Delius

Who is your favorite songwriter?	If music were not your profession, which would you now choose?	Who was your greatest influence?
ole Porter	Electronics	Franz Schoeppe, my teacher, and Wilbur Sweatman
uke Ellington	Personal management	Fats Waller
uke Ellington	Law	My father
uke Ellington	Real estate or practical medicine	Coleman Hawkins
uke Ellington and George Gershwin	Architect	Fats Waller
eorge Gershwin	Professional big game hunter	Louis Armstrong
uke Ellington	Law	Sonny Greer
arold Arlen	Real estate	Big Sid Catlett
o one in particular	Radio commentator on world news	Ben Webster
ole Porter	Writing	Dave Tough
uke Ellington	Commercial art	Coleman Hawkins and Duke Ellington
n Hendricks	Nightclub owner presenting deserving talent in the young	My father
ts Waller	Television director	John Kirby, Billy Taylor and Jimmy Blanton
o choice	Law	Fats Waller
eorge Gershwin	Writing about musicians	Major N. Clark, my bandmaster in Chicago
hnny Mercer for lyrics, George Gershwin for music	A doctor	Sidney Bechet
uke Ellington	Construction work	Jo Jones
uke Ellington	Real estate and insurance	My father
e Styne (I had so much luck with his songs)	Photography or education	Louis Armstrong
uke Ellington	Teaching	Fats Waller, Nat Cole and Count Basie
uke Ellington	Athletics	My mother
uke Ellington	Electrical engineer	Walter Page
eorge Gershwin	Accountancy	Mahatma Gandhi
dgers and Hart	I'd rather be dead	Bix Beiderbecke
orge Gershwin	Growing things	Lester Young
uke Ellington	Boxing	Lester Young, Louis Armstrong and Roy Eldridge
uke Ellington	Golf	Art Tatum
rold Arlen	Cabinetmaking	Lester Young

	Who is the greatest blues singer you ever heard?	Who is the greatest dancer you ever saw?	What other instrument would you like to be able to play?
BUSTER BAILEY (clarinet)	Buster Bailey	Baby Laurence	Piano
COUNT BASIE (piano)	I really have to put four or five on the same level	Baby Laurence and Fred Astaire	Tenor saxophone
AARON BELL (bass)	Joe Turner	Baby Laurence	Piano
HARRY CARNEY (reeds)	Joe Turner	Baby Laurence	Piano
AL CASEY (guitar)	Lonnie Johnson	Baby Laurence and Teddy Hale–they improvise	Cello, trombone or flute
BUCK CLAYTON (trumpet)	Ray Charles	Baby Laurence	Piano
COZY COLE (drums)	Bessie Smith	Baby Laurence	Vibraphone
JIMMY CRAWFORD (drums)	Bessie Smith and T-Bone Walker	Bill Robinson	Piano
LOCKJAW DAVIS (tenor saxophone)	Dinah Washington	Teddy Hale	Piano
BUD FREEMAN (tenor saxophone)	Bessie Smith	Bubbles, of Buck and Bubbles	Piano
PAUL GONSALVES (tenor saxophone)	Jimmy Rushing	Teddy Hale	Piano
AL GREY (trombone)	Jimmy Rushing	Teddy Hale	Piano
AL HALL (bass)	Bessie Smith	Freddie James	Cello (classical)
EARL HINES (piano)	Joe Turner	Bubbles	Trumpet
MILT HINTON (bass)	Mae Alix	Bill Robinson	Piano
JOHNNY HODGES (alto saxophone)	Joe Turner	Bill Robinson	Guitar
OLIVER JACKSON (drums)	Joe Turner	Bill Robinson	Piano
BUDD JOHNSON (tenor saxophone)	Bessie Smith	My wife	Piano
JONAH JONES (trumpet)	Bessie Smith	Bill Robinson and Baby Laurence	Trombone
NAT PIERCE (piano)	Jimmy Rushing	Baby Laurence	Tenor saxophone
RUSSELL PROCOPE (reeds)	Chippie Hill	Eddie Rector	Trumpet
GENE RAMEY (bass)	Blind Lemon Jefferson	Baby Laurence	Cello
ROGER RAMIREZ (piano)	I've heard too many	Baby Laurence for tap, Maria Tallchief for ballet	Guitar and clarinet
PEE WEE RUSSELL (clarinet)	Mamie Smith and Mae Alix	Fred Astaire	Cornet
ZOOT SIMS (tenor saxophone)	Jimmy Rushing and Ray Charles	Baby Laurence	Guitar
CLARK TERRY (trumpet)	Jimmy Witherspoon, Eddie Vinson and T-Bone Walker	Carmen De Lavallade and Baby Laurence	Piano
SIR CHARLES THOMPSON (piano)	Joe Turner	Baby Laurence	Tenor saxophone
FRANK WESS (saxophone and flute)	Jimmy Rushing and Joe Turner	Baby Laurence	Guitar

me a record you ay on that you pecially like	Name just one musician you consider underrated	What is your favorite brand?
ot one	Hilton Jefferson	Van Doren (reeds)
Veeds to Be Bee'd With	Just one! And offend ninety-nine others who know I know they are underrated	Harvey's Bristol Cream Sherry
ke Ellington's Suite Thursday	Harold "Shorty" Baker	J. & B.
ttle of the Saxes (Coleman Hawkins)	Harold "Shorty" Baker	Cutty Sark
dy and Soul Buck Jumpin', Prestige)	Harold "Shorty" Baker	Teacher's
dland Betty Buck and Buddy, Prestige)	Emmett Berry	Cadillac
escendo in Drums with Cab Calloway)	Hilton Jefferson	Chrysler Imperial
ve Me or Leave Me with Sammy Davis, Jr.)	Hilton Jefferson	Black and White, the integrated scotch
hirlybird with Count Basie)	Johnny Griffin	Cutty Sark
-Stars with Shorty Baker Prestige-Swingville 2012)	Bobby Hackett	Dewar's White Label
one with the Wind Verve V8225)	Harry Edison	Any drink in good company
Jut It Dad Argo 653)	Billy Mitchell	The Thinking Man's Brand
eeuner with Jimmy ones (Wax 111)	George Dorsey and Dick Vance	Fleischmann
t one	Budd Johnson	79 Smoking Tobacco
te for Brass by .J. Johnson (CBS)	Hilton Jefferson	J. & B.
arm Valley	Hilton Jefferson	Seagram's V.O.
y Bryant Plays Signature)	Tommy Flanagan	Beefeaters' Gin
es à la Mode Felsted)	Frank Foster	Old Grandad
se Room (Muted azz, Capitol)	Dicky Wells	Harvey's Bristol Cream Sherry
Jones Special Vanguard)	Clark Terry	J. & B.
ubert's Serenade with John Kirby)	Hilton Jefferson	Sunoco
dobon (with J.J. ohnson)	Me	Cutty Sark
ne	Johnny Hodges	Any good champagne over five years old
Walk (Commodore)	Let me out of this one	Miniature Schnauzer
ur Altos	Tubby Hayes	J. & B.
ne	Gerald Wilson	Selmer
ffy (with oleman Hawkins)	Clark Terry	Cadillac
ny Afternoon Prestige/Moodsville 8)	Billy Taylor (piano)	Pontiac

BANDS IN HARLEM THEATRES

The importance of employment in Harlem vaudeville theatres to big bands during the Swing Era may be gauged from the following lists compiled by Walter C. Allen and Jerry Valburn, whose permission to use them is gratefully acknowledged. Culled from advertisements in the N.Y. *Age* and N.Y. *Amsterdam News,* these lists represent a great many hours of painstaking labor. Gaps in the sequences are usually either the result of the theatre's summer closing, or the presentation of a revue for which a name band was not employed. Most engagements were for a period of one week. Similar theatres existed in, notably, Chicago, Philadelphia, Washington and Baltimore, so that together they offered very considerable work opportunities during the course of a year. The increasing use of small bands at the Apollo in the '40s is significant.

THE LAFAYETTE THEATRE, *2227 Seventh Avenue*

1931	March:	Edgar Hayes		August:	Pike Davis
	April:	Bennie Morton		September:	Mills Blue Rhythm Band
		Noble Sissle			
		Danny Small			Donald Heywood
		Dave Peyton		October:	Joe Jordan
	May:	Chick Webb			Lucky Millinder
		Eubie Blake			Billy Kato
		Blue Rhythm Boys			Bennie Morton
		Cab Calloway		November:	Chick Webb
	June:	Charlie Johnson			Blanche Calloway
		Fletcher Henderson		December:	Noble Sissle
	July:	Eubie Blake			Bennie Morton
		Zudie (sic) Singleton			Lucky Millinder

1932 *January:* Donald Heywood
              Sammy Stewart
              Sam Wooding
      February: Fletcher Henderson
      March: Earl Hines
              Eubie Blake
      April: Baron Lee's Blue
              Rhythm Boys
      May: Duke Ellington
              Mrs. Louis Armstrong
              Don Redman
              Cab Calloway
      June: Claude Hopkins
              Earl Hines
      July: Eddie Deas & Bos-
              ton Brownies
      October: Sammy Stewart
              Benny Carter
              Blanche Calloway
      November: Lucky Millinder
              Louis Armstrong
      December: Sammy Stewart
              Duke Ellington
              Don Redman
              Teddy Hill
1933 *January:* Cab Calloway
              Noble Sissle
              Hardy Brothers
      February: Chick Webb
              Earl Hines
              Benny Carter
              Billy Fowler
              Ralph Cooper
      March: Luis Russell
              Hardy Brothers
      April: Benny Carter
              Teddy Hill
              Baron Lee Blue
              Rhythm Band
              Emmett Matthews'
              Arcadians
      May: Sam Wooding
              Hy Clark Missourians
              Hardy Brothers

      June: Drake and Walker's
              Cyclonic   Jazz
              Band
              Sam Wooding
              Chick Webb
      July: Leroy Smith
              Ralph Cooper
              Sam Wooding
      August: Chick Webb
              Danny Small
      September: Bobby Neal
              Jimmie Lunceford
      October: Jimmie Lunceford
              Speed Webb
              Ralph Cooper
      November: Willie Bryant
              Mills Blue Rhythm
              Band
      December: Jimmie Lunceford
              Willie Bryant
              Ralph Cooper
              Chick Webb
1934 *January:* Teddy Hill
              Jimmie Smith
              Teddy Hill
      February: Fletcher Henderson
              Chick Webb
              Rex Stewart
              Wen Talbert
              Claude Hopkins
      March: Blanche Calloway
              Willie Lewis
              Earl Hines
              Baron Lee
              Charlie Johnson
      April: Teddy Hill
              Willie Bryant
              Chick Webb
              Leroy Smith
      May: Noble Sissle
              Hardy Brothers
              Mills Blue Rhythm
              Band
              Pike Davis

June:	Leroy "Stuff" Smith and His Sensational Buffalo Band	San Domingan Serenaders
	Jimmie Lunceford	*November:* Fats Waller
	Luis Russell	Kaiser Marshall
	Eubie Blake	Tiny Bradshaw
	Wen Talbert	'Bama State Collegians
October:	Teddy Hill	*December:* Willie Bryant

(The Lafayette Theatre and the Harlem Opera House came under the same management in 1934, and the former now discontinued stage shows.)

THE HARLEM OPERA HOUSE, *211 West 125th Street*

1933	*April:*	Lucky Millinder (house band)		thews
	May:	Lucky Millinder (house band)		Clarence Williams & James P. Johnson
	June:	Lucky Millinder		Teddy Hill
		Teddy Hill		Don Redman
	July:	Chick Webb	*March:*	Chick Webb
		Benny Carter		Willie Bryant
	August:	Hy Clark Missourians		(An interval of several weeks be-
		Teddy Hill		tween stage pre-
		Hardy Brothers		sentations
		Teddy Hill		resulted from a
	September:	Fess Williams		dispute with the
		Hy Clark Missourians		Musicians' Un-
		Sam Wooding		ion.)
	October:	Chick Webb	*June:*	Hardy Brothers
		Jimmie Smith & Night Hawks		Benny Williams
			July:	Lucky Millinder
		Hardy Brothers		Wen Talbert
	November:	Teddy Hill		Baron Lee
		Turner's Arcadians		Leroy Smith
		Fletcher Henderson	*August:*	Chick Webb
		Chick Webb		'Bama State Collegians
	December:	Hardy Brothers		
		Claude Hopkins		Jimmie Lunceford
		Benny Carter		Fletcher Henderson
		Willie Bryant	*September:*	'Bama State Collegians
1934	*January:*	Luis Russell		
		Blanche Calloway		Dave Martin
	February:	Turner's Arcadians, with Emmett Mat-		Eubie Blake
				Blanche Calloway

Billy Bowen's Cotton Pickers (with Cuba Austin)

October: Hardy Brothers
Mills Blue Rhythm Band
Francois & Chicago Band
Don Redman

November: Chick Webb
Jimmie Lunceford
Reuben Reeves
Fletcher Henderson

December: Frank & Milt Britton
Hy Clark Missourians
Louis Metcalf
Hardy Brothers
Cab Calloway

1935 January: Claude Hopkins
Fats Waller
Don Redman
Earl Hines

Blanche Calloway

February: Willie Bryant
Leroy Smith
Tiny Bradshaw
Cab Calloway

March: Chick Webb
Earl Hines
Teddy Hill
Tiny Bradshaw
Don Redman

April: Eubie Blake
Erskine Hawkins
Claude Hopkins

May: Noble Sissle
Mills Blue Rhythm Band
Jimmy Johnson
(Subsequently there were movies only at the Harlem Opera House.)

THE APOLLO THEATRE, *253 West 125th Street,*
opened as a "Negro vaudeville theatre"
on Friday evening, 26 January, 1934.

1934 January: Benny Carter
February: Valaida Snow & Twelve Syncopators
Sam Wooding

March: Charles Turner's Arcadians, with Emmett Matthews
Luis Russell

April: Charles Turner's Arcadians, with Emmett Matthews

May: Eddie South
Claude Hopkins
Don Redman
Luis Russell

June: Fletcher Henderson
Teddy Hill
Chick Webb

July: Willie Bryant
Teddy Hill
Tiny Bradshaw

August: Tiny Bradshaw
Willie Bryant
Claude Hopkins

September: Al Jenkins
Tiny Bradshaw
Fess Williams

October: Duke Ellington
Eddie South
Willie Bryant
Al Jenkins

	Mrs. Louis Armstrong	*August:*	Willie Bryant
November:	Charles Turner's Ar-cadians, with Emmett Matthews		Claude Hopkins
			Mills Blue Rhythm Band
	Eddie South		Luis Russell
	Charlie Barnet		Louis Armstrong
	Benny Carter	*September:*	'Bama State Collegians
	Billy Maples		
	Luis Russell		Noble Sissle
December:	Duke Ellington		Blanche Calloway
	Clarence Olden		Leroy Smith
	McKinney's Original Cotton Pickers with Wm. McKinney	*October:*	Duke Ellington
			Willie Bryant
			Teddy Hill
			Tiny Bradshaw
	Luis Russell	*November:*	Jimmie Lunceford
1935 *January:*	Jimmie Lunceford		Chick Webb
	Lucky Millinder		Don Redman
	Vernon Andrade		Mills Blue Rhythm Band
	'Bama State Collegians		
			Claude Hopkins
February:	Mrs. Louis Armstrong	*December:*	San Domingans
	Claude Hopkins		Fletcher Henderson
	Al Jenkins		Hardy Brothers
	Fats Waller		Willie Bryant
March:	Baron Lee	1936 *January:*	Fats Waller with Turner's Arcadians
	Luis Russell		
	Alberto Socarras		Erskine Hawkins
	Willie Bryant		Noble Sissle
	Fletcher Henderson		Doc Hyder
	Donald Heywood	*February:*	Teddy Hill
April:	Luis Russell		Duke Ellington
	Ralph Cooper		Earl Hines
May:	Mrs. Louis Armstrong		Luis Russell
	Leroy Smith	*March:*	Louis Armstrong
	Jimmie Lunceford		Leroy Smith
	Don Redman		Claude Hopkins
	Earl Hines		Jimmie Lunceford
June:	Blanche Calloway	*April:*	Willie "The Lion" Smith
	Luis Russell		
	Willie Bryant		Cab Calloway
July:	Erskine Hawkins		Willie Bryant
	Chick Webb		W. C. Handy St. Louis Blues Band
	Alberto Socarras		

May:	Hardy Brothers		Chick Webb
	Mills Blue Rhythm		Willie Bryant
	Band	*February:*	Jimmie Lunceford
	Willie Bryant		Mills Blue Rhythm
	Noble Sissle		Band
	Fats Waller & Tur-		Fletcher Henderson
	ner's Arcadians	*March:*	Earl Hines
June:	Earl Hines		Jesse Stone
	Blanche Calloway		Count Basie
	Chick Webb		Cab Calloway
July:	Teddy Hill	*April:*	Teddy Hill
	Valaida Snow		Chick Webb
	'Bama State Colle-		Don Redman
	gians		Claude Hopkins
	Luis Russell		Edgar Hayes
August:	Willie Bryant	*May:*	Willie Bryant
	Cab Calloway		Blanche Calloway
	Sunset Royal Enter-		Fats Waller
	tainers		Louis Armstrong
	Billy Hicks Sizzling	*June:*	Count Basie
	Six		Mills Blue Rhythm
	Claude Hopkins		Band
September:	Louis Armstrong		Duke Ellington
	Duke Ellington		Erskine Hawkins
	Jimmie Lunceford	*July:*	Eddie Mallory
October:	Fats Waller & Tur-		Jimmie Lunceford
	ner's Arcadians		Edgar Hayes
	Noble Sissle		Cab Calloway
	Chick Webb	*August:*	Sunset Royals
	Sunset Royals		Claude Hopkins
	Mills Blue Rhythm		Harlem Playgirls
	Band		Blanche Calloway
November:	Earl Hines	*September:*	Chick Webb
	Andy Kirk		Don Redman
	Blanche Calloway		Willie Bryant
	Don Redman		Duke Ellington
December:	Ovie Alston	*October:*	Mills Blue Rhythm
	Erskine Hawkins		Band
	Luis Russell		Tiny Bradshaw
	Claude Hopkins		Luis Russell
1937 *January:*	Teddy Hill		Eddie Mallory
	Willie Bryant		Fletcher Henderson
	Fats Waller & Tur-	*November:*	Count Basie
	ner's Arcadians		Andy Kirk

Edgar Hayes
Erskine Hawkins
December: Willie Bryant
Teddy Hill
Sunset Royals, with
Ace Harris
Mills Blue Rhythm
Band
Tiny Bradshaw
1938   January: Chick Webb
Noble Sissle
Duke Ellington
Claude Hopkins
February: Savoy Sultans
Don Redman
Earl Hines
Count Basie
March: Eddie Mallory
Willie Bryant
Buck & Bubbles Or-
chestra, with Em-
mett Matthews
Floyd Ray
April: Cab Calloway
Teddy Hill
Jimmie Lunceford
Fats Waller
Stuff Smith
Jesse Stone
May: Edgar Hayes
Count Basie
Don Redman
Chick Webb
June: Duke Ellington
Louis Armstrong
Tiny Bradshaw
July: Willie Bryant
Eddie Mallory
Edgar Hayes
Hartley Toots Rhythm
Rascals
Claude Hopkins
August: Savoy Sultans
Sunset Royals

Hot Lips Page
Luis Russell
September: Erskine Hawkins
Jimmie Lunceford
Eddie Mallory
Andy Kirk
Duke Ellington
October: Blanche Calloway
Lucky Millinder
Noble Sissle
Teddy Hill
November: Savoy Sultans
Chick Carter
Wen Talbert
Harlem Playgirls
December: Tiny Bradshaw
Stuff Smith
Ovie Alston
Louis Armstrong
Jimmie Lunceford
1939   January: Claude Hopkins
Earl Hines
Count Basie
February: Fats Waller
Andy Kirk
Tiny Bradshaw
March: Savoy Sultans
Cab Calloway
Don Redman
Floyd Ray
April: Edgar Hayes
May: Jimmie Lunceford
Chick Webb
June: Willie Bryant
Tiny Bradshaw
Earl Hines
Billy Hicks
Fats Waller
July: Benny Carter
Savoy Sultans
Erskine Hawkins
Teddy Wilson
August: Jimmie Lunceford
Teddy Hill

Willie Bryant's Band outside the Apollo Theatre L. to R.: Arnold Adams, Charlie Frazier, Stanley Payne, Glyn Pacque, John "Shorty" Haughton, George Matthews, Cozy Cole, Dick Clarke, Bass Hill, Jacque Butler, Taft Jordan, Johnny Russell, Roger Ramirez. Willie Bryant in front.

Back: Willie Bryant and the Apollo Theatre chorus line. Front: Moms Mabley (extreme left), Stump and Stumpy (centre).

	Ernie Fields		Andy Kirk
	Andy Kirk	*July:*	Louis Armstrong
September:	Lucky Millinder		Sunset Royals
	Don Redman	*September:*	Ella Fitzgerald
	Duke Ellington		Louis Prima
	Claude Hopkins		Roy Eldridge
	Roy Eldridge	*October:*	Erskine Hawkins
October:	Teddy Wilson		John Kirby
	Earl Hines		Count Basie
	Teddy Hill		Andy Kirk
	Tiny Bradshaw	*November:*	Claude Hopkins
November:	Noble Sissle		Fats Waller
	Fats Waller		Jimmie Lunceford
	Blanche Calloway		Cab Calloway
	Edgar Hayes		Tiny Bradshaw
December:	Charlie Barnet	*December:*	Count Basie
	Lee Norman		Duke Ellington
	Bunny Berigan		Lucky Millinder
	Cab Calloway		Ella Fitzgerald
	Jimmie Lunceford	1941 *January:*	Count Basie
1940 *January:*	Andy Kirk		Earl Hines
	Count Basie		Erskine Hawkins
	Erskine Hawkins		Louis Prima
	Les Hite		Blanche Calloway
February:	Savoy Sultans	*February:*	Les Hite
	Harry James	*March:*	Louis Jordan
	Earl Hines		Billy Butler
March:	Fats Waller		James P. Johnson
	Teddy Wilson	*April:*	Ella Fitzgerald
	Claude Hopkins		Earl Hines
	Ella Fitzgerald		Count Basie
	Bardu Ali	*May:*	Lucky Millinder
April:	Coleman Hawkins		Earl Bostic
	Savoy Sultans		Louis Armstrong
	Charlie Barnet		Andy Kirk
	Tiny Bradshaw		Savoy Sultans
May:	Leon Abbey	*June:*	John Kirby
	Louis Prima		Chris Columbus
	Cab Calloway		Ovie Alston
	Count Basie		Stuff Smith
	Erskine Hawkins	*July:*	Blanche Calloway
June:	Duke Ellington	*August:*	Sunset Royals
	Coleman Hawkins	*September:*	International Sweet-
	Earl Hines		hearts of Rhythm

	Ella Fitzgerald			Erskine Hawkins
	Fats Waller		*July:*	Benny Carter
	Lucky Millinder			Earl Hines
October:	Savoy Sultans		*September:*	Lucky Millinder
	Horace Henderson			Tiny Bradshaw
	Andy Kirk			Eddie Durham's All-
	Louis Prima			Girl Band
November:	Cab Calloway			Noble Sissle
	Tiny Bradshaw		*October:*	Louis Prima
	Charlie Barnet			Earl Hines
	Lionel Hampton			Cootie Williams
December:	Doc Wheeler & Sun-			Andy Kirk
	set Royals			Louis Armstrong
	Lucky Millinder		*November:*	Fletcher Henderson
	Earl Bostic			Hot Lips Page
	Jimmie Lunceford			Savoy Sultans
1942 *January:*	Claude Hopkins			Erskine Hawkins
	Count Basie		*December:*	Louis Jordan
	Sweethearts of			Fats Waller
	Rhythm			Charlie Barnet
	Earl Hines			Count Basie
	Chris Columbus		1943 *January:*	Jimmie Lunceford
February:	Louis Armstrong			Sweethearts of
	Ella Fitzgerald			Rhythm
	Fletcher Henderson			Earl Hines
	Erskine Hawkins			Cootie Williams
March:	Fats Waller			John Kirby
	Tiny Bradshaw		*February:*	Louis Prima
	Les Hite			Lionel Hampton
	Red Allen & Jay Hig-			Tony Pastor
	ginbotham			Eddie Durham's All-
April:	John Kirby			Girl Band
	Benny Carter		*March:*	Erskine Hawkins
	Jay McShann			Tiny Bradshaw
	Hot Lips Page			Fletcher Henderson
May:	Andy Kirk			Louis Jordan
	Red Norvo			Al Sears
	Cootie Williams		*April:*	Fats Waller &
	Sweethearts of			Muggsy Spanier
	Rhythm			Sunset Royals
June:	Doc Wheeler Sunset			Una Mae Carlisle
	Royals			Earl Hines
	Lucky Millinder			Charlie Barnet
	Claude Hopkins		*May:*	Teddy Powell

Cootie Williams

John Kirby

Cecil Scott

Milt Larkins

June: Erskine Hawkins

Andy Kirk

Eddie Durham's All-
Girl Band

Bob Chester

July: Lionel Hampton

Earl Hines

Buddy Johnson

Louis Jordan

Cootie Williams

August: Tiny Bradshaw

September: Eddie Robinson

Charlie Barnet

Earl Hines

Cab Calloway

October: Jimmie Lunceford

Count Basie

Eddie Durham's All-
Girl Band

Buddy Johnson

Georgia Auld

November: Al Sears

Lucky Millinder

Andy Kirk

Cootie Williams

December: Bobby Sherwood

Nat Towles

Teddy McRae

Lionel Hampton

Jimmie Lunceford

1944 January: Erskine Hawkins

Hot Lips Page

Louis Jordan

Don Redman

Benny Carter

February: Sweethearts of
Rhythm

Charlie Barnet

Earl Hines

Count Basie

March: Louis Prima

Fletcher Henderson

Louis Armstrong

Tiny Bradshaw

Buddy Johnson

April: Lucky Millinder

Boyd Raeburn

Erskine Hawkins

Eddie Durham's All-
Girl Band

Trummie Young

May: Cab Calloway

Georgie Auld

Noble Sissle

Ernie Fields

June: Andy Kirk

Roy Eldridge

Erskine Hawkins

Lucky Millinder

Lionel Hampton

July: Earl Hines

Luis Russell

Buddy Johnson

September: Luis Russell

Coleman Hawkins

Tom Reynolds

John Kirby

Cecil Scott

Andy Kirk

October: Roy Eldridge

Louis Jordan

Count Basie

November: Tiny Bradshaw

Sweethearts of
Rhythm

Benny Carter

Duke Ellington

December: Hot Lips Page

Eddie Heywood

Billy Eckstine

Jimmie Lunceford

1945 January: Earl Hines

Cootie Williams

Boyd Raeburn

	Frank Humphries	*March:*	Cecil Scott
February:	Luis Russell		Sweethearts of
	Andy Kirk		Rhythm
	Fletcher Henderson		

RELEVANT RECORDS

THE WORLD OF SWING,
 Volume 1. Compiled by the author especially to
 illustrate this book, the collection contains examples of the work of many of the musicians
 interviewed. In most cases the recordings are
 not otherwise available.   Columbia KG–32945

HENRY "RED" ALLEN
 Henry "Red" Allen (with Charlie Holmes)   RCA LPV–556

MILDRED BAILEY
 Her Greatest Performances   Columbia C3L–22 (3)

CAB CALLOWAY
 Penguin Swing   Jazz Archives JA–8

BENNY CARTER
 1933   Prestige S–7643
 Big Band Bounce   Capitol M–11057
 Swingin' the '20s   Contemporary 7561
 Further Definitions   Impulse S–12

DOC CHEATHAM
 Adolphus "Doc" Cheatham   Jezebel JZ–102 (2)

COZY COLE
 All Stars   Savoy 14010

ROY ELDRIDGE
 At the Arcadia Ballroom, 1939   Jazz Archives JA–14
 Swing   RCA LPV–578

Roy Eldridge   GNP Crescendo 9009
The Nifty Cat (with Nat Pierce)   Master Jazz 8110
The Nifty Cat Strikes West   Master Jazz 8121

BENNY GOODMAN
A Jazz Holiday   MCA 2–4018 (2)
Giants of Swing   Prestige S–7644
Small Groups   RCA LPV–521
Carnegie Hall Concert   Columbia OSL–160
Solo Flight (with Charlie Christian)   Columbia G–30779 (2)

TINY GRIMES
Profoundly Blue   Muse MR–5012

LIONEL HAMPTON
Swing Classics   RCA LPM–2318
Stompology   RCA LPV–575
Steppin' Out   Decca 79244E
Original Star Dust   Decca 74194E
Golden Favorites   Decca 74296E
Good Vibes   Harmony KH–32165

COLEMAN HAWKINS
Body and Soul   RCA LPV–501
Jazz Pioneers   Prestige S7647
Hawk and Roy, 1939 (and Roy Eldridge)   Phoenix LP–3
Hollywood Stampede   Capitol M–11030
Classic Tenors (and Lester Young)   Flying Dutchman 10146
The Tenor Sax (and Frank Wess)   Atlantic SD2–306 (2)
The High and Mighty Hawk   Master Jazz 8115
Night Hawk   Prestige S7671
Blues Groove   Prestige S7824
The Newport Years (with Roy Eldridge)   Verve V6–8829
The Hawk Flies   Milestone M–47015 (2)

ERSKINE HAWKINS
After Hours   RCA LPM–2227
Reunion   Stang M–51014

FLETCHER HENDERSON
Fletcher Henderson's Orchestra   Biograph BLP–C–12
First Impressions, 1924–31   Decca 79227
Swing's the Thing, 1931–34   Decca 79228
A Study in Frustration   Columbia C4L–19 (4)
Big Bands, 1933   Prestige S7645

BILLIE HOLIDAY
  The Billie Holiday Story, Vol. I   Columbia KG–32121 (2)
  The Billie Holiday Story, Vol. II   Columbia KG–32124 (2)
  The Billie Holiday Story, Vol. III   Columbia KG–32127 (2)
  Strange Fruit   Atlantic SD–1614
  Lady Love   United Artists UAS–5635
  The Newport Years (and Ella Fitzgerald)   Verve V6–8826

CLAUDE HOPKINS
  1932–1933–1940   Jazz Archives JA–4
  Yes, Indeed!   Prestige SW–2209
  Let's Jam   Prestige SW–2020
  Swing Time   Prestige SW–2041
  Soliloquy   Sackville 3003
  Crazy Fingers   Chiaroscuro CR–114

JONAH JONES
  Swing, 1946   Prestige 7604
  Back on the Street (with Earl Hines and Cozy
    Cole)   Chiaroscuro 118

GENE KRUPA
  Gene Krupa and His Orchestra (with Roy El-
    dridge)   Columbia KG–32663 (2)

JIMMIE LUNCEFORD
  Rhythm Is Our Business (1934–35)   Decca 79237
  Harlem Shout (1935–36)   Decca 79238
  For Dancers Only (1936–37)   Decca 79239
  Blues in the Night (1938–42)   Decca 79240
  Lunceford Special   Columbia CL–2715
  The Original Jimmy Lunceford Orchestra Perception PLP–35 (2)

MILLS BLUE RHYTHM BAND
  Keep the Rhythm Going   Jazz Archives JA–10

ROGER RAMIREZ
  Rampant Ram   Master Jazz 8123

DON REDMAN
  Master of the Big Band (and McKinney's Cotton
    Pickers)   RCA LPV–520

LUIS RUSSELL
  Luis Russell and His Louisiana Swing Orchestra Columbia KG–32338 (2)

SAVOY SULTANS, THE
  Jumpin' at the Savoy
                                        Decca DL–74444

ARTIE SHAW
  Featuring Roy Eldridge
                                        RCA LPV–582

STUFF SMITH
  Cat on a Hot Fiddle   Verve V–8339
  Have Violin, Will Swing   Verve V–8282

WILLIE SMITH
  Alto Saxophone Supreme   GNP Crescendo 2055

ELMER SNOWDEN
  Harlem Banjo   Riverside RLP–348

WALTER "FOOTS" THOMAS
  All Stars   Prestige S7854

"FATS" WALLER
  '34–'35   RCA LPV–516
  Valentine Stomp   RCA LPV–525
  Fractious Fingering   RCA LPV–537
  Smashing Thirds   RCA LPV–562

CHICK WEBB
  A Legend, 1929–36   Decca 79222
  King of the Savoy, 1937–39   Decca 79223
  Stompin' at the Savoy   Columbia CL–2639
  1937–39   First Time 1508

VARIOUS ARTISTS
  Big Bands Uptown (Claude Hopkins, Benny
    Carter, Don Redman, Lucky Millinder) Decca 79242
  Jazz Odyssey: The Sound of Harlem (Erskine
    Hawkins, Jimmie Lunceford, Fletcher Hender-
    son, Benny Carter, Claude Hopkins, Teddy
    Hill, etc.)   Columbia C3L–33 (3)
  Master Jazz Piano, Vol. I   Master Jazz 8105
  Master Jazz Piano, Vol. II   Master Jazz 8108
  Master Jazz Piano, Vol. III   Master Jazz 8117
  Master Jazz Piano, Vol. IV   Master Jazz 8124
  Swing Exercise (Al Casey, Billie Holiday, etc.) Capitol M–11035
  Stars of the Apollo Theatre   Columbia KG–30788 (2)
  The Tenor Sax (Chu Berry, Roy Eldridge, Lester
    Young, Ben Webster)   Atlantic SD2–307 (2)

Town Hall Jazz Concert, 1945 (Stuff Smith, Red
   Norvo, Don Byas, Teddy Wilson, Gene
   Krupa, etc.)   Atlantic SD2 310 (2)

TEDDY WILSON
   Teddy Wilson and His All Stars (Cozy Cole,
   Jonah Jones, Roy Eldridge, Benny Goodman,
   Billie Holiday, Benny Morton, etc.)   Columbia KG–31617 (2)

(Not all of the above are currently in catalogue, but most can be obtained from specialist jazz stores in the U.S. and Canada. Although jazz albums are very much subject to the dictates of the record industry's accountants, the number of deletions is usually matched by reinstatements.)

Don Redman's Band, 1932. L. to R.: Sidney De Paris, Benny Morton, Shirley Clay, Fred Robinson, Manzie Johnson, Langston Curl, Claude Jones, Horace Henderson, Redman, Ed Inge, Talcott Reeves, Bob Carroll, Bob Ysaguirre, Rupert Cole.

INDEX

Aarons, Al, 110
Abney, Don, 280
Applewhite, Bubber, 232, 233
Adderley, Cannonball, 339
Addison, Bernard, 33, 55, 67, 346, 351
Aiken, Gene, 54, 59
Aiken, Gus, 54, 59
Albright, Freddie, 184, 382
Alexander, Charles, 295
Alexander, Van, 387
Allen, A.G., 345
Allen, Bessie L., 161, 162
Allen, Henry "Red," 22, 84, 144, 148, 191, 211, 253, 259, 284, 306, 347, 352, 353
Allen, Moses, 97, 120
Allen, Snags, 198, 360, 365
Alston, Ovie, 22, 39, 235, 236
Alvis, Hayes, 135, 273
Amos 'n' Andy, 268
Andrade, Vernon, 246
Andrews, "Dope," 287
Andrews Sisters, The, 321
Anderson, Cat, 106, 220, 275, 282
Arbello, Ferdinand, 234
Archer, Bernard, 82
Armstrong, Lil, 167, 169
Armstrong, Louis, 3, 18, 19, 42, 56, 57, 59, 69, 79, 80, 84, 87, 92, 124, 131, 148–150, 152, 156, 161, 165, 167, 168, 176, 190, 194, 195, 196, 202, 215, 216, 254, 256, 259, 262, 268, 270, 273, 284, 287, 288, 290, 303, 309, 311, 325, 329, 347, 349, 355, 359, 391, 397
Ashby, Irving, 109, 275
Astaire, Fred, 175
Auld, Georgie, 210, 320
Austin, Cuba, 268, 295, 311
Austin, Hal, 174, 201
Autrey, Herman, 82, 357

Bacharach, Burt, 324
Bacon, Trevor, 381

Bailey, Benny, 276
Bailey, Buster, 11, 19, 139, 173, 184, 192, 273, 285, 306, 400–404
Bailey, Mildred, 387, 391–395, 397
Bailey, Pearl, 90, 123, 297
Baker, Alec, 167
Baker, Josephine, 33, 34, 67
Baker, La Vern, 382
Baker, Laverne, 381
Baker, Harold "Shorty," 201, 298, 314, 330, 331
Ball, Ronnie, 156
Balliett, Whitney, 62
Barbarin, Paul, 22, 253
Bardu Ali, 87
Barefield, Eddie, 88, 273
Barker, Danny, 211, 297, 371
Barksdale, Everett, 364
Barnet, Charlie, 93, 109, 228, 230, 325, 353
Barnett, Cliff, 129
Bascomb, Arthur, 193
Bascomb, Wilbur "Dud," 192–203, 204, 206, 210, 211, 214–216, 218–220
Bascomb, Paul, 193, 196, 198, 199, 204, 206, 207, 213, 214, 215
Basie, Count, 13–17, 23, 29, 54, 71, 105, 110, 125, 132, 147, 154, 183, 192, 196, 221, 227, 230, 240, 270, 271, 279, 283, 284, 289, 290, 299, 301, 304, 316, 317, 330, 331, 334, 336–339, 341–344, 346, 350, 378, 389, 390, 400–404
Bateman, Charlie, 381
Battle, Edgar, 25, 186, 187, 191
Bauza, Mario, 85, 87, 316, 386
Beason, Bill, 162, 256, 350, 379
Bechet, Sidney, 6, 33, 36, 75, 76, 242, 301, 304
Beckett, Fred, 275, 282
Beiderbecke, Bix, 3, 148, 150, 262, 395
Bell, Aaron, 400–404
Bellson, Louis, 88, 90, 105, 221

Belton, C.S., 196
Benford, Tommy, 211
Bennett, Bobby, 168
Bennett, Cuban, 28, 136, 137, 170
Bennett, Robert Russell, 189
Benskin, Sammy, 181, 211
Benson, George, 282
Benton, William, 295
Berigan, Bunny, 3, 6, 210, 394, 395
Berk, Sam, 174
Bernhardt, Clyde, 199, 259
Bernie, Ben, 168
Bernstein, Artie, 273
Berry, Chu, 28, 141, 172, 187, 227, 245, 246, 273, 277, 297, 314, 349, 369, 371, 394, 395
Berry, Emmett, 189, 230, 321, 330, 355
Bertrand, Jimmy, 265
Best, Denzil, 182
Best, Skeeter, 202
Bigard, Barney, 190, 207, 210, 309
Black, Bill, 202
Black Diamond, 47
Blair, Lee, 245
Blake, Eubie, 46, 48
Blake, Jerry, 256, 257, 310
Blake, Luther, 345
Blakey, Art, 173
Blanchard, Harold, 245
Blanton, Jimmy, 28, 210, 383, 395
Bleyer, Archie, 23, 138, 376
Bloomfield & Greeley, 267
Blue Rhythm Band, 346, 353
Bolden, Buddy, 384
Booze, Bea, 46
Booze, Eddie, 46
Borden, Ray, 335
Bostic, Earl, 273, 276, 282
Bowles, Russell, 162, 164, 167
Brady, Stump, 295, 304
Brannon, Teddy, 174
Brantley, Charlie, 379
Brecker, Lou, 38
Bricktop (Ada Smith), 34, 52
Briggs, Arthur, 67
Briscoe, Dan, 164
Briscoe, Sylvester, 165, 232
Britton, Joe, 245
Brookmeyer, Bob, 317
Brooks, Charlie, 184
Brown, Al, 173
Brown, Andrew, 297, 368, 371
Brown, Bob, 67

Brown, Bobbie, 120
Brown, Clifford, 193, 218
Brown, James, 25
Brown, John (alto saxophone), 247
Brown, John (bass), 17–30, 41, 43, 174
Brown, Lawrence, 72, 90, 267, 268, 297, 298, 343
Brown, Roy, 302
Brown, Ruth, 119
Brown, Scoville "Toby," 43
Brown, Steeplehead, 22
Brownie, 242
Brubeck, Dave, 337
Bryant, Marie, 359
Bryant, Ray, 156
Bryant, Wallace, 164
Bryant, Willie, 87, 187, 191, 227, 325, 381
Brymm, Lieut. Tim, 310
Buchanan, Charlie, 38, 39, 194, 254
Buckner, Milt, 275, 278, 281, 365
Buckner, Teddy, 270, 271
Bullock, Ernie, 54
Bunn, Teddy, 356
Burgess, Charlie, 38
Burke, Sonny, 104
Burnett, Bobby, 254
Burns, Bobby, 125, 127
Burrell, Kenny, 230, 282
Burroughs, Alvin, 273, 275
Bushell, Garvin, 58, 59, 368
Bushkin, Joe, 28, 173, 182, 322
Busse, Henri, 55
Butler, Jack, 68
Butterbeans & Susie, 119, 318, 319, 322
Butts, Jimmy, 365
Byas, Don, 190, 359.

Cage, John, 340
Caldwell, Lorenzo, 347, 348
Calloway, Blanche, 25, 186, 187, 190, 227, 303, 304
Calloway, Cab, 25, 28, 42, 83, 122, 172, 173, 181, 186, 187, 191, 194, 207, 213, 227, 230, 234, 296, 297, 299, 301, 304, 311, 314, 320, 342, 353, 366, 367–369, 371, 372, 374, 375, 376, 381
Calloway, Elmer, 234
Calloway, Jean, 213–215
Calloway, Ruth, 304
Carey, Dan, 242

Carmichael, Hoagy, 209, 392
Carney, Harry, 54, 90, 103, 168, 207, 210, 242, 243, 250, 251, 253, 273, 400–404
Carr, Les, 162
Carroll, Bob, 68, 76, 89, 162, 246, 356
Carroll, Joe, 339
Carruthers, Earl, 116, 167
Carry, Scoops, 152
Carter, Benny, 23, 28, 93, 106, 108, 135–140, 145, 147, 165, 170, 186, 187, 233, 235, 243, 245, 248, 251, 252, 273, 293, 296, 304, 311, 314, 320, 321, 325, 332, 342, 349, 350, 353, 369, 370, 385, 386
Carter, Betty, 276
Carver, Wayman, 85, 314, 319, 349
Casa Loma Orchestra, The, 71, 87, 178
Casey, Al, 273, 325, 355, 356–359, 400–404
Catlett, Sidney, 29, 59, 71, 124, 169, 190, 256, 273, 325, 327, 349, 359
Cats & The Fiddle, The, 361, 365
Cato, Billy, 245
Cato, Minto, 58
Cavanaugh, Dave, 174
Celestian, Jack, 25, 186
Challis, Bill, 39, 138
Cheatham, Doc, 44, 307–318, 321, 327, 368, 371
Cheek, Bobby, 245
Chittison, Herman, 295
Choo Choo Chasers, The, 61
Christian, Charlie, 22, 28, 272, 273, 281, 282, 356, 365, 366, 395
Clanton, Sammy, 398
Clark, Chester, 176
Clark, Doc, 67
Clark, Harold, 173
Clark, June, 346, 347
Clarke, Arthur "Babe," 202, 381
Clarke, George, 120, 167
Clarke, Kenny, 150
Clarke, Pete, 85, 89, 386
Clayton, Buck, 123, 173, 225, 270, 271, 337, 394, 400–404
Cleveland, Jimmy, 276
Clinton, Larry, 331, 332, 335
Cobb, Arnett, 155, 276, 282
Cole, Cozy, 17–30, 155, 156, 168–170, 172, 174, 175, 179, 181, 183–192, 273, 297, 314, 349, 353, 355, 371, 376, 400–404
Cole, Jay, 191
Cole, Nat, 273, 282, 325, 359
Coleman, Bill, 186, 246, 349
Coleman, Booker, 233
Coleman, Ornette, 107, 142, 316, 341
Collins, John, 147, 379
Collins, Mr. (restaurateur), 219
Collins, Renee, 41
Collins, Shad, 297, 314, 349
Coltrane, John, 142, 157, 277, 278, 330, 340
Comden, Betty, 320
Condon, Eddie, 287
Conyers, Walter, 59
Cook, Willie, 229
Coquatrix, Bruno, 127
Coss, Bill, 134
Costa, Eddie, 395
Courcy, Charlie, 25, 186
Cox, Baby, 119
Cox, Charlie, 334
Cox, Ida, 119
Crawford, Jimmy, 23, 97, 100, 104, 119–125, 192, 229, 230, 383, 394, 400–404
Crippen, Katie, 48
Crosby, Bing, 321, 353, 368, 392, 397
Crosby, Bob, 6, 387
Crosby, Israel, 355
Crumbley, Elmer, 196, 381
Cuffee, Ed, 296, 311
Cullamore, Winston, 173
Culley, Wendell, 243, 311
Curtis, King, 359

Dale, Jimmy, 138
Dandridge, Putney, 25
Daniels, Billy, 216, 359
Daniels, Herman, 36
Darr, Jerome, 17–30
Dash, Julian, 197, 207, 220, 222
Davis, Jimmy, 327
Davis, Lem, 321, 379
Davis, Eddie "Lockjaw," 141, 142, 152, 325, 342, 400–404
Davis, Meyer, 31, 47
Davis, Miles, 144, 325, 330
Davis, Sammy, Jr., 58, 127, 131, 174, 202, 298
Davis, Wild Bill, 275, 326
Davison, Wild Bill, 44, 284

De Faut, Volly, 262
Delaunay, Charles, 174
De Paris, Sidney, 315
De Paris, Wilbur, 67, 75, 144, 298, 310
Depp, Dr. Nathaniel, 348
Dial, Harry, 247
Dickens, Doles, 359
Dickenson, Carlos, 302, 306
Dickenson, Vic, 44, 75, 122, 229, 236, 284, 289, 290, 292, 301–306, 320
Diemer, Pops, 167
Diggs, "Apple," 242
Dillard, Bill, 173, 186, 349
Dixon, Charlie, 23, 81, 87, 225, 289
Dixon, Edward "Sharkey," 359
Dixon, Lucille, 90
Dodds, Johnny, 262, 272
Doggett, Bill, 199, 326, 381
Dolphy, Eric, 157
Domino, Fats, 248
Donaldson, Lou, 201, 202
Dorham, Kenny, 199
Dorsey, George, 75, 133
Dorsey, Jimmy, 184, 262, 295, 394
Dorsey, Tommy, 3, 22, 23, 39, 67, 103, 104, 107, 125, 127, 131, 169, 178, 184, 238, 295, 296, 304, 378, 380, 394
Dougherty, Eddie, 384
Douglas, Louis, 34
Doy, Daniel, 33, 67
Drake, Jesse, 381
Drayton, Charlie, 123, 379
Driggs, Frank, 392
Drinkard, Carl, 398
Drootin, Al, 44
Drootin, Buzzy, 44
Dudley, Jimmy, 311
Dudley, S.H., 36
Duffy, Bill, 39
Duke, Doug, 276
Dukes, Willie, 327
Dunn, Johnny, 287, 309
Durham, Eddie, 115, 131, 225, 346
Dylan, Bob, 337

Eckstine, Billy, 199, 239, 247, 334
Edison, Harry, 175, 337
Edson, Feets, 193, 194
Eglin, Duke, 233
Eldridge, Joe, 122, 148, 150, 152, 153

Eldridge, Roy, 22, 28, 59, 75, 118, 122, 133, 136, 137, 142, 143–145, 147, 148–155, 157, 160, 164, 165, 215, 227, 230, 246, 303, 330, 334, 355, 359, 360, 379, 380, 394
Elkins, Vernon, 267
Ellington, Duke, 14, 16, 29, 31, 46–49, 52–54, 56, 59, 69, 71, 72, 82, 83, 89, 90, 96, 103–106, 115, 122, 132, 141, 147, 150, 160, 172, 178, 179, 181, 187, 191, 193, 194, 197, 199, 201, 206, 207, 210, 215, 219, 221, 227, 230, 233, 238, 253, 254, 256, 268, 280, 296, 297–299, 317, 326, 329, 331, 334, 336, 338, 339, 342–344, 348, 349, 351, 353, 365, 367, 371, 382–384, 386
Ellington, Mercer, 228
Ellis, Don, 341
Ellison, Ralph, 9
Elman, Ziggy, 30, 273
English, Bill, 222
Englund, Leon, 84, 197, 207, 385
Escudero, Ralph, 47
Ertegun, Ahmet, 382
Europe, Jim, 285
Evans, Gil, 341
Evans, Gus, 282
Evans, Herschel, 270, 271, 273, 277, 337, 394, 395

Farber, Burt, 191
Farmer, Art, 276
Faulkner, Herbert, 45
Feather, Leonard, 139, 141, 225, 254, 398
Feldman, Al, 87
Fenton, Nick, 198
Ferguson, Maynard, 317
Fetchit, Stepin, 219–220, 272
Fields, Herbie, 276
Fields, Kansas, 381
Fields, Shep, 39
Fiorito, Ted, 262
Fitzgerald, Ella, 29, 69, 87, 125, 177, 181, 247, 280, 321, 325, 384, 387, 389, 390, 397
Flanagan, Tommy, 145, 157, 160
Foote, Bea, 33
Ford, Clarence, 167
Ford, Charles, Everett, 348
Forrest, Maudie, 33, 34
Forrester, Johnny, 67
Foster, George, 174

Foster, Marquis, 334
Foster, Pops, 253
Four Dots, The, 360
Fowler, Billy, 253, 283
Fowlkes, Charlie, 282
Fox, Charlie, 182
Francis, Panama, 172, 375–383
Fraser, Elwyn, 381
Frazier, Jake, 54
Freeman, Bud, 400–404
Freeman, Jeremy, 334
Fulford, Tommy, 89
Fuller, Walter, 247, 273, 275

Gaillard, Slim, 361
Galbraith, Frank, 381
Gale, Moe, 73, 87, 194, 196, 197, 199, 219, 220, 221
Garland, Joe, 56, 79
Garland, Red, 278
Garner, Erroll, 181, 326, 338
Garrette, Duke, 276
Garrison, Jimmy, 147
Garvey, Claude, 355
Gaskin, Leonard, 133
Gay, Leonard, 303
Gee, Matthew, 206
George, Karl, 274, 314
Georgia Minstrels, The, 345
Gershwin, George, 332
Gibbs, Eddie, 350
Gibson, Al, 297
Gibson, Andy, 130, 147, 199, 224–232, 236, 297, 371
Gillespie, Dizzy, 106, 145, 148, 172, 175, 193, 221, 222, 246–248, 273, 316, 325, 327, 330, 334, 335, 337, 338, 340, 359, 367, 371, 372, 380, 386, 391
Gillette, Miss, 295
Gilmore, Buddy, 36
Giuffre, Jimmy, 340
Gladstone, Billy, 184
Glascoe, Percy, 279, 280
Glaser, Joe, 42, 43, 197, 274, 276, 322
Gleason, Ralph, 62
Glenn, Tyree, 172, 187, 201, 233, 271, 297, 298, 320, 371
Glover, Henry, 239
Godfrey, Arthur, 69, 191
Godley, A.G., 176, 177
Gold, Sanford, 189
Goldkette, Jean, 19, 148, 295, 296

Golson, Benny, 276
Gonsalves, Paul, 93, 105, 141, 142, 145, 230, 400–404
Goodman, Al, 238
Goodman, Benny, 3, 22, 23, 30, 71, 90, 91, 92, 154, 169, 175, 189, 190, 192, 227, 238, 260–264, 271–274, 315, 318, 352, 353, 368, 378, 387, 389, 394
Goodman, Irving, 280
Goodman, Saul, 184
Goodwin, Henry, 33, 34, 76
Gordon, Dexter, 275, 278
Gordon, Max, 320
Gordy, Herb, 365
Gorham, Jimmy, 82, 83
Grainger, William, 164, 165
Granz, Norman, 153, 156, 181
Gray, Glen, 39, 170
Gray, Wardell, 395
Green, Adolph, 320
Green, Benny, 173
Green, "Big" Charlie, 68, 186, 284, 285, 296, 349, 386
Green, Claude, 22
Green, Rev. C.E., 345
Green, Freddie, 13–17, 273, 279, 350
Green, Urbie, 174
Greer, Sonny, 49, 50, 53, 56, 183, 192, 211, 273, 382, 383, 384
Grey, Al, 276, 299, 400–404
Griffin, Chris, 30
Griffin, Johnny, 142, 276, 278
Grimes, Tiny, 123, 190, 360–366
Grundy, Hense, 161, 162
Guarneri, Johnny, 109
Guerra, Marcelino, 314
Guillmet, Eustace, 282
Gumina, Tommy, 109
Guy, Freddy, 53, 55, 57, 348, 349, 350
Guy, Joe, 145

Hackett, Bobby, 284, 306
Hall, Al, 400–404
Hall, Archie, 165
Hall, Ed, 39, 123, 233, 235, 236, 304, 379
Hall, Henry, 139
Hall, Minor, 267
Hall, Sol, 191, 202
Hallett, Mal, 19, 190
Hamilton, Jimmy, 90, 379

Hamilton, Johnny "Bugs," 245, 356
Hamilton, Roy, 211
Hammond, John, 59, 61, 168, 187, 319, 320, 350, 392, 394
Hamner, Curley, 359
Hampton, Charles, 265
Hampton, Lionel, 71, 210, 265–278, 279, 280, 281, 368
Hardee, John, 365
Harding, Buster, 147, 152, 172, 174, 199, 225, 236, 297, 314
Hardwick, Otto "Toby," 47–50, 53, 58
Hardy Brothers, The, 165, 233
Hardy, Marion, 309, 310
Harris, Bill, 284, 292
Harris, Charlie, 282
Harris, Wynonie, 202
Harrison, Jimmy, 57, 63, 67, 68, 142, 143, 177, 284, 285, 287, 289, 296, 303, 385
Hart, Clyde, 152, 168, 179, 186, 187, 273, 379
Hartwell, Alan, 191
Hastings, Count, 223
Haughton, Chauncey, 87, 236, 280
Hawkins, Coleman, 18, 23, 56, 63, 68, 73, 106, 108, 120, 139, 140–147, 149, 153–157, 159, 184, 233, 252, 268, 273, 285, 290, 309, 311, 320, 321, 329, 351, 352, 355, 359, 385, 394
Hawkins, Erskine, 192–194, 196–198, 201, 203, 204, 209–211, 214–216, 218, 220–222, 380, 381
Hayes, Clifford, 164
Hayes, Thamon, 304
Hayman, Joe, 33, 35
Hayse, Al, 276, 282
Heard, J.C., 156, 172
Heath, Jimmy, 278
Hefti, Neal, 230
Helvey, Wesley, 165, 294, 295, 303
Hemphill, Shelton, 201, 298
Henderson, Fletcher "Smack," 3, 18, 19, 22, 23, 29, 39, 56, 57, 63, 66, 68, 69, 73–77, 88, 120, 136, 138, 139, 142, 143, 147, 150, 160, 161, 165, 170, 178, 184, 233–235, 238, 268, 273, 280, 283–285, 287, 289, 290, 292, 295–297, 303, 311, 314, 318, 319, 342, 343, 346, 350–353, 355, 367, 371, 386
Henderson, Glenford, 279

Henderson, Horace, 22, 67, 136, 138, 148, 162, 164, 165, 178, 225, 238, 243, 352
Henderson, Rosa, 61
Henry, Haywood, 197, 203–212
Henry, Lew, 253, 310
Herman, Sam, 16
Herman, Woody, 284, 331, 332, 335, 337–339, 344
Heywood, Eddie, 304, 307, 314, 317–324, 327
Heywood, Eddie, Sr., 307, 318
Hicks, Billy, 379
Higginbotham, J.C., 22, 68, 74, 303, 306
Hill, Alex, 225
Hill, Elton, 152, 297
Hill, Ernest "Bass," 33, 36, 349
Hill, Teddy, 22, 84, 150, 196, 199, 245, 246, 372, 386
Hines, Earl, 19, 23, 28, 38, 42, 83, 111, 156, 173, 190, 196, 203, 207, 211, 212, 214, 233, 241, 246, 268, 277, 303, 325, 326, 327, 334, 338, 359, 365, 380, 400–404
Hinton, Milt, 28, 119, 172, 187, 227, 229, 273, 297, 299, 314, 366–375, 400–404
Hite, Les, 265, 267, 268
Hite, Mattie, 47
Hobson, Gerald, 294
Hodges, Johnny, 19, 50, 96, 106, 107, 108, 139–141, 157, 168, 228, 241–243, 249, 251–254, 256, 259, 273, 289, 296, 301, 310, 330, 343, 348, 385, 386, 394, 400–404
Holiday, Billie, 168, 169, 321, 327, 334, 353, 359, 364, 368, 384, 389, 395–398
Holiday, Clarence, 351
Holland, Matthew "Red," 59, 162, 164, 165
Holland, Peanuts, 75, 176
Holley, Major, 145
Holliday, Judy, 320
Holman, Bill, 344
Holmes, Charlie, 22, 242, 243, 248–259
Holmes, Horace, 54
Holmes, Leroy, 382
Holstein, Caspar, 253
Hooks, Charles, 334
Hope, Elmo, 202
Hopkins, Claude, 22, 31–44, 48, 54,

58, 67, 233–236, 238, 240, 246, 280, 304, 320, 386
Horvath, Charlie, 296
Howard, Buddy, 213
Howard, Darnell, 309
Howard, Joe, 41–43
Howard, Paul, 267
Howe, George, 253
Hudson, George (trumpet), 16
Hudson, George (trombone), 212, 213
Hughes, Bill, 299
Humes, Helen, 162, 329, 391
Hunt, George, 191
Hyder, Doc, 82–84
Hylton, Jack, 145
Hyman, Dick, 191

Inge, Ed, 297
Irvis, Charlie, 53, 55, 296

Jackson, Alex, 54
Jackson, Cliff, 28, 48, 56, 61, 84, 314
Jackson, Dewey, 149
Jackson, Franz, 152, 379
Jackson, Fred, 295
Jackson, Mahalia, 288
Jackson, Milt, 201
Jackson, Oliver, 155, 156, 400–404
Jackson, Quentin, 172, 293–301, 311
Jackson, Wallace, 167
Jacquet, Illinois, 106, 172, 275, 278
Jacobs, Pete, 22, 36, 39, 235
James, Baby, 149
James, Benny, 346
James, Elmer, 369, 386
James, Harry, 30, 71, 93, 104, 105, 108, 109, 227, 273, 316, 336, 380
James, Ida, 209
James, Prof. Willis Lawrence, 206
Jazzola Band, The, 384
Jefferson, Hilton, 33, 67, 172, 187, 227, 236, 247, 296, 297, 314, 349, 371
Jenkins, Freddy, 310
Jenkins Orphanage Band, The, 165, 232, 287
Jeter, James, 176
Johnakins, Leslie, 229
Johnson, Archie, 380
Johnson, Bill (saxophone), 194, 197, 209, 215, 222
Johnson, Bill (bass), 267
Johnson, Bobby, 241, 249

Johnson, Budd, 196, 225, 228, 273, 297, 306, 400–404
Johnson, Buddy, 19, 221, 355
Johnson, Charlie, 22, 29, 48, 66, 150, 162, 186, 192, 251, 284, 310
Johnson, Clarence, 245
Johnson, Dink, 267
Johnson, Freddy, 56
Johnson, Gene, 235
Johnson, George, 189
Johnson, Gus, 380
Johnson's Happy Pals, 233
Johnson, Harold (drums), 110
Johnson, Harold "Money" (trumpet), 133, 196, 381
Johnson, Howard, 22, 241–248, 249, 251, 347
Johnson, James P., 25, 32, 57, 111, 245, 319, 324
Johnson, J.J., 69
Johnson, Keg, 172, 186, 297, 367–369
Johnson, Lennie, 335
Johnson, Manzie, 68
Johnson, Osie, 123, 173
Johnson, Percy, 32–34, 234
Johnson, Pete, 332
Johnson, Roy, 276
Johnson, Walter, (drums), 29, 56, 73, 75, 88, 351, 355
Johnson, Walter (piano), 241
Jolson, Al, 335, 366
Jones, Ben, 78, 79
Jones, Bobby, 133
Jones, Broadway, 53, 54
Jones, Claude, 233, 289, 292, 294–298, 302, 367–369
Jones, Elvin, 341
Jones, Isham, 83, 262
Jones, James W., 164
Jones, Jimmy, 181
Jones, Jo, 88, 147, 156, 173, 183, 192, 273, 351, 383, 394
Jones, Jonah, 17–30, 115, 122, 161–175, 179, 181, 187, 191, 227, 273, 314, 356, 374, 400–404
Jones, Leroi, 9
Jones, Max, 181
Jones, Quincy, 119, 125, 276, 298, 299
Jones, Reunald, 85, 303, 386
Jones, Rohmie, 287
Jones, Sam, 202
Jones, Thad, 338

Jones, Wallace, 90, 280
Jones, Walter "Joe," 234
Jordan, Joe, 44
Jordan, Louis, 88, 199, 222, 329
Jordan, Steve, 16
Jordan, Taft, 69, 72, 77–92, 201, 202, 306, 386
Josephson, Barney, 320, 324
Julien, Colonel, 42

Kahn, Roger Wolfe, 262
Kansas City Blue Devils, The, 19
Kansas City Five, The, 61
Kapp, Jack, 321
Katz, Dick, 147
Kaye, Sammy, 344
Keller, Gary, 277
Kelly, George, 191, 375, 376, 378, 379
Kenny, Nick, 39, 280
Kenton, Stan, 29, 231, 240, 344
Kessel, Barney, 62
Keyes, Joe, 186
Keyes, Lawrence, 355
Kilbert, Porter, 152
Killian, Al, 199, 298
Kincaide, Deane, 225
King, Teddi, 335
Kirby, John, 28, 39, 168, 192, 233, 256, 257, 273, 325, 394
Kirk, Andy, 165, 186, 219, 295, 303
Kirkland, Leroy, 221
Kirkpatrick, Don, 59, 254, 385
Kreisler, Fritz, 181
Krupa, Gene, 30, 71, 106, 152, 154, 190–192, 271–273, 334, 371
Kyle, Billy, 124, 256, 257, 273

Ladd's Black Aces, 303
Ladnier, Tommy, 234, 310
Lane, Morris, 276
Lang, Eddie, 176, 346, 392
Lanin, Lester, 174
La Redd, Cora, 167
Larkins, Ellis, 392
Lee, Bobby, 310
Lee, Buddy, 227, 295, 296
Lee, Nora, 355
Leonard, Harlan, 304
Lester, Norman, 59
Levy, John, 181
Lewis, Charlie, 111
Lewis, Ernie, 271
Lewis, Lockwood, 162

Lewis, Mel, 338
Lewis, Sylvester, 235
Lewis, Ted, 262
Lewis, Willie, 139
Liggins, Joe, 222
Lim, Harry, 109
Littauer, Joseph, 189
Locke, Eddie, 143, 145, 155–160
Lombardo, Guy, 207, 375, 381
Love, Clarence, 320
Louisiana Stompers, The, 325
Lowe, Sammy, 194, 202, 204, 209, 210, 212–225
Lovelle, Herbie, 211
Lowth, Eddie, 152
Lucas, Al, 314,
Lucas, Marie, 32, 47, 50
Lucie, Lawrence, 168, 186, 345–355
Lunceford, Jimmie, 14, 16, 23, 39, 43, 54, 71, 93, 96, 97, 100, 103, 108–120, 122–125, 127, 128, 130–132, 134, 162, 165, 167, 178, 179, 187, 192, 194, 210, 219, 225, 309, 334, 340, 342, 346, 353, 378
Lyles, Aubrey, 57, 58
Lynch, Willie, 346

McCain, Beau, 88
McCoy, Herman, 104
McCoy, Roy, 280
McFerran, Hal, 162
McGarity, Lou, 69
McGhee, Howard, 106
McIlvaine, William, 245
McKibbon, Al, 199
McKinney, Bill, 295
McKinney's Chocolate Dandies, 148
McKinney's Cotton Pickers, 19, 114, 148, 167, 178, 227, 235, 268, 293, 295, 296, 299, 303, 311, 342, 397
McLin, Jimmy, 41
McLinton, Charles, 282
McPartland, Jimmy & Marian, 306
McRae, Dave, 229
McRae, Teddy, 88, 167, 347
McShann, Jay, 365, 380
McVea, Jack, 275
Machito, 229, 314, 316
Mackel, Billy, 276, 279–383
Mallory, Eddie, 219, 310
Mann, Herbie, 315
Manne, Shelly, 123
Marable, Fate, 19
Margolis, Sam, 334

Mariano, Charlie, 335
Marrow, Esther, 339
Marsala, Joe, 173
Marshall, Joe, 122
Marshall, Kaiser, 29, 197, 207, 233, 289, 325
Marshall, Wendell, 276, 299
Martin, Bobby, 325
Martin, Dave, 350
Mason, Jack, 138
Mathhews, Al, 355, 358
Matthews, George (trombone), 289
Matthews, George (violin & saxophone), 241
Maxey, Leroy, 368, 371
May, Billy, 96, 106
Means, Delmas, 204
Metcalf, Louis, 177
Middleton, Velma, 190
Mikell, Eugene, 136
Miles, Tommy, 298
Miley, Bubber, 53, 55, 56, 136, 148, 150
Miller, Bill, 66, 67
Miller, "Devil," 66, 67
Miller, Flournoy, 57, 58
Miller, Glenn, 238
Miller, Prof. James, 66
Miller, Johnny, 270, 273
Miller, Mitch, 394
Millinder, Lucky, 75, 199, 227, 230, 353, 355, 380, 381
Mills Brothers, The, 306
Mills Blue Rhythm Band, 346, 353
Mills, Irving, 122
Mills, Lincoln, 82, 186
Mingus, Charles, 28, 173, 276
Mino, 256, 257
Minor, Dan, 299, 304
Mitchell, Freddy, 74, 75
Mitchell, George, 162
Mitchell, Jimmy, 204
Mitchell, "Razz," 380
Mole, Miff, 293, 303
Moncur, Grachan, 394
Monk, Thelonious, 62, 325
Montgomery, Ann, 97
Montgomery, Monk, 276
Montgomery, Wes, 28, 276, 282
Moore, Big Chief, 118
Moore, Billy, 131, 225, 230
Moore, Bobby, 380
Moore, Freddy, 29, 379
Moore, Monette, 61

Moore, Oscar, 273, 356
Morales, Noro, 381
Moran, Willie, 380
Morgan, Al, 366, 367
Morgan, Richard & Lavinia, 265
Morgenstern, Dan, 193, 229
Morris, Joe, 282
Morris, Marlowe, 273
Morrison, "Big" Jack, 214
Morrison, Montgomery, 295
Morton, Bennie, 75, 283–292, 297, 317
Morton, Bernice, 164, 165
Morton, Jelly Roll, 18, 25, 177, 184, 346
Mosby, Curtis, 267
Mosley, Snub, 120, 130, 177, 235
Moten, Bennie, 19, 116, 303, 346
Moten, Benny, 156
Mulligan, Gerry, 344
Mundy, Jimmy, 22, 104, 114, 225, 233, 236
Murphy, Turk, 61
Murray, Albert, 9
Myers, Herb, 154

Nance, Ray, 118, 179, 201, 298
Nanton, Joe "Tricky Sam," 56, 150, 210, 296, 298
Navarro, Fats, 142
Nelson, Oliver, 140
Nesbitt, John, 235, 295
Newman, Joe, 206, 275
Newton, Frank, 148, 246, 304
Nicholas, Albert, 253, 320
Nichols, Red, 149, 262
Nicholson, Eddie, 365
Noone, Jimmie, 262, 272
Norman, Fred, 39, 114, 225, 232–240
Norvo, Red, 199, 387, 392, 394, 395
Nottingham, Jimmy, 228
Nulasco, 50

Oberstein, Eli, 273
O'Day, Anita, 152
Oliver, Joe "King," 148, 215, 254, 309
Oliver, Sy, 19, 22, 23, 100, 102, 104, 110, 113, 115, 116, 122, 123, 125–134, 169, 178, 194, 225, 230, 238, 295, 303
Original Cotton Pickers, The, 150

Otis, Clyde, 238, 239, 240
Oxley, Harold, 117, 118

Pacque, Glyn, 325, 349
Paige, Clarence, 295
Paine, Benny, 297, 368, 373
Page, Dave, 282
Page, Oran, "Hot Lips," 284, 395
Page, Walter, 330
Panassie, Hugues, 203, 225
Panico, Louis, 309
Parenti, Tony, 156
Parker, Charlie "Bird," 93, 106, 107,
    108, 140, 145, 198, 199, 248, 325,
    327, 330, 334, 337, 340, 364, 380,
    384, 395
Parker, Jimmy, 22
Parrish, Avery, 193, 194, 196, 197,
    209, 210, 215, 216, 221, 222
Parrish, Curley, 209
Pasquall, Jerome Don, 241, 242
Payne, Sonny, 154, 199
Perkins, Bill, 109
Perry, Bay, 334
Perry, Doc, 47
Perry, E.V., 232
Perry, Joe, 334
Perry, Ray, 275, 334
Persiany, Andre, 173, 306
Phillips, Don, 302
Phillips, Reuben, 206, 222, 223
Peterson, Oscar, 28, 181
Pierce, Nat, 109, 329–344, 400–404
Pike, Bobby, 133
Pilars, Jeter, 120
Pillars, Chester, 176
Pillars, Hayes, 176
Pinkett, Ward, 177
Pittman, Booker, 186
Plater, Bobby, 276
Pleasant, Bu, 282
Pleasants, Henry, 1
Polk, George, 64
Pollack, Ben, 353
Porter, Cole, 220, 322
Potter, Jerry, 365
Potter, Tommy, 173
Powell, Baden, 62
Powell, Bud, 341
Powell, Mel, 189
Powell, Rudy, 347
Powell, Seldon, 202
Powell, "Specs," 123, 189
Powell, Teddy, 238

Prado, Perez, 315
Price, Sammy, 315
Prince, Henry, 270
Procope, Russell, 76, 325, 400–404
Proctor, Harold, 136
Profit, Clarence, 358
Pryor, Arthur, 285
Prysock, Arthur, 202
Prysock, Red, 365
Pulliam, Steve, 199, 381
Purce, Ernest, 380

Quebec, Ike, 172, 201, 329

Radcliffe, Freddy, 282
Raglin, Junior, 28
Rainey, Ma, 119, 307, 309
Ram, Buck, 223
Ramey, Gene, 156, 380, 400–404
Ramirez, Roger, 325–329, 400–404
Randolph, Irving "Mouse," 176, 273,
    311, 352, 368
Range, Bob, 204, 206
Ray, Ricardo, 315, 317
Reagan, Caroline, 33, 34
Redman, Don, 18, 83, 90, 114, 138,
    152, 178, 187, 206, 207, 235, 268,
    283, 289, 293, 295, 296, 297, 299,
    318, 319, 342, 353
Redman, Louis, 225
Reese, Rostelle, 267
Reeves, Arthur, 136
Reeves, Reuben, 211
Reich, George, 127
Reinhardt, Django, 282, 356, 366
Reynolds, Ellis, 82
Reynolds, Ellsworth, 252
Rhodes, George, 174
Rhodes, Todd, 295, 334
Rhythm Boys, The, 392
Rich, Buddy, 14, 36, 71, 210, 240
Richards, Chuck, 353
Richards, Johnny, 344
Richards, Red, 284, 306
Richardson, Ben, 130
Riddle, Gladys, 270–272
Riddle, Nelson, 104, 239, 329
Rinker, Al, 392
Roberts, Caughey, 270
Roberts, Howard, 173
Roberts, Luckey, 32, 61, 327
Roberts, Tommy, 248
Robeson, Orlando, 39, 236, 320
Robinson, Bill, 42

Robinson, Clarence, 48–50, 52
Robinson, Eli, 122, 149, 152, 229, 230, 379
Robinson, Fred, 296
Robinson, Jackie, 272
Robinson, Milton, 165
Robinson, Prince, 41, 56, 57, 79, 150, 152, 177, 207, 229, 311, 379
Robinson, Sugar Ray, 114
Rochester, Eddie, 267
Rochester, Joe, 46, 47
Rocking Highlanders, The, 365
Rockwell-O'Keefe, 39, 235
Rocky Mountain Trio, The, 61
Rodgers, Jimmy, 264
Rogers, Will, 290
Rolle, Ivan, 191, 376
Rollini, Adrian, 169
Rollins, Sonny, 142, 160
Roppolo, Leon, 262
Rose, Billy, 189
Rosenkrantz, Timme, 182
Ross, Alonzo, 233
Ross, Candy, 133
Rothstein, Arnold, 57
Rouse, Charlie, 142, 147
Rowles, Jimmy, 109
Royal, Ernie, 202, 220, 275
Royal, Marshall, 273, 275, 342
Rubinoff, Dave, 238
Rushing, Jimmy, 92, 341, 389
Russell, Jimmy, 345
Russell, Johnny, 186, 245
Russell, Luis, 22, 83, 246, 253
Russell, Pee Wee, 400–404

Sachs, Aaron, 173
St. Clair, Cy, 25, 39, 186
Saints & Sinners, The, 306
Sampson, Edgar, 2, 68, 69, 76, 85, 177, 225, 386, 387
San Domingans, The, 22
Sands, Bobby, 22, 39, 235
Sanders, John, 298
Sanders, Pharoah, 157
Saparo, Henri, 54
Sauter, Eddie, 225, 384
Savage, Henry, 295
Savoy Bearcats, The, 385
Savoy Sultans, The, 14, 73, 380, 381
Schelsinger, Milton, 184
Scott, Cecil, 19, 59, 150, 162, 168, 246
Scott, Hazel, 194, 219

Scott, Lanny, 174
Scott, Patrick, 62
Scott, Raymond, 41, 189, 239, 283
Sears, Al, 58, 129, 225, 259
Sebastian, Frank, 267, 268
Sedric, Gene, 356
Senior, Milt, 295
Sepia Serenaders, The, 61
Shannon, "Detroit," 265
Shavers, Charlie, 28, 169, 192, 211, 287, 325
Shaw, Artie, 152, 394
Shaw, Arvell, 190
Shaw, Billy, 213
Shearing, George, 174, 181, 365
Shepp, Archie, 341
Sherman, Jimmy, 168
Sherman, Joe, 275
Shirley, Jimmy, 356
Shoffner, Bob, 162
Shulman, Joe, 28
Silver, Horace, 340
Simeon, Omer, 273
Simmen, Johnny, 135
Simmons, Freddy, 282
Simon, Gene, 297
Simpson, Lieut., 285, 287
Sims, J.B. (Capt. Ed), 194, 204, 206, 207
Sims, Lee, 327
Sims, Zoot, 400–404
Sinatra, Frank, 125, 131, 189, 211
Singer, Harold, 156
Singleton, Zutty, 8, 29, 273, 320, 366
Sissle, Noble, 242
Skeete, Charlie, 36
Skinner, Frank, 320
Slats, 296, 385
Smothers, Richard, 378
Smalls, Cliff, 133
Smalls, Ed, 59
Smith, Bessie, 25, 47, 119, 307, 319, 376, 392, 395, 397
Smith, Bobby, 197, 222
Smith, Buddy, 133
Smith, Carroll, 164
Smith, Clara, 307
Smith, Chris, 58
Smith, Floyd, 394
Smith, Jabbo, 236, 304
Smith, Jimmy, 326
Smith, Joe, 22, 148, 150, 215, 284, 289, 295, 309, 311, 395
Smith, John, 356

Smith, Major N. Clark, 265
Smith, Mamie, 142, 302, 387
Smith, "Pinetop," 384
Smith, Raymond, 168
Smith, Russell, 19, 39, 73, 160, 170,
    172, 233, 236, 289, 297, 311,
    352
Smith, Stuff, 30, 97, 120, 130, 167,
    168, 169, 170, 174, 176–183, 187,
    191
Smith, Tab, 380, 381
Smith, Willie (saxophone), 93–110,
    111, 113–115, 117, 120, 122, 131,
    133, 213, 309
Smith, Willie "The Lion" (piano), 46,
    326, 327
Snaer, Albert, 235, 236
Snodgrass, 299
Snowden, Elmer, 36, 45–62, 150,
    245, 346, 351
South, Eddie, 179
Spanier, Muggsy, 262
Spellman, A.B., 9
Spikes Brothers, The, 267
Spirits of Rhythm, The, 22, 325, 356
Spitalny, Phil, 41
Spivak, Charlie, 104, 239
Springer, Joe, 364
Stabile, Dick, 168, 179
Stacy, Jess, 273
Stafford, George, 29, 192
Stafford, Mary, 47
Stamps, Charlie, 164
Stanfield, Lee, 204, 222
Stark, Bobby, 63, 68, 69, 71, 72, 74,
    87, 149, 233, 385, 386
Stearns, Marshall & Jean, 3
Steele, Joe, 243, 386
Stevenson, George, 75, 380
Stevenson, Tommy, 102, 116, 122,
    167, 220
Stewart, George, 164
Stewart, Luke, 164, 167
Stewart, Rex, 19, 22, 56, 57, 68,
    84, 149, 177, 273, 296, 311,
    325
Stewart, Slam, 123, 361, 364
Stitt, Sonny, 142, 201, 247
Stone, Jesse, 256
Strayhorn, Billy, 105, 221, 225, 230
Sturgis, Ted, 152, 198, 379
Sullivan, Joe, 273, 283
Swayzee, Edwin "King," 149, 176,
    177, 311, 371

Sweatman, Wilbur, 32, 49, 184
Synco Septet, The, 294, 295, 303

Tate, Erskine, 265, 310
Tate, James, 310
Tatum, Art, 123, 325–327, 332, 335,
    359, 361, 364
Taylor, Arthur, 202
Taylor, Billy (bass), 189, 296, 299,
    311
Taylor, Billy (piano), 123, 181, 190,
    326
Taylor, Sam, 172, 202, 207, 380, 382
Teagarden, Charlie, 184
Teagarden, Jack, 3, 184, 190, 284,
    303
Terry, Clark, 228, 317, 330, 400–404
Thomas, Andrew, 31
Thomas, George "Fathead," 268,
    295, 397
Thomas, Joe (trumpet), 43, 236
Thomas, Joe (tenor saxophone), 97,
    110, 115, 122, 133, 165, 167, 186
Thomas, Joe (saxophone and brother
    of Walter Thomas), 23, 186
Thomas, Louis, 31, 47, 52
Thomas, Walter "Foots," 25, 177,
    186, 187, 297, 311, 367, 368
Thompson, Benny, 167
Thompson, Sir Charles, 274, 365,
    383, 400–404
Thompson, H.O., 206
Thompson, Lucky, 139, 340
Thornton, Caroline, 32
Three Hot Eskimos, The, 61
Three Monkey Chasers, The, 61
Tibbs, Leroy, 31
Tijuana Brass, The, 336
Tinsley, Ted, 82
Tizol, Juan, 47, 50, 105, 106, 297, 317
Toliver, Buster, 241, 250
Tomlin, Sleepy, 149, 167
Tompkins, Eddie, 102, 103, 116, 118,
    122, 167, 213
Toots, Hartley, 233, 378
Tough, Dave, 104, 192, 273, 383,
    394, 395
Travis, Al, 213
Tremaine, Paul, 23
Trent, Alphonso, 120, 125, 130, 176–
    178, 235
Trenton, Prof., 206
Tribble, Earl, 295
Tristano, Lennie, 341

Trotman, Lloyd, 181, 182, 334
Trueheart, John, 19, 72, 346, 350, 351, 384–386
Trumbauer, Frankie, 3, 138
Tunia, Ray, 211
Turner, Charlie, 309
Turner, Henry, 39
Turner, Joe, 382
Tynes, George, 242

Vacchiano, William, 173
Vallee, Rudy, 346
Vance, Dick, 89
Vaughan, Sarah, 125, 175, 181, 239, 240, 287
Ventura, Charlie, 106
Venuti, Joe, 176
Victor, Frank, 346
Vinson, Eddie, 202, 256
Vodery, Will, 39

Walker, Frank, 239
Walker, Henry, 34
Walker, Mack, 168
Waller, Thomas "Fats," 28, 32, 48, 49, 57, 58, 111, 181, 238, 242, 245, 324, 326, 332, 338, 356, 357, 359
Walters, Teddy, 123
Walton, Greely, 246, 252
Ward, Joe, 36
Ware, Leonard, 356
Waring, Fred, 116
Warren, Earle, 223, 318
Washington, Booker, 119
Washington, Buck, 164
Washington, Dinah, 119, 202, 239, 275
Washington, Freddie, 222
Washington, Johnny, 168, 187
Washingtonians, The, 50, 55, 57
Waters, Benny, 251, 252
Waters, Ethel, 47, 58
Watkins, Ralph, 174
Watts, Joe, 314, 379
Watson, Billy, 83
Watson, Laurel, 152
Webb, Chick, 19, 22, 29, 58, 59, 63, 68, 69, 71, 72, 74, 77, 80, 84, 85, 87–89, 169, 177, 192, 196, 220, 251–254, 280, 283, 296, 303, 310, 343, 346, 350, 369–371, 376, 379, 380, 384–390, 395
Webb, Speed, 122, 149, 303

Webster, Ben, 93, 123, 186, 273, 304, 314, 320, 367–369, 371, 372
Webster, Freddie, 102, 380
Webster, Paul, 102, 116, 167, 220
Wein, George, 44, 61, 62, 306
Wells, Dicky, 8, 59, 135, 137, 143, 156, 161, 162, 197, 227, 229, 230, 246, 284, 289, 299, 304, 356
Wells, Gertie, 49
Wells, Henry, 116, 120, 167, 236
Wells, Joe, 326
Wellstood, Dick, 156
Wess, Frank, 400–404
Wettling, George, 395
Wexler, Jerry, 382
Whatley, "Fess," 214, 215
Wheatstraw, Peetie "The Devil's Son-In-Law," 169
Wheeler, De Priest, 371
Wheeler, Doc, 380
Whetsol, Artie, 36, 48, 49, 53, 317
White, Baby, 236
White, Freddy, 243
White, Georgia, 169
White, Harry, 76, 371
White, Morris, 371
White, Sonny, 17–30
Whiteman, Paul, 55, 178, 192, 262, 295, 346, 386, 392, 397
Whitlock, Elmer, 165
Whittet, Benny, 252
Whyte, Zack, 19, 100, 122, 125, 129, 130, 149, 225, 227, 230, 295, 303
Wilborn, Dave, 150, 295, 311
Wilcox, Ed, 97, 100, 110–118, 120, 131, 211
Wilder, Alec, 394
Wilder, Joe, 276
Willet, Chappie, 380
Williams, Al, 156, 202
Williams, Bert, 39, 236, 284
Williams, Bob, 152
Williams, Charles, 119
Williams, Cootie, 22, 74, 133, 160, 254, 256, 273
Williams, Dutch, 117
Williams, Earl, 202
Williams, Elmer, 33, 67, 69, 85, 86, 252, 385, 386
Williams, Ethel, 47
Williams, Francis, 202, 298
Williams, Joe, 275
Williams, John, 120, 178, 394

Williams, Mary Lou, 120, 133, 178, 225, 261, 332, 394
Williams, Mr. (bass), 267
Williams, P.M., 148
Williams, Rudy, 198, 199, 380
Williams, Sandy, 63–77, 87, 386
Williams, Teroy, 56, 67
Wilshire, Teacho, 356
Wilson, Derby, 184
Wilson, Gerald, 102, 104, 181, 336, 342
Wilson, Gus, 122, 149, 167, 303
Wilson, John S., 182
Wilson, Lester, 127
Wilson, "Shadow," 275, 380
Wilson, Teddy, 22, 28, 71, 122, 149, 167, 168, 186, 187, 271, 272, 283, 303, 314, 324, 332, 356, 368, 394, 397
Winterhalter, Hugo, 238, 322
Witherspoon, Jimmy, 222
Wood, Booty, 276, 282
Woode, Jimmy, 44, 299

Wooding, Russell, 48
Wooding, Sam, 234, 310
Woodman, Britt, 133, 276, 299
Woods, Phil, 147
World's Greatest Jazz Band, The, 284
Wright, Lammar, 172, 202, 297, 311, 367, 368
Wright, Lammar, Jr., 282
Wynken, Blynken & Nod, 360
Wynn, Al, 309

Yaged, Sol, 156
Young, Dave, 152
Young, Lee, 275
Young, Lester, 14, 16, 106, 108, 141, 225, 230, 277, 334, 337, 352, 384, 389, 395
Young, Snooky, 103, 276
Young, Trummy, 63, 104, 133, 190, 290
Ysaguirre, Bob, 54, 56, 299

Zeitlin, Danny, 341